INSPIRING PRIMARY LE

Inspiring Primary Learners offers trainee and qualified teachers high-quality case studies of outstanding practice in contemporary classrooms across the country. Expert authors unravel and reveal the theory and evidence that underpins lessons, helping you make connections with your own practice and understand what 'excellent' looks like, within each context, and how it is achieved.

Illustrated throughout with interviews, photos, and examples of children's work, it covers a range of primary subjects and key topics including creating displays, outdoor learning, and developing a reading for pleasure culture. The voice of the practitioner is evident throughout as teachers share their own experience, difficulties, and solutions to ensure that children are inspired by their learning.

Written in two parts, the first exemplifies examples of practice for each National Curriculum subject, whilst the second focuses on the wider curriculum and explores issues pertinent to the primary classroom, highlighting important discussions on topics such as:

- Reading for pleasure
- Writing for pleasure
- Creating a dynamic and responsive curriculum
- Creating inspiring displays
- Outdoor learning
- Pedagogy for imagination
- Relationships and Sex Education

This key text shows how, even within the contested space of education, practitioners can inspire their primary learners through teaching with passion and purpose for the empowerment of the children in their class. For all new teachers, it provides advice and ideas for effective and engaging learning experiences across the curriculum.

Roger McDonald is an Associate Professor at the University of Greenwich and has extensive experience in the primary classroom as a practitioner. Roger is also President Elect of the United Kingdom Literacy Association (UKLA).

Poppy Gibson is a Senior Lecturer at the University of Greenwich, and programme lead of the accelerated BA (Hons) in Primary Education Studies.

INSPIRING PRIMARY LEARNERS

Insights and Inspiration Across the Curriculum

Edited by
Roger McDonald
and Poppy Gibson

Routledge
Taylor & Francis Group

LONDON AND NEW YORK

First published 2021
by Routledge
2 Park Square, Milton Park, Abingdon, Oxon OX14 4RN

and by Routledge
52 Vanderbilt Avenue, New York, NY 10017

Routledge is an imprint of the Taylor & Francis Group, an informa business

British Library Cataloguing-in-Publication Data
A catalogue record for this book is available from the British Library

Library of Congress Cataloging-in-Publication Data
Names: McDonald, Roger, 1973- editor. | Gibson, Poppy, editor.
Title: Inspiring primary learners: insights and inspiration across the curriculum / Edited by Roger McDonald and Poppy Gibson.
Description: Abingdon, Oxon; New York, NY: Routledge, 2021. |
Includes bibliographical references and index.
Identifiers: LCCN 2020038927 | ISBN 9780367110642 (hardback) |
ISBN 9780367110659 (paperback) | ISBN 9780429024597 (ebook)
Subjects: LCSH: Primary school teaching-Great Britain. |
Education, Primary-Great Britain. | Effective teaching-Great Britain.
Classification: LCC LB1556.7.G7 I57 2021 | DDC 372.24/10941-dc23
LC record available at https://lccn.loc.gov/2020038927

ISBN: 978-0-367-11064-2 (hbk)
ISBN: 978-0-367-11065-9 (pbk)
ISBN: 978-0-429-02459-7 (ebk)

Typeset in Interstate
by Deanta Global Publishing Services, Chennai, India

CONTENTS

CONTRIBUTORS

James Archer has broad experience in supporting trainee primary teachers in primary Design and Technology. He has authored chapters on creative Design and Technology for both Sage's *The Primary Curriculum a Creative Approach* and Taylor and Francis's *Teaching Design Technology Creatively*. His career in Initial Teacher Education has spanned over ten years. He is Course Director for the BAH Primary Education Accelerated degree at Leeds Beckett University. Prior to his current role, it has been his privilege to work with trainee teachers and colleagues at Bradford College and Canterbury Christ Church University. He has a passion for creative child-centred enquiry. Before working in Higher Education James taught in both the primary and secondary phases in England and South Africa. In these settings he held various responsibilities for leading and co-ordination of Design and Technology. He has also been an advisor in primary Science supporting a cluster of schools.

Anthony Barlow is Principal Lecturer (Geography) and Programme Convenor for the BA Primary Education QTS programme at University of Roehampton, London. He worked in primary schools for 12 years in Hillingdon and Bolton. Anthony is Chair of the Early Years and Primary Committee of the Geographical Association (GA) and in 2020 he was awarded the Geographical Association Annual Award for Excellence. As a consultant he has led teacher development sessions for teachers around England. Anthony has written for the GA Gold award-winning *Teaching Geography Creatively* (Routledge, 2013/2017) and co-authored the Scholastic series *100 Geography Lessons: Years 3-4/Years 5-6*. His chapter for *Reflections on Primary Geography* (2017, Catling, S. ed) covered issues of plastic waste on a Mull beach combined with the importance of personal reflections on the importance of narrative and story in primary Geography. Hodder published *Geography Voyagers KS1: Geography* (2017), updated in 2019 as *Rising Stars: Primary Geography KS1*. His research interests are pupil, staff and student understanding and use of their immediate school surroundings and the importance of questions through an enquiry lens. With other educators he supports the @Humanities2020 campaign and builds links between the humanities subjects. He tweets @totalgeography and @EYPPC_GA. See also www.primarygeography.wordpress.com.

Michelle Best is a Senior Lecturer in Teacher Education at the University of Greenwich and has been developing her expertise as a teacher educator since 2010. After many years in the industry she thrived as a Further Education Lecturer and progressed to Programme Leader for Education Studies at a South East London University Centre. She developed her role in the Further Education sector and enhanced her experience in Primary Education studies. She is Senior Fellow of the Higher Education Academy and a Fellow of the Society of Education and Training. She is currently studying towards her Doctorate in Education exploring teachers' awareness of their identity as a beginner teacher. Her continued focus of the evolving teacher during and beyond Initial Teacher Training steered her to publish an article on perceptions of Further Education teachers in secondary schools and her interest in developing teachers continues.

Mark Betteney is a Principal Lecturer at the University of Greenwich and has worked in Teacher Training since 2005. Before teaching in HE, Mark was a primary school teacher for over 15 years, teaching in North West Kent and South East London. He led the teaching of Literacy and Music in two schools and emphasised to the children the importance of composition and performance. Mark was never happier than when teaching music structure through dance, not least because he experienced such powerful inclusive practice in that activity. Mark's teaching and research interests include inclusion; music; the connections between music and literacy; language acquisition; and student progression.

Ashley Brett is a Senior Lecturer in the School of Education at the University of Greenwich and has worked within the primary and early years foundation stage education sector for over 25 years. His previous roles have been as a primary school teacher, an education consultant for a local authority (also serving as a Lead Assessment Practitioner, involved with quality assuring practice for the authority) and a deputy headteacher. Ashley's doctoral research was focused on how primary school leaders support their teachers to be learners as part of school improvement, where links were made to transformative learning theory. This study has relevance for leadership teams and current or aspiring teacher practitioners. Besides lecturing, Ashley supports the University's 'Professionals as Researchers' (Action Research projects) for teachers improving their practice. In schools, Ashley led a variety of curriculum areas, including the Arts, Humanities, Religious Education and Mathematics. As a primary school teacher, he became inspired about promoting learning as intrinsically healthy, leading him to complete a Masters in Health Education and Health Promotion. Ashley is passionate about art, having completed a Foundation Course in art and design and gaining entry for a theatre design degree at top London art schools.

Megan Brown is an experienced primary school teacher, Phase Leader and Digital Learning Lead at Wingfield Primary School. She developed the use of technology within her school, gaining qualifications as an Apple Teacher and more recently as an Apple Professional Learning Specialist. Megan also gained her MA in Education at Greenwich University in 2019, focusing her research on effective approaches to training teachers in the use of iPad. Following her research, Megan has delivered professional development in technology to a host of schools and delivered guest lectures for trainee teachers. She continues to develop training in digital learning, working as a teacher and Professional Learning Specialist.

Kay Charlton is a trumpet player, educator, composer, and is Music Manager at Plumcroft Primary School where she teaches KS2 music, brass, and WCET. She completed an MA in

Music Education at Trinity Laban Conservatoire of Music and Dance in 2018 and was delighted to be awarded the Director's Prize for Excellence in Music Education. Kay has been guest lecturer on instrumental tuition at Leeds College of Music and Trinity Laban and has written resources for LSO Discovery and LPO Creative Classrooms. She is the author of *How to teach Whole-Class Instrumental Lessons, 50 Inspiring Ideas* (Collins Music, 2020). Kay plays trumpet with the Bollywood Brass Band who have toured and recorded extensively, and she leads on their education work. Her passion for making music fun and accessible for beginners has led to the composition of Bollywood brass/wind tutor books (Spartan Press) and examination pieces for Trinity College London. Her book of WCET repertoire and backing tracks *Are You Ready?* (Warwick Music) has been converted into a series of online tutorials by MusicGurus, and she has delivered workshops based on this repertoire at education conferences, the Music and Drama Education Expo and as CPD sessions for music hubs. See also www.kaycharlton.co.uk.

Poppy Gibson is a Senior Lecturer in Primary Education at the University of Greenwich. Poppy came to HE after over ten years working as a primary school teacher in and around London, with key responsibility roles including Head of Computing and Head of Modern Foreign Languages (MFL). Poppy is now Programme Lead for the two-year BA (Hons) in Primary Education (accelerated) as well as the MFL co-ordinator for the Primary team. Poppy's main research interests involve social media and mental health and well-being, and Poppy is currently working on several projects that explore the tensions between the online and offline self.

Alison Hales is a Senior Lecturer in Primary Education, with overall responsibility for the wider curriculum provision; she also jointly leads the Initial Teacher Education programme working with trainees, schools, and settings to develop practice-based learning and partnerships. She is also a Senior Fellow of the HEA. After completing her degree with South Bank University, she worked as a primary class teacher and as a member of the senior management team for several years, having experience across the primary age phase. Her area of expertise is within the Humanities and she has written and published widely on primary History, in particularly using local people and places as a way to develop historical knowledge and understanding with children. Alison is currently studying for her PhD and is researching young children's understanding of controversial issues and is looking specifically at war and conflict. Other research interests include the character education of teachers and children, identity, and the use of the local in primary History teaching.

Kristy Howells is a Reader in Physical Education and Sport Pedagogy at Canterbury Christ Church University. She co-leads the International Association of Physical Education in Higher Education Early Years Special Interest Group. Her research expertise is in the field of physical activity interventions, physical activity and mental health, as well as public health and nutrition. She is a member of the All Party Parliamentary Fit and Healthy Childhood Group and has contributed to the last four reports for this group. She has published numerous chapters on Physical Education, Physical Activity, and Health as well as the key book *Mastering Primary Physical Education*. She also is the co-editor of *Mentoring Primary Teachers a Practical Guide* (2020).

She lives and breathes sport, having achieved podium success at national, international, and world level in para- and able-bodied masters cycling, as well as podium success in national indoor lightweight rowing and para-triathlon.

Rachel Linfield has worked in education for over 30 years, teaching throughout the 3–11 age range and in Higher Education at both the University of Cambridge and Leeds Beckett University. As a Senior Lecturer at Leeds Beckett University, Rachel teaches Design and Technology, and Science, for undergraduate and postgraduate early years and Primary Education courses. She supports students on school placements and supervises students for final year dissertations. Rachel has written over 100 publications including: professional materials for early years and primary teachers; chapters in academic books; articles within peer reviewed journals; and non-fiction books for children. She was a member of the editorial board for *Primary Science Review* (Association for Science Education) for six years, and for four as the assistant editor.

Adewale Magaji is a Senior Lecturer at the University of Greenwich and course leader for the Science PGCE and Subject Knowledge Enhancement courses. He is a Fellow of the Chartered College of Teaching and a chartered Science teacher (CSciTeach). This is in recognition of his expertise in promoting the integration of research and classroom practices and contributing to solving problems facing teaching and learning. He has had extensive experience of teaching in several secondary schools as a Science teacher and lead professional. He is an International Committee member of the Association for Science Education and passionate about helping people to learn successfully as well as developing teachers. Ade's teaching and research interests include interactive pedagogy in Science education; assessment for learning; developing learning community; student-led learning and empowerment; teacher education; and teachers as researchers.

Sacha Mason is Head of Programmes for Education and Lifelong Learning at Bishop Grosseteste University, Lincoln. Sacha has been a class teacher in primary schools in West Sussex and Lincolnshire for a number of years, working with children aged 3–11 years. She has worked in Further and Higher Education with work-based practitioners in schools, early years settings, and the youth service. Her research interests are in relationships and Sex Education, with a particular focus on the primary phase. Sacha is co-author of *Relationships and Sex Education 3–11* (Bloomsbury, 2019) with Professor Richard Woolley. Her other research interests are in academic literacies in Higher Education. Sacha is a senior fellow of the Higher Education Academy.

Roger McDonald is an Associate Professor in the School of Education at the University of Greenwich. Roger initially worked as a primary school teacher for 16 years before moving to the University of Greenwich in 2012. Roger has a passion for literacy, particularly Drama and the use of picture books to enhance possibility thinking. In 2019 Roger was proud to have been appointed President Elect of the United Kingdom Literacy association (UKLA). Roger's research interests centre around the importance of creating opportunities for imagining within the primary curriculum.

Robert Morgan is a qualified primary school teacher who taught in schools in Torfaen, Southwark, and Bexley. He was appointed to the University of Greenwich in 2007, where he lectures in Education and Religious Education. Robert's doctoral (EdD) dissertation focused on the needs of trainee teachers working with teaching assistants during a school-based placement. Robert is a Senior Fellow of the Higher Education Academy and a member of the National Association for Primary Education. Robert is also involved in the promoting of Religious Education; he is the vice chair of the Royal Borough of Greenwich's Standing Advisory Council for Religious Education, where he chaired the writing of the new Agreed Syllabus.

Janet Morris is a Senior Lecturer in Primary Education at the University of Greenwich and leads on Early Years, teaching on both the undergraduate and postgraduate degrees. Prior to joining the university, Janet was a nursery teacher, reception teacher, and Early Years lead in a Lewisham primary school. Her interests are in early language and talk and engaging learning experiences. She is currently completing her EdD at the University focusing on early conversation within the home and community.

Gemma Parker is a qualified primary school teacher who has taught in South London primary schools, as well as in the Netherlands. Gemma has worked in Higher Education settings, lecturing in primary Mathematics and is now an independent primary Mathematics advisor. She is passionate about supporting schools to raise standards in primary Maths as it makes a difference to children's life chances. To this end, Gemma is constantly striving to understand more about how children and teachers learn.

Talia Ramadan studied Primary Education at the University of Greenwich and completed her literature review on the importance of Modern Foreign Languages in primary schools in England. Prior to her studies in the United Kingdom, she lived in Spain and worked as an English as a second language instructor for children aged 3–11; she also worked as a musical theatre teaching assistant in Spain, where children learnt the English language through the performing arts ages 3–18. Talia currently works as a Teaching Assistant, in South East London, where she is able to continue her own professional development and further her interests in inclusive education and language acquisition.

Deborah Reynolds is a Senior Lecturer in the School of Education at the University of Greenwich. Prior to her role at the university Debbie was a classroom teacher, a subject leader in Creativity and Literacy, and a Deputy Headteacher in the borough of Greenwich. She has worked on outreach community projects for Charlton Athletic football club and is a Drama Workshop Facilitator for the Greenwich and Lewisham Young Peoples Theatre. She has worked freelance in schools in London and Kent for over 20 years, delivering creative workshops with storytelling and Drama across all key stages; enriching the department and inspiring new teachers at the university with her experience. Debbie was part of the Poetry Champions Project (2012-2013), and Ways with Words Project (2013-2015), together with Professor Andrew Lambirth and the University of Greenwich English Team, working with Literacy Coordinators from a cluster of schools in Kent. Debbie works part-time at the university and also continues with her freelance work in schools.

L.D. Smith is a Principal Lecturer and programme leader at the University of Greenwich, who has worked in teacher training since 2014. Before teaching in HE she was a secondary school Science teacher for over 14 years, teaching in Outer London. She led the teaching of Science, and emphasised to the children the importance of curiosity and critical thinking. Her teaching and research interests include mentoring; innovation in Science education; outdoor learning; and personalised learning.

Sarah Smith is a Principal Lecturer and leads both the PGCE in Primary Education and the BA in Primary Education at the University of Greenwich. She is a Senior Fellow of the HEA. Sarah is an English specialist who has worked at the university for 13 years. Prior to this Sarah taught in primary schools, in both England and New Zealand, for 17 years. Sarah was a Leading English Teacher in Kent. She has published on poetry and digital literacy. She is currently completing her EdD at the University of Sheffield, researching primary teachers' use of digital literacy.

Kat Vallely is a Practitioner of Primary Teacher Education at the University of Greenwich and is the English and RSE subject lead for the BA and PGCE ITE programmes. Her teaching experiences were founded in the EYFS and KS1 stages of education where she taught for several years. Since moving to Higher Education, she has been interested in researching children's early writing development, with a tight focus on the relationship between teachers as writers, and writers as teachers. Her current research interests include the development of early literacy and communication skills within vulnerable groups of children, with a specific focus on multimodal forms of communication. Kat is the Regional Representative Coordinator for the United Kingdom Literacy Association (UKLA) where she leads a national team of dedicated and skilled English professionals, with an aim to improve literacy in every school through a range of informed research. Kat is currently studying for her Doctorate in Education at the University of Sheffield, where she is specialising in Early Childhood Education.

Rachel Wolfendale has been a Senior Lecturer in Primary Education at the University of Greenwich since January 2019 with teaching responsibilities on both the undergraduate and postgraduate Primary Education programmes as well as on the BA Hons Primary Education (Two-Year Accelerated Degree). In her academic study she has carried out research on home-school partnerships with a particular focus on school professionals' perceptions of 'disadvantage' and is exploring this further in her doctoral study with a focus on families' diverse cultural experiences and unique stories. In 2006, she re-trained as a primary teacher on the University of Greenwich PGCE programme, specialising in Early Years, which led to more than 12 years working as a teacher. In her SLE role, Rachel led a local hub of early years settings in a one-year action research project exploring ways to improve outcomes for identified groups of children.

Richard Woolley is Professor of Education and Inclusion and Deputy Head of the School of Education at the University of Worcester, UK. His career has spanned Primary, Further, and Higher Education including time spent coordinating a range of curriculum areas in primary schools in Yorkshire and the East Midlands, and as a deputy headteacher, and SENCo. He has been involved in both initial teacher education and a broader range of education courses at undergraduate and postgraduate level. His research and professional interests include student teachers' perceptions of the controversial issues they may encounter early in their careers, relationships and Sex Education, and social justice and values-focused education. He is author of *Tackling Controversial Issues in the Primary School* (Routledge, 2010), co-author of *Relationships and Sex Education 3–11* (Bloomsbury, 2019), and editor of *Values and Vision in Primary Education* (Open University Press, 2013) and Understanding Inclusion (Routledge, 2018). Richard was awarded National Teaching Fellowship in 2018.

Ross Young and Felicity Ferguson are the founders of The Writing for Pleasure Centre, authors of *Real-World Writers: a handbook for teaching writing with 7–11 year olds* (2020) and *Writing For Pleasure: theory, research and practice* (in press). Ross Young was a primary school teacher for ten years and holds an MA in Applied Linguistics in Education. He was the lead researcher on *What is it 'Writing for Pleasure' teachers do that makes the difference?* He now works around the UK and abroad helping teachers and schools develop young writers. Additionally, he is a visiting lecturer and a passionate writer-teacher.

Felicity Ferguson was a primary school teacher for 40 years, working as an EAL specialist, SENCO, deputy, and headteacher. She has MA degrees in Applied Linguistics and Children's Literature and has been involved in a number of literacy-based projects, including children's reading development. An avid writer herself, Felicity, along with Ross, was the series creator of the *Power English: Writing* approach written for Pearson Education (2019). Her current interest is in how classroom talk affects the development of children as writers.

ACKNOWLEDGEMENTS

We would like to thank all the students, staff, and partnership schools who have taken time to share their practice. It has been wonderful to be able to share ways in which schools have continued to inspire primary children through creating a love of learning and discovery. In particular we would like to thank:

Belmont Primary School, Erith, London: Special thanks to all the fantastic staff and children.

Bishop John Robinson C of E Primary School, Thamesmead, Royal Borough of Greenwich: Special thanks to Jo Richardson and all the fantastic staff and children.

Canary Wharf College, London: Special thanks to all the fantastic staff and children.

Charlton Manor Primary School, London: Special thanks to Tim Baker and all the fantastic staff and children.

Christ Church C of E Primary, Hertfordshire: Special thanks to Marianne Mitchell and all the fantastic staff and children.

Coopers Lane Primary School, Grove Park, London: Special thanks to all the fantastic staff and children.

Ealdham Primary and Nursery School, Eltham, London: Special thanks to Headteacher Christian York, Deputy Headteacher Lindsay Hance, Literacy Leader, Samantha Leslie, and all the fantastic staff and children.

Forster Park Primary School, London: Special thanks to Rebecca Gonsalves and all the fantastic staff and children.

Foxfield Primary School, Woolwich, London: Special thanks to all the fantastic staff and children.

Heronsgate Primary School, Thamesmead, Royal Borough of Greenwich. Special thanks to Renu Partap: RE subject lead and School Direct manager and all the fantastic staff and children.

Longlands Primary School, Broxbourne: Special thanks to Liliana Ioana Dudau and all the fantastic staff and children.

Plumcroft Primary School, Plumstead, London: Special thanks to Sophie Nichol and all the fantastic staff and children.

Sadie Phillips: Link up with Sadie through her social media channels: https://literacywith missp.com/2018/08/07/harnessing-the-power-of-working-walls/ @SadiePhillips literacy-withmissp.com

St Matthew's C of E Primary School, Birmingham: Special thanks to Headteacher, Sonia Thompson, and all the fantastic staff and children.

Thorntree primary school, Charlton, London: Special thanks to Lucy Brown and all the fantastic staff and children.

West Minster Primary School, Sheerness: Special thanks to Tina Ovenden, Holly Gransden, Danielle Cunningham, Wendy Kennedy, Kerry Woolnough, J. Malinauskas, Stacey Spokes, Krystina Barrett, Lisa Hardy, and all the fantastic staff and children.

Wingfield Primary School, Kidbrooke, London: Special thanks to all the fantastic staff and children.

Woodhill Primary School, Woodhill, London: Special thanks to all the fantastic staff and children.

Special thanks also to **Michael Green** who, through our regular conversations, sparked the inspiration to produce this book.

Introduction

Poppy Gibson and Roger McDonald

Thank you for choosing to read this book, which is an exciting collaboration between primary practitioners, university lecturers, and ITE experts. This book draws together detailed insights from UK primary schools in the form of case studies and vignettes from practicing teachers, together with an academic evaluative voice to support you in making connections and developing your own practice through a shared experience. The aim of this book is to offer the reader insights into schools' practice in inspiring primary learners across the curriculum.

We are proud that this book brings together experts from across the country including colleagues from Leeds Becket University, University of Roehampton, University of Worcester, Canterbury Christ Church University, Bishop Grosseteste University, Wingfield Primary School, Plumcroft Primary School, and the founders of the Writing for Pleasure Centre.

We have identified a need for this book due to many of the routes into teaching such as PGCE, BA, School Direct, Apprenticeship or SCITT placing students, for their extended practice, in schools based on a number of criteria which include location, age phase, and the need for a contrasting experience. There are, of course, many benefits to this but one possible limitation is the students' ability to discover insights into other excellent practices taking place in schools they will not have the opportunity to visit. This book provides, not only the insights, but a guided analysis and evaluation through the narrative provided.

In addition, we have seen a shift in pedagogy taking place in some primary schools with an increase in the objective led curriculum and a focus on testing due to pressures schools are experiencing. This shift has resulted in pedagogy sometimes shifting from one characterised by creativity, to teaching which, arguably, is compliant in nature. This book directly addresses this shift through the innovative way in which insights into practice are provided across the curriculum. Through each chapter you will be able to see a range of practices from a variety of schools in the UK which inspire primary learners.

Feedback from students regarding academic texts used on Initial Teacher Education programmes indicates that often the texts they are directed towards can be theoretically driven, and they struggle to make the connections with what they read and how this relates to practice and their experiences. A key feature of this text is that the book begins with the practice which is underpinned by the theory. The emphasis will be on practitioner voice; woven throughout each chapter in a variety of modes including interviews, reflections, thought pieces, and case studies. In addition, this book encourages student teachers to engage educational debates, prompted throughout the chapters in the form of critical questions.

Presented in two parts, you can take a journey through the subjects of the UK National Curriculum in Part One, and then through a range of wider issues and debates in Part Two. This book offers experience, expertise, and valuable insights into the primary classroom across the curriculum, reflecting on practice and strategies in order to help practitioners achieve educational excellence.

This book also offers the latest relevant insights into educational practice in UK primary schools through case study snapshots provided through the integral partnerships between a range of schools and the School of Education at the University of Greenwich, as well as the wider partnership the university has with other educational institutions. This partnership allows for the exciting culmination of valuable case studies with the experience and knowledge of lecturers in the field of Primary Education, who are equipped both with knowledge of the primary classroom, and the pedagogy behind training teachers at university level.

We hope that this book will compliment your experience as a student teacher, practitioner in school, or as a researcher. Its aim is not to provide a 'how to guide' or suggest that the case studies we feature are a holy grail. Instead we hope that the chapters will spark conversations through the insights given into other schools' practice. As professionals, we are all working in the same, often contested, space of education but with a clear aim to inspire primary learners. We hope this book will support you in your exciting, unique, challenging, and inspirational journey.

Whether you are here as a student, a primary school teacher, or a teacher educator, we hope you enjoy reading this book as much as the authors enjoyed writing it.

Be inspired!

Part 1

The primary curriculum

1 Empowering communication through speaking, reading, and writing

Deborah Reynolds, Sarah Smith, and Kat Vallely

Critical questions

When in the Early Years environment, how can you show children that you are actively listening to them with more than just your ears?

When providing children with talking opportunities, what skills do we need to encourage them to use?

When was the last time you felt fully included in a discussion? What made the conversation so inclusive, and what skills were you drawing upon?

What perspective(s) do you take your values around reading from?

How many children's picture books can you name with a BAME character or author that have been published in the past five years?

What purpose do children (and adults) have to write in the classroom?

Who is the audience for the writing?

In what way does the writing connect to children's own experiences?

Introduction

The subject of English in the primary school has been the focus of great debate for educationalists, politicians, and the general public. The news agenda is focused each year on the percentage of pupils in Year 6 who leave school 'being able' to read or write. Of course, those of us who work in education know that the vast majority of pupils leave being able to read and write. Whether they are able to meet an arbitrary mark in an outdated testing system is another matter. English, or 'literacy' as it is sometimes called, is on the political agenda. 'literacy' is seen as a valuable commodity which correlates with economic growth. Therefore the ability to 'measure' literacy has increasingly become important in order to justify the money spent on it. Successive governments have put education at the top of their agenda and made changes in order to evidence success. It could be argued though that the changes have led to an increasingly skills-based curriculum for the children in our schools.

In this chapter we will explore the areas of talk, reading, and writing to show how schools can develop inspiring learning opportunities based on principled pedagogy which permeate across the school to create meaningful learning experiences for the children. We start by exploring the spoken voice, introducing the practice at St Thomas a Becket Primary School before turning to look at how a love of reading can be developed through the case study of Ealdham Primary School. Finally, we focus on writing and how writing for meaning can create a desire to write for both children and teachers.

The spoken voice

Talking about what you are doing, in order to understand and learn, has been considered an important and effective part of good classroom practice for a very long time. As a primary pupil in the 60's, the expectation was to talk not only about what we were doing as we worked, discussing and justifying our thoughts and ideas in our groups, but also to be able to organise and present our work to others in the class and wider school community.

From the Bullock Report (DES, 1975), through the work of Douglas Barnes and the Hackney Link project (1991) to the work of Robin Alexander (2010), talk has been researched and proven invaluable to children's development and understanding. Indeed, included in the national curriculum of 1990 was a whole section on speaking and listening, heightening the profile of talk even further. In the new national curriculum (2014) this was changed to 'spoken voice', offering statutory criteria across the primary phases. Although this is still centrally important to every primary school teacher, it could be argued that, in the current standards-led and accountability culture, finding space and time to ensure the pedagogy of talk is embedded in classroom practice is becoming more challenging.

Within this section I will present a case study from St Thomas a Becket Primary School to celebrate how they ensure that talk is central to teaching and learning. I present the case study from an observer's point of view, having had the privilege of visiting the school and seeing how talk was embedded in the school from the Early Years to Year 6.

During my time visiting St Thomas a Becket it was clear that there was a determination to create a culture and practice throughout the school, to not only use effectively in the classroom, but to ensure that, as the children progressed through the school, the skills needed to make talk for learning successful were developed. This was evident from the Headteacher, Bernie Greally, who told me that she sees talk as 'one of the most complex areas for children to develop'. She is determined that from the moment the children enter the school they are 'allowed' to talk and have effective role models to develop the confidence and skills that lead to success. In addition the Deputy Headteacher, Jo Cooper, said that the inclusion of role play, Drama, and storytelling over many years, as well as the use of structured spoken word games and talk partners, group collaboration, class discussions, and debates, has built a philosophy within the school that has become part of their culture and practice.

The case study below documents my reflections as I visited classes in Early Years, Key Stage 1, and Key Stage 2.

Case study on St Thomas a Becket Primary School: Early Years and Key Stage 1

In the Early Years, I observed that within the free flow environment, the adults were listening carefully all the time. It was almost a physical thing – eye contact, a tilt of the head or a nod, a smile of reassurance – an action actually signalling to others around that they were listening to what one child was saying. This informal practice was constantly taking place throughout both the inside and outside areas. The Early Years co-ordinator told me that the children do not need to be asked to talk, in fact stopping them is sometimes near impossible! However, the adults listen and monitor how the talk is being used, scaffolding and modelling, asking questions and clarifying in order for the use of talk to be effective and focused on learning.

When the children came together for more focused activity such as fruit-time discussion, games, story, etc., the talking was more structured. However, I saw the children being asked to notice how things were said and why and how that might help them know what was going to happen, or what they thought about it. Talk itself was being talked about and modelled. All children in the Early Years were involved in singing, rhymes, dancing, shouting, explaining, and describing. All were building vocabulary, as well as understanding that what they say is important and interesting.

The Deputy Headteacher told me that as children move into Key Stage 1 the experience in the Foundation Stage, of talking being an important and taught part of the learning process, is built upon. The skills are described and discussed more directly, and the children begin to understand why they are asked to talk about their learning.

In the Year 2 class, I observed the teacher giving the children many opportunities to talk for a range of reasons and situations. The feedback written in their books from the previous lesson was read and shared with a friend, while the teacher, Emma Taylor, had conversations about the comments with several individuals. The talking opportunities were short; Emma told them how long they had, reiterated the focus and the purpose while she praised them for the skills they were using, reminding them of the skills they were using. Throughout the lesson she told the children why she was asking them to talk about things, reminding them of the purpose of the discussions.

The children in Year 2 knew how talk partners worked, but more than that, it appeared that many of them knew why the talking helped them. There was mighty enthusiasm for contributing to the feedback, many of them using statements like 'I thought that … but' or 'when he told me that, I didn't think the same'. I could hear some of the games and discussions I had observed in the Early Years class being used here. They were obviously beginning to consider the process of learning through talking, as well as just saying something themselves.

Both the Headteacher and Deputy Headteacher were passionate when we talked about the developmental journey that the children take at St Thomas a Becket. They are determined that talk is used across the whole curriculum, emphasising that, as a staff, they were continually considering the role talking plays in the wider curriculum, moving on from the routine of talk partners, to make the discussion part of the learning process valuable. They talked about the skills and understanding that children need to develop not only about what kind of talking to do, but also how it helps understanding.

From this case study you may wish to consider what skills Emma, the Year 2 teacher, was praising the children for when they were speaking with their talk partners. Also, you may want to question when was the last time you really listened to what a child was saying to you, and was able to extend their thinking through the conversation you shared.

The development of talk and the centrality of it in the Early Years and Key Stage 1 is crucial. The passion of individual teachers supported and exemplified by the senior leaders in a school is paramount to ensuring genuine conversations take place. At St Thomas a Becket Primary School it was clear that teachers were developing language though creating a stimulating environment and through giving the children opportunities to imitate (Skinner, 1957) the language they were hearing.

Language was used as a tool for learning (Vygotsky, 1962) where adults would ensure they talked about the importance of talk with the children in order to encourage them to have a metacognitive awareness of what they were engaged in. Language was not dumbed down but instead used in a way to expose the children to more complex patterns of language as it was recognised that the children could understand a greater range of language then they could use themselves (Bruner, 1986).

One of the most striking aspects of the talk taking place was the personal and genuine nature of it. The teachers were truly intrigued and immersed in the conversations they were having, and meaningful exchanges were taking place (Bearne and Reedy, 2018). Teachers listened to children, spoke with them, and extended their thinking through the conversations they had. There was no sense of teachers having to 'tick off' objectives, meet a certain number of conversations with each child or dig for specific vocabulary. It was greater and more meaningful than this – it was real.

Case study on St Thomas a Becket Primary School: Key Stage 1

In the Year 3 class I observed class teacher Faye Pellatt, introducing the lesson with clear instructions and reminders. The importance of talk was made explicit. I saw the children put into action talking to each other successfully in such a variety of ways. There was a lot of talking to each other, out loud and individually to the adults throughout the lesson. The room was filled with the quiet hum of thinking and learning. I didn't once see a child off task, but I did see children discussing their work and asking each other questions for help and clarification. These children knew they were allowed to talk, even when not specifically given a talking task, and they were using expression and consideration to learn about the focus.

Faye was a role model throughout. Her interest, enthusiasm, and expressive responses included almost no managerial language. She refocused individuals or groups by questioning, responding to what she had seen or heard (and she obviously knew where to focus and on what, as she was there at the moments she needed to be, with intervention and support). She occasionally addressed the class as a whole to remind them of their tasks: 'Remember you are talking to each other as you work to explain the method you are trying out, to help each other and to see if you can learn more about division today'.

The end of the lesson, on the carpet, wasn't just a plenary about the subject area, but included reference to how their learning was supported by each other and the resources they used, and they were encouraged and helped to reflect upon new skills and ideas.

Faye believes that letting the children talk through ideas and sharing, supporting each other, builds on their previous understanding. She told me that the school allows a teacher to be creative in planning and teaching, but that the support she has been given has let her develop the use of talk how and when she feels it's right and appropriate for the class. Faye feels that their attitude to and engagement with lessons that include talk is very high and continually challenges them by asking questions that make them consider and reflect on the way they learn best.

I made the decision to observe the year groups in order, so I began in Early Years and moved through the school. By the time I entered the Year 5 classroom, I felt I had already seen the progression in the use of talk that Jo Cooper and I had discussed when she spoke about the aims and philosophy of the school. But it was indeed a delight to watch a class of children genuinely appear to have ownership of their learning. This was evident through the way they understood what was expected of them when asked to discuss something, but also how they applied the experience to the tasks they were carrying out. Certainly, the children observed in Year 5 were using their talking in a more mature way than the younger children. It had developed and they appeared very aware of how to talk to support learning and why they were doing it.

The evidence from my observations seems to show a development in modelling and skills, teaching and expectation, based on the school's philosophy reading the importance of talk. There was a culture that encouraged teachers and pupils to reflect upon, not only what learning is, but how it happens successfully.

Siobhan McKiernan, the Year 5 teacher approached the lesson as a learner alongside the children. This was a joint affair. The whole class – adults and children alike – was a group of people completely engaged and engrossed in their focus. There was an atmosphere of a workshop; I could feel the learning going on. There was almost no point when they weren't discussing and putting forward ideas and suggestions. As a visitor, I too was included; the children were keen to share their findings and ideas, to ask for opinions and advice. I heard one group compare the work to something done the previous week. They reflected on how this was the next part of their learning, how now they knew more and understood it better. I didn't ask any questions I didn't need to; as I walked past groups excitedly shared what they were doing.

The sense of achievement was tangible, they were very proud of their work. Siobhan told me that: 'The use of talking partners, shared discussion, and verbal feedback from both peers and teachers is so important in a classroom setting as it gives the learner an opportunity to scaffold their ideas and sequence their thoughts'. She feels that:

It is extremely beneficial in supporting and developing the learner's investigative skills. Giving the learner an opportunity to discuss ideas with friends and create shared conclusions, in my experience, helps to produce more confident and fluent written work as well.

Reflecting on talk

Through my time at St Thomas a Becket Primary School I was privileged to see how talk developed throughout the school, underpinned by the knowledge and understanding of the senior leaders who ensured talk had prominence and permutated all aspects of school life. All staff understood the complex nature of talk and that it could not be reduced down in any way to a target sheet or set of criteria to evidence. The talk was 'in action' throughout every class, with teachers skillfully navigating their way, scaffolding and modelling talk between themselves as adults and with the children.

Research by Sinclair and Coulthard (1992) identified that the most common type of teacher-pupil interaction was the pattern of Initiation-Response-Feedback (IRF) where teachers are looking for the 'correct' answer to their question and once it is given will move on to another question or aspect of the lesson. At St Thomas a Becket Primary School I could identify a greater range of teaching talk taking place. Alexander (2008) identified five aspects of teaching talk as outlined below. He noted that it was the discussion and scaffolded dialogue where most learning would take place.

- **Rote** (teacher-class): The drilling of facts, ideas, and routines through constant repetition.
- **Recitation** (teacher-class or teacher-group): The accumulation of knowledge and understanding through questions designed to test or stimulate recall of what had been previously encountered, or cue pupils to work out the answer from clues provided in the question.
- **Instruction/exposition** (teacher-class, teacher-group, or teacher-individual): Telling pupils what to do, and/or imparting information, and/or explaining facts, principles, or procedures.
- **Discussion** (teacher-class, teacher-group, or pupil-pupil): The exchange of ideas with a view to sharing information and solving problems.
- **Scaffolded dialogue** (teacher-class, teacher-group, teacher-individual, or pupil-pupil): Achieving common understanding through structured and cumulative questioning and discussion which guide and prompt, reduce choices, minimise risk and error, and expedite 'handover' of concepts and principles. There may, or may not, be a right answer but justification and explanation are sought. Pupils' thinking is challenged and so understanding

is enhanced. The teacher is likely to share several exchanges with a particular child several times in order to move the thinking on.

(Alexander, 2008: 30)

With the knowledge and understanding from the senior leadership team and the principled approach taken at St Thomas a Becket Primary School it was clear to me that children were immersed in a talk environment which was stimulating, motivating, and enriching. Talk underpinned every aspect of the school with a prominence of discussion and scaffolded dialogue leading the teacher talk.

Reading

Learning to read is one of the most important, if not *the* most important learning activity that children will engage with during their first years of school. Primary schools, and more specifically teachers, play a fundamental role in developing children's abilities to read effectively for a whole range of purposes. However, controversy about teaching reading has a long-standing history and causes much confusion for teachers, educators, parents, and student teachers alike. Written almost 50 years ago, the Bullock Report (DES, 1975:77) is a reminder that 'there is no one method, medium, approach, device or philosophy that holds the key to the process of reading'. Now, more than ever, reading is dependent on the context – e.g. reading on a screen or paper – the experiences of the reader, and the communities in which reading takes place (Bearne and Reedy, 2018).

For the vast majority of us, reading has become an automatic process. Before leaving our homes in the morning our brains have read thousands of messages in the form of pictures, signs, symbols, posts on screens, emails, WhatsApp messages, books, newspapers, headlines, magazines … the list goes on. It is fair to say that reading is an essential part of our everyday lives and it is a skill we need in order to exist. But reading is so much more than this. Reading has the power to transport us to fictitious worlds, it allows us to imagine beyond our own existence, and it helps us form connections with imaginary characters, places, and ideas. If nurtured in the correct way, reading can be irresistible, highly addictive, and wonderfully liberating.

Sadly, for some, reading is none of the above and the thought of picking up a book or reading something on a screen fills some with a surge of overwhelming anxiety. Much of the academic research carried out into reading has explored the most effective ways, and preferred strategies, to teach reading. Bearne and Reedy (2018) have helpfully divided these strategies into two categories, learning to read and becoming a reader. *Learning* to read is about getting the words off the page, this is called decoding. For some this will come first, whereas for others, meaning will come first, with the preference to understand what a word means and then decode it. Whereas *becoming* a reader is about supporting young readers in developing a repertoire of reading behaviours, encouraging them to develop autonomy, choice, and agency in their selection of reading material, and helping them carve a reading identity. This approach is all about laying the foundations both in school and outside of school, so that children see the benefits that can be gained from a lifelong commitment to reading. And it is the teacher who has a fundamental role in nurturing this commitment to reading.

There are many different viewpoints on reading development, and we would strongly encourage you to explore these perspectives so that you can begin to see where your values as a reading teacher lie. The following is not an exhaustive list for you to aimlessly research, rather the perspectives are suggestions for you to dip in and out of within your own personal study:

- Skills and drills
- Cognitive-Psychological view
- Psycholinguistic view
- The Simple View of Reading
- Socio-political perspective
- Sociocultural view

Critical question

What perspective(s) do you take your values around reading from?

For the remainder of this section on reading, a sociocultural view will be taken. It is here where we turn to the work of Cremin et al., (2014) who have published prolific research into reading for pleasure. Findings from this fascinating study reveal that international policy seems to have emphasised the skills needed for reading, rather than children's engagement, motivation, and dedication to reading (that is 'learning to read', rather than 'becoming a reader'). If schools want to develop children as lifelong readers, they must ensure that their teaching incorporates strategies which promote the skill, but most importantly the will to read. Through the creation of a supportive classroom reading community, a reading for pleasure agenda, where children can learn to become readers, can be achieved. Such a community is most effective when it is led by a reading teacher – that is a teacher who reads, and a reader who teaches. Having reviewed literature around reading for pleasure, Bearne and Reedy (2018) and Wyse et al., (2018), suggest that in order for children to develop a love of reading, they need exposure to:

- Social reading environments (reading is not an act that is carried out in silence or isolation)
- High-quality books being read aloud to them (books that will offer them pleasure, not books that are designed for skills-based literacy teaching)
- Creative opportunities to explore books (e.g. through Drama and role play as this will help them gain a better understanding of the content and theme of a book)
- Informal book talk, inside text talk, and recommendations (a chance to pour over a book and have a good blather about it)

To help the reader understand how the above four points can be put into practice within the primary classroom, attention will now be given to a case study which explores the way in which a South East London primary school has used one book to promote reading across the school.

Background to the case study school

Ealdham Primary, is a two-form entry inner London school that is situated on the cusp of a deprived area of London and has a significantly high proportion of children receiving pupil premium, as well as a large majority of pupils who speak English as an additional language. The teachers at Ealdham have always been aware of the vital necessity to model and encourage reading in the most positive ways possible. Although reading was valued, discussions amongst the staff team revealed that they needed to develop the way in which they promoted and taught reading to their children. Together with a combination of reading initiatives, a project named 'One School – One Book' was introduced across all year groups. This project required all teachers from Nursery through to Year 6 to use the book *Malala's Magic Pencil* by Malala Yousafzai to produce a whole class written and artistic response that could be displayed across the school. Unlike other case studies that you will read in this book, the following case study does not focus on one or two particular professionals, rather it brings together the reflections of a number of teachers. This is because the case study is reporting on a whole school approach that involved all members of teaching staff and showcases how they had complete control over the work that was produced and were often led by the children's voices and their interests.

Case Study on 'One School – One Book', changing the way reading is promoted and taught across the school

At the end of the summer term headteacher Christian York read aloud *Malala's Magic Pencil* to all members of staff. When asked why he did this, he explained:

> I wanted to share my interpretation, but also it was important that the staff had the opportunity to sit back and really listen to the story without distractions. My staff team love being read to! By doing this, it meant that everyone was familiar with the story when they returned to it to plan their work.

The teachers were each given their own copy of the book to take home over the summer. During this time, they had the freedom to plan their own learning outcomes, objectives, and activities, without fear of judgement. When asked to share their views on this process, words like 'liberating', 'exciting', 'fun', and 'insightful' were often used. One Year 3 teacher reported:

> It was exciting, as it allowed me to tailor the lessons for the children and create a sequence of lessons that would spark their imagination and interest.

By taking the book home and reading it several times, the teachers became readers, and in doing so gained a deeper insight into the book. One Year 6 teacher went on to report that during the summer months, she also read the book aloud to familiarise herself with the language and flow of the book.

Staff and children returned from the summer break with renewed levels of energy, and excitement was bubbling behind classroom doors, as all teachers patiently waited to introduce the story to their class on the same day. This whole school approach certainly had a lasting impact and the children's interest was ignited even further when they soon realised that they were reading the same book as their siblings. This sparked deep and long conversations, with one Reception teacher explaining how parents were even commenting on the book because it has been discussed so much at home. One Year 2 teacher went on to say:

> children stopped me in the corridor and wanted to tell me about the book.

Having captured the children's attention and interest in the book, teachers were able to begin exploring the story in more depth. To do this a number of ideas were implemented. In Year 5 the teacher explained how she used active learning and groupings to tap into the story:

> We used drama as a way to explore the characters feeling and emotions and various elements of the story. And we then used role-play in mixed ability groups to bring the story alive.

Having facilitated creative opportunities for children to explore texts, teachers were keen to encourage children to respond creatively, and in many different ways, but knew this required additional time to read. For most teachers, this came through the facilitation of small group work where the children were provided with opportunities to build understanding in a social context. The teachers at Ealdham reported that by connecting with children through informed and respectful book talk, the children's participation levels increased. In addition to this, the group discussions could be tailored to suit the specific needs of the children.

A commonly reported benefit of making time to read in smaller groups was the way in which the children began to find a voice and question, ponder, analyse, and check their understanding. Through the creation of a safe space, children were more willing not only to share, but also to take risks with sharing some of their thoughts and opinions. One Year 4 teacher confirmed that his children had started to question more about what they had read. For one teacher in Year 1, it was also an ideal opportunity to assess the children's progress and note where additional comprehension support was needed. Interestingly for this teacher, the group discussions enabled her to share her own thoughts about the book. This teacher felt it helped the younger children, who had limited experience of this type of text, gain clarification on the author's key message. These fruitful discussions and dialogues were an essential part of the process and key in helping children really begin to understand and unpick the text. A Year 3 teacher offered the following response:

They were able to discuss some serious social issues in context of the book. The children were engaged throughout the work and developed critical thinking strategies in order to create pieces of writing.

From a socio-cultural perspective, it appears that this high-quality text helped the children at Ealdham move away from focusing on themselves, and rather shift their focus on the social and cultural context in which the story occurred (Hall, 2003). The words of one of the Year 6 teacher, eloquently expresses the way this project enhanced the reading culture at Ealdham:

> It had a big impact in a very positive way, it established reading as not only an essential tool in learning, but also as a pleasure, something we do because it is interesting, that it can fill us with joy, make us laugh or even cry, that it allows us the chance to have different experiences, to step into new worlds, and visit new places.

Discussion: 'One School - One Book'

When asked to reflect on the benefits of taking the 'One School - One Book' approach, teachers were very complimentary and in unanimous agreement that reading the book as a whole school created a real sense of community. A huge part of building such a community was dependent on the four factors that Bearne and Reedy (2018) and Wyse et al., (2018) previously mentioned (see above box). In relation to the case study each one of these factors will be discussed in further detail.

Social reading environments

Although not previously mentioned, discussions held with the literacy coordinator, Samantha Leslie, during a visit to the school revealed that funding had been given to restock all book corners in the classrooms. According to Medwell and Wray (2016), a classroom library supports the idea that for children to be literate, they need to have access to a rich range of reading materials, whilst being given time to indulge, explore, and experiment with the texts. Classroom libraries are a crucial source of reading material and an important means of encouragement for reading. In addition to this Samantha explained that they constantly reviewed and improved their whole curriculum to ensure, where possible, the books supported and complemented the teaching of other subjects. But she insists that all teachers still used their favourite, as well as the children's favourite texts, even if they were not felt to complement or enhance the current learning topic or theme. Familiarity and slipping into a sense of comfort is very important for the continuing growth of the schools reading community. But social reading environments are not just about the locality, they are also about the act of communicating with one another. Referring back to the case study, it is clear that the small group work facilitated a culture that encouraged reading as a social act, sometimes with two, but more often than not, with more than two children sharing their interpretations of the story.

High-quality books being read aloud

At the start of the case study, we learnt that headteacher Christian York read *Malala's Magic Pencil* to all members of staff. Reading aloud has always been a priority at Ealdham with Christian reporting that:

> teachers finish the day with read alouds and share their own favourite books with the children.

For these teachers reading aloud to their classes at the end of each day is seen as a crucial factor in modelling to, and engaging children in reading. When asked, all teachers confirmed that they ringfenced a good proportion of time each day to read the text aloud to their children.

When I visited the school as part of the case study work, the act of reading aloud was seen in a number of classrooms across all Key Stages. Most notably it occurred during a Year 6 guided reading session, where the class teacher was reading a long passage to the children in her group, instructing them to carefully tune into the words that were pouring out of her mouth as she read from the page. For Barrs and Cork (2001:39) when teachers read aloud, children are able to 'attend more closely to the language of the text', without having to focus on reading skills such as decoding. Reading aloud to her Year 6 children permitted this teacher to model the way that a reader can manipulate the tone, pitch, gesture, speed, intonation, and use of dramatic pause, as well as reading strategies and behaviours.

By reading aloud from *Malala's Magic Pencil*, the teachers were able to share their own interpretation and understanding of the story, allowing them to emphasise the clues and signs that were required in order to fill in the gaps, this was most evident from the reflections given by the Year 1 teacher. This in turn allowed the children to draw upon these as a way of understanding the narrative. Reading aloud in this way has been described as a soundtrack to a story (Gamble, 2019). Through the act of reading aloud, discussions can be shared as a whole class, or in smaller groups, making the reading process a very social activity. Building on the social nature of reading aloud, teachers were successful in facilitating creative opportunities for children to explore the text.

Critical question

When you next read aloud to a class of children, what reading strategies will you model to the children?

Creative opportunities to explore books

The case study revealed how one Year 5 teacher used Drama with her children to explore ideas and issues together. By doing this, the teacher helped the children to evoke imaginative empathy and explore worlds that were far beyond their reach. Bearne and Reedy (2018) warn that this approach to teaching is not for everyone, and I like to think of it rather like Marmite.

Some teachers – including myself – love it, whereas others hate it with a passion. But, regardless of one's viewpoint, setting up opportunities to explore stories through Drama and role play allows children to dig deeper into a story. In negotiating such opportunities for Drama, the children's agency and ownership of their learning can begin to imbue. When immersed in such creative contexts, children are prompted to become engaged as speakers, listeners, readers, and writers (Cremin et al., 2014). Role play is just one form of improvisational drama that can be used in the classroom. You may want to consider researching some of the alternative conventions:

Decision alley
Forum theatre
Group sculpture
Improvisation: small group
Mantle of the expert
Role on the wall
Thought tracking
Drawing
Freeze frame
Hot seating
Improvisation: whole class
Teaching in role

Informal book talk, inside text talk and recommendations

Gamble (2019) suggests that high-quality texts must be rich enough to support re-reading and have the potential for exploring layers of meaning – this means reading deeply. Margaret Meek (1988) argued that the specific texts that children experience are one of the most important aids to learning to read, because it is not simply being able to decode the words, it is far more concerned with understanding the meaning behind the words. Teaching through literature in this way has endless benefits. If the correct text is selected, it has the potential to stimulate and engage emotions, spark imagination, and develop empathy whilst enabling children to encounter and deal with real world issues (Gamble, 2019).

Literature offers 'mirrors, windows and sliding glass doors' (Sims Bishop, 1990) into real and fantasy worlds, whilst empowering the reader to gain a better understanding of themselves and others. It is essential that in all classrooms, diversity is represented and celebrated through the literature that you, as a reading teacher, bring to the classroom. Although considerations of diversity are improving each year, there is still a long way to go before there is equal representation in children's literature. In 2017, The Centre for Literacy in Primary Education (CLPE) revealed profoundly eye opening and shockingly worrying findings in their survey of ethnic representation within UK children's literature (CLPE, 2018).

They revealed that out of 9,115 children's books published in the UK in 2017, only 391 of these books featured BAME (Black, Asian and minority ethnic) characters. Furthermore, only 1% of these 9,115 books had a BAME main character. There is a clear cry to redress the imbalances in representation, so that young children see their realities reflected in the books they read, and not just problematic representations. *Malala's Magic Pencil* is one such book that enables children to feel valued and entitled to occupy the literary space. It is essential for reading teachers to begin to develop a growing knowledge of titles, as well as the names of authors who come from a range of backgrounds, who are both established and new, who can paint characters and worlds that are congruent with children's realities. Publishers who specialise in providing a broad range of books include:

Letterbox Library
Mantra Lingua
Nosy Crow
Tamarin Press

Critical question

How many children's picture books can you name with a BAME character or author that have been published in the past five years?

According to Gamble (2019), teachers need to be knowledgeable about books and to under-stand how they effectively deploy their knowledge through their teaching. Teachers at Ealdham reported rereading the book several times to become familiar with the language, closely examining the illustrations and jotting down ideas, creating thought showers regard-ing key themes, using internet sources to research the background of the book, searching for online reviews of the book – KS2 teachers even found relatable news articles and videos that could be used with their classes. It would appear this approach to reading enabled the teachers and the children at Ealdham to be active in the process of making meaning. Gamble (2019) argues that such an approach could be classed as dialogic, in the way that it allows for freedom and flexibility in the interpretations of meaning, and consequently opens up oppor-tunities to apply critical thinking skills.

Closing thoughts on reading

The teachers referred to in this case study have been inventive and resourceful in finding ways to navigate between the demands of intense pressures that fall on their shoulders from higher powers and a desire to make reading irresistible. A few of the many ways that you might want to begin to change the way that reading is promoted, modelled, and taught within your classroom and school have been explored in this section. But there is a plethora of ideas and suggestions readily available for you to tap into. To help you grow your effectiveness as a reading teacher there are a number of useful websites and resources that you can download. The Just Imagine Story Centre (www.justimaginestorycentre.co.uk) and BookTrust (www .booktrust.org.uk) are excellent at providing information about new and established texts.

Both websites include book reviews, author interviews, lesson ideas, and top tips for teachers to use when selecting and working with texts in the classroom. Other websites are included at the end of this chapter.

Writing

Teaching writing

Writing is a social act, when we write we are taking part in a social practice which is shaped by historical and social understanding of what writing is and how it operates (Cremin and Myhill, 2012). This approach dominates current theory, Cremin and Myhill (2012) consider that as teachers, we teach children what we value about the culture of writing. They feel that texts are socially constructed and that children develop their knowledge of language through their social environment. Dyson (1997:17) adds to this, explaining that becoming literate involves deliberately manipulating language to take part in 'culturally valued literacy events'. She goes on to say that, through participating in such events children learn the conventions of writing, they learn who writes and who they write to, why and how people write, and for what purposes they do it.

For the vast majority of children, their first writing experiences take place in the home, often involving interactions with family members and friends. Jones (2015) notes that such events are usually purposeful forms of communication with a responsive audience. Writing experiences at home usually involve a freedom of choice of what to write about and will include a variety of meaning making modes.

When planning writing activities for children it is important to consider what writing is and for what purposes we use it. The writing that we as adults do is usually set within a known context and writing is purposeful, we are aware of who our audience is and have learnt over time how to adapt our writing to engage the person that is to read it. Often, we share our writing with a friend to check that it is okay, and we sometimes have to write alongside someone which involves us in a collaborative endeavour. Much of the writing we do is digital, and our speed of writing develops alongside our keyboard skills.

When teaching children about the craft of writing it is important to try to create similar conditions and introduce them to the skills that they need to develop. It is vital to engage children in the writing process from the beginning and there are a variety of ways in which to do this. Writing is composed of two elements – composition and transcription – and it has been found that the majority of children perceive transcription to be the most important aspect of writing (Chamberlain, 2016). When teaching it is very important that their equal importance is shared with the children, as teachers we need to be careful that we do not focus too much on the technical aspects of writing and ignore the compositional aspect of it.

It is also very important to provide writing opportunities that are pleasurable for children. The National Literacy Trust (NLT: 2016) conducted a survey which noted that there has been a decline in UK children's enjoyment, desire, and motivation to write, both in and out of school. Nearly half of the children who responded to the survey indicated either an indifference towards, or a dislike of, writing. The report also found that many children who did not enjoy writing, wrote below their expected level, compared with those that enjoyed writing.

Young (2018), founder of Literacy For Pleasure, developed the Writing For Pleasure Manifesto in response to this, as he considers that there is no reason that children and young people cannot find the same pleasure in writing that they do in reading. He notes that National Literacy Trust's 2016 survey showed that for many years children's enjoyment and motivation in writing has declined or stagnated both in and out of school. He also quotes the National Literacy Trust who state that 'the findings highlight the importance of writing for enjoyment for children's outcomes and warrant a call for more attention to writing enjoyment in schools, research and policy' (2017:15). One way of creating pleasurable writing activities is to frame writing around a high-quality text.

The use of text to create a context for writing

The links between reading and writing have been widely established (Cremin and Myhill, 2012) and using a text to provide a context for writing is very effective. There are a number of types of texts that work particularly well:

- High-quality picture books and novels
- Film and digital texts including computer games
- Poetry
- Paintings and images

It is good to use a range of texts throughout the year including those that are more traditional alongside those that reflect children's popular culture and experiences of digital literacy.

Creating a sense of audience

Any writer gains a sense of satisfaction from having someone read and respond to their work, so it is important that children are given a sense of audience when writing. Cremin and Myhill (2012) emphasise the importance of knowing the audience that writing is aimed at, as what is written will be shaped by the intended audience. Jones (2015) agrees that children are highly motivated by authentic writing practices that encourage children to share their writing with others. This agrees with a study by Gadd and Parr (2017) who found that the most effective teachers involved the children in authentic writing tasks aimed at real audiences. Writing for an audience allows children to shape their writing for their reader and gives a purpose to their writing. The language choices they will make within the writing will be influenced by who they are writing for. There are a number of ways of creating an audience. With stories and poetic texts, it can be a good idea to aim the writing for either an audience of an older or younger class in the school. In this way writing becomes more real, as children can consider how their writing will engage the reader and keep them interested. Published work can be put in the book area so that others in the class can read it.

When writing non-fiction texts, audiences can be both real and created. A report on animals could easily be shared with peers or children in other classes. An audience for a letter could be created in response to a character in a book of film. For example, after watching the film *Paddington 2* a letter could be written to the judge apologising for the haircut that Paddington gives him. When modelling to the children, specific language choices can be explained and reasons for style discussed.

Writing across the curriculum

Writing across the curriculum provides both a context and purpose for children. Audiences can be both read and created. For instance, when studying the Ancient Romans children can write news reports of important events, letters between historical characters, and diaries of notable historical happenings. This allows the children to write in a supportive environment about a subject that they already have knowledge about. Reading can be used to gather the required information, KWL Books (Ogle, 1989) work particularly well. This allows children to express what they know, want to know and what they have learnt.

Modelling

Once the audience, purpose, and context of the writing activity have been established it is very important to support children through the actual process of writing. The better the input at this stage the better the result. Some suggestions as to how to do this are:

Modelled/shared writing: Either working alone or involving in the class model the type of writing that you would like the children to do. This allows the teacher to explicitly teach aspects of composition and transcription that are needed for the children to be successful. It is really important to 'think aloud' as you write so that the children can see your thought processes. The writing produced can be used as a model for the children to base their writing on.

Mini-plenaries: If you have access to iPads and an interactive whiteboard (IWB), a mini-plenary is an excellent way to keep children focused and help them to improve their writing. A photograph can be taken of some particularly effective writing and it can be displayed on the IWB as an exemplar for the children. This is especially effective when modelling the editing process.

Reflection on writing

As an English team we are passionate about teaching writing and ensuring that children are motivated to write and do so with enjoyment. As teachers we need to make sure that the writing we require children to do is purposeful, set within a meaningful context, and allows them to develop a sense of audience. We must bear in mind that children are learning in the 21st century and consider the tools that we use to engage them in writing.

Chapter summary

Instilling a love of learning is a crucial aspect of any teacher's role where children are encouraged, nurtured, and supported to talk, read, and write in a way which creates an emotional connection between themselves and the text, other people, or the environment. A school where children's literacy learning thrives and where they see the power of literacy is important. This takes resilient teachers and leaders who ensure principled pedagogy, informed by research, leads any changes or developments in the school where talk, reading, and writing for pleasure and purpose are at the heart of the curriculum.

Further reading

www.booksforkeeps.co.uk

https://www.carnegiegreenaway.org.uk/

https://childrens.poetryarchive.org/

https://lantanapublishing.com/

https://literacyforpleasure.wordpress.com/

https://literacytrust.org.uk/

https://researchrichpedagogies.org/research/reading-for-pleasure

---

References

Alexander, R. (2008) *Towards Dialogic Teaching: Rethinking Classroom Talk*. 4th ed. York: Dialogos.

Alexander, R. (2010) *Children, Their World, Their Education. Final Report and Recommendations of the Cambridge Primary Review*. Abingdon: Routledge.

Barrs, M. and Cork, V. (2001) *The Reader in the Writer*. London: CLPE.

Bearne, E. and Reedy, D. (2018) *Teaching Primary English: Subject Knowledge and Classroom Practice*. Abingdon: Routledge.

Bruner, J. (1986) *Actual Minds, Possible Worlds*. Cambridge, MA: Harvard University Press.

Chamberlain, L. (2016) *Inspiring Writing in Primary Schools*. London: Sage.

CLPE. (2018) *Reflecting Realities: Survey of Ethnic Representation with UK Children's Literature 2017*. London: CLPE.

Cremin, T., Mottram, M., Collins, M. F., Powell, S. and Safford, K. (2014) *Building Communities of Engaged Readers: Reading for Pleasure*. Abingdon: Routledge.

Cremin, T. and Myhill, D. (2012) *Writing Voices: Creating Communities of Writers*. London: Routledge.

Department for Education and Science. (1975) *A Language for Life. Report of the Committee of Inquiry Appointed by the Secretary of State for Education and Science (The Bullock Report)*. London: HMSO.

Dyson, A. H. (1997) *Writing Superheroes Contemporary Childhood, Popular Culture and Classroom Literacy*. New York: Teachers College Press.

Gadd, M. and Parr, J. (2017) Practices of Effective Writing Teachers. *Reading and Writing* 30(7), pp. 1551-1574.

Gamble, N. (2019) *Exploring Children's Literature. Reading for Knowledge Understanding and Pleasure*. 4th ed. London: Sage.

Hall, K. (2003) *Listening to Stephen Read: Multiple Perspectives on Literacy*. Buckingham: Open University Press.

Jones, S. (2015) Authenticity and Children's Engagement with Writing. *Language and Literacy* 17(1), pp. 63-83.

Medwell, J. and Wray, D. (2016) *Essential Primary English*. London: McGraw-Hill Education.

Meek, M. (1988) *How Texts Teach What Readers Learn*. Stroud: Thimble Press.

National Literacy Trust. (2016) *Writing for Enjoyment and Its Link to Wider Writing – Findings from Our Annual Literacy Survey*. 2016 Report. Available at: https://literacytrust.org.uk/research-services/research-reports/writing-enjoyment-and-its-link-wider-writing-findings-our-annual-literacy-survey-2016-report/ [Accessed 3rd April 2019].

Ogle, D. (1989) The Know, Want to Know, Learn Strategy. In K.D. Muth (Ed.), *Children's Comprehension of Text Newark*. Delaware: International Reading Association.

Skinner, B. (1957) *Verbal Behavior*. New York, NY: Appleton-Century-Crofts.

Sims Bishop, R. (1990) Mirrors, Windows and Sliding Glass Doors. *Perspectives: Choosing and Using Books for the Classoom* 6(3), pp. ix-xi.

Sinclair, J. and Coulthard, M. (1992) Toward an Analysis of Discourse. In: M. Coulthard (Ed.), *Advances in Spoken Discourse Analysis*. Abingdon: Routledge.

Vygotsky, L. S. (1962) *Thought and Language*. Cambridge, MA: MIT Press.

Wyse, D., Jones, R., Bradford, H. and Wolpert, M. A. (2018) *Teaching English: Language and Literacy*. 3rd ed. Abingdon: Routledge.

Young. (2018) *A Writing for Pleasure Manifesto*. Available at: https://literacyforpleasure.files.wordpress.com/2017/10/writing-for-pleasure-manifesto.pdf [Accessed 3rd April 2019].

2 A Teaching for Mastery Approach
Primary Mathematics

Gemma Parker

Critical questions

What does *deep conceptual* understanding of any given mathematical concept look like?

What experiences could a teacher provide to children to help them develop this?

What implications does this have for a teacher's mathematical subject knowledge?

Introduction

'Mastery' hit the headlines in 2014 when the first Shanghai–England teacher-exchange programme, funded by the Department for Education (DfE), took place. This signalled the DfE's intent (2016) to build upon a South Asian mastery approach to teaching mathematics within English schools. Indeed, funding of £41m was announced in 2016 to support the majority of English primary schools to adopt a 'teaching for mastery' approach (TfM). Use of textbooks, rapid extra-curricular intervention, and whole class teaching (NCETM, 2014a) characterise this Chinese pedagogy, however the roots and implementation of mastery are not limited to the typical Shanghai practices which are the foundation of the DfE's TfM approach. Indeed, mastery in mathematics is not a new idea and it pre-dates its 2014 rise to prominence in England (NAMA, 2015; Duckworth et al., 2015).

At the heart of mastery of mathematics is an 'emphasis on success for all, achieved by developing conceptual understanding in mathematics, with a focus on mathematical structures' (NAMA, 2015: 2). Put simply, it means acquiring a deep, long-term, secure, and adaptable understanding of the subject (NCETM, 2019). As a Maths Lead from Nottinghamshire says, 'it's just good teaching really. It's all packaged up as something quite mystical and magical but it's just common sense, a lot of it' (Patman, cited in NCETM, 2018b). Indeed, it is common sense that children should understand the mathematics that they are doing. In this way, a TfM approach could be considered to address concerns that too often children are required to rely upon memory instead of building a connected network of conceptual understanding (OFSTED, 2008).

Let us consider this in the context of short division. Reflect:

- How were you taught short division?
- How have you seen short division taught when observing in schools?
- How have you taught short division?

Complete 237 ÷ 6 as an exercise to remind yourself and talk through the steps. Did you start by saying '6 into 2 doesn't go', '6 into 23 goes three times' and continue in that vein? If so, it is likely that you are typical of generations of English-schooled children who are well-versed in remembering procedures. On closer inspection, such an approach to short division fails to draw upon an understanding of place value which is a feature of the mathematics National Curriculum from Year 1 onwards (DfE, 2013). It also fails to build upon understanding of division as *grouping* or *sharing equally between* as the language of 'goes into' doesn't make any links explicit. Instead, it is indicative of an approach which values speed and the correct answer, and one which diminishes the focus on mathematical structure, suggesting that in mathematics it is more important to remember than to understand. Such an approach can provoke maths anxiety and a belief that maths is something that some people simply 'can't do' (Boaler, 2015).

In contrast, consider the explanation in Figure 2.1 of the formal short division method for 237 ÷ 6.

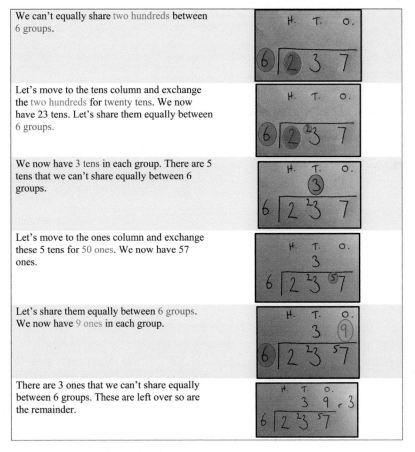

Figure 2.1 Short division with understanding

It is clear how this explanation is instead based upon understanding. It draws upon understanding place value, as well as *sharing equally between* as an underpinning structure of division (Haylock, 2014).

Critical question

Compare and contrast this example with your personal and professional experiences of short division, with respect to:

- Conceptual understanding
- Memory demands
- Sustainability/long-term learning

Skemp's (1976) seminal work on relational and instrumental understanding theorises the difference between the two approaches to short division that have been discussed so far.

Key reading

Skemp, R. (1976) Relational Understanding and Instrumental Understanding, *Mathematics Teaching*, 77, pp. 20-26

This seminal paper contrasts *relational understanding* whereby someone understands what they are doing and can explain why, with *instrumental understanding* which means rules and procedures are known, but not why or how they work.

A mastery approach to teaching mathematics aims to develop children's relational understanding by prioritising this list of indicative features (Askew et al., 2015):

- Use of multiple representations
- Clearly communicating thinking
- Relating concepts
- Independently applying understanding in order to access unfamiliar contexts

This chapter aims to support early career teachers to deepen their understanding of a TfM approach with a view to thoughtfully addressing the ongoing concern of improving standards in mathematics teaching and learning (Tidbury, 2019). Whilst this chapter aims to provide a broader window into mastery than the DfE's TfM conceptualisation, it is structured by the five big ideas (NCETM, 2017) as seen in Figure 2.2, which underpin the government funded TfM initiative (Boylan, 2019).

Teaching for Mastery

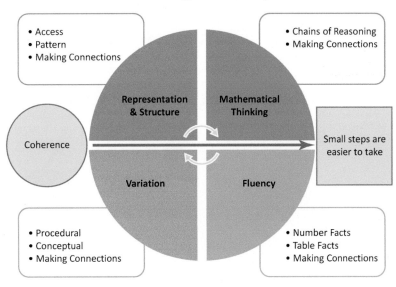

Figure 2.2 Five big ideas of teaching for mastery (NCETM, 2017)

Coherence

At the heart of a TfM approach is a focus on developing conceptual understanding in mathematics (NAMA, 2015). Such mathematical understanding can be conceived of as a conceptual network comprising of linked mental representations (Hiebert and Carpenter, 1992). Reasoning processes bridge the representations (Sierpinska, 1994) and the number and strength of the connections correlate with the depth of understanding (Hiebert and Carpenter, 1992). Barmby, Harries and Higgins' (2010) model illustrates such a connected picture and suggests that there is no boundary to understanding. Figure 2.3 is an adapted representation of their model.

This model illustrates the integral nature of connections between different ideas to conceptual understanding (Barmby, Harries and Higgins, 2010). Further, it is important to focus on connections between different representations of mathematical ideas (Bruner, 1960; Haylock and Cockburn, 1989; DfE, 2013). Such connections can be harnessed to illustrate the creative potential of maths and spark children's enthusiasm (Back, 2005). For example, tessellations and spirals both offer excellent links between mathematics and other curriculum areas. Over 20 years ago, Askew et al.'s (1997) seminal research identified a belief held by highly effective teachers that being numerate requires having a rich network of connections between different mathematical ideas. Read the full paper to explore this research in greater depth.

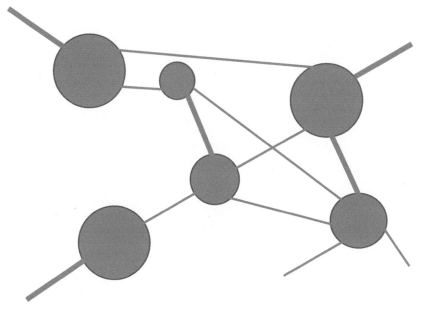

Figure 2.3 Representational-reasoning model of understanding (Adapted from Barmby, Harries and Higgins, 2010)

Research focus

Askew, M., Brown, M., Rhodes, V., Wiliam, D., & Johnson, D. (1997). *Effective Teachers of Numeracy: Report of a study carried out for the Teacher Training Agency*. London, King's College, University of London.

This research summarises that effective teachers of numeracy believe that being numerate requires having a rich network of connections between different mathematical ideas. Their subject knowledge supports this and they consequently connect different areas of mathematics, and different ideas in the same area of mathematics, using a variety of words, symbols, and diagrams.

The importance of connecting new mathematical ideas to existing ones is highlighted by Hodgen (2018) and referred to as *coherence*. Morgan (2016) expounds this, saying that coherence relies upon a 'comprehensive, detailed conceptual journey through the mathematics with a focus on mathematical relationships and making connections'. Indeed, it is suggested that planning for small sequential steps means that solid foundations can be built, leading to deep and sustainable learning (BBO Maths Hub, n.d). In order to plan for coherence and achieve a solid network of mathematical understanding, there are two related elements to be considered.

Firstly, the importance of deep subject knowledge is emphasised as critical when planning for a coherent approach. For example, when considering the objective 'to count objects', teachers need to be aware of the five counting principles (Gelman and Gallistel, 1978).

Critical question

Can you draw a connected map of understanding as in Figure 2.3, for the EYFS objective of counting out objects from a larger group (DfE, 2012)?

Secondly, a coherent approach which builds a connected network of conceptual understanding relies upon teachers selecting appropriate starting points, drawing links to prior learning, identifying next steps, as well as planning to deepen understanding, as opposed to accelerating through content. To summarise, using assessment for learning strategies is key (Hodgen, 2018).

Research focus

Black, P. & Wiliam, D. (1998) *Inside the Black Box: Raising standards through classroom assessment*, School of Education, King's College, London, United Kingdom.

This seminal piece of research explores how improving formative assessment can have a substantial impact on children's learning.

Ultimately, a coherent approach can support children to build a strong network of mathematical understanding. As such, it underpins and informs the other four TfM principles which will be addressed next.

Representation and structure

When first learning about halves, children will often fold or cut paper shapes into two equal pieces. Engaging with the concept on this practical level allows exploration of ideas to build a foundation for understanding $\frac{1}{2}$ as the abstract representation of one half. Concrete experiences of physically manipulating wholes into two equal pieces means the denominator 2 begins to take on a true meaning for the early learner. Bruner (1960) identified the importance of such an 'enactive' phase as the foundation of learning. Indeed, his seminal work provides the foundation for the current ubiquitous concrete, pictorial, abstract (CPA) spectrum in English primary schools (Boylan, 2019).

enactive	concrete
iconic	pictorial
symbolic	abstract
Bruner, 1960	Ban Har, (n.d)

Essentially, a CPA spectrum structures a comprehensive set of models and images during teaching sequences which expose and highlight the underlying structure of the mathematics; a key tenet of TfM.

Using concrete manipulatives supports learning (Rowland et al., 2010) and can help to consolidate cognitive connections between different mathematical representations which are critical to mathematical understanding (Haylock and Cockburn, 1989). The iconic/pictorial phase of learning requires children to begin representing mathematical concepts using models and images (Taylor, 2014) which, returning to the example of *halves*, may incorporate the following examples (see Figure 2.4).

Representations have the potential to provide access to mathematics which can otherwise be an abstract subject difficult for children to engage with, yet a common concern of teachers is that children may get stuck in the concrete stage. Evidence suggests however that use of representations results in them becoming part of learners' cognition and a tool for thinking with (Murata, 2008; Askew, 2012). That is to say that eventually children can visualise representations internally to assist their thinking (Rowland et al., 2010; Taylor, 2014), meaning there is no longer a need to touch or see them. Essentially, representations are mediators in developing abstract understandings (Bruner, 1974) and prematurely encouraging children to use abstract methods may mean they are not securely underpinned by understanding

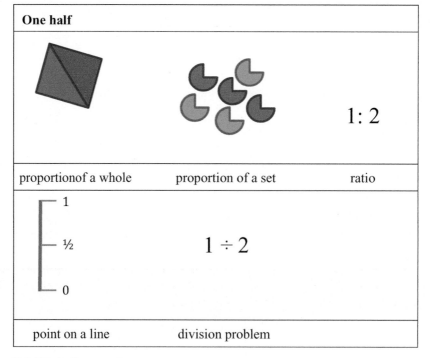

Figure 2.4 One half

and must simply rely upon fallible memories. Instead, a thoughtfully paced CPA approach can lead to a reliable network of conceptual understanding and Evans (2017) suggests that a flexible cyclical approach should replace an otherwise linear progression from concrete to pictorial to abstract.

Such a cyclical approach may mean that both older children and those who attain highly, who are typically less likely to experience concrete and pictorial representations, may still benefit. For example, children's understanding can be deepened by drawing upon varied representations to convince others that their abstract method is correct (Evans, 2017). Such reasoning is fundamental to mathematical thinking (Swan, 2011), indeed it is an aim of the national curriculum (DfE, 2013) and should be a high priority within classrooms. Secondly, using concrete manipulatives and pictorial representations can support access to more complex mathematics and problem solving. For example, the bar model is a pictorial representation which supports visualisation (Maths No Problem, 2019) by revealing the mathematical structure of a problem. Using it can allow children to gain insight and clarity as to how to solve problems (NCETM, 2014).

Ultimately, as a CPA approach can help develop conceptual understanding, it is likely to support positive attitudes towards maths as children experience success and feel empowered. Integral to this is the principle that children should be supported to select their own appropriate manipulatives, and not always be provided with what the teacher considers appropriate (Pepperell et al., 1999). Consider this case study to see how careful thinking about representation and structure supports children's understanding at Hillbrook Primary School.

Case study: Hillbrook Primary School

Hillbrook Primary School is committed to developing children's understanding of mathematical concepts. Kirsty, the Year 3 teacher, says 'the abstract nature of maths is often what makes it difficult, so it's about trying to give as much of it a meaning as possible'. The teachers understand the value of representing mathematical concepts and Jean, the Head of Year 2, explains one approach is to 'use concrete resources and get children to draw pictorial representations before moving onto the abstract'. Hannah, Head of Year 1, says that 'we use the concrete apparatus more heavily at the start as it helps with the visualisation and the reasoning'. Kirsty, Year 3 teacher, explains that 'even when I move onto the abstract, I'll show it on the board with the pictures first'. As an example, in Year 2, Jean says that 'for number bonds to ten, we used ten frames and Numicon'.

Alice, Head of Year 4, adds that for some children the use of the concrete and pictorial representations will decrease over time, but the Maths Lead, Amit, adds that 'manipulatives might help support the greater depth task'. For example, an investigation used at Hillbrook School explored totalling odd and even numbers. Children were asked to answer questions such as 'is the total odd or even when two odd numbers are added?' Critically, they were also asked to try to explain why.

Children were given lots of Numicon pieces to help their investigations. The Year 3 teacher Kirsty explains that 'these manipulatives support the child's understanding and reasoning'. By rotating and tessellating the pieces, children were able to see that the two odd pieces (composed of an even number +1) fit together to make an even number. This helped to generate explanations of why two odd numbers have an even total.

Within this case study, two ubiquitous manipulatives are used – Numicon and ten frames. Consider the two representations of numbers from 1 to 10 in Figure 2.5.

What different structures of the numbers do each emphasis? Consider the two investigations at Hillbrook:

- number bonds to 10
- odd/even totals

Which representation is best suited to each? Applying careful thought when selecting the most appropriate representation is important in order to suitably expound the key mathematical concept. It is this which lies at the heart of the representation and structure element of a TfM approach. If careful thought is put into presenting appropriate representations of specific mathematical concepts to children, then deep understanding is more likely to be built and sustained.

Key reading

'Tools' – Chapter 10 in:

Askew, M. (2012) *Transforming Primary Mathematics*, Oxon: Routledge.

This chapter explores the use of models, images, and artefacts in greater depth and will support classroom practice.

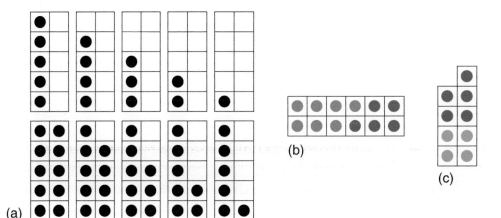

Figure 2.5 Numbers to 10

Variation

What makes a square a square? What does the set of squares in Figure 2.6 suggest are the important features? Jot down a list.

What about this set in Figure 2.7? Does this set of squares suggest different important features? Jot down a list and compare with your previous list.

Both lists should include *four equal sides* and *four right angles*. However, Figure 2.6 also suggests that all squares have horizontal bases and are blue. These irrelevant features are not fundamental properties of a square, yet are suggested to be important from this set of examples. Failing to ensure shared representations highlight the critical features of learning can carry a risk of children over-generalising as their conceptual understanding develops to include non-essential features. In this case, perhaps leading to a failure to recognise some shapes within Figure 2.7 as squares, instead believing them to be 'squares on their side', or 'diamonds'.

Consider the typical real-life examples in Figure 2.8 which are often employed to illustrate the concept of parallel lines to children. What do they suggest is important about parallel lines? This is a similarly narrow representation of parallel lines, so for what reasons might they suggest to children that the images in Figure 2.9 do not show parallel lines?

Figure 2.6 What makes a square a square?

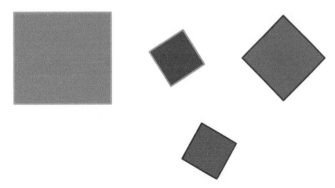

Figure 2.7 What makes a square a square?

Figure 2.8 Parallel lines

Figure 2.9 Parallel lines

Critical question

Can you think of any other mathematical concepts where children are often presented with a limited range of representations which can lead to misconceptions?

The start of this section has aimed to reinforce the idea that representations need to be carefully curated in order to avoid potential misconceptions and instead focus on deepening children's conceptual understanding. Doing so means that the critical features of a mathematical concept need to be identified and exposed through the shared representations. Teachers can then focus on 'helping learners focus their awareness on the critical features' (Askew, 2011) and design suitable 'varied set of examples, cases or questions' (Watson, 2016: 17). Such variation offers a systematic way to consider what is available for the learner to notice (Marton, Runesson and Tsui, 2003) and supports children's capacity to reason and generalise.

Variation supports pupils' deepening understanding by making connections between different representations and thinking about what different representations stress and ignore (Drury, 2015). The inclusion of non-examples is essential as they help to expound the critical features of a concept. For example, compare Figure 2.10 and Figure 2.11. Both are designed to illustrate what half of a whole is, but only one set incorporates non-examples.

On close inspection, Figure 2.10 suggests that one half is one of two parts, when in fact the critical feature is that one half is one of two *equal* parts. In Figure 2.11 the critical feature of the parts being equal is highlighted by some of the parts being unequal. By comparison, in Figure 2.10 this can be taken for granted as it is a common feature of all shapes.

Watson (2016) also raises the importance of how sequential presentation can make underlying relationships discoverable. Consider this exercise in Figure 2.12.

To accurately complete these questions, children are simply required to total the set and then divide by the number of items in each set. As an exercise, it exemplifies the traditional

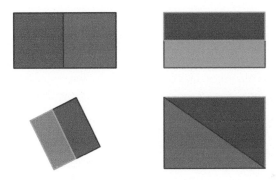

Figure 2.10 Half of a whole

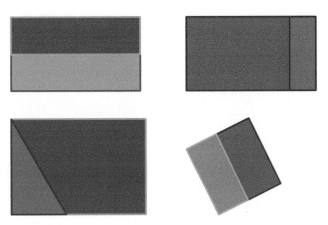

Figure 2.11 Half of a whole

Calculate the mean of the following sets of date:
1) 5, 3, 4, 2, 1
2) 11, 7, 1, 1, 5
3) 5, 1, 1, 2, 1
4) 1, 1, 1, 6, 1

Figure 2.12 Calculate the mean

Calculate the mean of the first date. How can you use the mean of set
1 to wotk out the mean of set?

1) 5, 3, 4, 2, 1
2) 10, 6, 8, 4, 2

Now, how can you use the mean of set 2 to work out the mean of set 3? And so on...

1) 15, 6, 8, 4, 2
2) 16, 7, 9, 5, 3

Figure 2.13 Calculate the mean

conception that maths is a set of rules children need to remember (McClure, 2013). If teachers want to deepen children's understanding of *mean* as a measure of average, then Figure 2.13 may be more useful.

A process of 'reflect, expect, check' (Barton, n.d.) can be applied to encourage children to think more deeply about *mean* as a concept rather than simply the result of an applied procedure.

REFLECT: What has changed between set 1 and set 2?
   Each piece of data has doubled.
EXPECT: How do you expect this to affect the mean of the set?
   As the total of the set has doubled, but the number of pieces of data has stayed the same, I would expect the mean to also double.
CHECK: Children can carry out the procedure of totalling the data and dividing by 5 to check their conjecture.

Such a process is reliant upon an intelligently designed sequence of examples which can help children develop a better understanding of a concept, and it allows potential for rich discussion too (Barton, n.d.). Askew (2011) likens contrasting exercises which are routinised and easy to do if the technique has been mastered, such as Figure 2.12, as being closer to knitting than mathematics.

In contrast, this type of variation is dynamic and encourages a focus on relationships rather than procedures. Children are able to draw conceptual connections and make generalisations. Such rich experiences can help deepen understanding and support progress and sustainable learning. However, there is a risk that children are able to complete the task by simply going 'with the grain' and following an obvious sequence without deep thinking. Consider Figure 2.14.

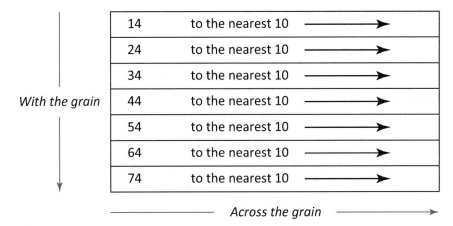

Figure 2.14 With the grain/across the grain

Whilst the sequential variation is essential to demonstrate the underlying mathematical structure, and one example would not be sufficient, the aim of the task should be to understand what is happening 'across the grain'. Instead, attention may be drawn to the 'with the grain' pattern (Watson, 2016) and it is easy to see how children may complete the answer column on autopilot by filling in sequential multiples of ten. Skillful teaching, including pertinent questions, is needed to ensure the balance between *across the grain* and *with the grain* is maintained and children's attention is drawn to what is important, not simply the continuation of a neat pattern.

In summary, variation can support deep learning by providing rich experiences rather than superficial contact. It supports a focus on conceptual relationships, making connections between ideas and reasoning. At its core is a requirement for teachers to identify the critical aspects of the mathematics as this informs important decisions about what to vary, and what the variation will draw attention to (Askew, 2012).

Key reading

'Variation Theory' – Chapter 6 in:

Askew, M. (2012) *Transforming Primary Mathematics*, Oxon: Routledge.

This chapter explores variation theory in greater depth and will support classroom practice and lesson design.

Fluency

Fluency is one aim of the mathematics National Curriculum (DfE, 2013) and is described as 'conceptual understanding and the ability to recall and apply knowledge rapidly and accurately' (DfE, 2013: 99). This statement clearly indicates that the dyad of understanding and recall is integral to fluency, however this principle can sometimes get lost in translation to practice. Firstly, fluency can instead be conflated with a disconnected memorisation of facts which can risk rising levels of math anxiety (Boaler, 2015). Secondly, McClure (2014) suggests that it can manifest as repetitive practice of formal algorithms. By exploring each of these common misinterpretations of fluency, this section aims to explore the nature of fluency and its importance as one of the five big ideas of TfM (NCETM, 2017).

Considering the topical issue of times tables, Stripp (2015) says that automatic recall of multiplication facts supports mathematical learning and understanding. He explains that automaticity can buoy children's confidence and free up cognitive space to learn new ideas and solve problems. This can allow access to more interesting and engaging mathematics (Askew, 2012) as well make it easier for children to focus on identifying connections (Meli and North, 2018; Motley, 2015). Indeed, there is wide agreement that it is useful to hold some maths facts in memory (Askew, 2012; Boaler, 2015; Stripp, 2015) and the triad of conceptual understanding, procedural fluency, and rapid recall can be mutually supportive. However, when they are divorced, children can be left with the impression that 'in maths you have to remember, but in other subjects you can think about it' (Boaler, 1998: 46).

Motley (2015) suggests that secure knowledge of facts which relies purely on memory can negate the need to focus on relationships. She suggests this can adversely affect children's understanding of structures of operations as they are instead content with recalling facts and thus unwilling and unmotivated to think about the underpinning conceptual understanding. In contrast, fluency demands that children understand *why* they are doing what they are doing (McClure, 2014) and mindful approaches should be prioritised over mindless practices such as repeated completion of formal algorithms. Take these questions from the Key Stage 2 national curriculum tests (STA, 2018) as in Figure 2.15.

It is easy to see how a child may use formal written methods to solve all four, particularly when their mathematical diet may have prioritised such strategies. It is also easy to see the potential for inaccuracy doing so may entail. A fluent child who is able to make sensible decisions about appropriate methods (McClure, 2014) is far more likely to be quicker and more accurate when answering these four questions. Indeed, the flexibility required to generate possible strategies and select an appropriate one is a key indicator of fluency (Russell, 2000).

Figure 2.16 contrasts one formal method with one informal method for one question from Figure 2.15. This highlights how the informal strategy exemplifies the components of fluency in a far more efficient way than the formal strategy. Essentially, a fluent child can make connections (McClure, 2014) and use relationships (Motley, 2015); the informal method requires

$838 \div 1 =$	$0.5 \times 28 =$
$270 \div 3 =$	$60 \div 15 =$

Figure 2.15 KS2 SATs, 2018

$$0.5 \times 28 =$$

28	$0.5 = \frac{1}{2}$
× 0.5	
14.0	$28 \div 2 = 14$
00.0	
14.0	

Figure 2.16 Choose a strategy

the application of a fraction-decimal equivalence, and the understanding that multiplying by one half is the same as dividing by two. Combined, they lead to a quick, reliable mental strategy. Compared with the formal written algorithm, it is clear to see the benefits.

Critical question

Can you create comparable tables to Figure 2.16 for the other questions in Figure 2.15?

Russell (2000) suggests that focusing on relationships between operations and numbers and, essentially, an understanding of the base ten system are paramount to developing fluency. Developing this number sense results from working with numbers in different ways (Boaler, 2015) across a range of appropriate contexts (Motley, 2015). Whilst it is suggested that varied and frequent practice can support pupils' fluency (DfE, 2013), this does not equate to robotically memorising facts (Boaler, 2015). Instead, prioritising decision making based upon efficiency, accuracy and flexibility is essential to develop children's mathematical fluency (Russell, 2000).

Mathematical thinking

Creative, curious, and collaborative are three words which might not spring to mind when thinking about mathematicians. Yet, alongside questioning, exploring, conjecturing, and proving, they are pertinent descriptors of mathematical thinking. Mathematical thinking requires systematic working, a logical approach, clear recording, and thoughtful decision making. Take the following question in Figure 2.17.

Three two-digit numbers total 201. The only digits used are 9 or 1.
What all the possible combinations?
(NCETM, 2014c)

Figure 2.17 Problem solving

Clearly, it is possible to solve this problem by adding three 2-digit numbers in a random fashion. However, a much more efficient strategy would be to first consider how the 1 in 201 can be created by totalling a combination of 9s and 1s. Would 9+9+9 work? What about 9+9+1? By identifying the ones digits of the three 2-digit numbers first, the tens digits can then be considered. By working in this fashion, the three critical features of mathematical thinking (Morgan, 2016) are employed:

- Problem solving
- Chains of reasoning
- Making connections

Making connections was addressed earlier in the chapter within the coherence section, however, *problem solving*, and *chains of reasoning* will now be addressed in turn.

Problem solving

Problem solving holds an intrinsic potential to motivate and engage children (Parr, 2011) and support the development of positive attitudes (Williams, 2008), as it is suggested that students learn better when they are curious, resourceful, resilient, and collaborative (NRich, n.d.). Indeed, Parr (2011) suggests that if an approach is taken whereby 'only when children have adequately mastered a vast number of skills and routines might they at some ill-determined time in the future get around to doing something useful with their mathematics', the majority will never willingly touch the subject again. Nevertheless, problems are 'often mistakenly thought of as something children can do only after they have learnt the "content"' (Askew, 2012). Such an approach fails to recognise that fundamentally, 'becoming a mathematical problem solver really is the point of doing mathematics' (Borthwick, 2018). Problem solving is one of three aims of the national curriculum (DfE, 2013), however it is often forgotten about or addressed as an afterthought (Borthwick, 2018). This is a long-standing issue, and nearly 40 years ago Cockcroft (1982) highlighted that children's abilities to recognise, represent, and solve problems languished behind their computational skills.

Genuine problems are ones which learners do not know how to solve; they are non-routine and new to the child (McClure, 2013). Hence, if children are told the method to use they are not problem solving and one child's problem is another child's routine exercise (Gifford, 2016). It is also important to note that problems do not have to be 'real world' applications, they can be within mathematics itself. Such rich tasks offer the opportunity to become fully immersed in the mathematics (Parr, 2011); consider this Magic V problem in Figure 2.18 (NRICH, n.d.).

Firstly, the Magic V provides great opportunities for teachers to model and explore a range of problem-solving strategies which Polya (1945) summarises as:

- Seeking solutions not just memorising procedures
- Exploring patterns not just memorising formulas
- Formulating conjectures, not just doing exercises

Completed the circles with the numbers 1–5 so that
both arms of the V have the same total.

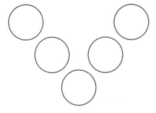

Figure 2.18 Magic V

Doing so is important as alongside multiplication facts, properties of quadrilaterals, and how to calculate a fraction of a number, for example, problem-solving skills need to be explicitly taught. Woodham (2014) suggests this comprehensive list as a good starting point:

- Working backwards
- Trial and improvement
- Conjecturing
- Pattern spotting
- Generalising
- Working systematically

Secondly, the requirement within the Magic V problem to employ a range of addition and subtraction calculation strategies, as well as knowledge of odd and even numbers, clearly 'demonstrates the power of learning content through problem solving' (Fosnot and Dolk, 2001). Such meaningful application of addition and subtraction strategies means that children are practising fundamental calculation skills within a context. Doing so is a far more engaging practice than completing a worksheet of meaningless calculations, and a good example of 'real mathematics' whereby children solve a problem (McClure, 2013).

Key reading

Woodham, L. (2014) *Using NRICH Tasks to Develop Key Problem-solving Skills*, Available online at: https://nrich.maths.org/11082 [Accessed 21st Feb 2019].

This article expounds the problem-solving skills mentioned by exemplifying them through a range of KS1 and KS2 problems. Engaging with it will deepen the reader's understanding of this selection of mathematical problem-solving strategies.

Chains of reasoning

Reasoning is another of the three aims of the Maths national curriculum (DfE, 2013). Its importance is supported by Nunes et al., (2009) who identify the ability to reason mathematically as the most important factor in a pupil's success in mathematics. Reasoning is fundamental to knowing and doing mathematics and is the 'glue' which helps maths make sense (NRICH, 2014a). It encompasses deducing, exploring, mapping, proving, sorting, explaining, pattern spotting, connecting, inferring, classifying (Hansen and Vaukins, 2011), evaluating situations, selecting problem-solving strategies, and drawing logical conclusions (NRICH, 2014a) … the list goes on!

Consider this question:

What is the largest 2-digit number you can think of which uses the digit 3?

It is a good example of a task which gives children something worthwhile to discuss mathematically which is essential as it allows children to rehearse their reasoning and listen to another's version (Askew, 2012). Doing so can support progression in reasoning which can be defined as moving from describing to proving (NRICH, 2014b).

Critical question

Consider a range of answers children could give for the above question, alongside their underpinning reasoning. Can you write an answer which would exemplify each of these progressive categories?

$$\longrightarrow$$

| describe | explain | convince | justify | prove |

There is a wealth of low threshold and high ceiling activities on the NRICH website which provide similar opportunities to reason. Once an appropriate activity has been selected, the key role of the teacher is to support the child to craft talk (Askew, n.d) which makes their thinking clear to themselves and an audience (DfE, 2013). To this end, good models of reasoning are important (DfE, ibid), as are strategies to scaffold the talk and writing (NCETM, 2016). Sentence starters, cloze procedures, shared writing, and vocabulary banks are all approaches and tools which can support children's mathematical communication. The emergent reasoning is central to a TfM approach because it deepens understanding (Askew et al., 2015), not least because it can support children to draw connections between mathematical concepts.

Read the following case study to see how a focus on mathematical thinking works in practice at Hillbrook Primary.

Case study: Hillbrook Primary School's Mathematical thinking

As a key element of TfM, Hillbrook School have a sustained focus on mathematical thinking. This has evolved to result in a focus on three key principles for teachers:

1. Children need to understand the mathematics.
2. Teachers need to model their mathematical thinking.
3. Children need to explain their mathematical thinking.

In order to implement these principles, the teachers at Hillbrook Primary School have moved away from an approach which solely focuses on providing the correct answer. Instead, they are interested in how children found their answer and they plan for children to explain what they are doing, which requires them to expound their mathematical thinking. In order to do this, teachers include investigative mathematics in their planning. The problems they set children are open ended with one/many solutions. In order to challenge children's mathematical thinking, the teachers structure children's investigative work by implementing the hierarchy, as seen in Figure 2.19.

Teachers at Hillbrook Primary have also changed the way they talk in maths lesson saying: 'I now talk through my thought process to model my thinking'. Such modelling is an important tool in helping children develop their mathematical thinking and the sharing of it. The teachers use a number of specific strategies:

'I might try something that I know is deliberately not right and ask them why'.

'We use clear sentence structures such as "there are 3 tens and there are 2 ones in 32"'.

The teachers' questioning is also very important (see Figure 2.20). Across the school, specific sentence structures are used.

There are also common questions which are routinely used across year groups:

How do you know?	Is this sometimes, always, or never true?
Do you agree with this reasoning?	Which is the odd one out? Why?
What do you think I was thinking?	What's the same, what's different?
What if … ?	Can you find another way to work it out?

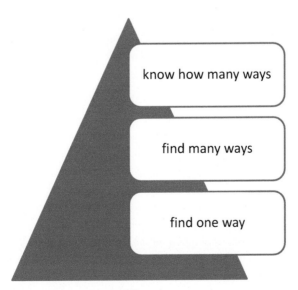

Figure 2.19 Mathematical thinking at Hillbrook

Sentence Structure	Example
I know... so ...	*I know $2/7$ of 168 is 48, so $2/7$ of _____ is 24.*
Prove it...	*Prove that 7 is an odd number.*
Show it...	*Show me that $1/3$ of the whole is smaller that $1/2$ of the same whole.*
Show me another way...	*Show me another way of working out 7×6.*

Figure 2.20 Sentence structures at Hillbrook

The coherence of this school-wide approach is clearly paying dividends as Ramsay, a Year 6 teacher, says that 'now we see children coming up much more able to explain their thinking'. Indeed, the children's perception of mathematics is changing as Jean, the Head of Year 2, says, 'children are becoming used to expecting there not to be just a one-word answer'. In agreement, Alice, Head of Year 4, says that now 'children are beating me to saying "because" by giving their reasoning as a matter of course. That's a big change'.

Fundamentally, a TfM approach aims to develop children's deep understanding and sustainable knowledge and skills (NCETM, 2019). As two key measures of this are the 'abilities to reason mathematically and to solve increasingly complex problems' (Askew et al., 2015: 4) it is clear to see why mathematical thinking is one of TfM's five big ideas (NCETM, 2017). Its reliance upon building connections between ideas through reasoning, and providing rich experiences rather than superficial contact, are just two ways in which it contributes.

Summary

- The essential idea behind a TfM approach is that all children need a deep understanding of the mathematics they are learning (Askew et al., 2015)
- The five big ideas of TfM (NCETM, 2019) can contribute in the following ways:
  - A coherent approach can support children to build strong connections within a network of mathematical understanding.
  - Appropriate representations can expose the structure of the mathematics.
  - Variation focuses on the underlying mathematical structures and demands teaching and learning is designed to address the critical question of 'what is to be learnt, and how it is going to be learnt through experiencing, or generating, and reflecting on a varied set of examples, cases or questions?' (Watson, 2016:17).
  - Fluency marries conceptual understanding and quick recall so it can support good decision-making and enable access to more complex mathematics.

   o   Mathematical thinking provokes and demands exploration of conceptual understanding through problem solving and reasoning.

References

Askew, M. (2012) *Transforming Primary Mathematics*. Oxon: Routledge.

Askew, M. (n.d.) *Private Talk, Public Conversation*. Available online at: http://mikeaskew.net/page3/page5
/files/Privatetalkpublicconverse.pdf [Accessed 1st March 2019].

Askew, M., Bishop, S., Christie, C., Eaton, S., Griffin, P. and Morgan, D. (2015) *Teaching for Mastery;
Questions, Tasks and Activities to Support Assessment, Year 5*. Oxford: Oxford University Press.

Back, J. (2005) *Creative Approaches to Mathematics across the Curriculum*. Available online at: https://
nrich.maths.org/4770 [Accessed 1st March 2019].

Ban Har, Y. (n.d.) *CPA Approach*. Available online at: https://mathsnoproblem.com/en/mastery/concrete
-pictorial-abstract/ [Accessed 30th May 2019].

Barmby, P., Harries, A. V. and Higgins, S. E. (2010) Teaching for Understanding/Understanding for
Teaching. In Thompson, I. (Ed.), *Issues in Teaching Numeracy in Primary Schools*, pp. 45–57. Berkshire:
Open University Press.

Barton, C. (n.d.) *Variation Theory*. Available online at: https://variationtheory.com/what-is-variation-theo
ry/ [Accessed 1st March 2019].

BBO Maths Hub (n.d.) *Mastery Overview*. Available online at: https://bbomathshub.org.uk/mastery/
[Accessed 27th March 2019].

Black, P. and Wiliam, D. (1998) *Inside the Black Box: Raising Standards Through Classroom Assessment*.
London: School of Education, King's College.

Boaler, J. (1998) Open and Closed Mathematics: Student Experiences and Understandings. *Journal for
Research in Mathematics Education* 29(1), pp. 41–62.

Boaler, J. (2015) *Fluency Without Fear: Research Evidence on the Best Ways to Learn Math Facts*.
Available online at: https://www.youcubed.org/evidence/fluency-without-fear/ [Accessed 25th
February 2019].

Borthwick, A. (2018) *What's the Problem with Problem Solving?* Available online at: https://nrich.maths
.org/13242 [Accessed 11th February 2019].

Boylan, M. (2019) Remastering Mathematics: Mastery, Remixes and Mash Ups. *Mathematics Teaching*
266, pp. 14–18.

Bruner, J. (1974) *Representation in Childhood in beyond the Information Given*. London: George Allen
and Unwin.

Cockcroft, W. H. (1982) *Mathematics Counts*. London: Her Majesty's Stationery Office.

Department for Education (2012) *Development Matters*. Available online at: https://www.foundati
onyears.org.uk/files/2012/03/Development-Matters-FINAL-PRINT-AMENDED.pdf [Accessed 31st
May 2019].

Department for Education (2013) *The National Curriculum in England and Wales*. Available online at:
https://assets.publishing.service.gov.uk/government/uploads/system/uploads/attachment_data/file
/425601/PRIMARY_national_curriculum.pdf [Accessed 1st March 2019].

Department for Education (2018) *Multiplication Tables Check: Development Update*. Available online
at: https://www.gov.uk/guidance/multiplication-tables-check-development-process [Accessed 22nd
February 2019].

Duckworth, L., Lawley, S., Siddiqui, M. and Stevenson, M. (2015) *Maths Hub, Mastery and Messy Research*.
Available online at: http://www.bsrlm.org.uk/wp-content/uploads/2016/02/BSRLM-IP-35-3-06.pdf
[Accessed 22nd February 2019].

Evans, S. (2017) *Examining the CPA Approach to Primary Maths*. Available online at: https://www.tes.com/
teaching-resources/blog/examining-cpa-approach-primary-maths [Accessed 22nd February 2019].

Gelman, R. and Gallistel, C. (1978) *The Child's Understanding of Number*. Cambridge, MA: Harvard
University Press.

Hansen, A. and Vaukins, D. (2011) *Primary Mathematics across the Curriculum*. Exeter: Learning Matters
Ltd.

Haylock, D. (2014) *Mathematics Explained for Primary Teachers*. 5th ed. London: Sage.

Hiebert, J. and Carpenter, T.P. (1992) Learning and Teaching with Understanding. In D. A. Grouws (Ed.),
Handbook of Research on Mathematics Teaching and Learning, pp. 65–97. New York: Macmillan.

Hodgen, J. (2018) *Guest Blog: Mastery and Maths - How Our Guidance Can Help.* Available online at: https ://educationendowmentfoundation.org.uk/pdf/generate/?u=https://educationendowmentfoundation .org.uk/pdf/content/?id=2252&e=2252&t=Guest%20Blog:%20Mastery%20and%20maths%20-%2 0how%20our%20guidance%20can%20help&s=&mode=embed [Accessed 27th March 2019].

Maths No Problem (2019) *Bar Modelling.* Available online at: https://mathsnoproblem.com/en/mastery/ bar-modelling/ [Accessed 4th March 2019].

McClure, L. (2013) *Problem Solving and the New Curriculum.* Available online at: https://nrich.maths.org /10367 [Accessed 21st February 2019].

McClure, L. (2014) *Developing Number Fluency - What, Why and How.* Available online at: https://nrich .maths.org/10624 [Accessed 21st February 2019].

Meli, R. and North, M. (2018) Using Maths Talks to Develop Fluency and Conceptual Understanding. *Mathematical Teaching* 26, pp. 28-31.

Morgan, D. (2016) *Five Big Ideas to Develop Mastery.* Available online at: https://nsmathshub.files.wordp ress.com/2016/04/4a_morgan-five_big_ideas_to_develop_mastery.pdf [Accessed 11th February 2019].

Motley, M. (2015) *Making Mathematical Connections – Part 2.* Available online at: https://www.nctm.org /Publications/Teaching-Children-Mathematics/Blog/Making-Mathematical-Connections---Part-2/ [Accessed 22nd February 2019].

Murata, A. (2008) Mathematics Teaching and Learning as a Mediating Process: The Case of Tape Diagrams. *Mathematical Thinking and Learning* 10, pp. 374-406.

NAMA (2015) *Five Myths of Mastery in Mathematics.* Available online at: http://www.nama.org.uk/Do wnloads/Five%20Myths%20about%20Mathematics%20Mastery.pdf [Accessed 28th February 2019].

NCETM (2014a) *Mastery Approaches to Mathematics and the New National Curriculum.* Available online at: https://www.ncetm.org.uk/teaching-for-mastery/mastery-explained/ [Accessed 6th February 2019].

NCETM (2014b) *The Bar Model.* Available online at: https://www.ncetm.org.uk/classroom-resources/ca-th e-bar-model/ [Accessed 24th October 2020].

NCETM (2016) *Primary and Early Years Magazine, Volume 89.* Available online at: https://www.ncetm.org .uk/media/thjevf3w/issue_89_primary_magazine.pdf [Accessed 1st March 2019].

NCETM (2017) *Five Big Ideas in Teaching for Mastery.* Available online at: https://www.ncetm.org.uk/ teaching-for-mastery/mastery-explained/five-big-ideas-in-teaching-for-mastery/ [Accessed 6th June 2019].

NCETM (2019) *Mastery Explained - What Mastery Means.* Available online at: https://www.ncetm.org.uk/ resources/49450 [Accessed 6th June 2019].

NRICH (2014a) *Reasoning: Identifying Opportunities.* Available online at: https://nrich.maths.org/10990 [Accessed 1st March 2019].

NRICH (2014b) *Reasoning: The Journey from Novice to Expert.* Available online at: https://nrich.maths .org/11336 [Accessed 13th April 2019].

NRICH (n.d.) *Developing Mathematical Habits of Mind – Primary Curriculum.* Available online at: https:// nrich.maths.org/12639 [Accessed 1st March 2019].

Nunes, T., Bryant, P., Sylva, K. and Barros, R. (2009) *Development of Maths Capabilities and Confidence in Primary School.* Oxford: DCSF.

OFSTED (2008) *Mathematics: Understanding the Score.* London: OFSTED.

Parr, A. (2011) *Rocking Chairs, Railway Games and Rayboxes.* Available online at: https://nrich.maths.org /7094 [Accessed 13th February 2019].

Patman, E. (2018) Cited in NCETM (2018b) *Teaching for Mastery: "Isn't it Just Good Teaching?"* Available online at: https://www.ncetm.org.uk/resources/49239 [Accessed 28th February 2019].

Pepperell, S., Hopkins, C., Gifford, S. and Tallant, P. (1999) *Mathematics in the Primary School; A Sense of Progression.* Oxon: Routledge.

Polya, G. (1945) *How to Solve It.* Princeton University Press.

Rowland, T., Turner, F., Thwaites, A. and Huckstep, P. (2010) *Developing Primary Mathematics Teaching.* London: Sage Publications Ltd.

Russell, S. J. (May, 2000). Developing Computational Fluency with Whole Numbers in the Elementary Grades. In Ferrucci, B. J. and Heid, M. K. (Eds.), *Millenium Focus Issue: Perspectives on Principles and Standards. The New England Math Journal.* XXXII (2), pp. 40-54. Keene, NH: Association of Teachers of Mathematics in New England.

Sierpinska, A. (1994) *Understanding in Mathematics*. London: Falmer Press.

Skemp, R. (1976) Relational Understanding and Instrumental Understanding. *Mathematics Teaching* 77, pp. 20-26.

Standards Testing Agency (2018) *Mathematics, Paper 1: Arithmetic*. Available online at: https://assets. publishing.service.gov.uk/government/uploads/system/uploads/attachment_data/file/710329/ST A187973e_2018_ks2_mathematics_Paper1_arithmetic.pdf.pdf [Accessed 13th April 2019].

Stripp, C. (2015) *It is Wrong to Tell Children that They Do not Need to Memorise Their Times Tables*. Available online at: https://www.tes.com/news/it-wrong-tell-children-they-do-not-need-memorise-t heir-times-tables [Accessed 25th February 2019].

Swann, M. (2011) *Improving Reasoning: Analysing Alternative Approaches*. Available online at: https:// nrich.maths.org/7812 [Accessed 4th April 2019].

Taylor, H. (2014) How Children Learn Mathematics and the Implications for Teaching. Chapter 1 in Tayler, H. and Harris, A (Eds.), *Learning and Teaching Mathematics*, pp. 0-8. London: Sage Publications Ltd.

Tidbury, F. (2019) A Mastery Approach: Taking the Long View. *Mathematics Teaching* 226, pp. 19-20.

Watson, A. (2016) *Variation: Analysing and Designing Tasks*. Available online at: https://www.atm.org.uk/ write/MediaUploads/Journals/MT252/MT252-16-04.pdf [Accessed 6th February 2019].

3 Science
Children as inventors

Adewale Magaji, L.D. Smith, and Michelle Best

Critical questions

What is the importance of scientific inquiry? Please give examples.

Discuss the relationship between scientific inquiry and children as inventors. Do you think scientific inquiry has any link to invention or promoting children as inventors?

How do teachers use Science as a tool to enhance independent thinking skills and problem solving among children?

Introduction

This chapter discusses the role of inquiry in primary science and shares best practice for helping children become independent thinkers, problem solvers, and inventors. The chapter covers the following:

- Who is an inventor?
- Links between scientific inquiry and promoting children as inventors
- Pedagogical approaches to supporting children as inventors
- Case study one: Exploring ways of carrying out inquiry and its link to promoting children as inventors
- Case study two: Creativity in the science classroom and the process of becoming an inventor

We will begin by exploring who an inventor is, with particular reference to children inventors, and why teachers should promote children as inventors by highlighting examples of the roles children have played as inventors. Case study one focuses on scientific inquiry and how it can promote children as inventors by exploring activities through inquiry such as investigations and problem-solving activities. This will highlight the roles of teachers and children in inquiry and draw upon evidence from literature to make a link between theory and practice. Thereby, creating opportunity to share good practices and improve teachers' pedagogical content knowledge. The second case study will highlight the processes involved in children becoming inventors and making links between creativity and inventions, and the importance of exploring children's concepts or ideas and how these could develop into a product. The chapter will end with an evaluation of pupil and teacher perceptions of inventors and their characteristics.

Who is an inventor?

While reading this chapter, you may ask yourself the question, 'who really is an inventor?' and it is likely you may even be one. The big question therefore is to consider how we can promote children as inventors. Bell et al., (2019) define an inventor as someone who is listed on a patent application and has intellectual property rights. Essentially an inventor is someone who creates or discovers a new method, form, device, or other useful means that becomes known as an invention. Bell et al., (2019) suggest that children whose families move to a high innovation area when they are young are more likely to become inventors. Exposure to innovation during childhood determines who becomes an inventor and the type of innovations they pursue. Interestingly, they consider role models – and arguably we could include teachers – as important factor in supporting children as inventors rather than the quality of schools attended or other capital accumulation of their parents.

On this basis, we therefore suggest that teachers should create awareness among children of what it means to be an inventor and cite examples of famous inventions by children to encourage them. The *Inventions Handbook* (2018) listed the following examples as famous inventions by children (Table 3.1).

A comprehensive process leading to various inventions by children is highlighted in the handbook and we would encourage teachers to go through this with pupils to encourage a 'can do' attitude and the mindset of an inventor. The process of becoming an inventor can be complex with probable interpretations in various forms, of who really is an inventor and how one could become an inventor. The first thought that may come to mind is a designer, engineer, technologist, or otherwise. However, in reality, there could be other forms of inventions that are not technology-based, thereby further instilling the concept of being an inventor

Table 3.1 Inventions by children

Child inventor	Age	Inventions	Inspiration
Philo Farnsworth	14	The electronic television	Shared his concept of an image transmitting device, an early prototype of the electronic television with his science teacher, and drawing diagrams in class.
Louis Braille	12	Braille writing system	A blind child was inspired to help other blind people to improve the way they read books by following raised letters.
Frank Epperson	11	The popsicle™	Mixed a fruit flavoured soft drink with soda powder and water to create a fizzy drink. The stick used in stirring the concoction became frozen overnight and resulted in popsicle.
Chester Greenwood	15	Earmuffs	Tried several ways to protect his ears from cold and this resulted in the creation of earmuffs.

Source: The Inventions Handbook (2018)

among children especially for those that may not be interested in pursuing science as a career.

Having cited examples of children inventors, we could argue that in order to develop children as inventors, learning should not be confined to the classroom only, but opportunities given to engage children in activities outside the classroom are vital to stimulate intellectual challenges beyond their cognitive domain. However, this would only be realised and informed by a pedagogical shift from a teacher-led learning to a more student-led and student-centred learning (Magaji, Ade-Ojo and Betteney, 2018) that allows opportunity for children's epistemological resource as a framework (Elby and Hammer, 2010) to explore the world around them and promote inventions. In the same vein, the Department for Education (DfE) (2013: 144) asserts that 'science education should provide the foundations for children to understand the world around them and be taught the essential aspects of the knowledge, methods, processes and uses of science'. We can argue, in this regard, that when children are given the opportunity to explore the world around them, it will discourage them from just being recipients of knowledge which is a transmission approach to learning (Elby and Hammer, 2010), to being students who are inquirers, creators of knowledge, and problem solvers. Therefore, in a quest to understand and promote children as inventors, we asked teachers the following question to seek their views 'who do you consider to be an inventor and why?' An excerpt from selected responses is as follows:

'Anyone who has an idea and a passion to develop it'

(Teacher, West Minster Primary School)

'Everybody because everybody has the ability to achieve'

(Teacher, West Minster Primary School)

'Thomas Edison because he invented the light bulb'

(Teachers, West Minster Primary School)

'Dyson helps save time and improved product'

(Teacher, West Minster Primary School)

'Edward Jenner – without his advancements in early vaccination, we would not be where we are now'

(Teacher, West Minster Primary School)

'Someone who developed a solution to a problem both physically and abstract concepts'

(Teacher 6, West Minster Primary School)

'Many people from past and present, and someone who can create, assess when something goes wrong, can think in and out of the box, alternative style, resilient and character'

(Teacher 7, West Minster Primary School)

'My friend is a food scientist and she developed new flavour and dishes'

(Teacher, West Minster Primary School)

'Problem solving and enquiry skills'

(Teachers, West Minster Primary School and Coopers Lane Primary School)

'Creativity, questioning, perseverance, resilience, and curiosity'

(Teachers, West Minster Primary School)

'Methodical thinkers'

(Teachers, West Minster Primary School)

'Perseverance - Thomas Edison, resilience'

(Teacher, Coopers Lane Primary School)

'Creative, perseverance/resilience, methodical'

(Teacher, Coopers Lane Primary School)

'Questioning'

(Teacher, Coopers Lane Primary School)

'Creativity, curiosity, perseverance, methodical thinker - steps clear - process'

(Teacher, Coopers Lane Primary School)

The teachers' responses show that anyone could be an inventor and what is crucial is the need to develop this 'inventor spirit' among children irrespective of their background and what career they intend pursuing in the future. This will be explored later in the section on children's perceptions of an inventor. Other salient but important attributes of an inventor are problem solving, passion, ability to think, creativity, and resilience. If teachers could identify these qualities associated with an inventor, the question to be asked is 'how can these qualities be promoted among children?' Is there curricular opportunity to further develop these qualities and if so, are teachers equipped with the subject and pedagogical knowledge required to promote these qualities and develop children as inventors? In contrast, some teachers cited examples of who an inventor is, by stating some of their inventions, therefore, the onus lies on the teacher to promote and create awareness among children on how to become one. Becoming an inventor requires helping children to develop investigative skills and this can be promoted by creating opportunities for them to be involved in scientific inquiry and helping them to understand the relationship between both processes.

Links between scientific inquiry and promoting children as inventors

Scientific inquiry, to a greater extent, has its pride of place in teaching and learning and helps teachers in promoting children as inventors. The DfE (2013: 147) promotes scientific inquiry in primary schools through the concept of working scientifically but with varying degree of complexity and skills that are required at each stage. In Years 1 and 2 the skills promoted among children involve:

- Asking simple questions and recognising that they can be answered in different ways
- Observing closely, using simple equipment
- Performing simple tests
- Identifying and classifying
- Using their observations and ideas to suggest answers to questions
- Gathering and recording data to help in answering questions

In addition to the above, in Years 3 and 4 (DFE, 2013: 155) pupils are also required to:

- Record findings using simple scientific language, drawings, labelled diagrams, keys, bar charts, and tables
- Report on findings from enquiries, including oral and written explanations, displays or presentations of results and conclusions
- Use results to draw simple conclusions, make predictions for new values, suggest improvements, and raise further questions
- Identify differences, similarities, or changes related to simple scientific ideas and processes
- Use straightforward scientific evidence to answer questions or to support their findings

While in Years 5 and 6, pupils are required to have the above skills in addition to the following:

- Planning different types of scientific enquiries to answer questions, including recognising and controlling variables where necessary
- Identifying scientific evidence that has been used to support or refute ideas or arguments

The DfE encourages schools to create opportunities for students to be involved in various learning activities that can promote all the aforementioned skills and be achievable by the end of Year 6. We could argue that these skills are required to support children as independent thinkers, problem solvers, and ultimately inventors. For children to be inventors, they must be curious and want to know how and why things appear the way they are, seek information, hypothesise, and develop concepts. Therefore, promoting curiosity among children is vital and has been highlighted as an important factor in scientific inquiry (Ofsted 2013; Van Uum, Verhoeff and Peeters, 2017; Van Schijndel, Jansen and Raijmakers, 2018) and drives the various learning experiences of children ranging from uncertainties in the inquiry process to knowledge creation and acquisition. This, in turn, prompts children to develop an interest in invention and find out information about the processes involved and how they might be developed.

During our discussions with the teachers and from the displays of children's work, it is clear that the schools celebrate children's work, and this could be a way to reinforce the 'inventor spirit' and boost children's confidence. This supports the views of Loxley et al., (2010) who suggest that teachers should model positive scientific attitudes and share enthusiasm for the work children are engaged in to shape the quality of their learning experience.

To make a link between scientific inquiry and children as inventors, we planned a well-structured lesson to provide children with the knowledge and skills that are required to work scientifically in line with the guidance of the DfE. They were involved in collaborative practical work on Darwin's finches (Hocking, Kennedy and Sochacki, 2008) such as collecting and analysing data, reporting findings, and evaluating outcomes from the practical work (this will be explored in the next section and the case study). An interesting element to this is that we created an opportunity for them to work collaboratively as inventors and to help each other during the design of bird beaks whilst evaluating the processes involved. In essence, we acted as facilitators who elicited information from the children, and where relevant, helped them to address misconceptions through prompts, rather than giving them answers, and in this case engaging them in the correct use of key words such as extinction, adaptation, and evolution.

Following on from this, we were interested in seeking information from the teachers to identify ways that they have been promoting scientific inquiry among pupils. The question asked was: 'what types of enquiry activities do children currently do in your school?' Responses include:

'Investigations and research'

> (Teachers, West Minster Primary School and Coopers Lane Primary School)

'Investigation, exploration and making igloos'

> (Teacher, West Minster Primary School)

'Classifying – when looking at plants/bulb seeds; observing animals over time, life cycle; growing own plants; problem solving – materials for different students'

> (Teacher, West Minster Primary School)

'Materials – testing properties; electricity-sabotage, children deliberately alter circuits and they have to work out what is changed'

> (Teacher, West Minster Primary School)

'Which surfaces generates the most friction; which rocks are permeable and what plants need to grow'

> (Teacher, West Minster Primary School)

'Testing, observing, making matches, classifying, and seeing discrepancies'

> (Teachers, West Minster Primary School and Coopers Lane Primary School)

'Materials in our environment, bug hotels, mini-beasts, plants, and trees; observation and growing'

> (Teacher, West Minster Primary School)

'In Year 6 children carry out research e.g. on Charles Darwin, Alfred Wallace's discovery, Mary Anning, pattern seeking, comparing, and testing, observation over time e.g. ice melting, chromatography, fair testing, and classification'

> (Teachers, Coopers Lane Primary School)

'Research/investigating and experiments'

> (Teachers, West Minster Primary School and Coopers Lane Primary School)

The above responses show that the teachers are not only engaged in promoting scientific inquiry in their classrooms in accordance with the guidance from DfE (2013) but are also supporting children as inventors by designing, making, and testing products, which could be considered as processes involved in inventions. In the same vein the teachers recognised the importance of promoting scientific inquiry in their classrooms and some of their responses included:

> it allows children to be curious and answer questions, test and prove theories, investigate, develop independence, predict results, observe and test, recording results and carry out fair testing and evaluate their findings

> (Teachers, West Minster Primary School)

pose lots of enquiry-based learning problems. Give children a problem and materials and allow them opportunity to come to a solution

(Teachers, Coopers Lane Primary School)

These skills are required in every science lesson to some extent, however, may not be fully promoted despite outcomes showing that the children have been supported with the relevant knowledge and resources required to meet the intended learning outcomes. Probable reasons could be teachers' subject and pedagogical knowledge (Dolan et al., 2010; Harrison, 2016) resulting in challenges for them to implement, contents to be covered in the national curriculum due to time constraints (Phillips et al. 2010; Harris et al., 2012), and increasing budget cuts on schools. From our experience of working with the children and discussions with the teachers, we could infer that learning to teach by inquiry is promoted and encouraged in the science class-room and teachers should be supported to develop and sustain this ability in order to promote children as inventors. This view is corroborated by Harrison (2016) who asserts that scientific inquiry may have been practiced in schools in the United Kingdom, but the progress associated with it is quite slow. In essence, various means are required to promote this element of learning in the primary classroom to prepare children for transition onto secondary education.

From the aforementioned, scientific inquiry has a greater role to play as a steppingstone towards children becoming inventors. Primary school teachers are pivotal in this learning process by creating awareness and making it explicit to children the relevance of being called inventors and making links to the projects they have developed in the classroom. Speaking to the teachers and the children during our visits shows that the teachers were enthusiastic about what they did with the children, in addition to being able to articulate this in their dis-cussions, and identifying the importance of scientific inquiry in children's learning.

Having highlighted the relevance of scientific inquiry in children's learning, we would like you to ponder over the questions in the box below.

Critical questions

What are the challenges of carrying out scientific inquiry in your classroom and are there any particular skills listed in the DfE requirements that would need more input from teachers or be rather difficult in achieving and how do you intend to achieve them?

List any skills you think children can develop from their science lessons and how does this link to promoting children as inventors?

Promoting curiosity among children is crucial in scientific inquiry. Discuss strategies you would use to promote curiosity among children and how can you model positive scientific attitudes in your classroom?

Pedagogical approaches to supporting children as inventors

Having explored the concept of scientific inquiry and its links with children as inventors, we envisage a pedagogical approach that would inform and clarify how to support children as inventors. The topic used in our case study is evolution and inheritance (DfE, 2013) as chosen by the schools and hopefully this would be vital in this process. The DfE (2013) statutory requirements of this topic are that children must be taught to:

- Recognise that living things have changed over time and that fossils provide information about living things that inhabited the Earth millions of years ago
- Recognise that living things produce offspring of the same kind, but normally offspring vary and are not identical to their parents
- Identify how animals and plants are adapted to suit their environment in different ways and that adaptation may lead to evolution

We focused on Darwin and his finches to explain the concept of evolution and inheritance, especially identifying how birds are adapted to their environment and how this relates to and provides substantial evidence of evolutionary process among living things. Prior to this, lessons taught in the schools have focused on activities that involve students exploring and creating own ideas; observing, comparing, experiments, science Week practical work; talking to students about inventors; and designing and inventing products such as tents, games, goggles, igloos, and investigating solutions to problems.

Case study: Coopers Lane Primary School and West Minster Primary School

Our lesson objectives focused on how beaks are adapted to different kinds of food and also to explain how evolution has led to changes in the sizes of birds' beaks. Children could call out the key words such as evolution, inheritance, extinction, adaptation, natural selection, survival of the fittest, and Galapagos Island to promote literacy and understanding of the terms. This activity was followed by a series of questions to check prior knowledge of the children, as we believe that some may exhibit forms of cultural capital that would contribute to the learning of others. We realised that they were not familiar with most of the key words, however one student said 'adaptation is when animals get used to their environment' and another student said 'evolution is when something changes'. Identifying these gaps in their knowledge meant that we were able to differentiate the resources and content to meet their needs.

It was important to listen to the children making links to the environment when describing adaptations, as it gave us an opportunity to further clarify how favourable variations among organisms could allow them to better adapt to their environment and survive, hence reproduce. However, we realised that it would be challenging to explain to them the relationship between the slow changes in the environment with how species evolve the necessary adaptations over generations. Therefore, the strategies adopted to support learning included using pictures of various finches and beak shapes and sizes to stimulate visual learners to be able to make a link to changes and variations among different finches. This also allowed us to direct them to the key words to work out the meanings for themselves, rather than providing them with the answers. This approach was not only useful to visual learners, but all children were able to make the link that we expected.

Misconceptions associated with the concepts of adaptation and evolution were clarified, especially pointing out to them that adaptation is a very gradual process which happens within a population rather than to an individual bird, a concept that may be above their cognitive level. This prompting was necessary as we realised that the children's perceptions of adaptation from general consensus is that it happens 'to a particular bird', and although they were able to identify various shapes and sizes of beaks of different finches provided, seeing them as belonging to the same species could have resulted in this confusion. The DfE (2013) stipulates that teachers should support children to understand that living things change over time and to identify how animals and plants are adapted to suit their environment in different ways but importantly, recognising that adaptation may lead to evolution.

Therefore, as teachers, we need to clarify and explain to children that all finches belong to the same species and that variations may have resulted in their appearances. The use of models in explaining key terms and making this link is useful to children, however, we also need to create awareness of the limitations of these models by discussing and probing them through questioning in order not to build up misconceptions.

Other strategies that we used involved storytelling (which resonates with the children's imaginations) of Down's House where Darwin lived and carried out his experiments, history and pictures of the Galapagos Island in real context so children can make the link to our discussion, and group practical work and questioning to close gaps in their knowledge. Our focus was to promote scientific inquiry among children as a means to becoming inventors. Therefore, we planned an investigation using a scientific model to simulate how birds' beaks are adapted to feeding by using various materials available to the students such as chopsticks, spoons, tweezers, and forceps to represent different types of beaks.

Children collected various food samples (such as nuts and seeds) using these beak types and then placed them in the bird's stomach (petri dish). The children had the opportunity to choose which type of beak they would use, and data was collected and analysed to make the relationship between beak shapes and the amount of food birds would eat. There was flexibility for children to choose types of beak shapes and sizes that they would like to explore and an opportunity to make predictions. All children chose to use spoon-shaped beaks, but a few children chose other types of beaks as well. They were asked to justify their decisions with some saying that spoon-shaped beaks would be able to pick more food than chopsticks and tweezers. The reasons given centred on survival of the birds as those that could not feed on a reasonable amount of food would die over a long period of time.

The knowledge and skills gained in this activity would be useful to them when creating their own beak shapes and sizes in case study two. Some children made reference to adaptation, extinction, and evolution in their discussions while others required support to be able to apply the key words used. Based on the outcomes from the practical work and discussions, misconceptions associated with the key words were further addressed. We ensured that whilst they were carrying out the practical, we went around asking questions and probing them to ascertain reasons behind their decisions and to give differentiated support to those that may have required it (see Figure 3.1).

Although we could argue that the dilemma faced by the children is how to link adaptation of birds to inheritance and evolution, a difficult concept that may not be uncommon at this stage of their development. Could this be due to the national curriculum not allowing children in primary school to be taught or given information on how genes and chromosomes work? Despite this, the national curriculum also stipulates that children should be introduced to the idea that characteristics are passed from parents to their offspring and variations over time can make some animals more or less able to survive in particular environments (DfE, 2013). For us, therefore, seeking ways to fully involve the children in their learning and promote skills such as problem solving, critical thinking, and independent learning becomes important to help them in becoming inventors. Therefore, we would encourage primary teachers to explore various models

Figure 3.1 Coopers Lane Primary School

Figure 3.2 West Minster Primary School

Figure 3.3 Coopers Lane Primary School

of classroom interactions that can help promote learning among children and support them in their journey towards becoming inventors. On this basis, we would encourage primary teachers to draw upon a more effective model of classroom interaction that is student-led and student centred as developed by Magaji, Ade-Ojo and Betteney (2018). This model involves a sequence of student initiation, student response, student probing, and student evaluation (SI-SR-SP-SE) and has been found to improve classroom interactions and attainment among science students. These sequences of interactions require supporting teachers' pedagogical knowledge to plan and structure lessons to allow children to get to their zone of proximal development and enable them to develop social capital that may further promote their skills in questioning and probing other children's views. Arguably, they would require these skills in order to become inventors (see Figures 3.2 and 3.3).

The bird beak design lesson activities were carried out in West Minster Primary School and Coopers Lane Primary School. However, the responses from pupils were distinct in both schools. The pupils from Westminster Primary School were able to talk about their designs with prompting and probing from the teacher and researchers. The pupils were able to articulate their varying ideas and adjust their designs with support. They seemed to be pursuing a process of invention without the explicit framework. This was partly through the class teacher guiding them each step of the way by questioning the purpose of their design and asking if the pupils could explain how the design would work. Teachers prompted pupils in their process of design to self-explain how their designs can be used and how the design would solve the problem presented. Rittle-Johnson (2006) suggests that this approach with pupils to getting them to self-explain was a means of improving the invention process to support pupils in developing new approaches. There is also an additional aspect to this where direct instruction from the researcher and teacher may also have avoided the development of less viable designs (Rittle-Johnson, 2006).

The pupils from Coopers Lane Primary School seem to have had experience of the process associated with invention indicated by the responses to questions such as 'you need to make a prototype', and 'you try out the prototype through trial and error'. This is demonstrated through the design in Figure 3.5 below, where the pupil has gone through a number of iterations of the design. The introduction of innovation and the process of inventing to children has a significant effect on children's tendency to identify as inventors and to invent (Bell et al., 2019). The teachers support in this school was less with regard to direct instruction for the activity as the invention process had already been embedded. The teacher took the role of the facilitator and has discussed the designs with the pupils to give them the opportunity to self-explain and evaluate their designs. This led to further developments in their designs to continue to improve them in light of their own evaluation and probing questions from the teacher (see Figures 3.4 and 3.5).

Figure 3.4 West Minster Primary School

Figure 3.5 Coopers Lane Primary School

Children's perceptions of inventors

Children's perceptions of inventors in each of the case study schools were influenced by the activities discussed in case studies one and two conducted in each environment. The pupils were motivated with the opportunity to be creative and try to solve a problem. The framework provided to pupils started with the examples of bird beaks and their design allowed pupils to demonstrate their prior learning about evolution and Darwinism. This provided a framework to support the introduction of the problem and the type of beak that would work in a particular context. From this point, the activity was open ended with the researcher and teacher becoming facilitators while the students took the lead on their designs.

During this time pupils were asked about their knowledge of inventors and how this knowledge led them to perceive who would be identified as an inventor (see Figures 3.6a and 3.6b for pupils' responses). It is interesting that the children's views of 'who an inventor is?' mirrors that of their teachers, as some of their comments include 'a person who creates something and tests it to see if it works; Galileo discovered gravity and Isaac Newton, Albert Einstein invented the fridge, Leonardo Da Vinci and the helicopter invention', etc. As with the teachers, children listed names of famous inventors when describing an inventor. This reiterates the need to encourage children to discuss not only the famous inventions that they are familiar with, but also to create awareness of other less familiar ones as means to promoting them as inventors.

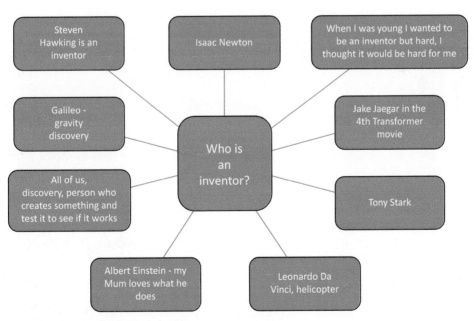

Figure 3.6a Who is an Inventor: West Minster School

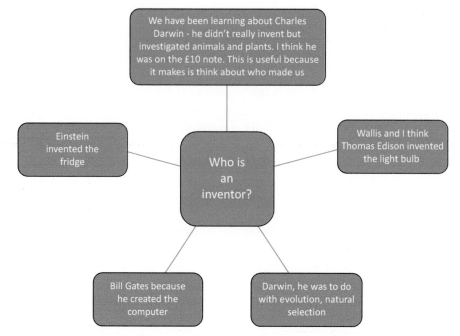

Figure 3.6b Who is an Inventor: Coopers Lane Primary School School

Most pupils identified mainly white male inventors from history. Similarly, Lee and Kwon (2018) suggest that pupils identify inventors as mainly male. This is supported by Bell et al., (2019) as they identified that 82% of inventors are males (over 40 years old), and mainly white (in the USA); up to three times more likely than those who are black. Riddy (2018) supported this picture in the UK based on the number of patents registered to males. Our examples of inventors in Table 3.1 gives credence to this notion and therefore, may further create the impression for our pupils that inventions are only made by a small group of individuals (Jordan Starko, 2014). However, there were very few contemporary inventors identified and one of them was fictional (Tony Stark – Iron Man). This may be an opportunity for primary school teachers to seek ways to promote inclusion and diversity as all children can be encouraged to view themselves as inventors and promote a love for creativity among them. To ensure that all children can view themselves in this way, the examples of inventors needs to be as diverse and inclusive such as Janet Emerson Bashen (inventor of software program Linkline), Hedy Lamarr (co-inventor of secret communication system in World War II), and Tim Berners-Lee (inventor of world wide web – means to link webpages using the internet), to name a few.

There were pupils who identified that anyone could be an inventor including themselves (see Figure 3.6b). Lee and Kwon (2018) concluded in their study that female pupils were more likely to draw female inventors, while male pupils were more likely to draw male inventors. This may suggest that pupils may be able to see themselves in the role of inventor, and this should be encouraged by the teachers who need to create a positive environment to motivate children and promote their interests in creativity. Bell et al., (2019) suggest that the home environment is also an influence where a parental inventor will increase the likelihood that their child would become inventors. In contrast to this, the pupil who indicated that it was too difficult to be an inventor may be feeling less confident in their own creative skills (Jordan Starko, 2014) and that is why the role of the teacher is crucial in this process of promoting children as inventors.

Critical questions

How could you enable all pupils to imagine themselves as inventors?
Identify a range of inventors from different ethnic groups and genders to expose your pupils to a wide range of inventors from different backgrounds and period of time (including contemporary inventors).
How can we build confidence in our pupils' creative skills?

Creativity and pupil/teacher perceptions of inventor characteristics

Creativity is viewed as the cornerstone of invention. This term is used in schools time and again to describe individuals and their work such as Picasso or in relation to creative writing. Referring to invention, Puccio and Cabra (2010) propose that there is a connection between creativity and innovation. Through the process of invention, creativity is a skill that is learnt and developed (Jordan Starko, 2014). The purpose of invention is to make products that are used by society as a means of providing solutions to problems (Lumsden, 1999; Puccio and Cabra, 2010). Pupils' perceptions of the skills of inventors also mirrors this perspective as seen in their comments in Figures 3.6c and 3.6d, in addition to other skills that they have identified. Therefore, case study two created opportunities for pupils to work in collaboration to refine their prototypes (as in Figures 3.4 and 3.5) and invent beaks that would be suitable to their chosen bird so it can feed and survive in its environment. It is this process of creativity and invention that would spur them into becoming inventors.

Teachers have taken a similar but also distinct perspective to pupils with regards to creativity and inventors. The teachers' perspectives were also being influenced by the scientific viewpoint as indicated by the fact that they identify scientific enquiry as a skill for inventors. Although these areas are very highly related, this perception may indicate a conflation between the role of scientists and inventors. However, both pupils and teachers appreciate that there is a need for determination and perseverance as there is the potential for failures as well as successes through trial and error and making revisions to the invention (see Figure 3.7).

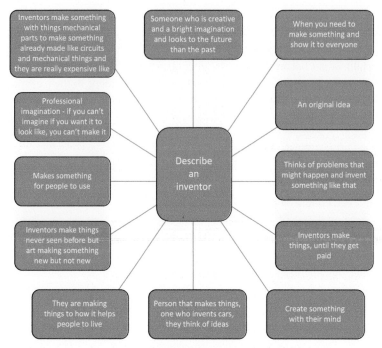

Figure 3.6c Describe an Inventor: West Minster Primary School

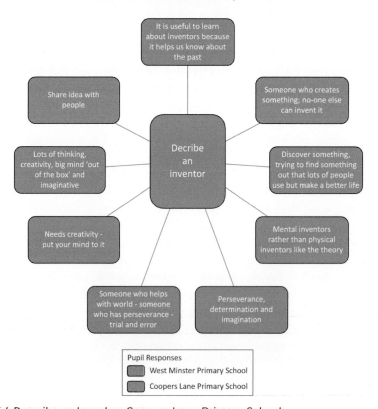

Figure 3.6d Describe an Inventor: Coopers Lane Primary School

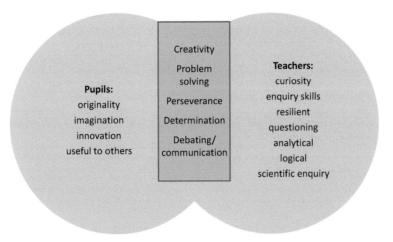

Figure 3.7 Skills identified as related to being an inventor

Critical questions

How are scientists and inventors different in their roles?

Why are determination, perseverance, and resilience important characteristics to have for inventors and scientists?

How can you build these characteristics in your pupils?

Further reading

Bell, A., Chetty, R., Jaravel, X., Petkova, N. and Van Reenen, J. (2019) Who Becomes an Inventor in America? The Importance of Exposure to Innovation. *The Quarterly Journal of Economics* 134(2), pp. 647–713. doi: 10.1093/qje/qjy028

Druin, A. and Fast, C. (2002) The Child as Learner. Critic, Inventor, and Technology Design Partner: An Analysis of Three Years of Swedish Student Journals. *International Journal of Technology and Design Education* 12, pp. 189–213.

References

Bell, A., Chetty, R., Jaravel, X., Petkova N. and Van Reenen, J. (2019) Who Becomes an Inventor in America? The Importance of Exposure to Innovation. *The Quarterly Journal of Economics* 134(2), pp. 647–713. doi: 10.1093/qje/qjy028

Department for Education (DfE) (2013) *The National Curriculum in England Key Stages 1 and 2 Framework Document*, September 2013. Retrieved on 23rd February, 2019 from: https://assets.publishing.serv ice.gov.uk/government/uploads/system/uploads/attachment_data/file/425601/PRIMARY_national_ curriculum.pdf.

Dolan, E. and Grady, J. (2010) Recognizing Students' Scientific Reasoning: A Tool for Categorizing Complexity of Reasoning during Teaching by Inquiry. *Journal of Science Teacher Education* 21, pp. 31–55. Doi: 10.1007/s10972-009-9154-7

Elby, A. and Hammer, D. (2010) Epistemological Resources and Framing: A Cognitive Framework for Helping Teachers Interpret and Respond to Their Students' Epistemologies. In L. D. Bendixon and F. C. Feucht (Eds.), *Personal Epistemology in the Classroom: Theory, Research, and Implications for Practice* (pp. 409–434). Cambridge: Cambridge University Press.

Harris, C. J., Phillips, R. S. and Penuel, W. R. (2012) Examining Teachers' Instructional Moves Aimed at Developing Students' Ideas and Questions in Learner-Centred Science Classrooms. *Journal of Science Teacher Education* 23(7), pp. 769–788.

Harrison, C. (2016) Bringing Inquiry into the Classroom through Action Research. *Education in Science* 266, pp. 30–31.

Hocking, S., Kennedy, P. and Sochacki, F. (2008) *OCR Biology, AS*. Essex, England: Heinemann.

Jordan Starko, A. (2014) *Creativity in the Classroom: School of Curious Delight*. 5th ed. Oxon: Routledge.

Lee, E. and Kwon, H. (2018) Primary Students' Stereotypic Image of Inventor in Korea. *Journal of Baltic Science Education* 17(2), pp. 252–266.

Loxley, P., Dawes, L., Nicholls, L. and Dore, B. (2010) *Teaching Primary Science. Promoting Enjoyment and Developing Understanding*. 1st ed. Abingdon, England: Taylor and Francis.

Lumsden, C. J. (1999) Evolving Creative Minds: Stories and Mechanisms. In R. J. Sternberg and J. C. Kaufman (Eds.), *Handbook of Creativity* (pp. 153–168). New York: Cambridge University Press.

Magaji, A., Ade-Ojo, G. O. and Betteney, M. (2018) Towards a Pedagogy of Science Teaching: An Exploration of the Impact of Students-Led Questioning and Feedback on the Attainment of Key Stage 3 Students in a UK School. *International Journal of Science Education* 40(9–10), pp. 1076–1093.

OFSTED (2013) *Science Teaching Must Maintain Pupils' Curiosity*. Press release. Available at: htt://www.ofsted.gov.uk/news/science-teaching-must-maintain-pupils-curiosity [Accessed 25 November 2013].

Phillips, R. S., Harris, C. J., Penuel, W. R. and Cheng, B. (2010) *Teachers Managing Students' Ideas, Questions, and Contributions in the Context of an Innovative Inquiry Based Elementary Science Unit*. Paper presented at the Annual Meeting of the National Association for Research in Science Teaching, Philadelphia, PA. March, 2010.

Puccio, G. J. and Cabra, J. F. (2010) Organizational Creativity. In J. C. Kaufman and R. J. Sternberg (Eds.), *The Cambridge Handbook of Creativity* (pp. 145–173). New York: Cambridge University Press.

Riddy, A. (2018) Why are only 7% of inventors female? *The New Statesman*. Available at: https://www.newstatesman.com/spotlight-america/skills/2018/07/why-are-only-seven-cent-inventors-women [Accessed on 16 July 2019].

Rittle-Johnson, B. (2006) Promoting Transfer: Effects of Self-Explanation and Direct Instruction. *Child Development* 77(1), pp. 1–15.

The Inventions Handbook (2018) *Famous Inventions Made by Kids*. Retrieved 18th July, 2018 from: http://www.inventions-handbook.com/inventions-made-by-kids.html.

Van Schijndel, T. J. P., Jansen, B. R. and Raijmakers, M. E. J. (2018) Do Individual Difference in Children's Curiosity Relate to Their Inquiry-Based Learning? *International Journal of Science Education* 40(9–10), pp. 996–1015.

Van Uum, M. S., Verhoeff, R. P. and Peeters, M. (2017) Inquiry-Based Science Education: Scaffolding Pupils' Self-Directed Learning in Open Inquiry. *International Journal of Science Education* 39(18), pp. 2461–2481.

4 How 'messiness' in Design and Technology can inspire creative teaching and learning

James Archer and Rachel Linfield

Critical questions

What is inspiring design and technology and what makes it distinctive as a subject in the primary curriculum?
How can design and technology inspire primary learners?
Where is the 'messiness' in primary design and technology and why is it important?

Introduction

Design and technology has the potential to be an inspiring, rigorous, and practical subject. Using creativity and imagination, pupils design and make products that solve real and relevant problems within a variety of contexts, considering their own and others' needs, wants, and values; this chapter helps highlight how.

What is primary design and technology?

As primary practitioners, it is important that we look at our own perception of each of the subjects that make up the primary curriculum. Chambers (1983) began a research phenomenon asking primary aged children to draw what they thought a scientist and engineer looked like. Further research has indicated that we hold stereotypical perceptions in relation to who can be an engineer and what they do. At the outset of this chapter, we would like to invite you to consider what perceptions you may hold and how this could influence your practice in primary design and technology.

Critical questions and personal reflections

What is your earliest memory of design and technology?
How has what you have learnt in design and technology been useful?
In your own words, how would you define primary design and technology?
How do your experiences link and influence your definition of primary design and technology?

The following pictures illustrate views of 'what someone who is good at design and technology' might look like. Interestingly all the artists, before drawing, wanted further clarification. Matthew aged six asked what design and technology was. He then said 'Oh I know. I'll draw Mr Sparks. He's good at maths too'. Thomas aged eight asked 'Can I draw me? I'm good at D and T!' Nate aged 15 based his picture on his father, an expert in all DIY jobs with tools to suit all problems. Soaibha, a trainee teacher, having experienced the subject at school and university decided to draw the lecturer who had taught the design and technology module. Rosie aged 22 felt design and technology happened throughout life. Her picture combined her father (the lab coat and mask), her mother (the tools), and appearance (the British Gas man who happened to be solving problems whilst installing a gas boiler on the day of drawing). The final picture by Kiera aged 15 recognised that most design and technology requires tools. She did not however feel there was 'a look for a D and T expert'.

The drawings indicate a move away from Chambers' research. They illustrate that a range of people can do design and technology. All participants, before drawing, wanted to talk more and based their pictures on real people showing the importance of role models (see Figure 4.1).

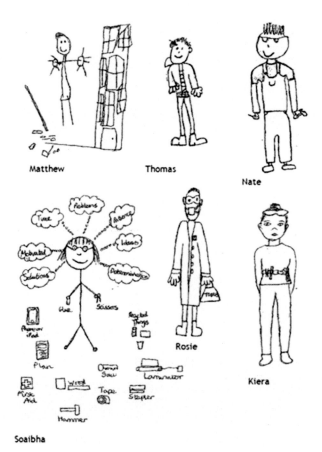

Figure 4.1 Depictions of being good at Design and Technology

As reflective practitioners, we often discover that the way in which we educate is influenced by our own educational and personal experiences. Values are developed throughout our lives that go on to influence the way that we teach. You can probably remember your least favourite experience in primary design and technology and may well be able to identify times when you were praised, and your confidence increased. Understanding the origins of teacher confidence and competence in primary design and technology is crucial if we are to fully appreciate the nature of primary design and technology.

Drawing can reveal our perceptions. By eliciting children's ideas about Design and designers, as well as any other manner of concepts, we are provided with a useful platform on which new learning can be built.

Research focus: Teacher confidence and competence in primary design and technology

The article below looks at the impact of the lived design and technology experience by the trainee teacher upon their future practice. Whilst the study focuses largely on secondary trainee participants the implications for those undertaking training in the primary sector are equally appropriate.

Read the following and consider how the findings might resonate with your own experience:

Bell, D. (2015). The reality of STEM education, design and technology teachers' perceptions: a phenomenographic study. *International Journal of Technology and Design Education*, 26(1), pp. 61-79.

Critical question

The research concludes:

> Where a teacher's own knowledge and understanding is deficient, findings indicate the potential for pupil learning is limited.

(Bell, 2015: 16)

In relation to this, what do you think the implications may be for your future education in design and technology?

The Programme of Study for Primary design and technology provides the following explanation for the subject's purpose:

> Design and technology is an inspiring, rigorous and practical subject. Using creativity and imagination, pupils design and make products that solve real and relevant problems within a variety of contexts, considering their own and others' needs, wants and values.

They acquire a broad range of subject knowledge and draw on disciplines such as mathematics, science, engineering, computing and art.

(DFE, 2013: 1)

This seems to imply design and technology might be seen as a little 'messy'. This messiness occurs because design and technology is an amalgamation of a wide range of disciplines. design and technology being a subject made out of a combination of subjects can provide scope in developing and fostering links with other disciplines. Understanding the constituent discipline elements that make up design and technology can help us develop a greater understanding of what design and technology is and what it is not. The following section will consider the impact of seeing design and technology as an art, and design and technology as a science.

Understanding what constitutes an Arts discipline is tricky as a there is very little agreement on a clear definition. All too often, there is a confusion with many people assuming that the Arts must have visual and aesthetic qualities. The National Advisory Committee on Creative and Cultural Education (1999) developed a pervasive definition of Creative Arts Education that still informs many people's understanding today. They suggest that a creative arts education is:

Imaginative activity fashioned so as to produce outcomes that are both original and of value.

(NACCCE, 1999: 30)

Such a definition may well be the reason for the misunderstanding of what is involved in Arts-based disciplines. Simply reducing the arts to physical activity, that produces outcomes that are valued, in the way that the quote above advocates does not fully appreciate the levels of cognition that are involved in Arts-linked subjects such as design and technology.

Davies and Howe (2003) speak about design and technology being 'wicked' inferring that a great deal of creative thought is essential to addressing design problems. design and technology as 'an art' is therefore much more to do with the thinking process rather than the embellishment of the end product. In addition, such a cognitive exercise may not always result in a tangible, physical form (for an example of design without the creation of a physical final product see case study 3).

The case study below explores the practices of two teachers. Which one do you think best represents a definition of design and technology as an art?

Case study: Art or design and technology?

Each year a primary school took their two reception classes to a safari park. Whilst preliminary work for both of the classes centred on wild animals, habitats, predators, and prey, the follow up work after an overcast, grey, May visit when animals tended to be asleep (classes spotted two crows, a blackbird, and three lions asleep!) also considered safari vehicles. The classes had been fascinated to see vehicles decorated with a range of animal patterns. Their teachers, however, steered the classes in different directions.

Figure 4.2 Model safari vehicle

Year 1 SB: Children were invited to make models depicting animal patterns. The focus was to research the patterns using iPads and then make models from boxes and jar lids. The majority of children stuck the 'wheels' on to their boxes with tape, few having the patience to let PVA glue dry. No wheels turned but patterns were effective for animal camouflage.

Year 1 RS: Discussion centred on the safari vehicles observed. Children were encouraged to analyse what makes something a vehicle. All were eager to make vehicles that would move with wheels that turned as well as have patterns that would provide camouflage for a specific animal. Children realised this included insects, birds, and the larger animals commonly seen at a safari park. Over several weeks children investigated ways to make wheels that turned. Final vehicles included a wide range of different mechanisms. Additional features included registration plates (see Figure 4.2).

Critical questions

Drawing on the discussion above, in which instance do you think the children engaged in design and technology as an art?

How could Year 1 SB be moved from engaging in arts and craft, to design and technology as an art approach?

Roden and Ward (2016: 6) define the sciences as 'A body of knowledge and a way of working'. The science in design and technology for many is perhaps, hidden. However, Science is very much connected with the conceptual knowledge of materials and physical processes. Importantly, the process skills, seen within the 'science way' of working exemplified in the investigation model, also contribute to our understanding of design and technology as a Science. Whilst there is not a definitive list of these process skills the two foundational skills of observation and questioning are fundamental to design and technology. Engaging in observation and the raising of questions generates ideas for products that meet genuine and authentic needs. However, the potential power of the process skills does not stop here. There are a number of process skills, that translate and transcend primary Science and design and technology. Progression in the process skills in primary science has been widely mapped. This progression can be neatly compared with the Programme of Study for Primary design and technology.

Roden and Archer (2017:11-12) have identified the progression in primary science across the primary phase. They use an approach known as 'One Science' that links the process skills to colourful icons. Children and teachers alike are known to draw on the symbols to help identify key areas of skills development. When planning teachers utilise the symbols to create a focus on a key skill in each individual lesson. Children are encouraged to employ the symbols to help plan enquiry and identify their learning focus in a particular learning episode (see Figure 4.3).

Critical question

How might these process skills assist learning within primary design and technology?

Look at the national curriculum programme of study for primary design and technology (DfE, 2013) and decide how these skills map into the skills required of those engaging in primary design and technology.

Being familiar with the requirements of the programme of study is essential if we are to be successful in our practice. In an era where teachers are known to have excessive workloads, the practice of searching for ways to expedite the planning process has become the norm. In addition, all too often practitioners report stretched timetables. Whilst we are not disputing these difficulties, adopting a scheme of work may inadvertently add to this problem. Familiarity with the national curriculum assists practitioners to appraise schemes of work in an informed way. Not only will this assist in developing a secure understanding of what conceptual knowledge is required at each phase, but this will assist you in developing a concrete understanding of the skills that are involved in design and technology and how these progress.

Key reading

Read and explore the Programme of Study for primary design and technology:

DfE (2013) design and technology programmes of study: Key Stages 1 and 2. London: DfE

In the subject content for both Key Stage 1 and 2 is states:

'Through a variety of creative and practical activities, pupils should be taught the knowledge, understanding and skills needed to engage in *an iterative process* of designing and making'.

(DfE, 2013 :2-3)

Process skill	KS 1	Lower KS2	Upper KS2
Questioning	Asking simple question	Asking relevant questions	Planning different types of scientific enquiries to answer questions
Observation	Observing closely	Making systematic and careful observations	Making systematic and careful observations
Prediction		Use conclusions to make predictions for new values, suggest	Using tests to make predictions
Selecting equipment	Using simple equipment Performing simple test	Setting up simple practical enquiries	Using equipment that assist observing and recording with increased precision, accuracy, and complexity (additional)
Selecting the one mode of enquiry		Using different types of scientific enquiries to answer questions eg. comparative investigations and fair tests	Planning different types of scientific enquiries including recognising and controlling variables where necessary Using tests to set up further comparative and fair tests
Recording	Gathering and recording data	Where appropriate taking accurate measurements using standard units with a range of equipment Gathering and recording in a variety of ways to help in answering questions Recording using simple scientific language, drawings, labelled diagrams, keys, bar charts and tables	Taking measurements, using a range of scientific equipment, increasing in accuracy and precision, taking repeat readings when appropriate Recording data and results in an increased complexity using scientific diagrams and labels, classification keys, tables, scatter graphs, bar and line graphs
Classifying	Identifying and classifying	Classifying in variety of ways to help in answering questions	
Presenting		Presenting data in a variety of ways to help in answering questions Reporting findings	Reporting and presenting findings including conclusions, causal relationships
Conleuding	Using observations and ideas to suggest answers to questions	Draw simple conclusions Use straightforward evidence to support findings	Identifying scientific evidence that has been used to support or refute arguments
Evaluating: Identifying barriers & ways forward		Identify barriers and suggest improvements and raise further questions Identify differences and similarities or changes related to ideas and processes	Evaluate the trust/reliability of findings

Figure 4.3 The 'One Science' approach

Critical question

Hope (2018) defines an iterative process as:

'A cyclical process. In design and technology this means that the designing and evaluating continue throughout the whole process of planning and making a product.'

(Hope, 2018 :5)

Considering this, how might this influence the amount of time that is required for the design and make process?

What are the benefits of design and technology?

The infamous design and patron to the design and technology Association (DATA) James Dyson suggested that:

'Design and technology is a phenomenally important subject. Logical, creative and practical … Policy-makers must recognise design and technology's significance for the UK economy and strive not just to preserve it – but to ensure it appeals to the brightest of young minds.

(DATA)

The benefits of design and technology are possibly too numerous to mention. However, we agree with the above that it is time that policy makers took the value of design and technology seriously. Beyond the pure economic benefits discussed in the quotation, design and technology has the potential to enrich lives, spaces and societies on a human level.

Critical questions and personal reflections

The following list suggests some of the wider benefits of design and technology. Do you agree with them? Are there any that you would change, adapt or erase? Are there any that you would add?

Once you have your statements, can you rank these from most important to least important?

Design and technology offers children the opportunity to:

- Be active learners
- Use problem-solving skills and to tackle problems in real life
- Learn and use approaches and processes that will be appropriate

Through school and beyond:

- Develop a broad range of key skills
- Look critically at the made world
- Foster links between subjects
- Be innovative and develop and demonstrate creativity.

You may have found this reflection to be a tricky task. Our values influence our responses to the task, but this does not necessarily mean that it is easy to champion one of the benefits above the rest. The listed benefits are integral threads that should be found within good design and technology practice. All of the listed benefits have value. Rather than producing a ranked list it may be helpful to see these benefits as key features which overlap and interlock. For example, at the heart of problem solving is the need for active learning that draws on appropriate approaches and processes is crucial. The case study below looks at this in further detail.

Case study: Classroom practice – the messy mat

Each September, a Cambridge primary school asks all children in the first week of the new school, academic year to make a 'messy mat'. Messy mats are pieces of A4 paper, decorated according to given criteria and then laminated to provide a wipe-proof mat. The reason for making the mats is two-fold: They are useful throughout the year for messy activities and they provide an invaluable way to assess skills such as the ability to use scissors, to design, to count and to follow instructions. Dependent on the year group the task can be changed. If mats are retained each year until the child leaves in the summer of the final year of primary school the mats can illustrate a child's development.

Thomas is a Year 5 child. He has been asked to do a mat based on a square that has 'exploded' into 16 pieces and told that he must use all the pieces. Analysis of Thomas' mat indicates that he has good scissor use skills. He can cut out intricate pieces with clean edges. When sticking, he uses the minimum amount of glue needed and all edges are secure. Thomas follows instructions – all pieces of the square are used and 16 have been cut (see Figure 4.4).

Figure 4.4 Exploded square messy mat

Critical question

What are the benefits of this activity?

Why might mapping progression in skills be an essential component in quality design and technology practice?

For further reading on assessment in primary design and technology read:

Hope, G. (2018) 'Assessing Children in design and technology'. Chapter 7 in Hope, G. (2018) *Mastering Primary design and technology*. London: Bloomsbury.

A brief history of design and technology

Design and technology has a chequered history. There have been periods of varied fortune in which design and technology has resulted in it taking different forms for different cohorts of children. It is likely that it is this reinvention, and repackaging, that has led to the uncertainty amongst practitioners regarding the aims and value of this important subject.

Reaching back into the early 1800s pioneers such as Steiner introduced the concept of 'Hand Craft' which emphasised making from natural materials that could be found in the locality. A variation of this is still prevalent in Nordic countries today, with children exploring traditional materials, products, and techniques as an essential part of the curriculum. Froebel developed resources known as 'gifts' that help geometry awareness as well as building skills. He also identified what he referred to as occupations which included building structures with peas and matches or sewing and weaving. This helped to reinforce the belief that there was great value in making. Looking back at this heritage it is possible to see that children have experienced an education that has involved making for centuries.

Before the formalisation of the curriculum there were several approaches that were adopted to a greater or lesser extent in local schools dependent on teacher interest. The tenets of needlework, woodwork, and painting were commonplace in many primary schools in the 1960s, which led to an innovation in practice through the introduction of junk modelling. Having not made great strides for several years a great hive of activity in the 1980s led to a real and significant change in practice. The 1987 'Craft, design and technology from 5 to 16' HMI report legitimised Craft and design and technology as a subject area and birthed the Craft and design and technology (CDT) movement. The intention here was to support a view that would engender a sense of mastery. For contemporary practitioners the concept of mastery has been made prominent through developments in Mathematics Education and is now largely understood. Unfortunately, at the time such an understanding was not prevalent and all too often the 'C' was interpreted simply as arts and craft.

After much international debate, the formalisation of the curriculum, through an act of parliament, saw the C (standing for craft) being dropped and the inception of design and technology in the first national curriculum (DESWO, 1988). Further iterations sought to refine and reduce the level of content. Rose (2009: 46) proposed the unification of Science and design and technology to form the scientific and technological understanding area of learning. Whilst the forming of a new government in 2010 meant that this plan did not come to fruition, it is important to note the political interest in unifying these subject areas. It is likely that this is a discourse which may well be revisited in future educational policy. History shows us that design and technology has been subject to change. Changes can be both positive and negative. The task of the primary practitioner is to know and understand what they believe to be the purpose of design and technology for themselves to ensure that primary school children continue to receive a quality education.

Critical questions and personal reflections

Based on your experiences as a learner and as a teacher if you were to create a new programme of study that included design and technology what would it be called and why?

Drawing on the brief history of education above, it appears that changes to design and technology policy including the national curriculum are likely to occur in your professional career:

- Why may the qualities of flexibility and resilience be important?
- What changes do you envisage happening in the future?

Many schools, due to time pressures, resort to occasional 'design and technology Days' or alternate the subject each term with art and design. What do you feel is ideal for design and technology? In order for it to encompass the 'iterative process' should design and technology be timetabled to happen every school week?

The process verses product debate

In the previous section, which discusses design and technology as an Art or Science, this chapter has begun to explore the ideas of process and product. These two concepts are central to a contemporary understanding of design and technology. Hope (2003: 88) discusses teacher tendencies to see designing as a single event in which children are invited to 'draw three and choose one'. She goes on to suggest that this is a rather unsophisticated understanding of design as a process. The figure is based on Kimbell's (1986) model of the design process. A key difference between our model and his is the integration of the identifying the

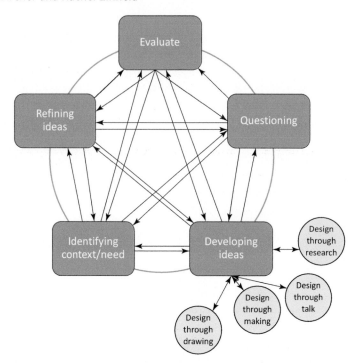

Figure 4.5 The development of ideas through the design process

context or need in the process. Our belief is that this can change through a design journey and that it is important to acknowledge this. In addition, we have increased the number of arrows which we feel best describes the flow and potential for change that occurs when designing. Finally, we have further exemplified how we believe ideas can be developed in the design process (see Figure 4.5).

Kay Stables (1997) argues that it is the design process that should far outweigh the creation of a final product. She also challenges the practice of children ending up with identical products, suggesting that any outcome should reflect and be as unique as the design journey that the child has courageously undertaken.

Critical questions and personal reflections

Looking at the model provided in Fig.1, why might it be impossible for children to end up with identical products after engaging in an authentic design process?

For further reading on designing through making and designing through drawing see:

Archer (2015) An introduction to design and technology, Chapter 4 in Driscoll, P., Lambirth, A. and Roden, J. (2015). *The primary curriculum.* 2nd ed. London: Sage.

Case study: Classroom practice – the case of the Christmas clothes hanger

A Year 2 class, in preparation for performing a play to celebrate Christmas was slightly perturbed when each morning they arrived at school to find their costumes on the floor. Many of the outfits, made from shiny, polyester type fabric had slipped over night from their clothes hangers. Whilst an observer might have felt a solution could simply be to place the costumes in carrier bags the class was adamant this should not be done because 'the clothes will crease' and, in the words of Connie, 'We shouldn't use carriers because they're not good for the environment'. This was the starting point for child-initiated designing based on a genuine, identified need.

The class discussed their concerns with their class teacher, during a 'carpet time'. The children offered reasons for why the clothes did not stay on the hangers. Stan thought a possible solution was to change the costumes to be made from 'not slippy fabric' but the angels were definitely not in agreement! Leanne, however, having closely examined a simple, metal hanger wondered whether the problem was for all hangers or simply the ones used. The following day children started to bring in different hangers for analysis.

A line was erected across the classroom and children added hangers. The only rule for adding a hanger was that each one had to be different from all others on display. By the end of the week, around 100 hangers were available for sorting. Children examined the materials, the shapes and special features such as added clips and padding. Hangers were then tested, overnight, but sadly costumes were still discovered on the floor each morning. As a result, children then started to design their own hangers and a variety emerged including ones with 'sticky pads that don't leave a mess', irons, 'anti-crease plastic', and 'anti-smell blobs'. Over a two-week period, the children were passionate in their desire to solve a problem and thoroughly engaged in their aim to create hanger designs that offered a solution.

Note: And in case you like a happy ending, you might wish to know a solution was, in the end, found. The cleaner was asked, when hoovering each night, to avoid the area where the clothes were hanging!

Critical questions

Which elements of the messy design process from Figure 4.5 were evident in this case study? Can you map this out following the arrows?

Considering that the children did not make the hangers, what do you feel was the value for the children in engaging in the design process?

Agency in design and technology

Pierre Bourdieu was one of the leading thinkers to consider identity. Mercer (2012) explores his idea of agency suggesting that it is the essential trait seen in human activity and that it is concerned with the individual's ability and capacity to act. Oswell (2012) furthers this idea suggesting that, in relation to children's education, agency is:

> Children's and young people's capacities to make a difference (rather than being constituted as difference)

> (Oswell, 2012 :6)

Fundamental to quality Design and Technological education is this notion of agency. Children being able purposely to manipulate, adapt and change the processes, ideas, concepts and materials that they come in contact with is the cornerstone to quality practice. It will result in individual rather than identical outcomes. The journey will be more involved and messier when children are enabled to act and make a difference in the design process. Often the difference between primary design and technology and 'real world' design and technology is the sense of authenticity. This can be achieved by placing the child centrally within the design process, seeking to let them solve real problems in their own way.

Design and technology for inclusion

As an Early Years practitioner, a clear success of quality design and technology is that it enables the benefits of child-initiated learning, which begins in the Early Years Foundation Stage (EYFS), to continue across the primary phase. This is key to its inclusive potential and helps to ensure that 'there are no barriers to <u>every</u> pupil achieving' (DfE 2013 :8).

In the following 'thought piece' Esther Cummins (SENDCo) reflects on the power of design and technology, to enhance inclusion, drawn from her experiences as Inclusion Manager within three primary schools. She had responsibility for SEND, EAL, and other Additional Educational Needs that arose within children's educational journeys.

Thought piece: Esther Cummins (SENDCo)

My experience in school has helped me to understand the complexity of 'inclusion'. The range of needs that children had predominately stemmed from how we 'do' learning in school rather than something being 'wrong' with the children themselves. One example of this would be the emphasis on writing within primary classrooms: Children who had dyslexia, were new to English, or who had some speech and language difficulties, may have needed additional support or differentiated learning activities during such lessons. However, teaching a broad curriculum in a more balanced manner would mean that some of these children would exceed their peers within subjects such as design and technology. I remember one child in Year 5 was working below age expectations in Maths and English who [during design and technology] created a very complex fairground system with Meccano – his sense of achievement was immense.

Beyond the interest and abilities that children may have in design and technology, I also recognise the importance of the subject for supporting children's development. I have worked with several children who had difficulties with fine motor skills, and commonplace activities such as holding a pencil was very challenging for them. When I worked in Early Years settings, I noticed that children who would usually shy away from writing would use the 'workshop' or the construction area. As they created, I realised that these were not ad hoc creations but taught through designs that reflected their lives and interests, such as garages made from Lego, pirate ships made from blocks, and wands made from recycled materials. The children were able to problem solve and create whilst developing their fine motor skills through placing blocks together, cutting, drawing, sticking, and pulling apart the Lego bricks. These vital skills were not only the pre-cursor for writing but also valid dexterities in themselves. As an Inclusion Manager, I realised how we often saw such activities as pre-writing only, instead of celebrating the successes that children had had when gaining these new skills.

For a child new to English, the primary classroom can be a daunting place. design and technology offers opportunities to access the 'known' whilst extending learning. I often feel that the designing of a sandwich is a brilliant example of how learning can be culturally and linguistically inclusive. Through exploring types of sandwich, children new to English can exchange words for bread, cheese, tomatoes, butter, and so forth, with their peers. The teacher can include fillings that do not segregate any learners (EAL or otherwise), such as avoiding meat that is not halal or kosher, or even providing purely vegetarian options. In addition, the range of bread can enable children to explore new and familiar options, as they can taste naan, pitta, granary, sourdough, rye, baguettes, and bagels. Through these opportunities, informal learning can take place without creating a false experience to learn about culture. These natural opportunities can go beyond the learning of skills that can be easily assessed, such as using a knife, and, I believe, can last into adulthood in the same way that learning to make a sandwich can.

Developing children's skills with tools and techniques is crucial in design and technology. Working with focus groups here can be key. In small groups children can work on Focused Practical Tasks (FPTs) that may assist children to develop skills that may be useful for the children to draw on when designing. Mapping this activity across a school can help to give an overview of the skills that the children are supported with and may have acquired. All too often children receive repeated input on basic skills. Children must be able to see how the challenge in skills progresses over their time in schools. During FPTs the teacher can draw on the school's skills provision map to help review what the children have previously engaged in and use this as the platform on which new skill acquisition can take place. FPTs can be successfully completed on a carousel, with children rotating around in small groups to different FPT inputs. Drawing on parent and carer support in such activities or inviting older children in from class in years above to model skills to children can be useful here. Acquiring these skills is essential in developing child agency in the design and make process.

Helping children to engage in the design process authentically involves acknowledging that there are many different ways to design beyond drawing. Indeed, Design drawing requires the child to work in abstract thought, turning this into abstract drawings after which the child has to take the large leap to see this become a concrete product. Alternatively, making as Design enables dialogue between abstract thought and the concrete action of making. This process often results in children refining and adapting ideas more easily. Creating mock-ups out of scrap materials such as newspaper helps children encounter the challenges their design will face. Challenges such as how one will join materials or ensure the product has the desired qualities become tangible and the child is forced to address these in a way that abstract thought and drawing alone would not. It could therefore be argued that this approach to design in the primary phase enables the greatest sense of agency.

Case study: Classroom practice – the design trolley

Hamish, a lower Key Stage 2 teacher was keen to develop a greater sense of independence in design and making for his class. Exploring practices seen in the foundation stage he was persuaded that it would be beneficial to look to create an environment for Design. With a limited budget he set about his own design and challenge to create a design and technology trolley for his classroom. The cost of a similar trolley from an educational supplier was far too great and often these products were much too small for the children in his class.

Hamish ordered a wooden vegetable trolley, a kitchen roll dispenser, plastic food storage jars, metal plant pots and used his drill and a few screws to create a design and technology trolley that was not only a quarter of the price compared the products he had looked at aimed at the EYFS but was also appropriate in terms of dimensions and resources for the age of the children in his class. Using the shelves, storage jars, and metal plant pots to separate out materials into groups and placing reels of tape on the kitchen roll dispenser, Hamish was pleased with the way the materials had been able to be organised into a single area, with the materials in clearly defined places. With the wheels on the trolley this could be moved to any position in his classroom.

Within a few days of being *in situ* in the classroom Hamish noticed how excited the children were to have a design and technology trolley. He observed that children were talking more about making things and were discussing their design ideas with each other at moments outside of design and technology sessions. The children also started to use the resources and materials in other lessons with a clear example being the children creating props when exploring stories orally together.

By the end of the year, design by making, became a natural part of the children's weekly experience even if they were not undertaking formal design and technology sessions. Hamish saw that the children grew in independence when designing by making, selecting the material and resources that they required themselves rather than having to ask an adult for these. This independence created a noticeable increase in the children being prepared to 'have a go' and try out ideas (see Figures 4.6 and 4.7).

Figure 4.6 The Design and Technology trolley

Figure 4.7 Talk and independence at the Design and Technology trolley

Critical questions

What do you believe the value may be in developing independent designers?
How could you seek to develop environments that promote Design?

The future and potential of design and technology

Anna Craft (2001) highlights that the unenviable task of the primary teacher is to prepare children for an uncertain future. She suggests that the best way in realising this
is through adopting approaches that seek to release children's creative potential and
capabilities.

In recent years, global and environmental issues have come to the forefront. We believe the
future of design and technology lies in its potential to help children explore the role of design
in tackling some of these environmental issues in creative and innovative ways. However,
Elshof (2005) warns that few pre-service teachers are fully aware of how to approach ideas
such as 'sustainable development'.

Case study: design and technology for sustainability - eco bricks

Lucinda, an upper Key Stage 2 teacher planned to explore the theme of 'Being a Friend
to our world'. This cross-curricular theme drew on the links with the programme of
study for primary geography, science and design and technology. From the start of the
academic year, she had held an after-school club to which children, parents, and carers
were invited. These sessions took the flavour of a community project with participants
working together to make 'eco bricks' out of plastic bottles and non-recyclable plastic
waste. The whole school was involved in collecting bottles, and bringing in washed and
dried plastic waste.

By the final term the group had built up an impressive number of eco bricks. Lucinda
presented these to her class and challenged them to work in small groups to design
and make products that would improve the school's environment. The class explored
www.ecobrick.org to find inspiration. Lucinda found that this was not only an important
step in the children developing an awareness of the product but was useful in connecting children to the big ideas, and other projects, from around the world adding a truly
global dimension to the work.

Using the materials and masking tape, the children began to develop their
understanding of how the materials could be joined and how structures could be
made. Designs for a table, chair, flower planter, and even a float for the school
swimming pool soon emerged. Working alongside some of the parents and carers
from the community project club, the children were able to realise their designs
(see Figure 4.8).

Figure 4.8 Making eco bricks out of plastic bottles and non-recyclable plastic waste

Critical questions

Who benefitted from the design and technology learning experience?
How might designing for sustainability within a school's provision in design and technology help release the subject's future potential?

Chapter summary

- Design and technology should be recognised as a separate subject from art and science. It goes far beyond the reaches of craft. It seeks to involve children in an authentic, iterative, purposeful process whereby consideration is given to the user and functionality of a 'product'. Throughout this process, children navigate a range of often-tricky design decisions
- Design and technology has had different guises since its formalisation as a discipline through the first national curriculum
- Contemporary research highlights the importance of confidence and competence. The literature suggests that quality practitioners in primary design and technology are aware of the progression in skills that should occur across the primary phase. They also seek to provide time for the iterative nature of Design

- Not all primary design and technology may result in a physical product. We have suggested that the design process is as important, if not more so, than the production of artefacts
- Through design and technology there is tremendous potential for agency for teachers and children. However, we suggest that a shift in practice may be needed to fully realise this
- The future for design and technology lies in its potential to meet real current and future issues head on including topics such as climate change and sustainability

---

Further reading

Hope, G. (2018) *Mastering Primary Design and Technology*. London: Bloomsbury.
Benson, C. and Lawson, S. (2017) *Teaching Design and Technology Creatively*. London: Routledge.

References

Archer, J. (2015) An introduction to design and technology. Chapter 4 in Driscoll, P., Lambirth, A. and Roden, J. (Eds.), *The Primary Curriculum*. 2nd ed. London: Sage.

Bell, D. (2015) The reality of STEM education, design and technology teachers' perceptions: A phenomenographic study. *International Journal of Technology and Design Education* 26(1), pp. 61-79.

Chambers, D. (1983) Stereotypic images of the scientist: The draw-a-scientist test. *Science Education* 67(2), pp. 255-265.

Craft, A., Jeffrey, B. and Leibling, M. (2001) *Creativity in Education*. London: Continuum International Publishing Group Ltd.

DATA (2019) [online] Available at: https://www.data.org.uk/campaigns/what-is-design-and-technology/ [Accessed 26 Mar. 2019].

Davies, D. and Howe, A. (2003) *Teaching Science, Design and Technology in the Early Years*. London: D. Fulton.

Department of Education and Science Welsh Office (1988) *National Curriculum Design and Technology Working Group: Interim Report*. [The Parkes Report.] London: HMSO.

DfE (2013) *Design and Technology Programmes of Study: Key Stages 1 and 2*. London: DfE.

HMI (1987) *Craft, Design and Technology from 5 to 16*. London: Crown copyright.

Hope, G. (2003) *Teaching Design and Technology 3-11*. London: Continuum.

Hope, G. (2018) Assessing children in design and technology. Chapter 7 in Hope, G. (Ed.), *Mastering Primary Design and Technology*. London: Bloomsbury.

Ishof, L. (2005) Teacher's interpretation of sustainable development. *International Journal of Technology and Design Education* 15(2), pp. 173-186.

Kimbell, R. (1986) *Craft Design & Technology*. Buckingham: Buckinghamshire Open University Press.

Mercer, N. (2012) Commentary: The future development of research on classroom talk. In Kaur, B. (Ed.), *Understanding Teaching and Learning: Classroom Research Revisited*. Rotterdam: Sense Publishers.

NACCCE (1999) *All Our Futures*. Sudbury: DfEE.

Oswell, D. (2012) *The Agency of Children*. Cambridge: Cambridge University Press.

Roden, J. and Archer, J. (2017) *Primary Science for Trainee Teachers*. London: Learning Matters.

Roden, J. and Ward, H. (2016) *Teaching Science in the Primary Classroom*. London: Sage.

Rose, J. (2009) *Independent Review of the Primary Curriculum: Final Report*. Nottingham: DCSF Publications.

Stables, K. (1997) Critical issues to consider when introducing technology education into the curriculum of young learners. *Journal of Technology Education* 8(2), pp. 50-65.

5 Putting the human back into the Humanities

Alison Hales

Critical questions

In light of the global pandemic, reassessment of local people and places and the value they bring to our communities has already begun. We are seeing and hearing of people and communities who have been, historically, hidden in history. How might this impact on our understanding, the importance, and the place of Humanities in primary schools?

How might you use the experiences and stories of people in 2020 in your teaching across the Humanities?

How important to you is the child's voice? How will you ensure the child's voice is heard in your planning and provision?

Introduction

Primary education is politically driven and value laden and the Humanities are no exception. The foundation subject curriculum areas have competed for time and attention in British primary schools since the introduction of statutory testing for the core subjects and the outcomes being held for public scrutiny, through league tables and Ofsted inspection visits. Whilst it is likely there will be resurgence in the importance of the foundation curriculum within primary schools, as a result of the revised Ofsted inspection framework, (which is welcomed) we still very much need to claim a genuine place for Humanities within the curriculum (Scoffham and Barnes, 2017). The Humanities are not only key to enriching children's learning but are a powerful way to bring about positive change and equality to the world.

Humanities are the collection of subjects concerned with the study of people and places and their interaction; it is the bringing together of local, national, and global. This chapter refers specifically to the study of history and geography, though it recognises that Religious Education and Citizenship Education are also inherent parts of the Humanities, and teachers should most definitely consider how and when they might be used alongside history and geography and each other; these areas will be covered separately in other chapters but reference will be made here where appropriate. The chapter considers the importance of the Humanities education through the collection of subjects, valuing and recognising the individuality of each, but also as a discipline in its own right. It endeavours to show primary school teachers and primary educators that the Humanities are an exciting, invigorating, and invaluable area of study for children, providing rich and meaningful learning opportunities for children to engage with people and places. It offers ways in which its unique interlocking and transferable concepts and skills can be made exciting and irresistible to children; thus, providing a tangible learning context in which wider understanding can be deepened and built upon. In the final section 'challenging history and geography' it will consider how emotive but significant issues, inherent in history and geography, can be explored in a safe and unbiased environment. It stresses the importance of not underestimating children, in both their understanding and their voice of such issues and the impact they themselves can have.

This chapter will explore the following areas with reference to specific examples from school case studies:

- Why the Humanities?
- Exploring rich and engaging experiences through local people and places
- Humanities and the child as a global citizen
- The child as a co-constructor of their learning – children's voice
- Challenging history and geography

Why the Humanities?

When considering 'why the Humanities?', we need to look no further to the summary offered by the Humanities Manifesto 20:20 which states: 'The challenges of globalisation and the need for sustainability and social justice in the 21st century raise important, often controversial, issues about identity, diversity and how to care for other people and the planet'(http://www.humanities2020.org.uk). Whilst we will unpick this further, it provides a justification and a starting point as to the importance and relevance of good Humanities teaching in the primary classroom.

Before we look at Humanities in the current framework, it is useful to briefly consider its origins, its emergence into the curriculum and why perhaps the philosophy underpinning it has hardly changed. Griggs and Hughes (2013) give a comprehensive historical overview of the Humanities, explaining how its origins lay with early philosophers and their 'new conception of humanity' considering 'what the human mind was for: namely to reason, seek out patterns and above all ask questions' (Kitto, 1951 in Griggs and Hughes, 2013). As a discipline, it can be traced back more than 2,500 years to the classical Greeks, with its relevance being overtly evident with Socrates (469–399BC), a leading philosopher, who proclaimed: 'the unexamined life is not worth living'. Coupled with this, we see evidence of familiar teaching approaches through his methods of use of sequential questioning to elicit understanding, later to become known as the 'Socratic Method', designed, as Griggs and Hughes suggest, to 'reach the heart of what pupils believed' (p.3). We can recognise these pedagogical approaches: asking questions, seeking patterns, and reasoning as very characteristic in an enquiry approach to the teaching and learning within the Humanities today. Hughes (2011 in Griggs and Hughes, 2013) offers the view that 'we think the way we do [about Humanities], because Socrates thought the way he did' (p.3). But we might also conclude that good educators throughout time have understood that it is not enough for children just to 'know' but rather they understand and reason about what they know.

The humanities within the primary classroom today holds as much importance as it did back in the days of Socrates. Whilst there is no single definition of the study of Humanities, there are common features that give it its distinct and prominent characteristics, notably people and places and their interconnectedness. These elements give children the opportunity to explore the complex nature of the world in which they live in a context that is meaningful and real. It allows children to begin to ask the questions of 'who am I and why am I?' (Usborne and De La Sablonniere, 2014).

Hales (2018) explores the importance of personal identity and its significance in children's understanding of the global world. She suggests that in a world where societies, communities, and families have multi-layered and multifaceted identities within a rapidly changing framework, children are faced with the difficult task of understanding. They struggle, she says of where and how their developing 'self' fits in. She goes on to describe the difficulties that emerge when children attempt to forge their own identity and argues that if children are deprived of experiences that enable them to explore identity in a coherent and comprehensive way, there is a danger they will feel isolated and disconnected from the world around them. Here, the inclusion of the Humanities is paramount. The interplay between people and places and the active nature of the study allows children to begin to explore and make sense of such complexities and so begin the formation of personal identities and how they can actively navigate and contribute to the world in which they live. This consideration of identity and recognising the experiences that children encounter enables them to: interpret situations; form personal and collective identities: make predictions; and understand potential. This is only possible if they know what came before and recognise the consequences after (history) and being able to relate this to the 'now' (geography) (Tosh, 2015; Hales, 2018).

Doull, Russell and Hales (2019) add another dimension, bringing our attention to the well-being of children and the role that the Humanities can play. They highlight the increasingly low morale prevalent amongst English school children as reported by the World Health Organisation, 2016 (cited in Barnes and Scoffham 2017). Figures suggest that children's mental and social well-being is on the decline in the UK, with them faring poorly against their European counterparts.

Critical question

What is your immediate response to the knowledge that our young children are increasingly reporting a negative attitude to schooling and as a result having their well-being compromised? What might be the causes here and how might we further mitigate them?

If we consider, what Scoffham and Barnes (2017) allude to, that the pressure of our current UK system with standardised testing, conformity, and a seemingly narrow approach to the curriculum is attributing to the dissatisfaction of our English school children we can agree with Doull, Russell and Hales (2019) when they say the foundation subjects can be instrumental in bringing about change: 'The multifaceted nature of the subjects allow schools to exploit these attributes and plan creatively and deliver opportunities to explore a wide range of issues' (p17) thus bringing the curriculum alive for children.

Barnes and Scoffham, (2017) discuss how the Humanities are further well placed to provide opportunities for children to explore human emotions, as well as to consider motives and challenges that people face in a world of increasing uncertainty and vulnerability; emotions that they themselves might be experiencing. They state that 'the positive sense of self and others which the humanities subjects offer children could and should be at the heart of the primary curriculum' (p.307). Eaude et al., (2017) offer a broader view based on a belief 'that learning through, and about, the humanities help develop the qualities and values associated with acting as an educated and empowered person in the context of diversity and change' (p.390).

Bringing the Humanities alive through local people and places

'People and places' is an obvious starting point in the planning of an enriching and exciting Humanities unit of study but considering history and geography through the local makes it more enticing for children. Local people and places make the study tangible and real and give children something they can connect with; putting the child at the centre of that learning in order that they are able to co-construct the learning is even more powerful.

Dixon and Hales' (2014) coin the phrase of 'the child as the local' suggesting that children come with an array of rich histories and geographies, some might be from their immediate local but others from 'locals' in the wider world. Working in this way and using the child as a starting point for planning enables children to understand how one local (people and/or places) may interact and impact on one another. It is a way to bring peoples' histories and geographies together, making connections, understanding how the local picture might fit into the global picture and wider world. All classroom teachers have a wealth of resources at their disposal – the children themselves.

The following case studies are taken from my own experiences and illustrate how the histories and geographies of children came together to provide rich learning experience for a Year 2 class and then how it was replicated later in Nursery.

Case study: Contrasting localities –Year 2

During a unit of work looking at contrasting localities, Stephen was keen to share that his family had their roots in the Seychelles, an archipelago country in the Indian Ocean. The children were excited to find out about their friend's family 'local' in the Seychelles and this prompted lots of questions for Stephen. It was here that I decided to abandon my original planning ideas already outlined on the medium-term plan and use Stephen's story as a real context for learning. His mum was a frequent visitor to the class and on school trips, so I was familiar with his family and was assured that approaching Stephen's mum about how she might enrich our learning of the class would be welcomed. The children's questions: 'where were the Seychelles? How might we get there? What features did the island have? Why did your family move to here?' prompted my planning and the direction I might take in their development of geographical skills and understanding. This also allowed me to consider how I might incorporate and engage with some of the enquiry skills associated with history, such as the use of oral history, questioning, and empathy, etc.

I was aware that many children in my class had not had direct experience of other countries or cultures, other than what they experienced in the media, so this was a good opportunity to address stereotyping and misconceptions. We began by exploring the children's perceptions of faraway islands and how such places are portrayed in the media travel companies by comparing a range of photos and written accounts.

Stephen's mum was keen to come in and work with the children and so we decided to have a 'Seychelle's morning'. Using an active learning approach, the children were given roles and areas to focus on to find out and collate information to build up a picture of what the island and life on the island was like. Stephen's mum brought in family photos to share with the children which added a nice comparison to the stereotypical view of the 'paradise island' and memorabilia from her past- toys, clothes, and objects that she had kept. This enabled them to consider change and continuity and how different her childhood was compared to their own. She also brought in food - both unprepared and cooked to share with the children, along with music typical to her culture.

This experience enabled me as the teacher to plan the rest of the term's work creating bespoke cross-curricular opportunities for learning resulting from the children's enthusiasm and interests, using the Seychelles as a starting point. We made our own musical compositions, designed fabric from both African and Western influences, created and cooked simple food dishes, and explored different types of homes and school systems. Stephen's mum's personal history (and willingness to share) allowed children to empathise and explore difficult concepts such as poverty and ways of life for some communities (some photos showed Stephen's uncle being bathed in a tin barrel and the inside of their house being sparsely furnished - very different from their experiences).

Case study: Bringing the world to the Nursery

I was fortunate to have a very diverse Nursery, with a range of languages and cultures within it, which I was eager to celebrate and use in the children's learning in order to make it relevant to them. I asked the children (with their parents' consent) to bring photos from the different places their families came from across the world. As part of the learning we made a very large papier-mâché world - so children could begin to understand about oceans, continents, and simple features of the world - and hung it up in our classroom. It became a central feature and an ongoing tool for learning. The pictures that the children brought in were then attached to the relevant parts of the world, highlighting the expanse and diversity of their families. The children themselves brought in family objects and personal items to share alongside their pictures. This also extended to members of the families themselves who were keen to come in and share with the children. For example, Leonardo and his family were from Lithuania. During Easter celebrations, Leonardo's mum came in to share their family's tradition of decorating and rolling eggs at Easter – the whole Nursery replicated the event by making and rolling their own eggs. She also told stories in Lithuanian which enabled Leonardo to join in, something he was reluctant to do when I read stories in English to the class. The children's continued interest and knowledge allowed me to plan for areas of learning within 'Understanding the World' depending on what was brought in, their questions and developmental needs. I was able to choose books and stories that individual children could relate to, share food from different cultures, and present an ethos of collaborative learning through local families and communities.

Both examples offer a way of learning which puts children and their histories and geographies at the heart. It shows spontaneity, echoing features of the now very popular 'in the moment planning', frequently used in Early Years, and illustrates that such an approach can be replicated in any Key Stage (Ephgrave, 2015).

The following case study illustrates a similar but whole school approach taken by Charlton Manor School, a South East London primary school which prides itself on its outdoor learning philosophy and advocates a very immersive and child-centred approach to the Humanities. Learning through local people and places is central to the curriculum at the school, ensuring that children are not only central in the learning but the ownership. When considering the Humanities curriculum, it offers an illustration of real-life experiences, and how they can deepen children's knowledge and understanding, and begin to build and develop self-identity.

Case study: Charlton Manor

The approach at Charlton Manor is very much about giving experiences that are real and contextualised, and offer deep learning for the children.

The headteacher, Tim Baker, is particularly passionate about history and geography and this is evident the moment you enter the school. For example, the playground has a 'street through time' where houses have been replicated across the centuries from their historical counterparts – showcasing roundhouses to modern day living. Children are not only able to see and compare changes but able to explore and use the rooms during learning and play. Opposite this is a market street where children sell the goods that are produced in the school's own secret garden and honey from its beehives. Children and teachers are trained as beekeepers and gardeners at their community garden allotment and tend the animals that they share with the local Woodland Farm Trust, as well as the chickens they have onsite. Teachers are encouraged to take the learning outside wherever possible so the children can use their skills from across the curriculum in a context that makes sense. The school has a working teaching kitchen with its own teaching chef. Here, children not only learn about the food grown in the garden, but they learn to cook food from around the world and throughout time. Their onsite restaurants enable children to become waiters and serve food to both school members and the wider community.

Charlton Manor not only prides itself on its community engagement but also on its international profile achieving the British Council's 'International School' award. They have several links with China, Nepal, France, Ghana, and Germany. Here we see the immersive experience for children really come alive. For example, for children to develop their language skills, they stay in France where they are encouraged only to use French. The visits develop their cultural understanding by visiting local markets, buying food, and communicating with local people. In Germany they engage with a Bavarian school on joint projects such as healthy schools, creating a food garden, and beekeeping. Each year they have a teacher/pupil exchange in which language and cultural similarities and differences can be explored. Links with China enable its teachers and children to visit to work alongside children in Charlton Manor, with teachers due to visit different provinces in China to learn about their education system and how practices might complement one another.

The school links across the world put the child's voice at the centre of the learning, with children being able to speak, listen, and work with each other across the world. Children are able to direct the learning and projects alongside the teachers, allowing them to take ownership.

Tim also considers it is very important for teachers to have the same contextual experiences, so that they themselves fully understand and appreciate the learning which is needed if learning is to be made relevant for children. The close links with schools and the 'Nepal Mary Child Help Centre' orphanage in Nepal allows teachers, who are actively encouraged and supported by the headteacher, the opportunity to visit and experience the way of life for the children there. This enables them to bring back understanding and empathy, to break down barriers and develop cultural awareness which is built into the curriculum for the children. This learning is summed up nicely, as seen from the school's international policy statement:

> Charlton Manor has developed a creative curriculum that encourages children to explore the world and develop into global citizens. We aim to remove cultural barriers and stereotypes and encourage positive communication. Our children will learn about a wide range of cultures and be able to think for themselves and be aware of changing times and worldwide problems. This will help develop their critical thinking.

Carpenter (2018) considers three domains of learning: the cognitive learning domain (CLD) the 'stuff' that children know; the affective learning domain (ALD), more about the why of learning and the personal connection children have to it; and the phychomotor learning domain (PLD) which concerns the 'specific-to-discrete' physical functions and skills that are practiced to embed learning (p.83). Traditionally, our education system focuses largely on CLD to prepare children for performance scores and league tables, seen not only nationally but internationally through the high-ranking PISA tests for example; something that Carpenter describes as the 'industrial approach to learning' (ibid). He offers an alternative model to learning in which a value-based ALD is at the heart, but one that continuously considers and weaves between the other two domains. His approach echoes that of the case studies, and a pedagogy advocated in this chapter, suggesting that deep learning happens through interaction and with 'people and connections with the wider world' (p.77). He highlights the need for learners to be morally and emotionally connected to the learning if learning is to be remembered (CLD) and practiced (PLD) 'the better we connect learning to moral purposes, the deeper the relationship between the learning and the learner' (p.78). Charlton Manor has embraced this learning through their creative curriculum, facilitating children to communicate and learn with each other, not just locally but globally. Carter et al., (2018) describes how curious teachers create curious learners; Charlton Manor school embraces their teachers' natural curiosity by actively supporting them to experience learning and contexts first hand and consider their own moral and emotional perspectives by working alongside different people and places. In turn they are able to encourage children's curiosity, through an enquiry approach to learning: asking the questions to find out about the 'why' and 'how', making connections between the local, national, and global, and developing a sense of identity through the study of people and places (Cooper, 2018, Hales, 2018).

Whilst it may seem idealistic for schools to send teachers and children on international trips, the use of technology is one way that other schools can achieve similar results if they want to embrace a global approach to teaching and learning. The following offers ideas for connecting with the global classroom:

- Google Earth can be used to zoom in to real places, offering children the opportunity to see how the local fits into the global
- Links can be made with schools around the world through organisations such as the British Council (https://www.britishcouncil.org/school-resources) who offer resources, ideas, and partnerships
- Webcams and Skype are excellent resources to set up classroom discussions both nationally and internationally
- Using local communities for both teaching and learning; all villages, towns, and large cities have rich and diverse communities – teachers should get to know their own environment and what it has to offer by spending time in and about local communities
- Bring people in from the community to work with children; in my experience people are more than happy to do this, it just takes someone to ask!
- Using events and happenings around the world as a focus for learning. Newsround (https://www.bbc.co.uk/newsround) and First News, a newspaper aimed at 8-13 year olds, offer starting points for discussion and further research which change daily. Picture-News also offers ideas and resources for using headlines in the classroom (www.picture-news.co.uk)

- Many of the major children's charities such as Save the Children, Banardos, and The Red Cross have opportunities for joint projects and involvement to consider global issues
- Forging links with local charities, organisations, and centres can provide children with real contexts. In my own school we had links with a local sheltered housing scheme. history and geography activities often involved visits to and from the home enabling children to develop a sense of community and responsibility
- Facebook, Instagram, and other social networks provide links for children to the wider world and this is a good way for teachers to model safe and effective use of technology to aid learning

The Humanities and the child as a global citizen

In a world that is continually changing and its connectedness becoming far more intricate and complex, it is vital that we prepare children as citizens of the global world.

Citizenship – and more recently global citizenship – have been the focus of several reviews since the latter part of the last century. The 'Advisory Group on the Teaching of Citizenship and Democracy in schools' commonly known as the Crick Report (1998) laid the foundations for citizenship education in UK schools. This was quickly followed by the Adegbo Report (2007) as another major review looking at diversity and citizenship across UK schools, and how the curriculum can and must be used as a starting point for global understanding and citizenship:

> By 'education for diversity' we mean teaching and learning – in both the formal and informal curricula – that addresses issues of ethnicity, culture, language and religion and the multiple identities children inhabit. It is education for mutual understanding and respect, which gives pupils a real understanding of who lives in the UK today, of why we are here, and of what they as pupils can contribute ... Education for diversity is key to preparing children and young people for the 21st century world, where borders are becoming more porous and global citizenship is an increasing imperative. It is about learning for life, ensuring that in adulthood pupils will be able to cope with social mobility, armed with the social skills that will help them flourish.
>
> (p.15)

Slightly later, Alexander (2010) also emphasised the importance of education for diversity in his report 'celebrating culture and communities', as part of the Cambridge review into education. In his review, he argues for an education which attempts to bridge the gaps in what he sees as a widening void in the understanding of cultural identity within communities. The report advocates a coherent and comprehensive citizenship education through a Humanities-based curriculum. However, despite these major reports, the principles for primary Citizenship Education has been lost with the withdrawal of the statutory Citizenship Education at KS2 replaced for non-statutory guidance for both Key Stage 1 and 2.

More recently we have seen a focus on the promotion of fundamental British values through the government document 'Promoting Fundamental British Values as part of the SMSC (social, moral, spiritual and cultural) curriculum' (2014). The title itself is arguably controversial, with the document using language such as 'tolerance' and 'acceptance' of other beliefs and religions, inadvertently suggesting a potential hierarchy in cultural values. This, I suggest, may further divide communities if the interpretation and meaning of the guidance is skewed; further emphasising the need for a strong and coherent approach to learning in the Humanities. Schools are in danger of children's global education for citizenship being compromised by a British citizenship education if global principles and practices are not kept alive through an active and relevant Humanities curriculum, one that embraces all cultures and communities across the world.

Critical questions

- What does fundamental British Values mean to you?
- How might you link this to the idea of being a global citizen?

To add to the discussion around the importance of global citizenship, it is important that we recognise the potential challenges that are inherent when dealing with people and places. With children being exposed to a multitude of images, perspectives, and opinions through the various influences of the media and technology, it is unsurprising that with it comes negativity, bias, and stereotyping. Rowley (2007, in Eaude et al., 2017) state that such ideas are usually formed by the time children reach the age of nine or ten, whilst Kelly and Brooks (2009) argue that this happens much earlier, with children entering pre-school with already formed values and ideas about the world around them – both positive and negative. It is therefore essential that we grasp a Humanities curriculum as early as possible in school, so that it is ready to challenge preconceived ideas and notions. By examining the events of today it can go towards preparing children for being the future global citizens of tomorrow.

Early activities such as those illustrated in case studies one and two can be used to have open and transparent discussions about different cultures and communities through a child-friendly and all-encompassing global curriculum; one in which children can explore, understand, and celebrate differences in a safe and informed way. Catling suggests that the different strands of the Humanities, offer children the opportunity to be:

> introduced to, become aware of, and learn to apply concepts, ideas and insights (spanning) beyond the humanities themselves. This involves children using skills to examine different perspectives and complex, challenging and contentious ideas, learning about different viewpoints and making judgements.
>
> (Catling, 2017: 357)

The child as a co-constructor of their learning: Children's voices

A recommendation of the Ajegbo report in 2006 (among others) was the promotion of the child's voice in Citizenship Education. It urged schools to engage in various mechanisms such as school councils, child-adult forums, pupil questionnaires, and debates to champion the views and opinions of children about identity, values, and belonging. As a result, the early part of this century saw the involvement of children's voice as being a prominent and significant part of the school curriculum. In KS 1 and 2, schools actively promoted children's voices, asking and taking their views on curriculum design, school democracy and participation. The following case study, however, shows how a Nursery in a South East London primary school extended this idea to young children and used the idea of children's voices to prompt the redesign of their classroom whilst engaging with early geographical skills and concepts.

Case study

During a planned refurbishment of the Nursery, the Early Years team were keen to ensure an environment which excited and engaged the children – both indoor and outdoor. The team were conscious that earlier designs in the setting were very adult influenced, based around preconceived notions of teaching and learning. Spaces were largely designed to echo the areas of learning within the Early Years Foundation Stage framework but did not necessarily echo the children as learners themselves. The physical environment – furniture, tables, and chairs – enabled teaching to take place without much consideration of how the children felt themselves.

In order to go some way in designing a child-friendly learning space, the teacher decided to engage the voices of the children. She talked about the plans for the Nursery with them, engaging them in a real conversation about the refurbishment, something they were evidently aware was happening. She was keen to keep spaces that children loved and used but introduce others which were more consistent with the learning needs and enjoyment of the children. In order to do this, she gave groups of children different ways to identify current areas in the Nursery they liked and areas they would like changed. Some had cameras, some used Post-it notes and stickers, and others worked with adults in the room to talk about the facilities and environment.

The activity enabled a multi-dimensional approach to learning, engaging many aspects of what we now recognise as the characteristic of effective learning: playing and exploring; being willing to 'have a go'; active learning and creating and thinking critically (EYFS, 2017). During the activity children used in directional and prepositional language, engaged in early mapping skills by representing places on a simple plan format and learnt about the world of work through roleplaying various 'people at work' – photographers, planners, and builders, etc.

The teacher and the Nursery team then went about collating information from the children. The exercise presented some surprises which were taken into consideration when redesigning the learning spaces: the children didn't see the need or want the array of tables and chairs which dominated the room, instead preferring to work in less formal spaces on the floor with cushions and soft furnishings. They wanted to be able to have spaces where they could, if they wanted to, be alone without the ever-watchful eye of the adult – choosing to move their library from the main area to a quiet room at the side. They liked displays where they could add their own work ('like the grown-ups') showing little interest to the very colourful adult initiated displays that tended to decorate the walls. Learning areas were aligned more to children's interests rather than specific curriculum areas; they liked to build and construct but have places where they could keep and return to their projects. They wanted to be able to access all resources and not have things 'put in cupboards' so they had to ask adults for access.

Children wanted a bigger outdoor area for digging, exploring, and growing. They liked having their own place to grow plants and vegetables and were keen to expand this. This led to a raised sensory garden, made from lorry tyres, donated by a local company, a wildlife area with its own 'bug hotel' that the children designed and built themselves, and a bigger vegetable patch complete with mud kitchen.

The most striking thing about the involvement of the children was their eagerness and the loudness of their voices when expressing ideas and opinions, something that was quite unexpected for very young children and something that took practitioners by surprise. Through drawings, discussions, and a simple voting system, children were able to collectively design and agree upon a shared learning space. This became 'their' Nursery, a safe and inviting space that was celebrated and respected by children and adults alike.

Haynes and Murris (2013) say that educational practitioners are living through a period of pedagogical unrest, with relationships between the child and educator being re-examined and questioned. They challenge teachers to the notion of considering the child *as* the educator, suggesting that children can be perceptive and insightful, 'having fresh eyes to look at the world' with 'the courage and freedom to ask political questions about humanity in the world' (p.218). This was something experienced in the Nursery class in case study four – not just about the children wanting certain things or areas in the Nursery, but why it was important to them (the children) about their environment and their needs as human beings.

Murris (2013) calls into question teachers' beliefs and perception of what they think children know and understand, something that she identifies as 'the epistemic challenge of hearing children's voice' (p. 245). She states, that despite listening to children, teachers often fail to *hear* what they are saying because of the internalised acceptance of Piagetian staged developmental theories of learning which still influence our current educational thinking today.

Critical questions

- What are your beliefs about how young children learn?
- Do you consider their input into what you are going to teach and how?

More recently, however, we are beginning to see children's voices making a resurgence in the wider public and educational arena, speaking about issues affecting people and places, locally, nationally, and globally. In a climate of global social, emotional, and physical uncertainty, never has this been so pertinent. We have children actively and independently campaigning about issues that threaten the environment and the health and happiness of people making their voices heard around the world and pioneering change. Children such as Malala Yousafzai, a Pakistani activist who, whilst a teenager, spoke out against the Tehrik-e-Taliban Pakistan's ban on the education of girls; Greta Thunberg an activist in campaigning against environmental climate change, and sisters Ella and and Caitlin McEwan persuading a leading food chain to discontinue plastic toys in their children's meals as a bid to cut down on unnecessary plastics in the environment (BBC, 2019).

I argue this is likely to be the result of a considered and child-centred Humanities curriculum born from the early principles of citizenship and the now global citizenship curriculum; one where children have a say in the issues and decisions they are interested in and subsequently lead the learning along with teachers who work with them to design a relevant and appropriate curriculum such as the one seen in case study three.

Challenging history and geography

When learning through a people and places curriculum we will inevitably encounter topics, issues, and events which are complex, often uncomfortable and sometimes controversial. However, 'controversial' is a difficult concept to define as the answer is largely dependent on people's perspectives – often driven by their values, ideals, and the personal connection they may have to the issue or topic.

Critical questions

- What is your understanding of controversial history or geography?
- Do you teach any topics/subjects that you might consider controversial? If so, what has been the impact in the classroom?

In order to consider why it might be important to include controversial issues into our humanities curriculum we can look to Claire and Holden (2007) for a thought to ponder on:

> Because controversial issues are rooted in values, beliefs and different Ideologies as well as personal interest, children can use historical (and geographical) analogies as the rehearsal ground for their own developing ethical and ideological standpoint. This is not indoctrination but education: they (can) weigh up serious ethical questions and decide where they stand.
>
> (p.29)

Dixon and Hales (2014) draw our attention to the complexities of potentially emotive history and geography but also to the importance of it, reminding us that children are continually bombarded with images, stories, and news from the media that may cause some confusion, discomfort, or distress. The question being: If we avoid such issues and therefore do not attempt to explore perspectives, emotions, or feelings is there a danger of adding to this distress or inadvertently fostering hidden biases or stereotypes? Douell, Russell and Hales (2018) remind us that the classroom can provide a 'safe and neutral environment' for children to explore issues with their teachers and with each other (p.24).

The intention here is not for teachers to be coerced into teaching issues that they may not feel comfortable with, or insist/suggest that they do, moreover to consider what benefits there might be in the teaching of challenging history and geography – children, after all, are curious about the world and will question what is going on around them. It is always recommended that teachers should check with their Humanities lead or senior leader if they are concerned or want to question whether a topic or issue may be relevant and of course this should be with full consideration of the children and families within the classroom. Teachers may also want to consider where challenges may already be present in their planning in order to prepare for possible challenging questions and lines of enquiry. For example, how do we present Guy Fawkes to children – a historical hero whom we celebrate each year or a terrorist of his time? How do we separate his actions to what is current today? Or do we? How might we justify the execution of Henry VIII's wives? It is naïve to think that children are not considering these questions and teachers therefore need to consider how they might answer such questions if they arise. This is where it is vital for teachers to have good subject and pedagogical knowledge, to ensure that such teaching is done expertly and confidently modelling to the children what is appropriate, what questions might be pertinent, and how to make informed and justified conclusions. Pedagogy being the 'fusion of theoretical knowledge, practical experience and intuitive response' (Barnes, 2007: 126).

If we consider earlier points made in the chapter, including controversial issues sensitively in our Humanities curriculum can be another rich element in which to engage children. Such issues allow them to question their values, present their voice, and develop a sense of belonging as a global citizen through which they can perhaps instigate change or go some way in alleviating many of the social injustices that are present in the world.

Summary

This chapter has argued for a Humanities curriculum which is visible and prominent and one that is not left within the tokenistic 'topic' area of the planned curriculum. It should be underpinned by real people and places of the past and present and relate succinctly to the future. It argues for children to be central in the teaching and learning, ensuring that the curriculum is planned around what interests them, and is applicable to their lives and experiences; children need to see themselves reflected in the learning. We must ensure inclusion in what we teach. We have a duty to represent those not present in our current history or geography curricular – those groups of people and places or that are hidden from our recording of history or geography – minority groups, women, children, Black History, the impoverished, the enslaved or the persecuted, and ensuring that their successes, challenges, and contributions are recognised and celebrated.

It argues for children to be co-constructors of their curriculum and to give them a voice in what they want to learn about and what is important. This is not in any way suggesting that statutory guidance is disregarded, rather that is it used alongside a child-led curriculum to enrich and re-energise learning.

References

Alexander, R. J. (2010) *Children, Their World, Their Education. Final Report and Recommendations of the Cambridge Primary Review*. London: Routledge.

Barnes, J. (2007) *Cross-Curricular Learning 3-14*. London: Sage.

Barnes, J. and Scoffham, S. (2017) The humanities in English primary schools: Struggling to survive. *Education 3-13* 45(3), 298-308.

BBC (2019) *Burger King Ditches Free Toys and Will 'Melt' Old Ones*. https://www.bbc.co.uk/news/business-49738889 [Accessed 14 October 2019].

Carpenter, R. (2018) *A Manifesto for Excellence in Schools*. London: Bloomsbury.

Carter, J., Whitehouse, S. and Vickers-Hulse, K. (2018) Curious teachers, create curious learners and great historians. *Education 3-13* 46(6), 648-660.

Catling, S. (2017) High quality in primary humanities: insights from the UK's school inspectorates. *Education 3-13* 45(3), 354-364.

Claire, H. and Holden, C. (2007) *The Challenge of Teaching Controversial Issues*. London: Trentham Books.

Cooper, H. (2018) What is creativity in history? *Education 3-13* 46(6), 634-647.

Dixon, L. and Hales, A. (2014) *Bringing History Alive through Local People and Places: A Guide for Primary School Teachers*. London: Routledge.

Douell, K., Russell, D. and Hales, A. (2019) *Mastering Primary History*. London: Bloomsbury.

Eaude, T., Butt, G., Catling, S. and Vass, P. (2017) The future of the humanities in primary schools - reflections in troubled times. *Education 3-13* 45(3), 386-395.

Ephgrave, A. (2015) *The Nursery Year in Action: Following Children's Interest through the Year*. Oxon: Routledge.

Griggs, R. and Hughes, S. (2013) *Teaching Primary Humanities*. Harlow: Pearson Education Limited.

Hales, A. (2018) The local in history: Personal and community history and its impact on identity. *Education 3-13* 46(6), 671-684.

Haynes, J. and Murris, K. (2013) Child as educator: Introduction to the special issue. *Studies of Philosophy in Education* 32, 217-227.

Hughes, B. (2011) *The Hemlock Cup: Socrates, Athens and the Search for the Good Life*. London: Vintage in Griggs, R. and Hughes, S. (2013) *Teaching Primary Humanities*. Harlow: Pearson Education Limited.

Humanities 20:20 (2019) *A New Vision for Primary Schools. A Manifesto*. http://www.humanities2020.org.uk/manifesto [Accessed 25th October 2019].

Kelly, D. and Brooks, M. (2009) How young is too young? Exploring beginning teachers' Assumptions about young children and teaching for social justice. *Equity and Excellence in Education* 42(2), 202-216.

Kitto, H. D. F. (1951) *The Greeks*. London: Pelican in Griggs, R. and Hughes, S. (2013) *Teaching Primary Humanities*. Harlow: Pearson Education Limited.

Murris, K. (2013) The epistemic challenge of hearing child's voice. *Studies of Philosophical Education* 32, 245-259.

QCA (1998) *Education for Citizenship and the Teaching of Democracy in Schools. Final Report of the Advisory Group on Citizenship*. London: DfEE.

Tosh, J. (2015) *The Pursuit of History: Aims, Methods, and New Directions in the Study of Modern History*. 6th ed. London: Pearson.

Ushborne, E. and De La Sablonniere, R. (2014) Understanding my culture means understanding myself: The function of cultural identity clarity for personal identity clarity and personal psychological well-being. *Journal for the Theory of Social Behaviour* 44(4), 436-57.

6 Painting a canvas of creativity

Ashley Brett

Critical questions

How does the creativity in art and design contribute to education? What might the value of this be to greater society?
How can primary schools use art to deepen their children's understanding within their curriculum provision?

For the purpose of this chapter, where the term 'art' has been used in isolation, it is intended to encompass the 'design' component.

Introduction

This chapter explores how art and design contributes to developing a depth of understanding in children's learning. The chapter extends the pertinence of art, beyond developing key technical skills and expressing their individuality and cultural heritage (Freedman and Stuhr, 2004), to help pupils reflect upon relevant and meaningful global themes which they may study within the curriculum. This underpins how art and design may contribute to the curriculum and beyond to future society, if children develop a deeper understanding of global issues presented through art and which may impact upon their future decisions. Creativity, inherent within Art and Design, is also considered to be essential as a 21st century skill (OECD, 2018) and creativity is acknowledged as an 'important element of economic prosperity' (Wyse and Ferrari, 2015: 30) and may particularly benefit those children who may struggle within traditionally academic subjects (Caldwell and Vaughan, 2012). The creative outcomes which children may demonstrate are shown in this chapter to be a reflection of a creative, innovative curriculum, in which teachers and children have ownership and flexibility to explore, experiment, reflect, and enjoy.

Aims

This chapter aims to support the reader to reflect upon:

- The value and contribution of art and design to education (and ultimately to society)
- How art and design can contribute to a deeper level of learning for pupils

- How art and design may be integrated as a key component within the curriculum
- How art and design may be showcased within the learning environment to demonstrate an ethic of striving for standards of excellence

Research informed practice

Two decades ago, the National Advisory Committee on Creative and Cultural Education (NACCCE, 1999) suggested that creative and cultural education was essential for the 21st century to provide an educational system that fosters the talents within all children. This subsequently initiated rich cross-curricular activities especially within the Arts (Craft et al., 2014). Research demonstrates that the Arts can transform the learning of students who are disengaged (see Caldwell and Vaughan, 2012), with creative pedagogy identified as enabling children and their teachers to be innovative, affording ownership and control, and promoting themes of relevance (Craft et al., 2014). Creative approaches enable connections to be made and curiosity to be fostered (ibid). Pavlou's (2013) study demonstrates how creating artwork requires an enquiry-based approach, involving decisions to be made, problems to be solved, and evaluation, and in so doing nurtures creative development. This chapter centralises art and design education within the primary national curriculum (DfE, 2013) as a vehicle in which to promote creative approaches to the curriculum and deepen understanding of other curriculum areas through integrated themes and topics (Craft et al., 2014).

Setting the scene

Arts education is foregrounded as a universal human right (UNESCO, 2006) as part of 'a comprehensive education leading to the full development of the individual' (p.3). The prominence, or lack, of inclusion of art and design within the curriculum is therefore an important and relevant educational issue. Some may relegate art to an inferior status and position within the curriculum, against more academic subjects such as English and Maths, because of national assessments and a performativity and accountability agenda (Ogier, 2017). However, this view belittles the fact that success in art and design may raise the self-esteem of a child, perhaps one who may struggle in more 'academic' areas. Indeed, if lip service is paid to creativity, then this can deny children the opportunity of reaching their potential, engender issues for their mental health and well-being, and impede their ability to question and be critical (ibid). The creativity underpinning art and design can benefit the skills necessary for a 21st century workforce and for a successful economy, and enhance cultural understanding from appreciating diversity, and engender social justice and equality (Ogier, 2017). This chapter illustrates how two primary schools, Foxfield and Woodhill, in the London Borough of Greenwich, promote art and design, as part of their curriculum. They consider the subject to be a valuable and critical component of their children's education and foreground its status because it contributes to exemplary standards of work and deepens the pupils' understanding of curriculum topics related to themes of global importance.

The case for and value of creativity within art and design

Critical question

How does the creativity in art and design contribute to education? What might the
value of this be to greater society?

Creativity

This section explores the role and nature of creativity within education before situating this
within the domain of art and design. Creativity has been suggested as being '*the* crucial 21st-
century skill needed to solve pressing contemporary problems' (Newton and Newton, 2014:
575). Thinking creatively requires higher cognitive skills, including the ability to critically and
innovatively reason (Stavridi, 2015). 'Creativity' as a term is contested and it is important to
differentiate between teaching creatively (how a teacher plans engaging lessons to interest
and motivate learners) and teaching for creativity (for pupils to develop their creative thinking) (Newton and Newton, 2014). The former does not necessarily lead to the latter. Jeffrey
and Craft (2004) proposed 'creative learning' as a more apt term for 'teaching for creativity'
as it is broader and incorporates creative thinking.

Davies et al. (2013) highlighted the following as contributing to creative learning environments: partnerships with external agencies; exposing children to a range of appropriate
materials; making effective use of the physical environment; enabling child autonomy as
part of a pedagogical environment; establishing relationships of mutual respect and 'modelling creative attitudes' (p.88) between teachers and learners; and use of external environments, including art galleries. The researchers' recommendations included a consideration
of enabling 'teachers to focus upon the processes of creative skills development rather than
outcomes' (p.89).

Opportunities for creativity have been aligned with situations promoting 'personal
interest, involvement, enjoyment and engagement with challenging tasks' (Beghetto and
Kaufman, 2013: 13), and involve 'posing questions, making connections, being imaginative,
exploring options and engaging in critical reflection [and] evaluation' (Pavlou, 2013: 72).
Additional characteristics include opportunities to be innovative, collaborative, curious, and
autonomous (Craft et al., 2014) within an environment in which children may solve problems and 'take risks, but at the same time feel secure' (Newton and Newton, 2014: 580).
Craft et al. (2014) reported upon how two English primary schools maintained pedagogy for
creativity during a change of educational policy which emphasised knowledge and achievement. School characteristics aligned with co-construction of the curriculum content between
pupils and teachers, enabling agency and choice and a meaningful 'emphasis on real-life contexts and relevance' (p.23). Arts were also recognised as being motivational, and connections
pupils made between learning and the processes involved within the learning journey were
also valued. High expectations were maintained in fostering the skills needed for creative
engagement and appropriate staff training was delivered.

However, there is ambiguity about the role of creativity and its position within education (Blamires and Peterson, 2014). On the one hand, the creativity inherent within the Arts has gained prominence over the last two decades. Evidence of this has included government funded initiatives, papers, and policies, which have emphasised the need for education to nurture talent for the country's creative industries (ibid). In particular, this developed from NACCCE's (1999) advice which promoted creativity and Arts education and prompted creative cross-curricular activities. Simultaneous to raised expectations about the importance of Arts and creativity, however, there has been concern about an erosion of them within the curriculum (Blamires and Peterson, 2014; Ogier, 2017). Whilst the educational community, businesses, and society generally endorse the value of creativity, the place of creativity remains dependent upon political preferences (Wyse and Ferrari, 2015). Inclusion of creativity in the current programmes of study is generally lower than in previous versions (ibid). A culture of test results, generation of school league tables, inspection regimes, performance management, and target setting have meant that teachers show unwillingness to 'risk deviating from the expected, since it is possible to meet expectations without making the effort to exercise the students' creativity' (Newton and Newton, 2014: 581). Nevertheless, it would be remiss to negate the positive role of the creative Arts on impacting upon pupils' academic achievement in the primary phase, including those from lower-achieving pupils. For example, Caldwell and Vaughan's research (2012) demonstrated how Arts education enhanced the academic performance of primary school pupils. Meanwhile, Davies et al. (2013) reviewed literature of the impact of pupil achievement from creative environments, though acknowledged that additional research would prove useful. 'Understanding the value of arts and culture: The AHRC Cultural Value Project' (Crossick and Kaszynska, 2016) foregrounds how Arts benefit pupil learning. They are seen as contributing to general habits of mind, so as to foster curiosity, possibility, and inner critique. Whilst evidence that Arts education causing enhanced attainment on standardised tests is limited, and indicates only small benefits, other factors such as developing confidence, motivation, and positive behaviour are promoted as benefitting all learning, including problem solving, remembering, and communication (Crossick and Kaszynska, 2016). Certainly, problem solving, as part of creativity, is as relevant to art and design as to more academic subjects. Indeed, problem solving, which may have a qualitatively different approach in Mathematics than art and design, may still be promoted as a thinking skill as part of a creative approach to the curriculum (Wyse and Ferrari, 2015).

Zhao's foreword in Caldwell and Spinks (2012) captures the disheartening situation in which the Arts have been eroded from the curriculum, and which cannot be afforded outside school. He cautions of the danger this poses 'when artistic capabilities and creativity are becoming even more cherished assets and when arts are the only experiences that engage some children' (pp. ix–x). This, he concludes, is morally unacceptable and creates a dichotomy in an educational system, where the wealthy are presented with a balanced curriculum, whilst the poor have a limited educational experience of literacy and numeracy. Moreover, whilst OFSTED's school inspection framework (2019) comments on 'the importance of schools' autonomy to choose their own curriculum approaches' (p. 42) and design, there is a caveat that Key Stage 1 should stay focused on the ability to 'read, write and use mathematical knowledge, ideas and operations' (p. 42). OFSTED only acknowledges the need to see a 'broad, rich curriculum' (p. 42) from Key Stage 2 onwards because it has a 'disproportionately negative effect on the most disadvantaged pupils' (p. 42) linked to SATs testing (see OFSTED and Spielman, 2017). It could be argued that a rich, broad curriculum, incorporating creative approaches, is as necessary for Key Stage 1 as it is for Key Stage 2, to maintain children's excitement in, and passion for, learning.

Creativity in art and design

The current English primary national curriculum for art and design (DfE, 2013) seems limited on statutory requirements and guidance, and could lead to misinterpretation by those teachers lacking confidence (Ogier, 2017). Nevertheless, since the current English curriculum is only partially detailed by the government, this has enabled creative pedagogies to continue (Craft et al., 2014). Indeed, one of the national curriculum's (DfE, 2013) aims is to help 'engender an appreciation of human creativity and achievement' (p. 6) with art and design spotlighted as embodying 'some of the highest forms of human creativity' (p. 176). Essentially, 'a high-quality art and design education should engage, inspire and challenge pupils, equipping them with the knowledge and skills to experiment, invent and create their own works of art, craft and design' (p. 176). One could also assert that 'Creativity is polymorphic: its form depends on the discipline and context, although these forms have some common attributes' (Newton and Newton, 2014: 580). This may be considered against a backdrop of fostering creativity across the curriculum.

In producing an art piece, an artist engages with creative activities involving 'decision-making, problem-solving, information-gathering, experimental and evaluative activities' (Pavlou, 2013: 72). Within a small-scale study of 7–8-year olds, Pavlou considered the relationships between art viewing (to question, to hypothesise and uncover meaning), creative development in children's thinking (via imagination and possibility thinking and to make connections) and artmaking. Pavlou emphasised that deep level reflection about art viewing activities was essential to encourage creative learning in art. By introducing children to reading, understanding, and critically interpreting art pieces, we promote their visual literacy – the language we employ to 'read' something (Ogier, 2017). Meanwhile, Stavridi (2015) asserted that visual art enables creative thinking because 'works of art demand thoughtful attention to discover what they have to show and say' (p. 2275). This includes the use of interactive digital art for exploration, discovery, and enhancing knowledge – developing critical thinking – in other subject areas.

Key (2009) proposed that creative approaches in art, with a sense of curiosity, may be developed with reference to the teacher, curriculum, and pupils against the themes of being flexible, ambitious, and developing trust (to enable risk-taking). He suggested that a teacher could be assigned a supportive role, rather than one who regularly gave interventionist – didactic – approaches. This, he claimed, enabled a more spontaneous and personal response to creative expression from children and prevented children from having art 'taught out' of them and an 'I can't draw' attitude. There is a flexibility enabled through not having a set end, but one that changes and evolves and may be revised. This necessitates a conversational and reflective approach between teachers and pupils and being open-minded to allow personalisation. An ambitious approach is fostered by posing questions such as 'What will happen if...? What might happen when...? I wonder what this might look like?

How could these things be combined?' (p. 126). Trust is nurtured when, as teachers, we trust our instincts and feelings and trust pupils and their ideas as they produce 'personal and meaningful responses' (p. 126). Key cautioned that this approach may be challenging in light of inspection and curriculum recommendations but can prove valuable in bringing about creativity. Although Key's suggestions date back a decade, they are still relevant to the current curriculum. A curriculum flexibility does not propose a homogenous outcome, but allows children to respond with diverse, personal approaches; this goes beyond mere teaching of just knowledge, skills, and understanding to enable personal enquiry and response. The ambition and trust within the curriculum are grounded within an open and flexible approach of a pupil-led, rather than teacher-dominated, pedagogy to enhance child ownership. If teachers and the curriculum develop in such a way as Key presented, this enables children to nurture a belief in themselves.

Parsons (2004) highlighted that a cross-curricular approach (an integrated curriculum) benefits a socially relevant curriculum, which can help pupils to begin to grasp some of the rapidly changing aspects of society and the problems it faces, and to relate these to their experiences. This may be facilitated through skills which may be promoted within art: Self-reflection and active inquiry. Examples which Parsons referred to included environmental awareness, war (and its cultural and racial presentations), gender (and how it is advertised in popular media), and identity. Similarly, Freedman and Stuhr (2004) emphasised that art education should broaden in line with that reflected through our increasingly pervasive visual culture. This included art promoted through digital technology and artefacts and artistic pieces we create on a range of scales and in a range of forms such as architecture or media. art within a global visual culture can transcend to promoting ideology, aesthetics, and spirituality, including environmental education and human rights (ibid). It can inform beliefs, attitudes, and actions, and illustrates a key component of democracy within education 'to promote the development of responsible citizens who think critically, act constructively in an informed manner' (Freedman and Stuhr, 2004: 824).

Research and theory synopsis

Pavlou (2013) - 'Investigating interrelations in visual arts education: Aesthetic enquiry, possibility thinking and creativity'. *International Journal of Education through Art*, 9(1), 71-88.

Pavlou (2013) undertook a small-scale, though powerful, study which explored how 7-8-year olds viewing and responding to artwork could benefit their creativity necessary for artmaking. Aesthetic enquiry was a necessary feature, which incorporated opportunities for Pavlou to work collaboratively with the class teacher in planning and partially delivering the lessons.

Initial opportunities to enquire about artwork facilitated the children to 'envisage new possibilities, new ways of being creative in their thinking and in their representations' (Pavlou, 2013: 84). A model which explored relationships between art viewing, aesthetic enquiry, possibility thinking, and creativity is central to this article and represents useful constructs to use in practice by teachers in planning learning sequences for children in art.

Stavridi's (2015) research proposed that digital technologies in primary education should be utilised within art activities (painting, drawing, sculpture, and architecture) to enhance learning and children's creativity in subject areas such as geometry to support mental visualisation and reasoning or to help understand scientific ideas. Technology can act as 'tools of the mind' (Stavridi, 2015: 2279). Academics have claimed that an Arts integrated curriculum can support teaching in-depth understanding, though there is caution about asserting proof that this and creativity can improve academic performance (assessed via tests) and make children more innovative (Stavridi, 2015). Nevertheless, it has been emphasised that there can be benefits to the 'educational value of learning as a process matter, "to know and understand"' (Stavridi, 2015: 2278). The imaginative flexibility afforded in creative artistic endeavours to consider possibilities translates into other subject areas (ibid).

Stavridi's research analysed 40 'edtech' applications and web-based art, assessed by educators, which support 'critical thinking skills … and rev up creativity' (p. 2279).

Background to the case study schools

Critical question

How do Foxfield and Woodhill use art to deepen their children's understanding within their curriculum provision?

Foxfield and Woodhill primary schools are part of an Inspire Partnership Academy Trust and their curriculum has developed around seven global themes of importance which include human rights, identity and global sustainability. Each half term, there is a focus on a theme, but year groups may select different themes to one another. Once a year there is an 'Arts fortnight', where there is an agreed focus across the schools. The schools promote key values and each month there is a focus on one of them. The values are: Friendship, kindness, effort, forgiveness, integrity, responsibility, love, resilience, collaboration, respect, and excellence. There is an integrated dimension to the curriculum using a framework of cross-curricular topic themed lessons, planned backwards to incorporate knowledge, skills, attitudes and habits to achieve clear outcomes. This has been inspired by the approach suggested in 'Outstanding Teaching: Teaching Backwards' (Griffiths and Burns, 2014). Art is not conceived as a bolt-on but provides a vehicle in which to explore topics in further depth to also convey important and sometimes subliminal messages.

Throughout the schools' corridors and classrooms, high quality work is displayed (termed 'publishing' by the school), of which art is a key component and which act as a celebration of the outcomes and mastery of skills developed within the process of creating artworks. Art activities incorporate drawing, painting, printing, textile work, 3D construction, collage, use of Information Technology, and knowledge of artists and their techniques. Both schools have used artists-in-residence to support planning and teaching aspects of the art curriculum which have included the following: Team teaching, medium-term planning, documentation demonstrating exemplification of standards to support the teaching of key skills and staff training, advice about artists to include within topics, art development of workshops for teachers to run after school, and taking different groups of children to produce big installations or canvases as part of an art topic's final outcome. Whilst Foxfield and Woodhill subscribe to the same ethos and principles, the content itself and the way in which it is interpreted is personal to the school, year group, class, and individual pupil. Similarly, it is important to recognise that whilst the examples of practice presented within the case studies are illustrative of excellent practice, it is not intended that the ideas are copied directly, but instead adapted to suit the reader's situation. The case studies presented are subdivided against key themes which the teachers raised: Promoting deeper understanding of oneself and the world, process and expression, showcasing within a learning environment, developing the curriculum, celebrating cultural diversity, feedback, and community links. An analysis following each case study accompanies each sub-theme.

The teacher practitioners contributing to the case study from Foxfield were: Mikala, art and design Lead and phase leader of Key Stage 1 and Year 2 teacher; Sarah, a Year 5 teacher who is beginning a co-art lead role; and Candice, who teaches Year 4 and is lower Key Stage 2 phase leader. The teachers from Woodhill were: Owen, who is Deputy Head and, amongst his duties, holds responsibility for teaching and learning, curriculum development, and assessment; Tayo, the art and design lead, drama lead, and Year 5 teacher; and Kamaria, a newly qualified teacher in Year 1.

Case study on Foxfield Primary School: Promoting deeper understanding of oneself and the world

> Art helps them to understand the topic in a different way; it shows mastery of different skills so they can articulate in a different way, e.g. making art from recycling – so it is not just about creating a final piece of art, but looking at the process of recycling.
>
> (Sarah – Year 5 teacher and recently appointed co-Art Lead)

Mikala explained that engaging with art and design contributed to children developing a growth mindset. She highlighted that resilience and perseverance were fostered because of the staged nature of the processes they worked through when developing the skills and strategies within art. This was facilitated through a whole school teaching philosophy endorsing that it was acceptable to make mistakes. Sarah asserted that children's creativity was nurtured if children were 'willing to make mistakes, because that creativity is coming out of your comfort zone – you need to just give it a go'. She also associated this with the artwork transformed and depicted in the video clip 'Austin's butterfly' (see EL Education, 2016), shown to her class and which supported her children to evaluate and offer productive feedback whilst benefitting self-esteem. Sarah further commented that making mistakes, adapting work, and trying again – which she models to the children – should be valued as part of creativity – 'it might not look perfect to everybody, but that is what art is – *your* interpretation'.

The importance attached to pupils' personal interpretation and developing an inquisitive mind was promoted by Mikala. She explained that art could help children expand their 'awareness of the world with open eyes and see what they can do to change it to make it better'. She commented on this in relation to the English contemporary artist Grayson Perry, whose alter-ego is female. The artist was selected so that children could consider that it was acceptable to be different, which linked to their topic exploring human rights. The art techniques, based around producing a pot, developed from children initially recording some of Perry's designs. They then extended the artwork and incorporated the theme of gender and individuality by using computer technology to take photos of each other, tearing these in half and re-combining with another half from their peer (whether male or female), and working these ideas into the pot design. Meanwhile, Candice's class celebrated diversity and valuing differences by considering how standards of beauty contrasted with each other according to the views held by different societies. Her pupils made collages using different sections of editorial portraits because they wanted to reflect that there was no universal standard of beauty.

Another example of how art prompted deeper-level thinking was captured by Sarah who related how her class reflected upon the work of an American graffiti artist, Jean Michel Basquiat (who went from being homeless to selling a $110.5 million painting), when covering the topic of homelessness. The theme of graffiti was further discussed with the children when they saw homeless people (in London and in videos) who used art (sometimes starting with graffiti) as a form of therapy or a way in which to pass the time. They then sold the artwork for money. During a school trip at a later point in the year, the pupils noticed some graffiti which stimulated debate as to whether art or vandalism was displayed, and how it may act as a unique way to distinguish the homeless person's place to sleep. In terms of art outcomes, the children created art pieces based on Basquiat's designs, by using 'found objects' such as cardboard, wood, or plastic which would be accessible by homeless people.

Inclusion through process and expression

We know there are so many artists out there, that's their way of life, that's their living – we want to encourage that with children, because not everyone is an academic, some people are absolutely flawless at creating art and we want to encourage that and give them every opportunity.

> (Mikala – Year 2 teacher, art and design leaf,
> and phase leader of Key Stage 1)

Sarah and Candice valued how art could help children, who might struggle academically, to express themselves successfully in a way which they may find easier than through the written form. This, Sarah acknowledged, was facilitated through the school's philosophy that it was acceptable to make mistakes, as part of the process of learning, and which she reinforced through her modelling of art techniques. Sarah suggested that such an approach enabled children to gain confidence to experiment and appreciate that 'art is not fixed'. Candice presented a similar view: 'Art allows expression; it's that freedom of being able to express yourself, be immersed in a topic, analysing, evaluating, but in a different way, where it's not just writing'. Nevertheless, Candice also acknowledged that developing the creative, artistic skills of children who performed well academically was also important, because it might not be regarded with such importance at home.

Showcasing within a learning environment

> It is about expressing yourself and trying, and I am proud that every single child in my class does their best with art. And they are encouraged to try and what they produce, as long as they have tried their best, is good enough.
>
> (Candice – Year 4 teacher and phase leader of lower Key Stage 2)

Displays, combining English and art, are refreshed on an ongoing basis in a half-termly cycle across the year, alternating between classroom and corridor-based displays, to continually showcase pupils' learning and achievement from the global topics. The teachers highlighted that because the learning environment and displays exemplified standards of excellence, this prompted pupils' motivation during lessons and triggered pride and enthusiasm when showing visitors around. The displayed artworks reflected learnt techniques (processes of art) and important messages to help increase children's awareness of key issues and guide their future choices. For example, within the Arts fortnight, Mikala explained that Year 1 focused on conservation linked to the art of recycling. After discussion about plastic pollution, they used recycled materials to construct a 3D turtle (see Figure 6.1); the art evoked emotional responses from the children who produced it and for others viewing the display, as it prompted reflection upon the underpinning, subliminal message of the effects of pollution.

Mikala's class produced artwork linked to conservation and the process of recycling – note the materials used in the two depictions of the turtle involve plastic, which echoes the powerful message conveyed recently in the media about plastic killing sea life.

Figure 6.1 Conservation and the process of recycling

Discussion: Foxfield Primary School

Promoting deeper understanding of oneself and the world

The teachers at Foxfield captured the way in which the art helped children to develop personal characteristics and deepened the children's understanding of the topics in which they were engaged. The themes of resilience and perseverance, referred to by Mikala, complemented the literature about creative thinking to develop the ability to critically and innovatively reason (Stavridi, 2015), and to explore alternatives and take risks (Key, 2009; Newton and Newton, 2014). This literature was also salient to Sarah's comments about children venturing out of their comfort zone to produce a personal interpretation for art, by taking risks and feeling that they can make mistakes, and about children developing the confidence to evaluate their work and engage with peer feedback. Moreover, Sarah's description suggested that she fostered child autonomy, mutual respect, and creative attitudes to promote an environment for creative learning (Davies et al., 2013).

All of the teachers gave examples about how art contributed to a deeper level of understanding of the topic being studied by the children, and how this was a reciprocal relationship, with the topic contributing to a deeper understanding of art appreciation, the process of art, and the outcome. The examples foregrounded the creative approaches embraced by Foxfield and echoed the connections which children could establish between areas of learning (Craft et al., 2014). This was mediated as part of a cross-curricular approach, which could help to explore the concepts of self and identity within the real daily world and socially relevant issues (Parsons, 2004). This was also facilitated by the way in which the artists used by the teachers inspired the children's art by initiating and promoting debate and discussion (Pavlou, 2013; Stavridi, 2015).

Inclusion through process and expression

Sarah and Candice considered the theme of inclusion in relation to those children who may flourish through the process of expressing themselves within art, as opposed to more traditionally academic subjects. This also touched upon an equity in their provision of art and other subject areas as part of a balanced curriculum. These themes echoed Zhao's (2012) tribute to the importance of Arts education which might be the sole experience to engage some pupils (see also Caldwell and Vaughan, 2012). Moreover, Sarah and Candice's notion that art and its outcome was fluid complemented Key's (2009) suggestion that teachers and pupils may come together on an equal level to journey together, to ask and respond to exploratory questions, and to personalise the children's expression of art in a more pupil-led, as opposed to teacher-centred, pedagogical approach.

Showcasing within a learning environment

Alongside how art could deepen the understanding of a topic during lessons (e.g. Parsons, 2004; Pavlou, 2013; Craft et al., 2014), as discussed earlier, Mikala emphasised how displays which showcased learning enabled similar reflection. Moreover, the displayed work within the learning environment symbolised how the school provided a motivational force to the children to strive for excellence. The displays also engendered an embodiment of pride for the pupils. These important characteristics reflected a national curriculum (DfE, 2013) aim to 'engender an appreciation of human creativity and achievement' (p.6), and specifically for art and design to promote 'some of the highest forms of human creativity' (p. 176).

Case study on Woodhill Primary School: Developing the curriculum

> I am most proud of the mere fact that the art has been sustained in light of the additional pressures of the curriculum and assessment; and the fact that the art is so impactful – it gives us a great sense of pride that so many people comment positively on the art and at the end of the day that's the children's learning and that's an opportunity that we're providing for the children; and there's some stunning pieces.
>
> (Owen – Deputy Head, with responsibilities which include teaching and learning, curriculum development, and assessment)

Owen acknowledged that as political educational agendas altered, so did the school's response to their curriculum to incorporate both skills and knowledge components. Additionally, the school was mindful that they wanted their curriculum to be 'purposeful, meaningful and relatable', so that children could appreciate 'their place in the world and that they can make a difference'. Owen explained that the project-based learning – linked to a key text explored in literacy – and generally occurring in the afternoon, entailed initial stages of exploring and deepening and could help children make links between curriculum areas. For the exploring stage, there might be a historical, geographical, or Science focus. The deepening stage might be facilitated by incorporating art, as a key component to support the understanding. For example, Year 1 used a key text around *Dougal's Deep-Sea Diary* (Bartram, 2004) as a stimulus for exploring recycling. Art and science were linked together where children painted animals using watercolour and noted the characteristics of the animals.

Owen described that the artists and their artistic styles which they chose to inspire the children may be considered a bit 'edgy' – i.e. they extended beyond traditional, popular artists and styles, to incorporate genres including pop art, digital art, and photography. Tayo explained that an artist's work was reflected upon and could inspire the children once they had engaged in discussions to fully evaluate the artist's work and reflect upon their own perceptions.

Celebrating cultural diversity

> You can use your own teaching style – I like being creative and using colour. I can have ownership and teach it in a way which engages the children. The art co-ordinator presents ideas for the term through the key book [driving the topic] and draws out ideas and themes linked to the book and discusses ideas with me, but there is openness for me to develop my ideas and do that journey with the children.
>
> (Kamaria – newly qualified teacher and Year 1 teacher)

Kamaria and Tayo noted that art could provide a means for children to express and celebrate their individuality and cultural roots alongside developing their understanding of a topic. Kamaria reflected that during diversity week some children in her class brought in traditional Nigerian fabrics which they presented and discussed in Circle Time. This led to discussions about how artwork could be based on the fabrics and how the children could represent the patterns through different media. When the children were working on landscapes, they incorporated some of the colours displayed within the materials which reflected links they had made between the art and their own lives (see Figure 6.2). This personal meaningfulness and association was also echoed by Tayo. She referred to some of her pupils who were refugees from the Middle East. Art was used as a vehicle in which to tackle gender stereotyping, using the book *The Breadwinner* (Ellis, 2014) about female roles in Afghanistan, as a stimulus; the female central character dressed up like a boy to be able to provide for her family. Ideas about challenging stereotyping were incorporated into vase designs. The children were inspired by Grayson Perry's art (similar to the children in Foxfield) to show that art did not have to be gender specific and it could reflect who you were as a person rather than who the world wanted you to be. On the vases, the children showcased both male and female representations to challenge gender stereotyping.

Figure 6.2 Personal Connections – Landscapes influenced by Nigerian fabrics

Kamaria's class worked on landscapes influenced by Nigerian fabrics, which reflected personal links between some of the children and their cultural roots.

Feedback

Some children would get distressed at the beginning of the year, but now they have developed their confidence through peer feedback to keep going and continue to develop their pieces of artwork.

(Kamaria – newly qualified teacher and Year 1 teacher)

Similar to Sarah in Foxfield, Kamaria was proud of the progression which the children had made in relation to their increased confidence in giving peer feedback to support their next steps to develop their artwork. In sketchbooks, learning objectives were detailed along with success criteria. Whilst teachers' written comments were not indicated in sketchbooks or the back of artwork, teachers gave verbal feedback, undertaking 'live' marking with the children. This enabled the pupils to consider and make instant improvements in response to evaluations and recommendations.

Showcasing work and community links

Children will walk round to monitor the standards of display on a morning and with the artist in residence will touch up areas in the afternoon; it shows pride of their learning environment. Within classrooms, displays shows a standard of work to aim for too with a new class and can inspire them – when work goes up it is truly appreciated by the child as work to be proud of.

(Tayo – Art and Design Lead, Drama Lead, and Year 5 teacher)

Figure 6.3 Arts Fortnight exhibition

As part of an annual Arts fortnight, there is an affordable art fair held at Woodhill (and to which Foxfield also contribute some of their pupils' artworks). Each teacher selects the three best art outcomes from the year to place in a gallery (see Figure 6.3). Artists known to the school are also invited to display their work, alongside local artists, and even teachers. Most recently, some of the children's works of art were printed on postcards and sold for an affordable price, to enable the children to make purchases. Parents are also invited to contribute and display craft work in a lower hall. Meanwhile, junior leadership teams in the upstairs hall (the art gallery) welcomed visitors and showed them around.

Discussion: Woodhill Primary School

Developing the curriculum

Owen's reflection about the school curriculum's development aligned with Craft et al.'s (2014) documentation of how two schools maintained creative pedagogy with a focus on meaningful 'real-life contexts and relevance' (p. 23). Woodhill School (as does Foxfield) presents a curriculum approach which enabled a depth of understanding – creative thinking (Newton and Newton, 2014) – within art and design and which was shown to contribute to other curriculum areas as part of a cross-curricular approach. The inclusion of digital art within the curriculum, referred to by Owen, was similarly highlighted by Stavridi (2015) as supporting creative thinking for exploration, discovery, and enhancing knowledge. This theme also complemented Freedman and Stuhr's (2004) suggestion of how digital technology broadened art forms in line with our visual culture, such as computer technology or photography, which could be used to explore and inform our beliefs, attitudes, and actions on important world issues.

Owen and Tayo foregrounded how the critical analysis of artists' work by children could inspire their work. This reflected Pavlou's (2013) assertion about how deep reflection of art viewing activities encouraged a visual literacy, creative learning and responses to the creation of new art.

As part of the Arts fortnight, Woodhill and Foxfield display the children's artwork in an exhibition.

Celebrating cultural diversity

The importance of a socially relevant, cross-curricular approach to teaching and learning (e.g. Parsons, 2004; Craft et al., 2014) was captured by Kamaria and Tayo. Kamaria's example of how art was used within diversity week, to celebrate the children's cultural backgrounds, was conducive to how relationships of mutual respect (Davies et al., 2013) and situations involving personal interest and involvement (Beghetto and Kaufman, 2013) may contribute to creativity. Through art, Tayo facilitated self-reflection and active enquiry within the critical exploration of cultural, racial, and gender stereotypes to explore identity (ibid). This also complemented how art education within a global visual culture could transcend to a consideration of human rights and empower people to be responsible citizens (Freedman and Stuhr, 2004). Attention to affective dimensions, relevant to celebrating identity, are noted as supporting pupils to take risks, an important dimension of creativity (Newton and Newton, 2014).

Feedback

The value of teacher and peer feedback were relayed by Kamaria (and Sarah at Foxfield). They demonstrated qualities conducive to a creative environment – relating to establishing ambition and trust, and pupil autonomy rather than teacher-led pedagogy – to enhance personal responses and reflection and the creation of artwork (Key, 2009).

Showcasing work and community links

The annual celebration of the children's art within an exhibition as part of the Arts fortnight embodies an aim of the art and design curriculum to appreciate achievement and creativity (DfE, 2013). This event is characteristic of how the school motivates pupils and promotes opportunities for self-esteem (similar to how Mikala described the learning environment at Foxfield) by showcasing the children's work. The exhibition reflects the engagement, inspiration and challenge which pupils experience within the curriculum to produce their own work (DfE, 2013) and expose their creativity. Together with the community involvement, the exhibition exemplifies a successful local economy, cultural understanding, social justice, and equality (Ogier, 2017).

To conclude, this chapter has explored how two schools conceived art and design as a key component within their meaningful curriculum to support creativity and provided a depth of understanding to global themes within a cross-curricular approach. It has been argued that creativity is a critical component of the 21st century and that the subject of art and design has an important contribution to play. The artistic skills and the processes of art involved in the creative learning journey have been promoted (Davies et al., 2013), having equal importance to the outcome. The showcasing of children's work to celebrate their artistic skills, learning processes, and outcomes demonstrated the excellence with which these schools have striven to enable children to reach their potential. Moreover, the use of an external agency (resident artist) and collaborative group work (promoting one of the schools' values) promote creative endeavours (Craft et al., 2014). It could also be asserted that the collaboration mirrors a global environment in which collaborative action and a social conscience can help to solve world problems in a creative way. This brings us full circle to Newton and Newton's (2014) highlighting of the need for creativity to solve society's contemporary problems.

Summary

To provide a rich art and design curriculum, schools could:

- Develop technical skills within a context-rich curriculum which is meaningful and purposeful for the children and which can be personalised to reflect cultural diversity
- Consider how art may contribute to a depth of understanding about oneself and the world, and make this explicit to pupils within the teaching episodes
- Emphasise the importance of the art process as well as the outcome to the children
- Use art as an integral component of a cross-curricular approach
- Value the role of art and celebrate its importance by giving it prominence within the curriculum, and appreciate how it may engage pupils with their education
- Consider the role of collaboration in art
- Develop the autonomy they afford to children within the artistic process
- Showcase artwork to motivate children and enhance their self-esteem through displays and formal exhibitions
- Use displays to develop children's thinking around global themes
- Develop an art curriculum which embodies the school's values
- Employ a resident artist to provide training to teachers, support curriculum planning, support teaching, and provide opportunities for large-scale group work
- Provide focused staff training (including that for showcasing children's work) delivered by the art and design Lead
- Broaden the opportunities of art to include digital technology

- Use a range of traditional and non-traditional artists (contemporary and non-contemporary) to include those who will have relevance for children, and use critical reflection of artistic work to explore underpinning messages as well as artistic technique
- Use feedback to enable children to take risks with their learning in art

---

Further reading

Key, P. (2009). 'Creative and imaginative primary art and design'. In A. Wilson (Ed.) *Creativity in Primary Education. Exeter: Learning Matters.*

Key's chapter proposes a challenging but worthwhile exploration of our teaching pedagogy within art and design, one which encourages curiosity and creativity through the teacher and curriculum, and pupils being flexible and ambitious and developing trust. A case study which is presented is powerful in illustrating the key themes of what this might look like for the teacher.

Ogier, S. (2017). *Teaching Primary Art and Design*. London: SAGE Publications Ltd.

This book positions the teaching and promotion of art and design within the current curriculum demands. It provides practical advice to support practitioners with developing their confidence with integrating art across the curriculum as well as refining specific art techniques. Case studies and reflective exercises help the reader to make connections to their own practice, and website links help the reader to delve further into areas of interest.

National Advisory Committee on Creative and Cultural Education (NACCCE) (1999) *All Our Futures*. London: DfEE.

Whilst a dated document, this publication suggests some valuable pedagogical ideas to inform creative practice. It is useful if you are completing an assignment on creativity or if your school is exploring ways in which creativity may be nurtured.

Caldwell, B. J. and Vaughan, T. (2012) *Transforming Education through the Arts*. Oxon: Routledge.

This inspirational book explains how the arts inspired disaffected pupils and transformed their educational experiences. Evidence also suggests increases in academic attainment. The publication is useful if you are exploring how creative interventions may support children.

References

Bartram, S. (2004) *Dougal's DeepSea Diary*. Surrey: Templar Publishing.
Beghetto, R. and Kaufman, J. (2013) 'Fundamentals of creativity'. *Educational Leadership*, 70(5), 10–15.

Blamires, M. and Peterson, A. (2014) 'Can creativity be assessed? Towards an evidence-informed framework for assessing and planning progress in creativity'. *Cambridge Journal of Education*, 44(2), 147-162.

Caldwell, B. J. and Vaughan, T. (2012) *Transforming Education through the Arts*. Oxon: Routledge.

Craft, A., Cremin, T., Hay, P. and Clack, J. (2014) 'Creative primary schools: developing and maintaining pedagogy for creativity'. *Ethnography and Education*, 9(1), 16-34.

Crossick, G. and Kaszynska, P. (2016) *Understanding the Value of Arts & Culture: The AHRC Cultural Value Project*. [Online] Available at: https://ahrc.ukri.org/documents/publications/cultural-value-project-final-report/ [Accessed 28th February 2019].

Davies, D., Jindal-Snape, D., Collier, C., Digby, R., Hay, P. and Howe, A. (2013) 'Creative environments for learning in schools'. *Thinking Skills and Creativity*, 8, 34-41.

DfE (2013) *The National Curriculum in England: Key Stages 1 and 2 Framework Document*. Available at: https://www.gov.uk/government/publications/national-curriculum-in-england-primary-curriculum. [Accessed 3rd December 2016].

EL Education (2016) *Austin's Butterfly: Models, Critique, and Descriptive Feedback*. [Online] Available at: https://www.youtube.com/watch?v=E_6PskE3zfQ [Accessed 3rd March 2019].

Ellis, D. (2014) *The Breadwinner*. Oxford: Oxford University Press.

Freedman, K. and Stuhr, P. (2004) 'Curriculum changes for the 21st century: Visual culture in art education'. In E. Eisner and M. Day (Eds.), *Handbook of Research and Policy in Art Education*. New Jersey: Lawrence Erlbaum Associates, Inc.

Griffith, A. and Burns, M. (2014) *Outstanding Teaching: Teaching Backwards*. Camarthen, UK: Crown House Publishing.

Jeffrey, B. and Craft, A. (2004) 'Teaching creatively and teaching for creativity: Distinctions and relationships'. *Educational Studies*, 30(1), 77-87.

Key, P. (2009) 'Creative and imaginative primary art and design'. In A. Wilson (Ed.), *Creativity in Primary Education*. Exeter: Learning Matters.

National Advisory Committee on Creative and Cultural Education (NACCCE) (1999) *All Our Futures*. London: DfEE.

Newton, L. and Newton, D. (2014) 'Creativity in 21st-century education'. *Prospects*, 44, 575-589.

OECD (2018) *The Future of Education and Skills 2030*. [Online] Available at: https://www.oecd.org/education/2030/E2030%20Position%20Paper%20(05.04.2018).pdf [Accessed 3rd March 2019].

OFSTED (2019) *School inspection handbook. Draft for Consultation - January 2019*. [Online] Available at: https://assets.publishing.service.gov.uk/government/uploads/system/uploads/attachment_data/file/772065/Schools_draft_handbook_180119.pdf [Accessed 6th March 2019].

OFSTED and Spielman, A. (2017) *HMCI's Commentary: Recent Primary and Secondary Curriculum Research*. [Online] https://www.gov.uk/government/speeches/hmcis-commentary-october-2017 [Accessed 6th March 2019].

Ogier, S. (2017) *Teaching Primary Art and Design*. London: SAGE Publications Ltd.

Parsons, M. (2004) 'Art and integrated curriculum'. In E. Eisner and M. Day (Eds.), *Handbook of Research and Policy in Art Education*. New Jersey: Lawrence Erlbaum Associates, Inc.

Pavlou, V. (2013) 'Investigating interrelations in visual arts education: Aesthetic enquiry, possibility thinking and creativity'. *International Journal of Education through Art*, 9(1), 71-88.

Stavridi, S. (2015) 'The role of interactive visual art learning in development of young children's creativity'. *Creative Education*, 6, 2274-2282.

UNESCO (2006) *Road Map for Arts Education. Report from The World Conference on Arts Education: Building Creative Capacities for the 21st Century in Lisbon, 6-9 March 2006*. [Online] Available at: http://www.unesco.org/new/fileadmin/MULTIMEDIA/HQ/CLT/CLT/pdf/Arts_Edu_RoadMap_en.pdf [Accessed 3rd March 2019].

Wyse, D. and Ferrari, A. (2015) 'Creativity and education: Comparing the national curricula of the states of the European Union and the United Kingdom'. *British Educational Research Journal*, 41(1), 30-47.

7 Music

Composing, performing, listening, and structuring (all without fear)

Mark Betteney and Kay Charlton

Critical questions

How might music be taught within the parameters of the current national curriculum?
How helpful is the national curriculum for music?
What is it to be musical?

Introduction

In trying to respond to these critical questions, this chapter is a celebration of how music might be taught within the parameters of the current national curriculum documentation. We are not claiming that music *should* be taught like this, but we are offering a perspective for ways in which children might engage in musical activity and learning, a perspective based upon consultation with a number of primary school music teachers. The chapter explores the purpose of music lessons and what might be learnt from them. It also identifies through case studies and literature what cognitive, intellectual and social opportunities participation in music can afford. The chapter is designed to encourage generalist teachers, as well as specialists, to have confidence in teaching music. We identify the status of the subject, and of teachers' attitudes to the teaching of music. The chapter may serve to reduce any lurking guilt that teachers may feel about what 'ought' to happen in music lessons, but may not in theirs, and aims to broaden teachers' approach to what music teaching might include.

Having said all that in a most bullish manner, it would be very easy to imagine that music has become something of a Cinderella subject in today's primary schools. For example, at first sight a simple numerical analysis of the national curriculum (DfE, 2013) is not encouraging for those who highly value the teaching of music. Table 7.1 identifies the number of pages given over to each KS 1 and 2 subject within the document.

The entire subject content for primary music is presented in ten bullet points: four for KS1 and six for KS2. No other subject is given less prominence in the national curriculum (DfE, 2013), although two others share music's numeric status. However, we argue that this is absolutely not a negative feature, or a cause for doom and gloom. The opposite is true. We

Table 7.1 National Curriculum (2013) KS1 and 2 subjects by number of pages

Subject	Total pages	of which are programmes of study or subject content	of which are appendices and glossary
English	85	31	49
Mathematics	44	39	2
Science	31	28	0
Art and design	2	1	0
Computing	2	1	0
Design and technology	4	3	0
Geography	4	3	0
History	5	4	0
Languages*	3	2	0
Music	**2**	**1**	**0**
Physical education	3	2	0

* KS2 only

would argue that this brevity is a good thing for those of us who are looking to give children musical experiences which are not constrained or directed centrally, but instead are tailored and informed by the interests, cultures and experiences of the children. A lack of prescription demands creativity. How many ways might there be to allow children to 'play tuned and untuned instruments musically' (DfE, 2013: 258, KS1) or to 'improvise and compose music for a range of purposes' (DfE, 2013: 258, KS2)? Any number! The teaching of music is not shackled by the prescriptive demands of the programmes of study which direct the learning and teaching of maths, english, and science. You will not find a reference to a systematic method of teaching notation. As a result, one of the most exciting aspects of the teaching of music is that the teacher has a good degree of autonomy. This is a responsibility, and a privilege.

De Vries (2010), for example, suggests that a teacher might choose, or not choose, to use contemporary popular music over other styles of music as a starting point or a resource; to use new media technology over traditional instruments; to establish how much choice to allow children in what they learn and compose and perform, as well as how they present their learning or compositions. A teacher can even choose to allow children the choice to perform or not to perform. Such flexibility is not in the gift of the teacher of systematic synthetic phonics, or early maths. In today's schools, to teach music is to teach creatively, because there is no set rubric from which to work.

This is all well and good for the teacher who is confident in teaching music, but where is a musical novice to start: a novice who may not know what to choose or how to choose it? Many schools have specialist music teachers, and this decision potentially negates the need for generalist teachers to teach music at all. Many generalists may heave a sigh of relief at this, but of course this policy reinforces the notion that music is for 'special' or 'specifically talented' people, an unvoiced message to children that music is hard, optional and niche. Hennessey (2017) puts it well when she observes that:

> those [teachers] who are confident in their own subject knowledge and skills and feel strongly about music are more likely to negotiate time to teach music and make it part of

their professional identity. Those who are less confident will not be challenged to try and may conclude that music is a subject that class teachers do not teach.

(p. 609)

This chapter intends to alleviate such a lack of confidence.

To this end, when developing the chapter, we undertook a small-scale study, interviewing four primary teachers of music about their priorities for teaching music. This study also explored such things as how helpful the teachers found the national curriculum (2013), how they assess music and the resources they found most useful. A pattern emerged that one of the most useful resources each of the teachers in this study used was the children themselves. Three of the teachers expressed without prompting that the use of body percussion is a superior resource to tuned or untuned instruments, certainly for warm-up activities, as the children need less-developed coordination or fine motor skills to be able to successfully engage in an authentically musical way. There are also, perhaps, fewer behaviour management problems than when multiple instruments are involved.

Question and answer activities (for example, copying a body percussion phrase); group improvisations; body movements on the pulse of a recorded or sung melody or song; sound pictures; sequenced movements to a given work, song or rhythm: these are all musical activities which children and generic teachers can easily work together with.

Henley (2017) explores a theoretical framework of what is meant by being 'musical' and identifies six interlinked perspectives – being musically active; having musical experiences; doing music; feeling musical; musical contributions; and developing musical expertise. She summarises these characteristics by arguing that '[this] theoretical framework underpins the viewpoint … that being musical means being engaged in active music making' (p. 746). Such a call for teachers to be seen by the children as active music-makers resonates with Welch (2005), who asks teachers to be musical role models – to engage and learn with the children – in order to erode the myth that music is an exclusive pursuit, engaged in only by the especially talented. Just as Cremin and Oliver (2017) are helping teachers to see themselves as writers, so Henley (2017) urges teachers to be seen as musicians.

Key reading

Incorporated Society of Musicians' (2018) *Consultation on the future of music education* London, ISM

This is a useful overview of where Music Education is now and its journey since the publication of the Henley Review (DfE/DCMS, 2011a) and the subsequent National Plan for Music Education (DfE/DCMS, 2011b). It includes powerful and useful statistics on the size and value of the music industry in the UK and Music's positive effect on well-being, countered by research into the recent decline in uptake of GCSE in music and the arts.

Fautley, M., Kinsella, V. & Whittaker, A. (2017) *Whole Class Ensemble Teaching Research Report*. University of Birmingham.

This detailed document is a comprehensive, nationwide research report, covering the delivery and outcomes of WCET.

Department for Education (2013) *The national curriculum in England: Key Stages 1 and 2 framework document* © Crown copyright 2013

What this document does not say about music is as significant as what it does. It contains affirming aspirations, and allows teachers to be creative about the short-term provision of music in their own schools, as the subject content descriptors lack specificity.

Critical question

What am I trying to achieve in a music lesson?

Teachers' priorities in music

We interviewed four teachers about their teaching of music – their starting points, aims and priorities. Without exception the teachers did not feel directed, influenced or constrained by the national curriculum (2013). Instead, they used words such as 'nebulous', 'vague', and 'harmless' to describe the subject content attainment targets for music, and no teacher was worried that they might be unable to fulfil its content, or that the curriculum might oblige them to work in a way in which they were not comfortable, or would emphasise one aspect of music over any other. The study found that throughout the school year, no teacher in our research study referred to the national curriculum regularly when planning, because each knew that their chosen activities and learning intentions would satisfy any number of the curriculum's learning areas.

Another reason why the teachers in this study did not refer to the curriculum was because, also without exception, they identified enjoyment and inclusivity, as their two most influential priorities for the teaching of music, and these are words not found in the music curriculum. For the teachers in this study, music teaching was as much about developing positive attitudes in children towards music as it was about developing their knowledge and technique. The teachers did not hold negative views towards the national curriculum. Each strongly subscribed to the national curriculum's purpose of study which reads 'A high-quality music education should engage and inspire pupils to develop a love of music and their talent as musicians, and so increase their self-confidence, creativity and sense of achievement' (DfE, 2013: 257). If anything, their feeling was that the subsequent single page of national curriculum subject content was surplus to requirements, almost antithetical, to that statement of intent.

The case studies below are indicative of the way in which the teachers felt that class music is best taught as a group exercise, not as an individual pursuit. All four teachers in this study agreed that a sense of teamwork, and the need for participating children to bring different phrases, rhythms, motifs or sounds to a performance, lent uniqueness to the teaching of music, which the children valued. Linked to this was the teachers' experience of assessing music. None of the four teachers kept detailed data on individual pupil progress, because (in their view) a non-specific curriculum does not lend itself to summative assessment. Instead they tended to assess groups, group compositions and group performances. Strategies were used for self- and peer-assessment (see the second case study, below), and one teacher felt that the fact that she did not assess children individually contributed a great deal to the children's enjoyment, as a lack of fear of judgement added to the children's willingness to take risks and to contribute. All teachers agreed that this lack of individual assessment did make report writing at the end of the year difficult, because, with only a few exceptions, the best they could honestly do was to make reference to a child's engagement and attitude to music, but since these were also the teachers' priorities, this would be inevitable. If the aim was to 'increase [children's] self-confidence, creativity and sense of achievement' (DfE, 2013: 257) through music, then that at least could be reported.

Critical question

Is Whole Class Ensemble Teaching effective as a method of instrumental learning?

Is Whole Class Ensemble Teaching effective as a method of instrumental learning?

Charlton (2016) has explored the literature around the effectiveness of Whole Class Ensemble Teaching (WCET, also known as First Access), which is part of a national programme of instrumental tuition. It was originally known as 'Wider Opportunities' and evolved from the pledge made by the government in 2000, that 'over time, all pupils in primary schools who wish to, will have the opportunity to learn a musical instrument' (David Blunkett, Secretary of State for Education, 2000; Ofsted, 2004). It is one of the core roles of music education hubs to 'Ensure that every child aged five to 18 has the opportunity to learn a musical instrument (other than voice) … for ideally a year (but for a minimum of a term) of weekly tuition on the same instrument' (Arts Council England, c.2017).

Music education hubs were established in 2012 as a result of the Henley Review (DfE/DCMS, 2011a) into Music Education in England and the subsequent National Plan for Music Education (DfE/DCMS, 2011b). Hubs are funded by Arts Council England and are charged with ensuring that the National Plan is delivered – via the school curriculum and by arts organisations in their area. Hubs are 'groups of organisations – such as local authorities, schools, other hubs, art organisations, community or voluntary organisations – working together to create joined-up music education provision'. (Arts Council England, c.2012). Although there is no standard model for delivering WCET, a range of models were piloted from 2002 and schemes evolved in music services with many regional variations such as:

- Whole classes learning one instrument together
- A 'class band' learning a variety of instruments together
- Classes split into two or three groups learning different instruments
- A carousel model of taster sessions on different instruments

Most WCET programmes are delivered to children in Year 3 or 4 (Fautley, 2017: 15) with no cost to children. Fautley's report showed that the five most popular instruments taught are violin, trumpet, clarinet, recorder and ukulele.

The question of what constitutes a good WCET programme remains open as, given the variety of models, there is no comprehensive agreement on the definition of WCET. Fautley (2017) cites the oft-quoted phrase that it is 'learning music through the medium of an instrument' (p. 54), and it is often the case that for many schools instrumental learning is regarded by school leaders and teachers to be the delivery mechanism for the whole of the national curriculum for music (Instrumental and Vocal Tuition at KS2, 2007: 5).

Hallam (2016) urges that, as in any good lesson, the focus should be on engaging children through a variety of differentiated activities and repertoire and teaching the foundation of good instrumental technique. She notes that inspiring and enthusiastic teaching leads to successful lessons, and she maintains that 'musical learning prior to the commencement of WCET is critical' (2016: 17) if the ensemble teaching is to be effective. For example, the national curriculum for music identifies that 'children should be familiar with playing together and understand how to keep a pulse' (DfE 2013: 2). As such, WCET should be viewed as one component of a school's music provision, not its vehicle for the whole curriculum throughout the school. Hallam (2016) concluded that it is possible to implement WCET in ways that lead to high standards of instrumental playing and high continuation rates as long as lessons are of high quality, tutors have high expectations, high quality resources are used and there are frequent performance opportunities.

The choice of repertoire is fundamental to a successful WCET programme, with the 'inclusion of different types, styles and genres of music' (Fautley & Daubney, 2018: 219). There is very little published repertoire specifically written for WCET, and this lack of resources can be challenging for tutors. Evidence shows that the use of high-quality teaching materials is crucial to success (Hallam, 2016: 35), and Charlton has developed quality resources (case study three) based on her research into how the choice of repertoire can contribute to children's decisions about whether or not to continue playing the instrument after the initial WCET programme.

The period immediately following a term-long or year-long WCET phase is critical to a child's continuation with the instrument, or with an interest in music. If continuation is to be meaningful then progression routes need to be in place and will 'support children in making the transition from a class-based activity to one where they identify themselves as musicians' (Hallam, 2016: 10). Fautley (2017: 93) was surprised to discover that although 83.1% of headteachers using Music Education hubs to deliver WCET considered it was 'important' or 'very important' that children should want to continue with their musical instrument playing, 11.2% stated that it is of little or no consequence to the success of a WCET programme. For many hubs, continuation is seen as a key success indicator and crucial to fulfilling their core roles as detailed in the National Plan for music education (The Importance of music, 2011).

Case study: the use of online resources

Lucy Brown at Thorntree primary school, uses the 'BBC Ten Pieces' resources with her Year 5 and 6 classes. The Ten Pieces explore a range of musical styles and periods, from classical to modern. For Lucy, a series of lessons begins with a video (5-8 minutes typically) taken from these resources, on which she is able to build performance and composition activities for the children in her classes. For example, the composer Kerry Andrew explores how she wrote a specially commissioned song for the BBC series, ('No Place Like') involving not just singing, but also humming, beat-boxing, body percussion and arm movement, and she invites children to perform the song, and to add to it. The song is ambitious in structure, as in places it contains sections with different groups of children articulating different words, chants, rhythms or recreating environmental sounds. This song can be learnt and performed as written, but there are also opportunities for children and classes to insert their own interpretations of important features of what it is, and what it sounds like, to be 'home'. All of the six KS2 national curriculum subject content indicators can be nurtured and developed through engagement with this song.

Another example from this resource that Lucy felt effectively allowed children to learn, perform and compose musically, is a work entitled 'Connect It' (Anna Meredith, series 2), an example of a work through which children explore and develop musical patterns. This piece allows self-differentiation, as the children create layers of pattern and sequence according to their own musical ability, using only body percussion.

Both of these works from the BBC's Ten Pieces require children to perform as a member of a group. The success of the performance is dependent upon the concentrated success of each individual contributing a respective part, just as is required in any band, choir, orchestra, ensemble or music group. Lucy felt that this interdependency of children to create a coherent performance from their independent contributory parts was a fundamentally important aspect of music teaching, not found consistently in many other national curriculum subjects. music teachers might also be interested in exploring Charanga's Musical School (Casson, 2018), another online resource which is informed by the specific needs of the national curriculum.

Case study: the effect of the use of recording equipment

Kay Charlton at Plumcroft primary school planned a series of lessons for a Year 5 class based upon Grieg's *In the Hall of the Mountain King*, a piece that uses a repeated motif which becomes increasingly frenetically played as the piece builds. Having familiarised themselves with the music, the class watched two contrasting YouTube clips:

1. An orchestra playing the original piece
    https://www.bbc.co.uk/programmes/p02b5bwl

2.   A 'dubstep remix' created digitally
     https://www.youtube.com/watch?v=M1fWCFUMFwE

The children were asked to identify the difference between the sound and performance of the two versions, instilling in them a sense of 'historical periods, genres, styles and traditions' (National Curriculum, DfE, 2013). Having asked the children to listen and identify key melodic and rhythmic features of the music, Kay arranged the whole class so that they were able to create their own alternative version of this piece. Using body percussion to create a 'remix' beat, before then transferring this to wood blocks, maracas, tambourines and drums and a simplified melody was played on xylophones. As the piece became more frenetic, the untuned instruments became increasingly significant to the performance. Using a digital video recorder, Kay was able to record the children's rendition, play it to them on the interactive whiteboard and ask them for their comments.

   In terms of musical progress, in Kay's view, the initial quality of the performance is of less importance than the identification (by the children) of ways to improve the performance. The children were pleased with their performance but felt it could be improved by keeping a steadier pulse as they recognised that some children were ahead or behind others. When asked how this might be achieved, they suggested that watching the conductor might help, which indeed it did in their subsequent rendition.

The recording of the children's performance was a key motivational and educational aspect of this series of lessons. The children became their own audience and critic, which had four significant effects. Firstly, it embedded the children's learning, as critiquing their own work reinforced their concept of what was important in the piece, and of their role within it. Secondly, it gave them much more confidence when it came to performing the piece for another 'real' audience (another class, or perhaps the whole school in an assembly). Thirdly, recording the performance focused the children's immediate concentration, and reduced behaviour management problems, as children did not want to 'get it wrong'. Kay is convinced that the use of recording devices is a positive motivator for increased musicality, as well as improved learning behaviours. Fourthly, viewing their own performance enabled the children to become aware of the contributions of others, and how their own contribution fitted in with the whole performance. Kay agreed with Lucy's opinion that one of the unique aspects of music was the way it allowed children to work collegiately and as a team.

Case study: action research project

'Specially-Composed Musical Repertoire for Key Stage 2: its Impact on Progression and Engagement', research carried out by Kay Charlton for a Masters in Music Education (Trinity Laban Conservatoire of Music and Dance, 2016).

There is very little readily available, specific repertoire for WCET at KS2, and to address this, Charlton composed a set of progressive repertoires for trumpet with teachers' notes and backing tracks ('Are You Ready?' – published by Warwick music, 2016). The hypothesis of her report was that by using specially composed repertoire in WCET lessons there would be a positive impact on the engagement and progression of pupils.

Her research was based on 85 pupils in Year 4 who learnt trumpet and guitar through WCET from January to July 2015, and on 90 children in the next cohort from September to December 2015. The study's aim was to assess the efficacy of specially composed repertoire, and the data corroborated her hypothesis, that by using material she had specifically composed with the needs of WCET in mind, there was a positive impact on engagement and progression from the children who learnt the trumpet and played her repertoire. Charlton tried out her compositions on the children and took their feedback into account, making revisions and then testing it again. When children from the second cohort chose which instrument they would like to continue with until the end of Year 4 data showed that trumpet was more popular in all three classes, with an average of 60% choosing to continue with trumpet rather than guitar.

At the end of the WCET year (July 2015) all children from the first cohort filled out a questionnaire which produced quantitative results indicating that participants across both cohorts were engaged; 70% said they 'loved' music lessons and 57% said they would like to continue learning an instrument.

Did you enjoy doing Whole Class Ensemble music over the past year? (See Figure 7.1).
Did you like the music [repertoire] you learnt? (See Figure 7.2).
Do you want to carry on playing an instrument? (See Figure 7.3).

Interviews with children also produced qualitative data corroborating the positive reaction to the trumpet repertoire. By January 2016, in the subsequent academic year, 21% of the first cohort had continued with an instrument after the WCET programme (a little over a third of those who indicated in the questionnaires that they aspired to). However, the proportion is significantly higher than those who had continued in the previous year (14% of the cohort).

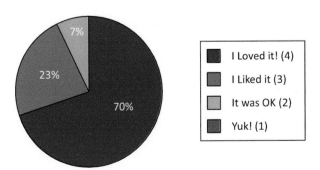

Figure 7.1 Results to the question 'Did you enjoy doing Whole Class Ensemble Music over the past year?'

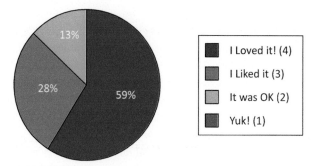

Figure 7.2 Results to the question, 'Did you like the music [repertoire] you learnt?'

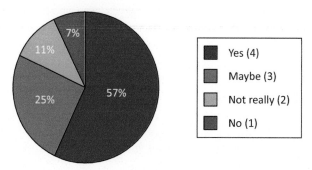

Figure 7.3 Results to the question, 'Do you want to carry on playing an instrument?'

In July 2017 the children Charlton studied were in Year 6 and 14% of the continuers were still playing an instrument. Four trumpet pupils continued learning with her, two achieving Grade 2 and professed a desire to continue at secondary school.

The repertoire comprises of simple melodies in various styles, each with a lively backing track with lyrics and actions to aid aural learning. Each tune has differentiated parts in order to ensure that every child can take part, and improvisation and copy-back sections to enable creativity. It starts with one note and gradually progresses to five, scaffolding children's learning through activities based on prior knowledge. This research shows that the right repertoire, taught in the right way, is crucial to children's enjoyment of learning an instrument and can lead to increased continuation rates.

Summary

- The national curriculum (2013) content descriptors for music are very brief and broad, allowing teachers a great deal of autonomy and flexibility about what they teach and how they teach it
- Inclusion and inclusivity are hallmarks of good music teaching. Children who struggle with paper-based subjects, or who have language challenges, often thrive in music lessons

- Music is best taught, developed and experienced when children are composing and performing as a group or even as a class. There is a great deal of social constructivism in an effective music lesson
- The downside of this social aspect of teaching a music class is that, as a subject, music is difficult to assess on an individual basis
- Music lessons can be at their most effective when children are the main resource. In particular, body percussion is an effective way of engaging children with musical sequences, patterns and layered textures within songs and performances
- Making use of visual and audio digital recording equipment (for use exclusively within the school of course) is a highly motivational tool for children's self-appraisal. It also can improve children's learning behaviours
- There are some excellent online resources available which can be used as a starting point for creative activities, or as a basis for recreating or accompanying those resources
- Whole Class Ensemble Teaching is an important feature of modern school life, but should not be the full strategy for a school's music provision

---

Further reading

Ofsted (2013) *Music in Schools: What Hubs Must Do. The Challenging Conversation with Schools*. London: Crown Copyright.

This document identifies Ofsted's 2013 long-term vision for the breadth and rigour of music provision in primary schools. In particular it states the extent to which hubs should be leaders and champions of music in schools, not a menu service from which schools can pick and choose their involvement.

The Importance of music: A National Plan for Music Education (2011). Gov.uk.

This plan introduced wide-ranging changes to the structure of music education in England, including the introduction of music education hubs.

Swanwick, K. (1999) *Teaching Music Musically*. London: Routledge.

This book is a classic text in music education. Swanwick questions the nature of music itself and considers the fundamental principles of how music can be taught in schools and colleges. This book is especially useful to read if you are completing an assignment about how formal music education in institutions may adapt to a changing world.

References

Arts Council England (c.2017) *Music Education Hub Core and Extension Role Guidance*. Available at: https://www.artscouncil.org.uk/sites/default/files/download-file/Music%20Education%20Hub%20Core%20and%20Extension%20Role%20Guidance.pdf

Arts Council England (c.2012) *Music Education Hubs*. Available at: https://www.artscouncil.org.uk/music-education/music-education-hubs#section-1

Casson, M. (2018) *Charanga Musical School Programme*. https://charanga.com

Charlton, K. (2016) Are you ready? *Warwick Music*. https://www.warwickmusic.com/p/UhjG

Cremin, T. and Oliver, L. (2017) Teachers as writers: A systematic review. *Research Papers in Education* 32(3), 269-295.

De Vries, P. (2010) What we want: The music preferences of upper primary school students and the ways they engage with music. *Australian Journal of Music Education* 4(1), 3-16.

Department for Education (2013) *The national curriculum in England: Key Stages 1 and 2 framework document*. London: Crown copyright.

DfE/DCMS (2011a) *The Henley Review: Music Education in England* © Crown copyright 2011.

DfE/DCMS (2011b) *The Importance of Music: A National Plan for Music Education* © Crown copyright 2011.

Fautley, M. and Daubney, A. (2018) Inclusion, music education, and what it might mean. *British Journal of Music Education* 35(2), 19-221.

Fautley, M., Kinsella, V. and Whittaker, A. (2017) *Whole Class Ensemble Teaching*. Research Report. Birmingham: University of Birmingham.

Gibb, N. (2018) *Announcement of Expert Panel for a Model Music Curriculum*. Crown Copyright. https ://www.gov.uk/government/news/government-backs-young-musicians?fbclid=IwAR0NhYOMrxg_3 cWkGCc86tJpGQoJqb_7sFiSS9IrY7zz4EK7iR1RHh7XKjw

Hallam, S. (2016) *WCET-Final-Report*. London: UCL Institute of Education.

Henley, J. (2017) How musical are primary generalist student teachers? *Music Education Research* 19(4), 470-484.

Hennessy, S. (2017) Approaches to increasing the competence and confidence of student teachers to teach music in primary schools. *Education 3-13* 45(6), 689-700.

Incorporated Society of Musicians (2018) *Consultation on the Future of Music Education. Results of the Incorporated Society of Musicians' (ISM) Surveys Conducted over Summer 2018*. London: ISM.

Ofsted (2004) *Tuning In: Wider Opportunities in Specialist Instrumental Tuition for Pupils in Key Stage 2: An Evaluation of Pilot Programmes in 12 Local Education Authorities*. Crown Copyright 2004.

Ofsted (2013) *Music in Schools: What Hubs Must Do. The Challenging Conversation with Schools*. London: Crown Copyright.

Welch, G. F. (2005) We are musical. *International Journal of Music Education* 23(2), 117-120.

8 Physical Education and Health Education

Kristy Howells

Critical questions

How can a Physical Education and Health Education pedagogy be embedded within
school practice?

What strategies could a class teacher use to develop a love for physical activity to support physical and mental wellbeing?

Where can I access research focused on Physical Education and Health Education?

Introduction

Health Education features within the statutory curriculum in England, from autumn term 2020, as part of Relationships Education, Relationships and Sex Education (RSE) and Health Education curriculum (see also Chapter 10 for further details on relationships education). The Health Education aspect of the curriculum aims to teach 'pupils about physical health and mental wellbeing' and 'to give them the information that they need to make good decisions about their own health and wellbeing' (DfE, 2019: 31). The reasoning behind this new focus is that 'physical health and mental wellbeing are interlinked, and it is important that pupils understand that good physical health contributes to good mental wellbeing and vice versa' (DfE, 2019: 31). The key areas that are focused upon within Health Education include:

- Mental wellbeing
- Internet safety and harms
- Physical health and fitness
- Healthy eating
- Drugs, alcohol, and tobacco
- Health and prevention
- Basic first aid
- The changing adolescent body – that actually occurs physically from the age of nine – and includes both physical and emotional changes

It is recommended within the guidance that Health Education can be supported through wider education on healthy lifestyles through for example Physical Education, sport, and extra-curricular activities. Hence the links in this chapter between Physical Education and Health Education.

Physical Education itself aims 'to provide opportunities for pupils to be physically confident in a way which supports their health and fitness' (DfE, 2013: 198), as well as ensuring that all pupils 'are physically active for sustained periods of times' and 'lead healthy, active lives' (DfE, 2013: 198).

There seems so much potential offered for primary school children within their curriculum. Yet according to ukactive's (2019) report 'generation inactive 2', today's children are the least active generation ever, which may explain the real current need for both Physical Education and Health Education curriculum to help educate children (and teachers) more about the importance of a fit and healthy lifestyle. In England one in four boys and one in five girls meet the 60 minutes of recommended physical activity each day of moderate to vigorous intensity by the Chief Medical Officer (ukactive, 2019). YoungMinds (2019) report that one in three children have mental health issues, which increases to one in four children if emotional distress is also included.

Physical activity interventions, school sport, Physical Education, physical activity, and movement within school time have been shown to help mental health issues (Bailey et al., 2018; Howells and Bowen, 2016) as well as sleep difficulties. A lack of sleep can impact children's cognitive function and their ability to focus within school settings. According to the Association of Physical Education (AfE, 2015) health position paper:

> physical education contributes to public health and personal wellbeing through the physical learning context that it provides for every child. Health and wellbeing should be viewed holistically to compare physical, psychological / mental and social aspects of health which contribute to people's quality of life.

(p. 4)

The experience of Physical Education and physical development within primary school is core to ensuring life-long and life-wide (Howells and Jess, 2019) participation in physical activity which will enable good physical and mental wellbeing into adult life. Therefore, role models within school are key to sharing the passion, excitement as well as knowledge and understanding of both Physical Education and Health Education.

The benefits of Physical Education and Health Education

It is important for us to be able to identify the benefits of Physical Education and Health Education. This chapter will argue that we should dedicate time every day for Physical Education as well as Health Education so that it becomes embedded as a valued subject across the whole school and being physical becomes a habit that is formed within primary school. Physical Education is one of the few subjects that has been a statutory subject across all Key Stages and phases of children's learning, from Early Years through Key Stages 1 to 4. The OECD International Curriculum Analysis (2019) identified that previously England had limited links to Health Education as a specific aspect of the curriculum, in comparison to the other countries within the analysis who had embedded Health Education into multiple subjects or combined with Physical Education. Both Scotland and Wales have Health and Wellbeing as the subject name. It is therefore important to understand the impact of these new and changing dynamics of including Health Education on pedagogy.

Research evidence has highlighted the benefits of movement to support mental health and well-being. The All Party Parliamentary Group (APPG) on Fit and Healthy Childhood Report (2019) on Movement and Mental Health identified that movement within Physical Education, physical development, physical activity, and school sport can be a positive experience for children and help in particular to increase confidence and self-esteem through regularly participating in movement. They also propose that children learn to experience the world through their bodies, therefore it is important for children to focus on both Physical Education and Health Education as this will enable children to develop social and emotionally through physical learning (APPG, 2019).

Harris (2018), in her call to make Physical Education a daily core subject, proposed that high quality Physical Education can help contribute to children's confidence, self-esteem, and self-worth – as well as enhancing social development. She suggested that children need to have the opportunity to develop physical competencies to ensure they can move efficiently, effectively, and safely. School has the potential to help support children's Physical Education as well as Health Education, as children spend 7,800 hours within school it is a critical place, yet 90% of school leaders have recently reported an increase in number of children experiencing anxiety or stress over the last five years (YoungMinds, 2019).

Decline in play and physical activity

Play is a basic human right of the child, but recent evidence from the Association of Play Industries (API, 2019) have found that children are physically weaker than previous generations and that 80% of 5–15-year olds are not getting enough physical activity to keep themselves healthy. For many, this is due to a decrease in access or opportunities to play or a lack of opportunities for sport and physical activity beyond the school day. There has been a 44% decrease in spending on playgrounds and local play areas/parks since 2017. 35% of playgrounds have shut or closed due to neglect in recent years. Parents reported in the report by API (2019) that 26% of children have sleep difficulties. Such play areas are needed to enable children to explore and engage in movement to learn what their bodies are capable of and how to move in a variety of different directions. If these play areas are being shut outside of school then there is a need to have these within the outdoor environments in schools.

Howells (2016) proposed that the outdoor environments in schools were key to developing physically and learning physically and aired caution in how outdoor environments were developed to ensure they posed risks and challenges to help educate the children physically as they had to critically engage in the obstacles they were faced with. Ridgers et al., (2006) previously support this idea and identified the outdoors as being important especially for infant aged children, as they can spend up to a quarter of their school day in the outdoor environments. Ridgers et al. (2011) in later work identified that time spent outdoors is associated with increased physical activity.

According to Play Scotland (2019) in their position paper, children are entitled to play every day, and this right is recognised by the UN Convention – a right that is often potentially forgotten in the pressure of testing and curriculum timings. Yet play and physical activity can help build healthy and happy children, who are then able to learn about resilience and how to cope with challenges through movement opportunities. A lack of these opportunities would mean less experiences of being able to cope with change, challenge, and stress, impacting on children's lifelong wellbeing. The Steiner Waldorf Education (2011) support the use of movement opportunities to help children learn and suggest that physical activity as well as play is the way children make sense of the world and support and develop children's thinking.

Oliver et al., (2007) propose that physical activity has been visibly recognised as being fundamental to health and wellbeing of school-aged children. Physical activity can enable a positive sense of identity, within international research it has been shown that being part of a sports team is associated with lower depressive symptoms, lower levels of isolation and loneliness, lower perceived stress, and better self-rated mental health in young people (Bailey, Howells and Glibo, 2018). The researchers (Bailey et al., 2018) also found that physical activity, in particular frequent vigorous activity, had protective measurements against feelings of hopeless and suicide risk in adolescents, especially males.

Principles for pedagogy

Physical Education is a place within the school day in which attitudes and interests can be fostered as well as an understanding of a healthy lifestyle. It is also a place for developing the children holistically, physically, socially, emotionally, and cognitive, through a physical means (Howells, with Carney, Castle and Little, 2018). Within their work (Howells et al., 2018) suggest there are '7Ps for perfect pedagogy' – which are adapted from the work of Launder (2001) – for making Physical Education irresistible. These include:

- Preparation
- Pace
- Participation
- Progression
- Practice and Performance
- Personalised
- Positivity.

(p. 62)

Howells et al., (2018) discuss the three elements to consider within a lesson when considering best practice. These include effective process (how you teach) and appropriate product (what you teach), but with the people (who you teach) as the central focus of every interaction (p. 56). This is reinforced by earlier work by Howells (2015, 2018) who identified four essential principles of pedagogy. These include:

- Pace
- Structure
- Transferable skills
- Competition

Howells (2015, 2018) identified that pace and structure are quite closely linked within her principles, and that subject knowledge and understanding is essentially to allow the teacher to share the links between the skills and for the children to understand how to apply balance and changing of weight within gymnastics as well as tag rugby, for example. Ní Chróínín, Fletcher and O'Sullivan (2018) also identified five principles in their work which focused on supporting pre-service teachers to learn how to facilitate meaningful Physical Education experiences and suggested these to be:

• Planning
• Experiencing
• Teaching
• Analysing
• And reflecting on meaningful participation

(p. 117)

They also turn to Kretchmar's earlier research, (2001, 2006) which discusses the features of Physical Education experiences that make them meaningful for children. These are:

• Social interaction, emphasising shared positive participation with others
• Challenge, involving engagement in activities that are 'just-right' (not too easy, not too difficult); Increased motor competence, including opportunities for learning and improved skilfulness in an activity
• Fun, encompassing immediate enjoyment in the moment
• Delight, experiencing more sustained pleasure or joy as a result of significant engagement and commitment

(Ní Chróínín, et al.: 119)

It may be useful to consider your own practice when developing skills and movement opportunities. Do you focus more on traditional sporting skills and activities, or on developing range of movement opportunities to extend skills such as agility, balance and coordination? There needs to be a shift in mindset of the traditional (for example) six weeks of dance followed by six weeks of athletics, and for school schemes to place more focus on challenge and cooperative physical activities that do not need to be longitudinally sport focused.

This chapter has reviewed the research highlighting the importance of both Physical Education and Health Education and sign-posted readings to support and enable class teachers and schools to embed a culture of physical development, physical activity, Physical Education, and Health Education for life. The final part of the chapter will put this into practice by showcasing examples of teachers who have adopted Physical Education and or Health Education into their school.

Introduction to the case study examples

The three case study examples will offer three distinct perspectives on developing Physical Education and Health Education pedagogy within the classroom and throughout the school. The first case study explores how physical activity interventions can be embedded within the class to support children's wellbeing. The second case study is from an experienced researcher and primary school teacher, who explains strategies he has used for enhancing children's understanding of Health Education by focusing on the element of diet that is often forgotten, fluid intake. The final example is from class teacher who is also Head of Physical Education and a special educational expert who explains the strategic approach to ensuring Physical Education is accessible for all.

Case study one: Jo Bowen – Year 6 lead class teacher and head of Numeracy in a school in the South East of England

In this case study class teacher Jo Bowen, who is also Year 6 lead, and head of Numeracy, (who previously specialised in Physical Education and Physical Activity within her Primary Education degree) shares ways in which she has embedded the daily mile as a physical activity active mile initiative within her class. As part of the government's plan to significantly reduce childhood obesity by supporting healthier choices, in their childhood obesity plan for action (DH, 2018) it is recommended that active miles are completed each day and propose the daily mile as one of the ways in which this could be done, as it can 'improve the physical, social and mental wellbeing of our children, regardless of age, ability or circumstances' (p. 5). At the time of the interview Jo had previously completed a research project on the long-term benefits of a physical activity intervention for one child over a five month period, through the use of shot put and hammer throwing and had found improvements in academic achievements, social connectedness, and wellbeing. The case study child had shown significant improvements in his interest and ability in Physical Education as well as improvements in both his physical and mental health and wellbeing (Howells and Bowen, 2016). Jo had then continued to implement physical activity interventions to a whole class to see if they could support in the say way as they did for the case study child.

What does the active mile mean to you?

In its essence the active mile means getting the children moving and being active every day to give them a love for physical activity, more engaged in Physical Education, and link to Health Education of understanding fitness and health. It is something that I have to plan in daily to the children's timetable. I found that it was important to visually indicate when the children were going to undertake their daily mile as otherwise the children became concerned as to when they would be undertaking it.

I shared The Daily Mile Foundation principles with the children: That the daily mile would take place outside, only take 15 minutes, and be self-paced – so this could be running, walking, or jogging each day of approximately one mile and can be undertaken three times a week (The Daily Mile Foundation, 2019). Yet when I explained the principles children expressed confusion, they commented that they felt they were being lied too, if a) 'we're not reaching a mile' and b) 'we're not doing it daily'. In their words 'it didn't do what it said on the tin', so I adapted the principles outlined by the foundation so that the children would indeed complete a mile and for us to undertake it every day, no matter what the weather. That was the agreement with the children, this then helped to prevent any confusion.

I found that the time and space within the outdoor environment really benefitted the children. I focused on recording aspects of their behaviour to see the impact on the children. I recorded their wellbeing levels, their academic achievement, and their social connectedness – in particular their ability to work together, as this was an aspect that the children were struggling with within the classroom set up.

Could you give examples of how the active mile impacted the children?

There are so many important elements that I found throughout the year with the children. Time and space were key to their social developments. I had one girl who had extra interventions for handwriting and fine motor skill development. She used the time and space outside to practice her shapes in the air, as she had to practice, and she described the active mile as her safe place to practice. Overtime, her friends also joined in with writing shapes in the air and encouraged the girl to draw for longer and longer as they could see how it was helping her fine motor skills when they were back in classroom. For one of the boys, he used the time outside being physically active to practice his joke telling, in particular to the teacher, but it encouraged him in two ways. Firstly, to be creative and try to make up his own jokes and secondly to read and find new jokes, so he could keep telling them as they were out completing the mile.

For me, I found that introducing physical activity daily the following occurred:

- 92% of the children improved their levels of wellbeing
- 8% of the children stayed at their starting levels of wellbeing
- Social connectedness improved, the children continued their discussions about problem solving or asked each other questions about the activities they were undertaking in class, through nurturing critical thinking skills and time for thinking skills
- It helped support teamwork, as they encouraged and motivated each other to finish their miles
- It allowed children to be competitive, and increase their levels of physical activity intensity, through offering choice of the speed of movement
- The children also improved their academic achievements

What has been the impact of the active mile pedagogy for you and your class?

The impact of including and developing the active mile within my daily routine and within my class pedagogy has made movement just part of the day – it has incorporated it into their way of life, rather than being an extra part. The most interesting finding of following the children and their improvements and questioning what the benefits would be of implementing such a new pedagogy was that the children became quite agitated as we neared the end of term or the end of each half term. They were becoming worried about how and when they would continue their daily mile within their day. I found that I needed to develop connections with the home networks and encourage the children to pair up or to group up and to plan out if they were going to go out together as a community during the non-school time or to go out with their family and make it part of family routine. I didn't expect the children to become quite so focused on it within the school day.

I have been able to share my findings with the rest of the school and I have started it again with my new class this year – they were keen to start as they had seen my previous class out during various times of the day walking, running, and jogging. My new class described them as laughing during lesson time and they wanted to experience this too.

The impact on me has also been huge. It has made me reflect and realise the importance of physical activity and physical activity interventions both on individuals, collectively as a class, and on me personally. I have continued to strive to make the mile exciting, through introducing problem-solving activities to help the children critically engage and think whilst outside. It has also made me more aware of the weather and being able to time the dry parts of the day. I have appreciated the different times of the year more.

I feel it is important to continue to research your own practice and not to just accept new initiatives, but to question why and how this will benefit my teaching and my children's learning, especially allowing myself to identify and recognise the unexpected learning and experiences that occur. This has allowed me to then influence practice and policy within my own school and also disseminate my research with a wider audience (Howells and Bowen, 2016, 2018; Howells et al., 2019). This has earned me a reputation of credibility with both parents and my headteacher.

What advice would you give an early career teacher who says they do not have time for active miles?

Physical activity is fundamental to children finding a passion and enthusiasm for Physical Education. When children are physically active, they are able to explore what their bodies can do and to learn the ways in which their bodies work. Children carry their bodies around all day and every day, and it's important to enhance every possibility possible to help children who may be overweight or obese and rely on interventions within a school setting to help support them. Some children do not have access to active transport and so Physical Education lessons and break times are their only forms of exercise. Within my local area up to 30% of children are regarded as overweight and obese, and I feel it is our responsibility as teachers to help where we can. I want to also reassure early career teachers that the 15 minutes a day really doesn't mess your day up, the benefits massively outweigh any impact you might perceive from having the break. The children come back in refreshed and reengaged and I found it helped improve their cognitive as well as social skills.

Jo provides a fabulous insight into embedding physical activity interventions as part of her Health Education and Physical Education pedagogy in her class. The case study offers reassurance as to the benefits of applying daily physical activity and recognising the importance of such activity to both the physical and mental wellbeing of the children within her class. Jo shows us how she has reflected on embedding this practice and the importance of questioning the benefits and encouraging others to also find time and space within their class.

In the next case study, we meet Josh Williamson. Josh completed his degree in Primary Education, and then continued on to complete a Masters by Research, as he was really interested in the impact of Health Education – specifically how much young children understood about fluid intake, in terms of knowing when to drink, what to drink, and how much to drink. His passion for investigating fluid intake comes from specialising in both Early Years and Physical Education during his degree and also from his experiences as both a teaching assistant and his placements as a student teacher where he observed that children struggled to understand drinking. Diet is key within the Early Year Learning Goal 5 (DfE, 2014a) – Health and Self-care focuses on the 'children knowing the importance of good health of physical exercise and healthy diet' (p. 10). As well as in the new Health Education (DfE, 2019), in which pupils should know 'what constitutes a healthy diet' (p. 34). At the time of the interview Josh's research had been published within International Journal of Nutrition (Williamson and Howells, 2019) and had been cited within the new 'All Party Parliamentary Report for the Fit and Healthy Childhood group on Dietary Patterns and the Way Forward' (2020), as well as previously being cited in the 'Health Families: The Present and Future of the Supermarket' report (2020).

Case study two: Josh Williamson – Primary Teacher and Health Education Researcher

Josh Williamson has been researching fluid intake for two years. Firstly, he investigated children's understanding within one class for his dissertation and final year placement during his Primary Education degree, in which he specialised in physical development within EYFS (DfE, 2014a). He then upscaled his research within his Masters by Research in Physical Education and Physical Activity degree and investigated and compared children's understanding across four coastal schools within the South East of England. The children were aged four and five years old. He used a Google document questionnaire and physical visual representations to aid question comprehension.

What is important within Health Education for children to understand about drinking, isn't the focus on food?

Drinking and the impact of fluid intake is often the forgotten part of food and diet. Water is a foundation for life according to Krecar, Kolega and Kunac (2014) but it is the most commonly ignored aspect as a dietary essential. Sufficient hydration is essential for maintaining children's health (European Food Safety Authority, 2010). Adequate hydration is essential for children, as they may not correctly replace fluid loss. Edmonds and Jeffes (2009) found children had higher levels of happiness when they had greater access to water and when fluid intake was promoted by teachers within their educational settings. This indicates the importance of fluids and fluid intake in children's overall wellbeing. Edmonds and Burford (2009) found that children experience 10% improvements in cognitive wellbeing when they maintain good fluid intake.

Why is drinking water important now? You've highlighted that the importance of it has been known for a while, so why now?

The DfE (2019) have recently suggested that school governors should encourage a healthy eating ethos and have for the first time in guidance also recommended water consumption. Yet there is no specific guidance on how to improve fluid intake for young children. Therefore, I believe that we need to help our children, our teachers, and the parents/carers as well as the governors understand what 'recommended water consumption means'. The last time there was a campaign in school related to fluid intake and water was 'water is cool in school' campaign which was in 2007, which means that we have the potential of a whole new generation of teachers who they themselves may have missed out on this campaign within their own school and we can't assume that they know and understand fluid intake. For this reason, I wanted my research to raise awareness of what children did know and how teachers could support.

The other key reason for identifying the importance of fluid intake is that it isn't easy for children to learn, they need help and support in this area of Health Education. This is because children experience a 45 minutes physiological delay in their thirst reflex, in terms of them recognising that they feel thirsty. This may explain why children often come back in after lunch time, when they have had ample time to have a drink, but they haven't recognised that their bodies need or will need a drink, and in the afternoon, their thirst reflexes kick in and they are all asking for drinks. I know that this can frustrate teachers, and feel like it breaks the afternoon up, with drink stops, but I don't think teachers know the delay that occurs physiologically. We need to help children to understand the signs that they need to drink. Through developing this awareness, understanding, and knowledge of fluid intake there is potential for massive changes in the health and wellbeing of children.

Could you explain what you found from your research?

First of all, my research found that four and five-year old children were quite confused about the amount that they should be drinking a day. They reported great contrasts in their estimates from this was shown that on average 46.9% of children believed they should be drinking only up to 500ml or 36.2% of children thought they should be drinking over two litres a day. The actual amount that is recommended by the World Health Organisation (2004) is 1.1–1.3 litres of fluid a day to maintain effective hydration status. This suggests that the young children are not gaining the knowledge from their curriculum. They also really struggled with explaining *why* you should drink fluids. Their answers included:

'Don't know'
'Something to do with being healthy'
'To help you go for wees'
'To stop you dying'
'Just because'.

If children do not know why it is important to drink, then habits won't be formed. I really feel that more time in curriculum is needed to explain why children should be drinking. This is additionally important to air caution on responses to those children who thought you needed to drink to stop you from dying – because what happens to their mental well-being if they are not allowed or prevented from drinking at some point? Does this potentially then cause panic that they will die?

The children were also able to say who supported them in terms of telling them to drink or reminding them to drink. Only 39.6% of children in the study said teachers told them when to drink. The stronger influencers were actually family members. This suggests that teachers may think that children know when to drink, when actually at this age range they are still learning and need teachers to keep supporting them in recognising both the signs and the delayed signs of thirst.

What are your recommendations? Could you give two examples of how you have implemented fluid intake in your classroom.

One example that is easy to implement would be drink breaks scheduled into the day – perhaps after playtimes/break times or lunch times – when the children may have been losing more water from their bodies due to running around. This would teach them that they need to replace the lost fluid from exercising. This would then help habit forming and relate to exercise, and linking to needing a drink when also consuming food at lunch times. This could be implemented by the children having a water bottle and sips from their water bottles during the register in the afternoon to prevent any learning disruptions.

Another example would be to plan drinking breaks into morning learning time, so that children recognise that it is an acceptable and positive aspect of learning, and can help with their cognitive thinking. According to Adan (2012) it only takes two minutes for cognitive benefits to occur once fluids have been consumed, therefore could help learning, rather than being a hindrance. It is necessary to try and change the mindsets of teachers to show the importance of understanding Health Education.

It is easy to hear the enthusiasm Josh has for integrating drink breaks into everyday class time, for this to become part of the pedagogy across the school, and not to be seen as a hindrance. Josh is also currently seeking funding for development of community hydration packs cited as a recommendation in the APPG (2019) report, to help parents/carers and children within the community better understand the importance of fluid intake.

In the final case study, we hear from Rhys Wintle who is Head of Physical Education across his federation of schools and has worked within speech and language units across Kent. Rhys shares how he has used a variety of strategies to help support children with special educational needs to excel within Physical Education.

Case study three: Rhys Wintle – class teacher and head of Physical Education across a federation of schools in the South East of England

In this case study class teacher Rhys Wintle, who is also Head of Physical Education across his federation of schools. Rhys specialised in Physical Education and SEND within his Primary Education degree. He completed his final placement within a speech and language unit and continues to be an expert in working with children who have language difficulties. He shares some of the ways he supports the learning of all children within his classes and how he has supported other teachers as well as teaching assistants across his federation. He outlines how he has utilised the Primary Physical Education and Sport Premium, that was first introduced in 2013, to improve the provision of Physical Education and Sport in primary schools in England – such as upskilling teachers and improving the levels of physical activity for all (DfE, 2014b). We are currently awaiting to see if the funding, set to run out in 2020, will be renewed by the government. Both the Youth Sport Trust and the Sport Recreation Alliance call for long-term funding from the government in order for schools to deliver sustainable improvements (Sport and Recreation Alliance, 2019).

For children with speech and language difficulties what do you have to consider in terms of pedagogy for Physical Education?

When I'm working with children who have specific speech and language difficulties, I have used verbal prompts and buddy systems as well as sign language – as recommended by the Training and Development Agency for Schools (2009). I also make sure my instructions are short and clear as this can help all children within Physical Education, not just those with speech and language difficulties. Teachers have a tendency to talk and over describe skills and movements, just make it very clear as to how you're going to be completing the activities. One strategy is to clearly plan out your teaching points and to practice describing them, so you don't become confusing by long-winded instructions. Additionally, getting a colleague to time you when you're teaching Physical Education to see how often and for how long you talk. All children need to have sustained physical activity according to the national curriculum (DfE, 2013), so don't let it be you that prevents the children from being physically active.

You may be teaching them a brand-new skill, so it is important to take smaller steps as this will help to include everyone. Having another child or you first performing the skill can help so they can see what it should look like. Williams (2017) highlights that the power of visual demonstrations and how you can bring the movement alive for all. Using questioning after you have given instructions can help you evaluate if the children have understood what is expected and then you are able to give them more help if needed. In addition, when teaching outside, make sure you give your instructions with you looking into the sun, not the children, and try not to wear sunglasses, as children need to see your eyes still. This is the best for all children, but especially any with speech and language difficulties, as they may need to watch your full facial expressions and will be watching your face and lips to help them understand. This will be tricky for them if they are looking into the sun or if you are wearing sunglasses.

What would be your top three actions for ensuring Physical Education is accessible for all?

The top three actions I would recommend for ensuring Physical Education is accessible for all include: As mentioned earlier, **short and clear instructions and steps** that can ensure the lesson is accessible for all. Ensure that you break a task, activity, skill, or movement down into smaller chunks and steps. This allows those who may struggle to build up the skills needed. You can encourage those who understand by showing them the next step or take a mastery approach and get them to complete that same step in a different way. For example, using their weaker foot while passing a football.

The second action that I would suggest is that, with all lessons, **differentiation** is key. Physical Education lessons should be no different to other lessons, yet at times teachers do forget to differentiate. This is something that I've worked with my teachers on, within the federation, to ensure that they differentiate all aspects of their Physical Education lessons. It is important to know where the children are, as this allows you to ensure they can all take part. Being able to simplify or progress a task will ensure they are all engaged. This will allow them to become physically confident and to engage in a range of increasingly challenging situations, as they should be undertaking within the curriculum (DfE, 2013). By modifying and providing activities at an appropriate skill level we are then using an inclusive teaching style, as Tant and Watelain, (2016) remind us to use.

Finally, the third action that I would highlight is staying on top of your **formative assessment** as this will help you support those who need it and then you can push those who are more able. You can undertake this with practice and ease through continuously circulating around the activities within the lesson and questioning the children. This will give you an idea of who is accessing the lesson in the way you had hoped and planned. It will also help you plan the next lesson.

Could you give examples of changes you have made to implement a more inclusive Physical Education pedagogy in your school?

One step that I have brought into the federation of schools that I have worked in, is to have a *Physical Education teaching assistant*. Their role is to work with children that have special educational needs. This was brought in as it became apparent that these children were often not accessing Physical Education for a number of reasons. By having a member of staff working one-to-one with them allowed them to fully take part in the lesson. Studies from Werts et al. (2001) and later by Conreoy et al. (2004) have shown that academic engagement increased when students with substantial disabilities had staff within three feet. On task behaviours also increased and disruptive behaviours decreased, in comparison to when there were no staff in proximity. These members of staff were hired using the Physical Education and Sports Premium funding given to each school. At time of writing it is not known if the funding will continue after 2020.

However, this introduction of a Physical Education teaching assistant has not been possible in all the schools I have worked with. In these schools I have also brought in planning throughout the school that is developed and clearly shows the progression throughout each year and between year groups. This has allowed the teachers to adapt accordingly to ensure they can include all, following the advice mentioned earlier on differentiation. I have also led staff meetings on ways to teach Physical Education and always tried to reiterate the strategies I've previously described. These staff meetings follow on from Tant and Watelain (2016) recommendations that there is a need for professional training as this will enable an easily adapted curriculum for physical activity that aids inclusive Physical Education teaching.

What has been the impact of your Physical Education pedagogy for you and your children, in particular those with speech and language difficulties?

I have been able to include all children in my lessons by following the steps mentioned previously. By ensuring that all children feel included, it builds their confidence and allows them to work with their peers more closely. The full participation in Physical Education 'may add valuable information to academic, social and emotional outcomes for students in need of special support' (Maxwell et al., 2018). Physical Education is a subject that can be accessible for all students when differentiated and presented correctly. Working closely with children with speech and language difficulties has actually improved my teaching of Physical Education in general. By having to break skills and processes down into smaller chunks, as well as multiple demonstrations and the use of signs and symbols, has enabled me to understand how to progress and cement these skills further. Through giving clearer instructions and support mechanisms to help children understand what is going to happen, as well as letting them indicate a preference or choice and means to communicate (Primary National Strategy, 2005), all children have improved in their physical learning.

What advice would you give a school that says they struggle with Physical Education for children with special educational needs?

Many of the approaches that a school would use to ensure inclusion in the classroom can be used within Physical Education too. As Medcalf (2012) proposes we always ensure that all the staff are aware of the needs of each pupil, and then differentiate appropriately and set suitable learning challenges for all. This should be the basis to build the Physical Education lesson from. Staff knowing and being confident in their expected outcomes helps with the planning and therefore can help ensure they are inclusive in their Physical Education teaching. Avoiding competition with others, in particular, can also help children with special education needs to engage and stay engaged in their Physical Education lessons. Competitive situations are often trigger points and can be challenging for children with special educational needs. Although competition is within the national curriculum, I would recommended a refocus to be on inspiring all pupils to succeed and excel (DfE, 2013) first, before putting them off and disengaging them with the introduction of competitive elements. Activities that reduce exclusionary competitive games and promotes collaboration are important for students to feel engaged and socially successful in Physical Education (Garn et al., 2011).

Is there anything else you want to note that is specific to your experience?

Physical Education can truly be one of the most inclusive subjects to teach in a Primary School. There are numerous studies that show how important Physical Education is for children's learning across all subjects (AfPE, 2016), so ensuring all are included is vital. Having worked closely with children with a range of needs has improved my teaching of all pupils.

Chapter summary

This chapter has sought to explore the importance of both Physical Education and Health Education, not only in the primary phase range, but also for young children within the EYFS (DfE, 2014a). It has also considered how to support and engage children with special educational needs. We have heard how experienced class teachers, Heads of Physical Education, and key researchers within Health Education have ensured that Physical Education and Health Education is at the heart of their practice. Each case study drew on research, theory, and practice to support the examples and how the class teachers analysed and reviewed their practice. These experts have highlighted the need to embed a Physical Education and Health Education pedagogy within schools and shown the importance of developing a love for physical activity to support physical and mental well-being to both the children's and the practitioners/teachers' benefit.

Further reading

All Party Parliamentary Group on a Fit and Healthy Childhood (APPG) (2019) *Mental Health through Movement*. Available at: https://royalpa.co.uk/wp-content/uploads/2019/10/mentalhealththroughmovement_301019.pdf [Accessed February 2020].

Bailey, R., Howells, K. and Glibo, I. (2018) Physical activity and mental health of school-aged children and adolescents: A rapid review. *International Journal of Physical Education* LV(1) 1st Quarter, pp. 1–14.

Howells, K., with Carney, A., Castle, N. and Little, R. (2018) *Mastering Primary Physical Education*. London: Bloomsbury.

References

Adan, A. (2012) Cognitive performance and dehydration. *Journal of the American College of Nutrition*, 31(2), pp. 71–78.

All Party Parliamentary Group on a Fit and Healthy Childhood (APPG) (2019) *Mental Health through Movement*. Available at: https://royalpa.co.uk/wp-content/uploads/2019/10/mentalhealththroughmovement_301019.pdf [Accessed February 2020].

All Party Parliamentary Group on Fit and Healthy Childhood (APPG) (2020) *Healthy Families: The Present and Future Role of the Supermarkets*. Available at: https://royalpa.co.uk/wp-content/uploads/2020/02/SUPERMARKETS-REPORT-Feb2020.pdf [Accessed February 2020].

All Party Parliamentary Group on Fit and Healthy Childhood (APPG) (2020) *Dietary Patterns and the Way Forward*. Report number 17, September 2020.

Association of Physical Education (AfPE) (2015) *Health Position Paper*. Available at: http://www.afpe.org.uk/physical-education/wp-content/uploads/afPE_Health_Position_Paper_Web_Version2015.pdf [Accessed February 2020].

Association of Physical Education (AfPE) (2016) *The Difference Physical Education Makes*. Available at: http://www.afpe.org.uk/physical-education/wp-content/uploads/Importance-of-PE-Poster-FINAL.pdf [Accessed March 2020].

Association of Play Industries (API) (2019) *Play Must Stay. A Childhood Crisis*. Available at: https://www.api-play.org/wp-content/uploads/sites/4/2019/08/Play-must-stay-4-pager.pdf [Accessed February 2020].

Bailey, R., Howells, K. and Glibo, I. (2018) Physical activity and mental health of school-aged children and adolescents: A rapid review. *International Journal of Physical Education* LV(1) 1st Quarter, pp. 1–14.

Conroy, M. A., Asmus, J. M., Ladwig, C. N., Sellers, J. A. and Valcante, G. (2004) The effects of proximity on the classroom behaviors of students with autism in general education strategies. *Behavioral Disorders* 29(2), pp. 119–129.

Department for Education (DfE) (2013) *The National Curriculum in England*. Key stages 1 and 2 framework document. London: Crown.

Department for Education (DfE) (2014a) *Statutory Framework for the Early Years Foundation Stage. Setting the Standards for Learning, Development and Care for Children from Birth to Five*. London: Crown.

Department for Education (DfE) (2014b) *Guidance, PE and Sport Premium for Primary Schools*. Available at: https://www.gov.uk/guidance/pe-and-sport-premium-for-primary-schools [Accessed March 2020].

Department for Education (DfE) (2019) *Relationships Education, Relationships and Sex Education (RSE) and Health Education. Statutory Guidance for Governing Bodies, Proprietors, Head Teachers, Principals, Senior Leadership Teams, Teachers*. London: Crown Copyright.

Department of Health (DH) (2018) *Childhood Obesity: A Plan for Action*. Chapter 2. London: Crown Copyright.

Edmonds, C. J. and Burford, D. (2009) Should children drink more water? The effects of drinking water on cognition in children. *Appetite* 52(3), pp. 776–779.

Edmonds, C. and Jeffes, B. (2009) Does having a drink help you think? 6-7-year-old children show improvements in cognitive performance from baseline to test after having a drink of water. *Appetite* 53(3), pp. 469-472.

European Food Safety Authority (2010) Scientific opinion on dietary reference values for water. EFSA panel on dietetic products, nutrition and allergies (NDA). *European Food Safety Authority Journal* 8(3) pp. 1459-1507.

Garn, A. C., Ware, D. R. and Solmon, M. A. (2011) Student engagement in high school physical education: Do social motivation orientations matter? *Journal of Teaching Physical Education* 30, pp. 84-98.

Harris, J. (2018) *The Case for Physical Education Becoming a Core Subject in the National Curriculum.* Available at: http://www.afpe.org.uk/physical-education/wp-content/uploads/PE-Core-Subject-Paper -20-3-18.pdf [Accessed February 2020].

Howells, K. (2015) Chapter 13: Planning physical education in the national curriculum. In Sewell, K. (Ed.), *Planning the Primary National Curriculum. A Complete Guide for Trainees and Teachers.* London: Sage, Learning Matters (1st edition) pp. 262-276.

Howells, K. (2016) Chapter 10: Supporting physical development, health and well-being through the use of outdoor environments. In Ritchie, C. (Ed.), *Exploring Learning for Children Aged 3 – 11 Years.* London: Routledge, pp. 142-160.

Howells, K. and Bowen, J. (2016) Physical activity and self-esteem: 'Jonny's story'. *Education 3-13: International Journal of Primary, Elementary and Early Years Education* 44(5), pp. 577-590.

Howells, K. and Bowen, J. (2018) 'Beyond Jonny's Story', - a whole class physical activity intervention. *International Society for Physical Activity and Health*, London, October 2018.

Howells, K., Bowen, J., Mannion, K. and McMartin, C. (2019) The adoption of daily mile as an active mile initiative. The children's and teachers' voices. *Practice Matters. Physical Education Matters.* Autumn 2019, pp. 37-39.

Howells, K. and Jess, M. (2019) The complexity of young children's physical education. *AIESEP (International Association of Physical Education in Higher Education) International Conference Building Bridges for Physical Activity and Sport*, New York, June 2019.

Howells, K., with Carney, A., Castle, N. and Little, R. (2018) *Mastering Primary Physical Education.* London: Bloomsbury.

Krecar, I., Kolega, M. and Kunac, S. (2014) The effects of drinking water on attention. *Procedia - Social and Behavioral Sciences* 159, pp. 577-583.

Kretchmar, R. S. (2001) Duty, habit and meaning: Different faces of adherence. *Quest* 53(3), pp. 318-325.

Kretchmar, R. S. (2006) Ten more reasons for quality physical education. *Journal of Physical Education, Recreation and Dance* 77(9), pp. 6-9.

Launder, K. A. (2001) *Play Practice: The Games Approach to Teaching and Coaching Sports.* Champaign, IL: Human Kinetics.

Maxwell, G., Granlund, M. and Augustine, L. (2018) Inclusion through participation: Understanding participation in the international classification of functioning, disability, and health as a methodological research tool for investigating inclusion. *Frontiers in Education* 3(41), pp. 1-16. doi: 10.3389/feduc.2018.00041

Medcalf, R. (2012) Chapter 12 - Towards a more inclusive provision. In Griggs, G. (Ed.), *An Introduction to Primary Physical Education.* Oxon: Routledge.

Ní Chróínín, D., Fletcher, T. and O'Sullivan, M. (2018) Pedagogical principles of learning to teach meaningful physical education. *Physical Education and Sport Pedagogy* 23(2), pp. 117-133.

OECD (2019) *OECD Future of Education 2030. Making Physical Education Dynamic and Inclusive for 2030. International Curriculum Analysis.* Paris: OECD.

Oliver, M. O., Schofield, G. M., Kolt, G. S. and McLachlan, C. (2007) Physical activity in early childhood: Current state of knowledge. *New Zealand Research in Early Childhood Education Journal* 10, pp. 47-68.

Play Scotland (2019) *Play Builds Children.* Children's Play Policy Forum Statement. Scotland: CPPF.

Primary National Strategy (2005) *Speaking, Listening, Learning: Working with Children Who Have Special Educational Needs.* London: Crown Copyright.

Ridgers, N., Stratton, G. and Fairclough, S. J. (2006) Physical activity levels of children during school playtime. *Sports Medicine* 36(4), pp. 359-371.

Ridgers, N. D., Carter, L. M., Stratton, G. and McKenzie, T. L. (2011) Examining children's physical activity and play behaviours during playtime over time. *Health Education Research* 26(4), pp. 586-595.

Sport and Recreation Alliance (2019) *Government Must Commit to Long-Term Funding of PE and Sport Premium*. Available at: https://www.sportandrecreation.org.uk/news/politics/government-must-commit-to-long-term-funding-o [Accessed October 2019].

Tant, M. and Watelain, E. (2016) Forty years later, a systematic literature review on inclusion in physical education (1975–2015): a teacher perspective. *Educational Research and Review* 19, pp. 1–17.

The Daily Mile Foundation (2019) *Core Principles*. Available at: https://thedailymile.co.uk/steps-to-success/ [Accessed September 2019].

The Steiner Waldorf Education (2011) *Guide to the Early Years Foundation Stage in Steiner Waldorf Early Childhood Settings*. East Sussex: The Association of Steiner Waldorf Schools in the UK and Ireland.

ukactive (2019) *Generation Inactive 2. Nothing About Us, Without Us*. London: ukactive.

Werts, M., Zigmond, N. and Leeper, D. (2001) Paraprofessional proximity and academic engagement: Students with disabilities in primary aged classrooms. *Education and Training in Mental Retardation and Developmental Disabilities* 36(4), pp. 424–440.

Williams, B. (2017) *Louder than Words*. Available at: https://coachad.com/articles/coaching-athletes-visual-demonstration-body-language/ [Accessed March 2020].

Williamson, J. and Howells, K. (2019) Young children's understanding of fluid intake. *International Journal of Nutrition* 4(4), pp. 1–8.

World Health Organization (2004) *Guidelines for Drinking-Water Quality: Recommendations (Vol. 1)*. Geneva: World Health Organization.

YoungMinds (2019) *Wiseup to Wellbeing in Schools*. London: YoungMinds.

9 Computational thinking and technology-enhanced learning (TEL)

The power of Computing in the primary classroom

Poppy Gibson and Megan Brown

Critical questions

What is the purpose of the current Computing curriculum (2014)?

In what way did it emerge and evolve from the previous 'Information Communication Technology' provision?

What are the online risks and opportunities posed for children using the internet?

What does 'technology-enhanced education' mean and what might this look like in the primary school?

Introduction

In the Western 'digital culture', children are born into the world of technology and social media (NAEYC, 2012). Prensky (2001) initially labelled these children as 'digital natives', implying that these children inherited a natural relationship with computers, the internet, and technological tools from birth, and thus are 'native speakers' of digital language. This chapter refutes that idea, arguing that technology is introduced to children – who must develop skills in order to use these tools – and thus disputing Prensky's claim. The one element that is true, however, is that there is often a familiarity between children born into our digital age and these devices. From the first days after birth, to their first steps, or the first school play, most children watch their parent or caregiver taking photographs and sharing these images with friends and family online via social networks; a term known as 'sharenting'. It is natural that young children will imitate this behaviour, as with any other.

Over the last decade, there has been a substantial increase in internet usage by children under nine years of age (Holloway et al., 2013). While the internet offers numerous benefits for children – as they can use it to learn, communicate, develop, create, and explore the world around them – young people can also face risks online which need to be addressed (NSPCC, 2017: 40). These risks are detailed further in the section below.

Online risks and opportunities

Several research studies have pursued the identification and classification of online risks (Dönmez et al., 2017), and the content of these categories and lists have evolved, as outlined in Table 9.1.

'How Safe Are Our Children' (NSPCC, 2017) deemed as the most comprehensive overview of child protection in the UK, and the fifth annual report of its kind, was conducted by the NSPCC to establish indicators that impact upon children and young people and their health and safety. It states that, in 2016/17, there were 12,248 Childline counselling sessions about online safety and abuse, which was a 9% increase on the previous year.

In addition to this figure, 30% of reviews by young people of the most popular social networking sites, apps, and games 'reported seeing violence and hatred' (NSPCC, 2017: 40); this means that one in three young people taking part in the study have witnessed upsetting images, footage, or interactions online. A similar study was conducted by Ofcom (2016), exploring children and parents' attitudes towards media use. One of the key themes that emerged from the report highlighted that social media, a central medium for both pre-adolescent children and teenagers, 'creates new opportunities and new pressures' (Ofcom, 2016: 3) (see Figure 9.1).

Children's interactions with **social networking sites (SNS)** (see Glossary at end of chapter) are continually evolving, which can bring both creative opportunities and also risks (as discussed in Table 9.1). The latest trend identified in this qualitative study (Ofcom, 2016) showed that children are increasingly using group messaging services including **WhatsApp**, **Instagram**, and **Facebook Messenger** but although opportunities involve support with homework and peer enjoyment, risks can involve offensive banter or bullying (see Table 9.1 for further identification and classification of online risks for children).

Table 9.1 Risks of online use for children

Author(s)	Risks of online use for children
Jantz and McMurray (1998)	Two broad themes of 'content-related' and 'communication-related'
Aftab (2010)	Six themes composed of inappropriate or harmful content, cyber-stalking, online harassment, the disclosure of sensitive information, cyber-grooming, and online-purchase frauds
Poftak (2002)	Five themes including pornography, hacking, copyright issues, cyberbullying, and inappropriate relationships with adults
Boulton et al. (2016)	A list of seven risks associated with 'inappropriate contacts, content, and conduct' (Boulton et al., 2016: 610) categorised as: 1. People may not be whom they say. 2. Meeting strangers. 3. Deliberately sharing personal information. 4. Accidentally sharing personal information. 5. Cyberbullying. 6. Sharing personal photographs. 7. Computer viruses.

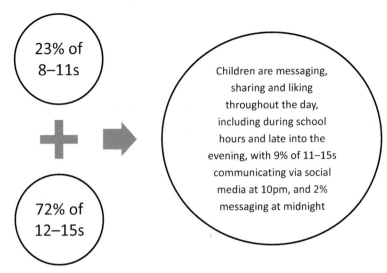

Figure 9.1 Children's social media use (adapted from Ofcom, 2016: 3)

Of current debate is the idea of 'toxic' childhood. Concerns in some literature warn that the modern world is 'damaging' our children, with at least 'one in five children in the developed world' diagnosed as having 'developmental or behavioural problems', and that number is rising by 25% each year (Palmer, 2007). 'Toxicity' is therefore defined for this study as something harmful or detrimental to well-being, which is the ability to function properly and feel generally positive on a daily basis.

In a thoughtful twist on this debate, Alexander (2007) argues that viewing contemporary childhood through a 'toxic' lens is unhelpful and can, in fact, be detrimental to children's learning. If children are 'obliged to begin from the premise that their culture – the building blocks from which their identities are created – is "toxic"' (Alexander, 2007: 57) they can become passive rather than active learners in their cultural world. Children learn to be cautious about dangers in their environment from birth, and if they end up fearing the introduction of new cultural tools, such as modern technology, for example, children may avoid incorporating such tools into their lives. Avoiding cultural artefacts could reduce an individual's autonomy and thus hamper opportunities to learn and develop.

Alexander (2007) states that we should instead consider the 'vitality' of modern childhood, seeing both the negative but also the positive opportunities that living in the 21st century presents, such as globalisation and the integration of technology. To build upon Alexander's point, although the cultural artefacts and daily tools used by children during childhood may have changed, it is through the exploration of children's adoption of these cultural artefacts that we can better understand contemporary childhood. Through the lens of 'vitality' rather than 'toxicity', it is exciting to see how children can become active sculptors of their childhood.

Livingstone (2013) warns that, in fact, the effects of childhood experiences are not yet fully understood, and thus we cannot even begin to assert or assess the risk or toxicity involved in children's use of online media. Even the data shared above cannot give a true picture of the risks of harm experienced online, due to issues of confidentiality, reporting, or children's own understanding of what they have experienced. Livingstone muses:

On the internet, we do not know how many children are hurt, or how severe are the consequences; there are no accident figures. If the offline were like the online, it would be like knowing, only, how many children report crossing a road and perhaps, how many report that something bad happened in consequence. On the other hand, if the online were like the offline, we would also know the online equivalent of how many cars were on the road and how fast they were driving (e.g. exactly what pornography they saw or how they were cyberbullied or groomed); most important, we would know whether an accident resulted (i.e., whether the child suffered harmful consequences, for how long and with what severity).

(Livingstone, 2013: 18)

Digital literacies and becoming 'social media literate'

Digital **media** is radically changing the way people communicate and influencing the thought processes and experiences of both children and adults. New technologies pose a challenge to the educational process (Globokar, 2018), yet also an opportunity. Literacy practices for children are constantly developing due to the advances in digital media, and this means that the implications for how children deal with the influx of digital information that they receive are far reaching (Burnett, 2016). As previously discussed, digital devices are part of everyday life for many children and can be some of their earliest literacy experiences (Gibson and Smith, 2018: 4). Young children are engaged in a variety of multimodal, multimedia practices from an early age, and it is imperative that educators help them to manage the amount of information they receive and how they portray themselves online. Many texts that they encounter are from outside of school or family and are often formed around popular or consumer culture. Their engagement with these electronic texts can allow them to outmanoeuvre or subvert the instructions of adults (Carrington, 2005).

Critical question

So, what does this all mean for the Computing curriculum? What has happened in the past and what is the shape of excellent Computing teaching in the primary school today?

Key readings

Livingstone, S. and Sefton-Green, J. (2016) *The Class: Living and Learning in the Digital Age.* Connected Youth and Digital Futures. An intimate look at how children network, identify, learn, and grow in a connected world.

Buckingham, D. (2007) *Youth, Identity and Digital Media.* Cambridge MA: MIT Press. Contributors discuss how growing up in a world saturated with digital media affects the development of young people's individual and social identities.

Computing in the primary school

Time is constructed into ages. Distinctively there are three ages: The agricultural age, the industrial age, and our current time period – the digital age. The names of these ages are characterised by the application of a new knowledge. The agricultural age focused on the use of farming tools to produce food; the industrial age was named thusly due to the application of machinery to produce goods; and now the digital age. The current age commenced between 1950 and 1970 and is defined by the introduction of the personal computer and subsequent technology which introduced the ability to transfer information freely and quickly. The last 20 years in particular have seen a society in transition, where changes in technology are rapid and relentless: 'the changes seem to accelerate, leaving us all just a little bewildered' (Wheeler, 2015: 6).

With this change, the role of the educator has similarly had to adapt with teachers being expected to adapt and introduce a variety of new technologies to accelerate their classroom alongside the accelerations of modern society. Incredibly, educators have been attempting to enhance the learning experience with technology since the 1600s: The Magic Lantern was the first ever projector, used to view images, one slide at a time, on a board or wall. Even more unbelievably, computer programming was in fact taught during the 1700s across the UK through the use of The Jacquard Loom – a device designed to weave silk through the use of punch cards that controlled the actions of the device. Students were taught to programme these machines through thinking about the order of the cards. Between the 17th and 18th centuries, technologies such as the typewriter, the film projector, the radio, and the overhead projector were all trialled in classrooms. However, the greatest accelerations in technology can be seen from the 1700s onwards. In the latter part of the 1970s, the very first computer was integrated into schools and by the early 1980s, when IBM created the first PC, nearly 20% of schools in the UK and the US had computers in use. (OurICT, 2017). The installation of PCs led to a rise in anxiety of teachers, often worrying about their future and whether one day teachers would be replaced with technology (Wheeler, 2015).

The next largest booms in technology in the 20th century for education came with the internet in the early to mid 1990s and the interactive whiteboard in the late 1990s. Both opened up opportunities in the classroom which had previously not been heard of – the ability to research and learn anything and share it immediately with a class of children on a board which you could touch. Even though these innovative technologies appeared to open up a world of knowledge and opportunities, if you look closely at the classroom dynamics, they stayed the same: The teacher stood at the front sharing information and ideas, whilst the children sat in their seats, facing the teacher and completed their learning. On occasion there would be the rare opportunity for the class to venture to 'the computer suite' where students could conduct their own research.

The 21st century has only just begun to really advance and change the classroom. Laptops bring the PC into the classroom; tablets and iPads allow for portable learning, including outside of the classroom; and Virtual Reality can literally transport children into locations never even dreamed of before. However, most education systems do not respond quickly to technological advances. Educators are reluctant to use the digital tools of a technological age without evidence of its benefits to children's development and without clear guidance (Abbott,

2001). This reluctance can be seen with the development and employment of the iPad. The inception of the iPad in 2010 was revolutionary. However, it was only in 2015, five years later, that interactive mobile apps became the centre of the effective learning classroom (OurICT, 2017). The same delayed implementation can be seen within the curriculum. Until September 2014, children were taught ICT – how to use software such as Word and Excel without any understanding of how programmes were made. It was only after the re-writing of the national curriculum in 2013 that Computing teaching was compulsory from ages 5–16 to introduce computational thinking from an early age. Considering the advances in technologies and computer programming outside of the education system, this incorporation of Computing into the curriculum could be seen as very delayed.

In just two decades technology has brought vast improvements in teaching and an availability of equipment that empowers educators and enhances learning. The 2018 classroom is now more accessible for all learners, has the potential to be more engaging, and readily encourages collaboration between all learners, not limited to the classroom, school, or country. Educators, however, now have a great responsibility to not only teach children skills such as coding, alongside English and Maths, but to also educate children about the growing world of technology, the appropriate use of technology, and to generally prepare them for a future that is going to be in a perpetual motion of progression. In the current climate, teachers need to be risk takers, try new technologies out to see if it works not only to support engagement, creativity, and learning, but to also model to children the importance of adaptability in a society of change and advancement. Without this, we will be stuck in 20th century teaching and doing a disservice to children within the education system.

Constructivism: Educational theory and computational practice

Constructionism places an emphasis on building knowledge through constructing or producing. There are many tools that we can do this with today and a variety of activities – podcasting, screen casting, presentations, mind-mapping, animations, infographic tools, etc. – but, at the time this was written about, the focus was on Logo (a programming language we will come across, albeit briefly). The heart of this argument is that learning happens best when learners construct their understanding through the process of constructing things that they share with others. When students explain what they have created and why, their own learning is consolidated and deepened – children learning through producing creative artefacts.

The theory of constructionism guides much research on how and what children learn when they work on a computer. The educational strategy of computer game programming with children is based on constructionist learning, which holds that learning happens when people are actively engaged in making a meaningful product. More specifically, constructionist learning is a process of making knowledge their own and identifying with it (i.e. appropriation), engagement with others, and the belief that understanding is more important than memorising rules or procedures (Mayer, 2003; Harel and Papert, 1991).

A constructionist approach to understanding learning combines individual level cognitive processes with the social and cultural contexts in which learning takes place (Kafai, 2006). From this perspective, it is not simply the act of making games that makes a constructionist learning environment – it is making games for and with other students.

Young people today have lots of experience ... interacting with new technologies, but a lot less so of creating [or] expressing themselves with new technologies. It is almost as if they can read but not write.

(Resnick, 2013: 23)

Resnick also builds on this idea of fluency as being more than a passive consumer or, in his words, a reader. Kafai tells us that technological fluency is about making things of significance, while Resnick points us towards this idea too – adding that it is a way for children to express themselves, as writers and as **producers of digital content**. This may be something new and original to them in a big way, or can simply be taking what has gone before, remixing it in some way and sharing it again. Digital technology can provide an authentic context for that, as well as an audience. What we can tease out of this is that we want children to be involved in the creation of something that they can share, discuss, probe, and admire. They put something **out into their world**. Technology provides several vehicles and platforms upon which pupils' creations can be constructed; the benefits of these are discussed more fully in the following section.

The role of the teacher in the Computing curriculum

Taking the theories of constructivism and social constructivism into account, technology has many benefits, but it is the role of that teacher that controls the way that this technology is utilised in the classroom. In an earlier section in this chapter we spoke about 'digital literacy' and children's ability to access what they read in digital spaces. Educational systems, it has been noted, still function on traditional models of teaching, with linear testing and strict outlines of subject knowledge (Collins and Halverson, 2018). Craft (2010) highlighted how creativity is critical within 21st century teaching – infusing creativity into the education system is viewed as highly important (Harris, 2016; Runco, 2014). However, due to the current education climate as commented on previously, incorporating creativity into the curriculum is becoming increasingly more challenging. This is because the complex nature of creativity presents a challenge for many schooling systems who are bound to national standards and standardised testing (Csikszentmihalyi and Wolfe, 2014; Henriksen et al., 2018). Henriksen et al. (2018: 411) suggest that creativity can often be enabled through the use of technology; there is an apparent connection between innovation and digital technologies. The prominence of new media, digital tools, and devices within the 21st century is creating a world of new opportunities in which people can more freely connect, share, imagine, and innovate (Zhao, 2012; Mishra and Deep-Play Research Group, 2012), thus implying the growing importance and need of 21st century technologies within the classroom.

The role of pupil autonomy and child-centred or child-led pedagogy in Computing

Children's experiences with technology will have significant implications for their future lives (Kaye, 2017).

The rate at which technology develops is exponential. The ability to produce more powerful and faster processors for use in smaller and more affordable devices has led to the proliferation of smartphones, table computers, and other ultra-portable devices which are all becoming a part of everyday life.

Technology is about more than supporting traditional ways of learning. IT provides new ways of engaging children – new shared resources for representing things differently and for scaffolding children's thinking.

- Allow children to engage positively in imaginative, active learning
- Offering instant feedback to children in a variety of forms
- Motivating and encouraging children to persist and take next steps
- Presenting ideas in dynamic and stimulating ways
- Providing resources for adults to use with children in their learning

We need to consider new and unfamiliar ways to teach and learn with technology.

What does excellent Computing teaching look like today?

The authors of this chapter argue that Computing in primary schools needs to involve pupils accessing appropriate tools and employing computational thinking and problem-solving skills to develop confidence and autonomy with these tools through a child-centred, child-led approach. In the next decade, teachers and other educators must establish new forms of practice, enhanced and supported by the most modern and productive technology tools available (Barron et al., 2011).

> it follows that children need the skills, competences and enthusiasms to function and flourish in the world in which they are growing up.
>
> (Plowman et al., 2012)

> all educators will need to know how pedagogy should change to meet students' needs in this disruptive era of technology and new working environments ... teachers will not achieve these quests by being timid, or reluctant to engage with technology. Nor, on the other hand, will they fully understand the benefits of technology is they believe that it is the only answer.
>
> (Wheeler, 2015)

Schools are full of cupboards filled with technology that teachers have bought without fully knowing what to do with it – they are following a trend. The most important implementation of technology in the classroom is that which is meaningful to the children. Before using technology, teachers should consider: 'Is this adding something to the learning or merely enhancing it? What is the purpose? What extra will this bring to the learning today?'

When we update our technology but simply incorporate them into old systems, tech is simply a 'research tool' or a 'show off' product in the lesson. To use technology effectively and to its fullest potential, teachers' pedagogies must change and adapt accordingly.

Six learning designs

There are six learning designs that we can consider when planning and implementing Computing lessons as identified by Laurillard (2012): Acquisition, discussion, investigation, practice, collaboration, and production.

Learning through **acquisition** is what learners are doing when they are listening to a presentation or podcast, reading from books or websites, and watching demos or videos. This is probably still the most common type of learning in formal education. The student is playing a relatively passive role while the teacher uses the transmission mode of teaching. We cannot avoid learning through acquisition. Students need to learn what others have discovered, to hear about expert ways of thinking and practising, and what is known already about the subject. Enabling students to build on the work of others is fundamental to formal education and the progressive development of ideas.

Learning through **discussion** requires the learner to express their ideas and questions, and to challenge and respond to the ideas and questions from the teacher, and/or from other students. The discussion may or may not end with a consensual outcome. The pedagogic value is the reciprocal critique of ideas, and how this leads to the development of a more elaborated conceptual understanding.

Learning through **investigation** guides the learner to explore, compare, and critique the texts, documents, and resources that reflect the concepts and ideas being taught. Rather than having to 'follow the storyline', as in learning through acquisition, they are in control of the sequence of information and can 'follow their own line of inquiry'. This makes them more active and gives them a greater sense of ownership of their learning, taking a critical and analytical approach, and thereby coming to a fuller understanding of the ideas.

Learning through **practice** enables the learner to adapt their actions to the task goal and use the feedback to improve their next action. Feedback may come from self-reflection, from other students, from the teacher, or from the activity itself – if it shows them how to improve the result of their action in relation to the goal of the activity. This helps them to develop, understand, and use the knowledge and skills of a discipline, like 'learning by doing' or 'learning through experience'. It is one of the most powerful ways technology can enhance learning for children but it requires always considering what exactly the children are learning: Technology versus content.

Learning through **collaboration** embraces mainly discussion, practice, and production. Building on investigations and acquisition, it is about taking part in the process of knowledge building itself. It is distinct from learning through practice because although it builds something, this is necessarily done through participation and negotiation with peers. It is distinct from learning through production, because although it produces something this is through debate and sharing with others.

Learning through **production** is the way a teacher motivates the learner to consolidate what they have learnt by expressing their current conceptual understanding and how they used it in practice. Producing an output generates a representation of the learning enabled by the other types. In its simplest form it is the learner's expression of their current thinking, which enables the teacher to see how well they have learnt, and to respond with feedback, guidance, and further explanation. The audience is motivating (Henderson et al., 2010).

Each of these six learning types (Laurillard, 2012) corresponds to different learning experiences the can be achieved through different activities, often combining several types, and using conventional technologies (e.g. books) or digital technologies (e.g. iBooks). It is important to look at the uses of digital technology critically, as well as being appreciative of the innovation they bring to teaching.

These types of learning help us to evaluate what digital technologies offer. The best learning environments combine all these types of learning.

Research focus

'After the Reboot – Computing Education in UK Schools' https://royalsociety.org/~/med ia/events/2018/11/computing-education-1-year-on/after-the-reboot-report.pdf

This Royal Society report, 'After the Reboot – Computing Education in UK Schools', explores the challenges and issues facing the subject in primary and secondary schools since the subject was introduced to schools in 2014.

December 2017's 'Life in "likes"'. This UK Children's Commissioner report on the effects of social media on 8–12-year-olds examines the way children use social media and its effects on their well-being.

While 8–10s use social media in a playful, creative way – often to play games – this changes significantly as children's social circles expand as they grow older. This report shows that many Year 7 children are finding social media hard to manage and becoming over-dependent on 'likes' and 'comments' for social validation. They are also adapting their offline behaviour to fit an online image, and becoming increasingly anxious about 'keeping up appearances' as they get older.

Case study: Wingfield Primary School

Wingfield Primary School began its technology journey in the autumn term of 2017/18. With a school-wide move to a new building, new technologies were incorporated into everyday life. Classrooms were equipped with flat screen TVs (Apple TVs) and each teacher was given a MacBook and an iPad to teach from. Shortly following this, the school invested in 240 iPads for the children; with the aim to build digital literacies and proficiencies and become an 'Apple School'. Three classes were given one-to-one iPads (one Year 4 class and two Year 5 classes) in the spring one term. Gradually, teachers began incorporating technology into daily teaching and trialled innovative ideas to teach using the iPads.

Within the one-to-one classrooms, the app Showbie was put to particularly good use with teachers setting tasks and sharing activities for each lesson via the app. Children were able to log on and immediately view their task for the day and work through the activities at their own speed. Teachers commented that the app supported them with tailoring learning to suit individual needs as they could write comments, leave voice notes, or draw images to guide the children through their learning.

Largely noted by all teachers using the one-to-one iPads was the effective use of technology to aid reading. Through the apps Book Creator and Showbie, teachers were able to create stories for reading lessons and share them with every child in the class, with specific reading questions tailored to them. Before the implementation of this in the Year 4 classroom, children were given a mid-year assessment during spring two. Between this and summer two, the children had daily reading lessons using the iPads to read the same texts and answer comprehension questions in whole class guided reading. At the end of the year, the children sat another reading test where 82% of the class had made progress in their results and boys in particular made good progress between the testing (see Table 9.2). The three children who made negative progress had diagnosed SEN and were receiving support for reading outside of the classroom.

Overall, teachers commented that during the reading lessons children appeared more engaged in the texts – in particular the boys who had often been a struggle in the past. They also commented on the benefits of the technology with regards to accessibility. For example, children were able to zoom in to the text to make the writing clearer. Those who struggled to read independently could choose voice over options, so the iPad would read with them. Additionally, they could mark-up the writing with thoughts and ideas, highlighting key words to support them in their understanding. The most frequent comment from teachers with regards to the benefits of the technology, was the role of independence in their classroom; children from all abilities were able to access the texts and comprehensions independently, giving them confidence and faith in their own abilities (see Table 9.2).

Table 9.2 Year 4 reading data spring/summer 2018

	Year 4	Reading				
	Name:	Spring 2 Scores (/50)	Spring 2 percentages	Summer 2 Scores (/40)	Summer 2 Percentages	Percentage progress
Boys	Boy A	18	36%	21	53%	17%
	Boy B	0	0%	2	5%	5%
	Boy C	37	74%	37	93%	19%
	Boy D	16	32%	10	30%	-2%
	Boy E	39	78%	39	98%	20%
	Boy F	23	46%	27	68%	22%
	Boy G	23	46%	32	80%	46%
	Boy H	32	64%	29	73%	19%
Girls	Girl A	41	82%	39	98%	16%
	Girl B	22	44%	9	23%	-21%
	Girl C	34	68%	17	43%	-25%
	Girl D	28	56%	27	67%	11%
	Girl E	35	70%	37	93%	23%
	Girl F	6	12%	14	35%	23%
	Girl G	22	44%	23	58%	14%
	Girl H	13	25%	18	45%	20%
	Girl I	8	16%	24	60%	44%

Three teachers from Wingfield, across different year groups, explore below what effective and transformational use of technology looks like to them in the classroom. All teachers interviewed teach in KS 2, with one teacher (Jack Delaney) using the iPads in a one-to-one context. Each teacher has only been using iPads to support learning for around a year and discuss the differences they have seen through the implementation of this technology.

What does effective Computing look like to you?

Tim Arding:	Effective Computing is fully embedded across the curriculum and provides children with practical and useful skills that will allow them to navigate the electronic world that they live in. It is accessible – allowing all pupils to make progress – and targeted, ensuring for faster, more responsive feedback from teachers. And it is engaging – providing an enriching, enjoyable form of learning that is relevant to this generation of students in the way that crusty old pen and paper and textbooks will never be.
Dennis Mitakos:	An environment for differentiation based on apps where we prepare pupils for the modern world.
Jack Delaney:	Effective computing is when the children are enhancing or accessing their learning in a way that they wouldn't be able to without iPads i.e.: Translating, recording sentences to write out, or researching, etc.

What are the best ways to incorporate the computing curriculum into your daily teaching?

Tim Arding:	Bluntly – the best was is for children to have daily, continuous access to technology. If this is the case, children will develop their aptitude and personal responsibility towards the devices, apps, and online world that they access. You can have great practise as a teacher (know all the latest apps, be able to use your screen/tablet/laptop), but if children aren't using it regularly themselves, it's as useless as shouting at the wind. All you are doing is presenting the same old pedagogy with some frills on it; students need to be living a fully embedded computing curriculum in order for it to have relevance.
Dennis Mitakos:	Using a variety of apps to ensure engagement is a mainstay. Using technology to help pupils progress – particularly greater depth level pupils – and finding alternative methods to teach pupils who may need visual representations for their learning.

Jack Delaney:	Children using the iPads in all curriculum areas is the best way to incorporate computing into daily teaching. Examples include children developing their Keynote skills by using an iPad to create an RE presentation, or publishing their writing on Pages, using the editing features and becoming increasingly confident in their use of these apps.

What apps would you recommend for new teachers to use?

Tim Arding:	Showbie was a revelation and completely allowed me to provide dynamic, targeted feedback on lessons where there was an exceptional level of engagement with the tasks I set via the app. I have found Popplet to be very useful when structuring the thoughts of pupils with SEND. I think Paper is a useful tool for creativity, and Padlet allows for some high-level questioning in your teaching.
Dennis Mitakos:	Showbie allows for the lesson to progress based on the pupil's ability to understand an AFL question – this in particular is useful in Mathematics. Paper-to-model writing and making amendments to improve work. Padlet to allow pupils share a variation of thoughts/outcomes at a fast pace.
Jack Delaney:	Showbie, Paper, and Classroom are the best apps for new teachers to use. Showbie for its paperless and resource-less effectiveness, Paper for modelling and AfL, and Classroom for control and overseeing the children's learning.

What would you say are the benefits of using technology within the classroom?

Tim Arding:	It is relevant – it reflects the world children are actually living in (the online world, constant social media, and being surrounded by technology) rather than the world I grew up in. It is more responsive – feedback and task-setting can be quicker and specified to the student's need. And it is in the long run eco-friendlier and cost saving, as you no longer spend hours wasting paper with the daily deforestation that comes with photocopying.
Dennis Mitakos:	Technology motivates the pupils in a variety of ways: it is stimulating and therefore ensures engagement is a constant. A variety of apps allows pupils to share information visually; it inspires both independent and shared work on a range of challenging platforms; it allows for work to be shared instantaneously and therefore allows learning to progress and move forward.

Jack Delaney: The benefits include:

- Children are much more likely to access learning
- Opens up learning opportunities
- Increases children engagement
- Promotes positive use of internet and safe web use

What are the best ways to teach e-safety? Why is it important?

Tim Arding:	It has to be safe - children have to be free to share their experiences of the online world. It has to be child-led; social media is moving so rapidly, that you have to prepare resources relevant to what the children are actually using (i.e. Minecraft was the rage 18 months ago, and is now almost forgotten about). And it has to be taught with passion - there is a vast disconnect between what children say in the safety of the classroom and what they actually do on their phones when they are in their bedroom at home. Children have to understand the very real difficulties, dangers, and stresses that come with being online.
Dennis Mitakos:	Regularity of conversations ensuring that both pupils/parents are kept up to date regarding the regulation of different apps/games. Children can create a role play to portray the negative cycle of not following the e-safety regulations and the subsequent and varied outcomes that can ensue thereafter. A successful method is to have older pupils support younger students in understanding this.
Jack Delaney:	E-safety is best taught through daily practise i.e.: Pretending to write a tweet incorrectly or asking the children what they would do in certain situations.

How has Computing/technology in your classroom changed since you began teaching?

Tim Arding:	When I started teaching SMART boards were revolutionary - now they are obsolete. I am sure that the technologies I am passionate about now will also prove to be obsolete in a worryingly short space of time.
Dennis Mitakos:	Technology is omnipresent at all times in lessons - whether that is annotating the correct/incorrect learning or simply sharing information so that all pupils can access information. Teachers are generally more confident due to professional development training and opportunities to transfer and implement skills promptly - this is due to the software/hardware being readily available.

| Jack Delaney: | Computing has changed because it is not about using coding apps like Scratch Jr anymore but about children's ability to access all apps and independently use them to enhance their learning or assisting them to access the curriculum. |

Analysis of teach voice and discussion of key themes that emerge

From this in-depth case study of Wingfield Primary School, key themes that emerge revolve around teacher knowledge, purpose of tools, and pupil autonomy.

Teacher knowledge

There are some caveats, particularly the suggestion that 'simply allowing them [pupils] to use their iPads, or providing them with classroom sets of iPods, does not implicitly mean they will be learning educationally beneficial material' (Peluso, 2012, p. 127). Teachers must be familiar with a range of both hardware and software in order to ensure, therefore, that pupils are given the best tools for the job. It is hoped that teachers will carefully consider the selection of tools for purpose rather than convenience, and that through these selections pupils will find independence and autonomy.

Purpose of tools

Accessibility is one of the key benefits of technology, in that the information is always available whenever the learners need to use it. This includes immediacy, the information can be retrieved immediately by the learners; interactivity, the learners can interact with peers, teachers, and experts efficiently and effectively through different media; and context-awareness, the environment can adapt to the learner's real situation to provide adequate information to learners. For these skills to develop, the correct tool must have been selected in the first place. This links back to the first part of this section, and the role of teacher knowledge and understanding of the computational tools available.

Pupil autonomy

The idea that students can work anywhere in a classroom, in a school, or at home with this tool makes it a compelling choice for many (Hutchison, Beschorner and Schmidt-Crawford, 2012, p. 23). Heinrich (2012) looked at the instruction of iPads into a large (970 pupil) academy for 11-18 years. They concluded that since 'the majority of pupils at the school now having iPads there has been a significant and very positive impact on learning together with further significant and still developing changes in pedagogy' (p. 4). The adoption of a personalised device such as an iPad significantly transforms access to and use of technology inside the classroom with many attendant benefits (Burden et al., 2012, p. 9). Personal 'ownership' of the device is seen as the single most important factor for successful use of this technology (ibid).

Chapter summary

- Technology should be used to enhance and support learning, with clear reason and purpose
- There should be pupil choice over which apps to use when possible, as this can develop pupils' autonomy when deciding on apps or platforms in the future
- eSafety must be relevant and show awareness of the apps and sites that the children being taught are using
- Three themes must be carefully balanced to ensure success in computing: Teacher knowledge, purpose of tools, and pupil autonomy through a child-led pedagogy

---

Further reading

Lessons in Teaching Computing in Primary Schools [Book]. Bird, J., Caldwell, H. and Mayne, P. (2017) Sage Publications Ltd: London.

Lesson planning and subject knowledge go hand-in-hand in this exciting new edition, covering all teachers need to know to confidently teach the Computing curriculum as well as explore opportunities for cross-curricular teaching. Whether you are currently teaching or training to teach the primary computing curriculum, you need to know what effective teaching of Computing in primary schools actually looks like. The current Computing curriculum is explored in manageable chunks and there is no 'scary' tech speak – everything is explained clearly and accessibly. You will find example lesson plans alongside every element of the curriculum that can be adapted to suit different year groups and different schools. This resourceful guide inspires an approach to teaching Computing that is about creativity and encouraging problem solving using technology as a tool.

Teaching Computing Unplugged in Primary Schools: Exploring Primary Computing Through Practical Activities Away from the Computer [Book]. Caldwell, H. SAGE Publications.

Teaching primary Computing without computers? The Computing curriculum is a challenge for primary school teachers. The realities of primary school resources mean limited access to computer hardware. But Computing is about more than computers. Important aspects of the fundamental principles and concepts of Computer Science can be taught without any hardware. This book shows you how you can teach Computing through 'unplugged' activities. It provides lesson examples and everyday activities to help teachers and pupils explore computing concepts in a concrete way, accelerating their understanding and grasp of key ideas such as abstraction, logic, algorithms, and data representation.

References

Abbott, C. (2001) *ICT: Changing Education*. London: Routledge Falmer.
Aftab, P. (2010) *What is Cyberbullying?* Available online at: http://www.stopcyberbullying.org/pdf/what_is_cyberbullying_exactly.pdf (September 14, 2010) [Accessed 02/05/2019].

Alexander, P. (2007) 'Rethinking the "toxicity" debate: The vitality of contemporary childhood', *Education Review*, 20(1), pp. 57-64 [Accessed 02/05/2019].

Barron, B., Cayton-Hodges, G., Bofferding, L., Copple, C., Darling-Hammond, L. and Levine, M. (2011) *Take a Giant Step: A Blueprint for Teaching Children in a Digital Age*. New York: The Joan Ganz Cooney Center at Sesame Workshop.

Boulton, M., Boulton, L., Camerone, E., Down, J., Hughes, J., Kirkbride, C., Kirkham, R., Macaulay, P., and Sanders, J. (2016) 'Enhancing primary school children's knowledge of online safety and risks with the CATZ cooperative cross-age teaching intervention: Results from a pilot study', *Cyberpsychology, Behaviour and Social Networking*, 19(10), pp. 609-614 [Accessed 02/05/2018].

Burden, K., Hopkins, P., Male, T., Martin, S. and Trala, C. (2012) *iPad Scotland Evaluation*. Hull, England: Faculty of Education, University of Hull.

Burnett, C. (2016) 'The digital age and its implications for learning and teaching in the primary school: A report for the Cambridge primary review trust', CPRT supported by Pearson, available at: http://cpr trust.org.uk/wp-content/uploads/2016/07/Burnett-report-20160720.pdf

Carrington, V. (2005) 'New textual landscapes, information and early literacy', in Marsh, J. (Ed.), *Popular Culture, New Media and Digital Literacy in Early Childhood*. London: RoutledgeFalmer, pp. 13-27.

Collins, A. and Halverson, R. (2018) *Rethinking Education in the Age of Technology: The Digital Revolution and Schooling in America*. New York City: Teachers and College Press.

Craft, A. (2010) *Creativity and Education Futures: Learning in a Digital Age*. Staffordshire: Trentham Books.

Csikszentmihalyi, M. and Wolfe, R. (2014) 'New conceptions and research approaches to creativity: Implications of a systems perspective for creativity in education', in M. Csikszentmihalyi (Ed.), *The Systems Model of Creativity* (pp. 161-184). Berlin: Springer.

Dönmez, O., Ferhan Odabaşı, H., Kabakçı Yurdakul, I., Kuzu, A. and Girgin, Ü. (2017) 'Development of a scale to address perceptions of pre-service teachers regarding online risks for children', *Educational Sciences: Theory & Practice*, 17(3), pp. 923-943, (viewed 14/09/2018).

Gibson, P. and Smith, S. (2018) 'Digital literacies: Preparing pupils and students for their information journey in the twenty-first century', *Information and Learning Science*, 119(12), pp. 733-742. doi: 10.1108/ILS-07-2018-0059

Globokar, R. (2018) 'Impact of digital media on emotional, social and moral development of children', *Gulhane Medical Journal*, 60(4), pp. 545-560.

Harel, I. and Papert, S. (Eds.). (1991) *Constructionism*. New York: Ablex Publishing.

Harris, A. (2016) *Creativity and Education*. Dordrecht: Springer.

Heinrich, P. (2012) 'The iPad as a tool for education', *NAACE*. Available at https://learningfoundation.org.uk/wp-content/uploads/2015/12/Longfield-The_iPad_as_a_Tool_for_Education.pdf

Henderson, M., Auld, G., Holkner, B., Russell, G., Seah, W. T, Fernando, A. and Romeo, G. (2010) 'Students creating digital video in the primary classroom: student autonomy, learning outcomes, and professional learning communities', *Australian Educational Computing*, 24(2), pp. 12-20.

Henriksen, D., Henderson, M., Creely, E., Ceretkove, S., Ćernochnová, M., Sendove, E., Sointu, E. T. and Tienken, C. H. (2018) 'Creativity and technology in education: An international perspective', *Technology, Knowledge and Learning*, 23, pp. 409-424.

Holloway, D., Green, L. and Livingstone, S. (2013) *Zero to Eight. Young Children and Their Internet Use*. London: EU Kids Online.

Hutchison, A., Beschorner, B. and Schmidt-Crawford, D. (2012) 'Exploring the use of the iPad for literacy learning', *The Reading Teacher*, 66, pp. 15-23. doi: 10.1002/TRTR.01090

Jantz, G. L. and McMurray, A. (1998) *Hidden Dangers of the Internet: Using it without Abusing it*. Chicago: Harold Shaw Publishers.

Kafai, Y. B. (2006) 'Playing and making games for learning: Instructionist and constructionist perspectives for game studies', *Games and Culture*, 1(1), pp. 36-40. doi: 10.1177/1555412005281767

Kaye, L. (2017) *Young Children in a Digital Age: Supporting Learning and Development with Technology in Early Years*. London: Routledge. Available at: http://public.ebookcentral.proquest.com/choice/pub licfullrecord.aspx?p=4568570

Laurillard, D. (2012) *Teaching as a Design Science, Building Pedagogical Patterns for Learning and Technology*. London: Routledge.

Livingstone, S. (2013) 'Online risk, harm and vulnerability: reflections on the evidence base for child Internet safety policy', *ZER: Journal of Communication Studies*, 18(35), pp. 13-28. ISSN 1137-1102.

Mayer, R. E. (2003) 'Elements of a science of E-learning', *Journal of Educational Computing Research*, 29(3), pp. 297–313. doi: 10.2190/YJLG-09F9-XKAX-753D

Mishra, P. and Deep-Play Research Group. (2012) 'Rethinking technology and creativity in the 21st century: Crayons are the future', *TechTrends*, 56(5), pp. 13–16.

NAEYC (2012) *Technology and Interactive Media as Tools in Early Childhood Programs Serving Children from Birth through Age 8*. Available at https://www.naeyc.org/sites/default/files/globally-shared/downloads/PDFs/resources/topics/PS_technology_WEB.pdf

NSPCC (2017) *Net Aware Report 2017: "Freedom to Express Myself Safely" How Young People Navigate Opportunities and Risks in Their Online Lives*. Available at https://www.nspcc.org.uk/services-and-resources/research-and-resources/2017/net-aware-report-freedom-to-express-myself-safely/   (Viewed 05/01/2018).

Ofcom (2016) *Children and Parents: Media Use and Attitudes Report*. London: Office of Communications. Available at https://www.ofcom.org.uk/__data/assets/pdf_file/0034/93976/Children-Parents-Media-Use-Attitudes-Report-2016.pdf [Viewed 16/05/2018].

OurICT. (2017) *Technology Education History*. Available at http://www.ourict.co.uk/technology-education-history/

Palmer, S. (2007) *Toxic Childhood: How the Modern World is Damaging Our Children and What We Can Do about it*. London: Orion.

Peluso, D. C. C. (2012) 'The fast-paced iPad revolution: Can educators stay up to date and relevant about these ubiquitous devices?', *British Journal of Educational Technology*, 43, pp. E125–E127. doi: 10.1111/j.1467-8535.2012.01310.x

Poftak, A. (2002) 'Net-wise teens: Safety, ethics, and innovation', *Technology & Learning*, 22, pp. 36–45.

Plowman, L., McPake, J. and Stephen, C. (2012) 'Extending opportunities for learning : The role of digital media in early education', in S. Suggate and E. Reese (Eds.), *Contemporary Debates in Child Development and Education* (pp. 95–104). Abingdon: Routledge.

Prensky, M. (2001) 'Digital natives, digital immigrants', *On the Horizon*, 9(5), pp. 1–6. Available at emeraldinsight.com/doi/abs/10.1108/10748120110424816 [Viewed 02/05/2018].

Resnick, M. (2013) 'Learn to code, code to learn', *EdSurge*, May 2013 [Spanish version].

Resnick, M. (2013) 'Lifelong Kindergarten', *Cultures of Creativity*. LEGO Foundation.

Runco, M. A. (2014) *Creativity: Theories and Themes: Research, Development, and Practice*. Amsterdam: Elsevier.

Wheeler, S. (2015) *Learning with E's: Educational Theory and Practice in the Digital Age*. http://public.eblib.com/choice/publicfullrecord.aspx?p=1918927

Zhao, Y. (2012) *World Class Learning: Educating Creative and Entrepreneurial Students*. Thousand Oaks, CA: Corwin Press.

10 Inspiración y oportunidad

Purpose and strategies for teaching Modern Foreign Languages in the primary classroom

Poppy Gibson and Talia Ramadan

Critical questions

Why should we teach other languages when English is the dominant language of both our country and our country's national curriculum?

Is there still time and place for Modern Foreign Languages (MFL) in an already over-crowded and time-limited curriculum?

How can the teaching of MFL succeed when many pupils may be children with English as an Additional Language (EAL), or have Special Educational Needs and Disabilities (SEND)?

Introduction

At the writing of this chapter, in the year of 2019, the Brexit deal, the withdrawal of the United Kingdom from the European Union, is of current fiery debate. Who knows how things may sit as you read this from the future? It is most likely that Brexit has been finalised, and the UK is no longer a member of the EU. It may be that the deal took a variety of forms, a possible 'no-deal' Brexit, that other elections followed, or that, by some strange series of events, the UK may remain in the EU or have mysteriously returned. Regardless of the outcome, which cannot be known as we write these words, one thing is certain: Brexit has brought into light several discussions about the part that the UK plays in the wider European landscape, and the roles of our members of society in the bigger picture of the world. Essentially, to communicate with others, whether in the same country or 100 miles away, some form of language is needed.

This chapter hopes to address why Modern Foreign Languages (MFL) should have a more secure and consistent role in the primary timetable (currently, MFL is only statutory from Key Stage 2). Background history on the subject of MFL in the UK system is shared, leading to a discussion on the current face of MFL in our schools. Case studies, practitioner thought pieces, and practical strategies will help to offer an insight into excellence in the primary classroom.

Why teach/learn MFL?

In the 2014 national curriculum (Department for Education, 2014), MFL aims to develop inter-cultural competence and linguistic skills for the future, as well as the ability to communicate proficiently in the chosen second language (L2). The 'Purpose of Study' in the current national curriculum claims:

> Learning a foreign language is a liberation from insularity and provides an opening to other cultures. A high-quality languages education should foster pupils' curiosity and deepen their understanding of the world. The teaching should enable pupils to express their ideas and thoughts in another language and to understand and respond to its speakers, both in speech and in writing. It should also provide opportunities for them to communicate for practical purposes, learn new ways of thinking and read great literature in the original language. Language teaching should provide the foundation for learning further languages, equipping pupils to study and work in other countries.
>
> (DfE, 2014: 1)

The European Commission support language learning for the countries that are part of the European Union, which had some influence on MFL being included in the first curriculum of study in England, when England was still a member of the European Centre for Modern Languages (Dobson, 2018). Meanwhile, Holmes (2017) suggests that language learning post-Brexit is as important as ever, for broadening pupil's horizons, and negotiating the new terms. Tinsley (2017) might argue that the divisive aftermath of the Brexit vote, and the monolingual mentality, could be amended by educating and using languages to reinforce inclusivity. The more common benefit of learning MFL in the PS, which has been highlighted in the national curriculum (DfE, 2013), is the opening of minds to other worlds, which is becoming essential in the 21st century (Myles, 2017). Vetrinskaya and Dmitrenko (2017) described in the journal of *Training Language and Culture*, the importance of sociocultural understanding for the future employment in the business world, and discussed how misunderstandings of how language is used in different contexts can easily offend another, especially as it is not something pupils will innately learn from language lessons. A small-scale study (Costley et al., 2018) concluded that the many teachers feeling unprepared are missing out on opportunities to use pupils, with English as an additional language, as a facilitative tool for learning about other cultures – especially when faced with pressures of attainment targets.

In the 2014 report, 'School approaches to the education of EAL students: Language development, social integration and achievement' (Arnot et al., 2014), it was highlighted how in England there are over 300 languages being used, including variations of Sign Languages, and therefore, there are varying degrees of bilingualism and being bimodal within our classrooms. However, exam entries in secondary schools are at an all-time low for languages (Tinsley and Doležal, 2018). Swanwick (2016) might suggest the time has come to move further away from a deficit model of assessment, towards a system that validates diversity in all its forms, embracing the different cultures, and languages available within our classrooms, and develop our already multilingual pupils, implementing an assessment system that supports all lessons and modes of communication.

Critical question

Why should we teach other languages when English is the dominant language of both our country and our country's national curriculum?

Interestingly, when we look at the aims set out in the current national curriculum (2014), the focus appears to be not on the language itself, which essentially can be chosen by the primary school, but is on the value of communication and understanding of the role of language as a whole. The aims are shared below:

The national curriculum for languages aims to ensure that all pupils:

- Understand and respond to spoken and written language from a variety of authentic sources.
- Speak with increasing confidence, fluency, and spontaneity, finding ways of communicating what they want to say, including through discussion and asking questions, and continually improving the accuracy of their pronunciation and intonation.
- Can write at varying lengths, for different purposes and audiences, using the variety of grammatical structures that they have learnt.
- Discover and develop an appreciation of a range of writing in the language studied.

(DfE, 2014: 1)

Standard English is the sociolect of most of school environments. This might be influenced by the assessment system in England, which requires pupils to complete standardised tests in English and Mathematics, while MFL is a foundation subject with no formal assessments (DfE, 2013). Issa and Hatt (2013) discussed in their book on language and culture, how Gove had promoted the use of MFL to further cement and explore English grammar. The National Literacy Strategy, which had been incorporated into schools from the late 1990s (Bunting, 2000), took a very narrow and prescriptive view as to how languages might be taught, underpinned by the basic skills agenda, which favoured the grammar of one dialect of spoken English. It could still be argued, however, that not allowing pupils access to another language, if not multiple languages, is doing the pupils a great injustice in later life, even more so, in an ever-growing multilingual world and economy (McLelland, 2018). Although, English is still the *lingua franca* of the world, the ability to speak a second language not only allows pupils to access a wider range of literature, thus ideas, but perhaps prepares them for an attitude of acceptance and openness (Tinsley, 2017).

The latest Language Trends Survey (see also boxed feature 'Research Focus' for further details) published by Tinsley and Doležal, investigating MFL in schools across the education system, might suggest that of the pupils leaving secondary school most are not able to hold a conversation in their L2 (Tinsley and Doležal, 2018). This mirrors similar concerns drawn from the Nuffield Report (2000), which had reviewed and devised strategies for very similar barriers to language teaching across England over a decade ago. While the benefits and aims of learning a MFL are certainly not limited to conversational skills, Sharpe (2001) has suggested that perhaps the emphasis should be, at the very least, on the acknowledgement of foreign languages, as well as the development of metacognitive skills to talk about language itself, while gathering a repertoire of sounds as a foundation to decode different languages in the future. It has been suggested that differentiating certain sounds and tones in a language is easier to pick up on at a younger age (Issa and Hatt, 2013). Although, according to the CALP and BICS in the Cummins (2005) language learning model, it takes more than seven years to fully comprehend a second language. That said, exposure, attitude, and amount of practice can be a variant in language learning too (Myles, 2017). Myles (2017) challenged the belief that learning languages from a younger age is better, by arguing that without proper train-ing and provision, despite MFL being supported by policy to be taught compulsory from Key Stage 2, teachers without sufficient MFL knowledge might still be facing hurdles. Although, data suggests just over half of all primary schools now have access to specialist expertise (Tinsley and Doležal, 2018), since the Department for Education released the new national curriculum (DfE, 2013) for schools to follow from 2014, the underlying objectives for learning Modern Foreign Languages have remained ambiguous – implicating the provision provided and support networks available to teachers.

Research focus: The language trends survey

Language Trends is an annual survey of primary and secondary schools in England, designed to gather information about the current situation for language teaching and learning. Its aims are to assess the impact of policy measures in relation to languages and to analyse strengths and weaknesses based both on quantitative evidence and on the views of teachers.

(Tinsley and Doležal, 2018: 2)

Policy background and context

The 2018 Language Trends survey responds once again to ongoing concern about the level of participation in language learning since the subject was removed from the compulsory curriculum at Key Stage 4 in 2004. The proportion of the cohort taking a language GCSE dropped from 76% in 2002 to 40% in 2011. This year's sur-vey gathers information about how schools and pupils are responding to the new A level syllabuses and the separation ('decoupling') of AS from A level. Language teaching became compulsory in primary schools in England in 2014 and high expectations of what can be achieved at Key Stage 2 underpin the whole National Curriculum Programmes of Study for languages. Previous Language Trends surveys identified significant disparities in provision between primary schools and barriers to achieving smooth transition to secondary school, which would allow pupils to build successfully on their prior learning. The 2018 survey again explores these issues. With the UK's relationship with the countries whose languages are most commonly taught in schools about to undergo a significant realignment, the survey also sought to gather information on the impact of the Brexit process on school policies, teacher supply, international links and the attitudes of parents and pupils.

(Tinsley and Doležal, 2018: 2)

The 2018 Language Trends survey can be downloaded for free at:

https://www.britishcouncil.org/sites/default/files/language_trends_2018_report.pdf

Additionally, the surveys from previous years can also be found archived on the British Council's website.

Background to MFL

Modern Foreign Languages and Ancient Languages were historically associated with elite secondary schools (Sharpe, 2001). Learning a second language was usually used in order to access literature in an Ancient Language, rather than to communicate effectively. Tinsley (2017) found that MFL is still associated with schools with more academic success, and in the highest socioeconomic band. MFL was freely taught before the national curriculum was gradually imposed onto schools, following the implementation of routine OFSTED inspections (Dobson, 2018). While there have been various initiatives supporting language learning, such as the national language strategy 'Languages For All; Languages For Life' (Department for Children Schools and Families, 2003) to encourage and support schools lacking in MFL teaching, not all have been continued. In 2009, the Department for Children, Schools and Families released the 'Developing Language in the Primary School: Literacy and Primary Languages' report which supported that the inclusive pedagogy which should be used for teaching MFL was advantageous for English as additional language learners and pupils with special needs too (Woodgate-Jones, 2015). These non-statutory guidelines were released by a Labour government, which reflected many of the aforementioned Nuffield Foundation recommendations. These guidelines had long-term goals for MFL to be taught in all primary schools by 2011. However, conflicting agendas may have restricted the advancement of teaching MFL (Dobson, 2018). The European Commission encourages many countries in Europe to extend the compulsory study of MFL, from the beginning to the end of compulsory education. In the 'Teacher education for linguistic diversity' Colloquium for the ECML, many countries in Europe came together to discuss the positive impact of beginning to learn a second or third language from a younger age, and highlighted how the policies implemented by governments, in the countries with a high standard of L2, have been consistently supported throughout the education system over the years (ECML, 2017). This process can be long and requires a lot of patience, but it links to the British Values, where being tolerant and accepting also requires guidance and time – this is arguably essential for any good education (Woodgate-Jones, 2015).

The 'Language Learning at Key Stage 2' report was initiated by a Labour government. Coleman (2009) suggests that sceptics perceived this as an attempt to make up for the previous decision to make MFL an optional area of study at Key Stage 4. McLelland (2018) poses, however, that the intention was to relieve struggling secondary school pupils of MFL, in order to refocus their abilities in other subject areas. This, however, resulted in a steady decline in examination uptake. A coalition government in 2010 would finalise and release the report, and in 2013 the new NC would be released – making MFL compulsory at Key Stage 2. The new NC still emphasised the importance of languages. However, the coalition government by that time had abolished many of the infrastructures in place including the withdrawal from CILT (The National Centre for Languages) and the National Language Strategy (Dobson, 2018). The government began to prioritise putting the Literacy and Numeracy strategies into place, maintaining that English and Maths should be regarded as the core subjects (Bunting, 2000). Perhaps this demonstrates how changes in government can disrupt long-term goals for the education system as a whole, if there is no cohesion on purpose for learning, especially for those delicate subjects with no formal assessments (McLelland, 2018).

It has been noted how teachers' attitudes regarding MFL remain mixed (Costley, 2018; Finch et al, 2018; Sutton, 2017). MFL in primary schools will compete alongside seven other foundation subjects for time in the school curriculum (Dfe, 2013). This has perhaps resulted in teachers finding it difficult to incorporate MFL into lesson plans, thus, exposure and pedagogy being used to teach MFL varies throughout schools in England (Finch et al., 2018; Woodgate-Jones, 2015; Sharpe, 2001; Bunting, 2000). Specialist language teachers are rare in more remote areas of the country – sometimes a collateral damage to the cuts being made in public funding – so the money intended solely for language initiatives is now being directly transferred into a school's general budget (Dobson, 2018). Thus, after the collapse of many initiatives and the breakdown of infrastructure, it can be difficult for teachers and schools to find the right support.

When Her Majesty's Government, in 2018, debated the position of MFL in schools and universities, it was concluded that MFL could be regarded as an area of study as important as a STEM subject and an advantageous employable skill for the future. The debate agreed that research carried out by the British Council regarding languages should be taken into consideration during policy change. Strengthening and sustaining England's language departments is a priority in order to begin growing England's pool of language graduates, rather than outsourcing provision from other countries. Many agreed upon the complexities that lie ahead because of the breakdown of the networks used to support language learning for all. There is no doubt that mastering a second language is beneficial for social, academic, and cognitive purposes (Sutton, 2017; Swansick; 2016; Bialystock and Kroll, 2009), however, due to a lack of support and consistency, the uphill battle to sustain the MFL stature in schools will continue to face barriers previously seen throughout the history of MFL (Dobson, 2018; McLelland, 2018). The barriers include that of isolation for teachers and schools. Language itself is the portal we use to connect and open doors to communicate with and support each other, usually restricted to our own linguistic networks. Modern Foreign Languages itself could allow us to broaden our platforms encouraging pupils, teachers, and schools to connect and share more support and ideas to engage MFL learning and teaching.

Case study: Longlands Primary School, Hertfordshire

Longlands Primary School and Nursery is a one-form entry school in Turnford, Herfordshire, which recently acquired the outstanding qualification from Ofsted in all areas.

Longland's website states how:

> Our School serves a community which is socially, culturally and linguistically diverse and we consider this diversity to be an asset, which enriches the educational experience we can offer our children. We also have a very strong commitment to inclusion.
>
> (Longlands, 2019: 1)

At Longlands Primary School French is being taught in each KS2 class every week for at least 30 minutes by the MFL Coordinator, Liliana Dudau, and several other teachers.

Longlands Primary School intends to open a Spanish club in the future.

MFL teacher, Liliana Dudau:

I am proud to be part of a wonderful, hard-working team who have extremely high expectations of what pupils can achieve, who plan their lessons with great skills, enabling children to make excellent progress.

I have worked at Longlands since 2016 (as an employee). Before being employed, I used to work as a supply teacher at Longlands (from 2013–2016). Since 2017, I have been MFL subject leader. To ensure that French is taught efficiently across KS2, every term, I scrutinise the French books to monitor if there is evidence for differentiation; if children produce work of an exceptional standard; if children understand the comments that the teachers make in their books; and if the work is presented neatly and clearly in accordance with the Presentation and Feed Forward Marking Policy. I also undertake observations and provide feedback to my colleagues on good practice and on next steps in teaching French, to ensure increasingly successful learning. Every term, randomly selected pupils from every KS2 class complete a survey. Data are discussed in staff meetings and areas for improvement are suggested. In my learning walks, I observe whether children are engaged in the lesson and having fun; I look at the French displays, e.g. the objective for the half term, key vocabulary used in the unit displayed, and celebration of success displayed. At Longlands, all the staff have the required knowledge to teach French.

I have strong knowledge about French and take any opportunity for professional development to improve my skills as an MFL subject leader. I hold a BA in English Literature and Language and French Literature and Language, and MA in Translation Studies and Interpreting (French and English).

What do you love about teaching MFL?

I love when children make mistakes and learn from their mistakes and have a growth mindset (we use this model across the whole school). I love when children tell me: 'I'm not sure how to pronounce it but I'll give it a try'. I love when children tell me 'I want to know French like you!', 'I want to speak like you!' and I love when parents stop me and ask me 'what game did you play yesterday? My daughter told me she had so much fun. Can you please give me the link so she can play more at home?' I love that children have a genuine love for learning French. I love that they want to find out more about what they are studying, that they take new opportunities to deepen their knowledge and understanding. Sometimes, children excitedly tell me that they've got a book in French or a dictionary which they would like to show the whole class, or they practised their numbers in French at home or they played a French game at home that they would like to share with their classmates.

Tell us about any resources or schemes you use to teach MFL.

We subscribed to www.languageangels.com and we use the plans and resources that are provided on the website. These fun lessons provide a strong sequence of learning, enabling children to apply what they have learnt in French to other subjects as well.

We also use the BBC online French resources (especially games). BBC – Learn French, with free online lessons.

Tell us about one of your favourite MFL activities to do with the children.

My favourite activities are those related to speaking because this is a great opportunity for me to develop a growth mindset in children. In my French lessons, I value any effort a child makes to try to speak French. I constantly praise them for their effort to pronounce a word, a phrase, or a sentence. I reiterate that making mistakes is a wonderful thing and its part of our learning. Thus, children feel more confident to speak and learn new things. The Language Angels resources are great as they embed French in other subjects: Geography (Continents, Countries, Types of Habitats), History (Ancient Britain, The Romans, The Tudors, World War Two), Literacy (Stories: Little Red Riding Hood, Goldilocks and the Three Bears), Music (Instruments), PE (The Olympic Games), PSHE (Healthy Lifestyles), and Grammar.

Why do you think it is important for children to learn MFL?

I believe that learning a foreign language equips children with amazing listening, memory, thinking, and concentration skills. It also helps them understand and improve their own language. Consequently, their English vocabulary and grammar skills increase. For instance, when I asked children to guess the meaning of 'J'habite a Londres', they immediately linked the French word 'habite' with the English word 'habitat'. Another example is when we discussed the French articles *le, la, les* and possessive determiners *mon, ma, ton, ta*, etc. Through examples, children understood the function of these determiners, they made the link with the English language and thus secure their grammatical knowledge in both English and French. Also, learning a foreign language makes children aware of the French culture. At Longlands, understanding others' cultures is a priority in many subjects, French included, and consequently, pupils show good understanding.

What do you think an excellent MFL classroom/lesson looks like, i.e. attitudes, the atmosphere, etc.

An excellent MFL lesson is when children are engaged, have fun, and never feel embarrassed about how they pronounce a word. It's a lesson where children are highly motivated to try their best in their work and children have an excellent attitude to learning French. It's a lesson where I ensure that children have time to practise what I am teaching so that their understanding and skills are secure. An excellent lesson is when I smile from all my heart and I have an excellent attitude towards my teaching and when I genuinely enjoy what I am teaching. It's a lesson where I use questions to extend children's thinking and encourage debate and discussion.

Key themes running throughout Liliana's interview (case study one) include pupils' attitudes, teachers' attitudes, and the need for a community that supports autonomous learning and resilience.

Case study: Belmont Primary School and Nursery

Belmont Primary School and Nursery is a two-form entry school in Bexleyheath, which recently acquired the good qualification from Ofsted in all areas, and outstanding in personal development, behaviour, and welfare. The report stated that:

> Pupils' moral, spiritual and cultural education is rich and wide-ranging. Opportunities within the curriculum celebrate differences in faith, language and culture. Pupils show a strong understanding and commitment to everyone having the right to feel safe at school and in the wider community.
>
> (OFSTED, 2018: 6)

At Belmont Primary School, French and Spanish are being taught in each KS2 class every week for at least 30 minutes, by several teachers with good subject knowledge of their language. One of the Belmont Primary Parliament's pledges this year was to work together to promote French and Spanish further across the school (see Figures 10.1 and 10.2).

Teacher voice: Katia, Year 3 teacher

Modern Foreign Language lessons are an opportunity for my pupils to not only begin to grow in confidence speaking a second or third language, for some, but to begin to open their minds to new cultures.

Figure 10.1 A colourful Spanish display in the classroom

Figure 10.2 Class names celebrate places around the world

Generally, I encourage the children to participate in the lessons through songs and games, in order to promote engagement and recall of simple vocabulary. By using a lot of repetition, the children get used to the sounds of the words and begin using the language in different contexts. Once they become familiar with the vocabulary, we can begin to explore patterns and similarities between the languages. When introducing more complicated words we will discuss the new vocabulary and try to link it with something the pupils are familiar with emotionally or use a visual cue to engage them in the learning. An important part of the learning is giving all pupils a chance to participate in the lesson.

The school has a lot of resources available for us to use, which supports us in our teaching, and also allows pupils to access the language outside of the designated language timeslot. Many of the teachers at the school, including myself, speak a second language, and we will encourage pupils to use greetings and reinforce other simple vocabulary around the school and during lunchtimes.

Every class is named after a different country and each class studies the country they are named after for the first few weeks of term. We will explore the country as a class investigating the culture, language, and customs. This is an exciting way of familiarising the pupils with the many different countries, which links in with their geographical knowledge and expands their wider understanding of the world. Our core values ensure children develop respect for every person – developing strong and lasting relationships that enable the community to be strong and cohesive.

I think generally our school offers our pupils a variety of languages to practice, listen to, and to hopefully grow a little more curious about.

Linking theory to practice

Key themes running throughout Katia's interview include pupils' confidence, teachers' experiences and skill, and the need for a school network that involves a shared vision and shared values.

Comparing the themes across both of the case studies presented in this chapter, there are clearly three levels of support needed, with space for development of knowledge, understanding, and skill within each level. These levels are:

- The united school community
- Teachers that are part of a learning network
- Pupils that receive strong role modelling to develop confidence and autonomy

Firstly, perhaps most importantly, there must be a shared vision within the school that emphasises the relevance of MFL in our society, and the value of celebrating different languages and cultures. As mentioned earlier in the chapter, links can be seen here to the Fundamental British Values document, which encourages tolerance and respect for all.

Secondly, MFL teachers need to be part of a supported network, either within the school with other MFL staff, or with MFL staff at other schools. Sharing knowledge and teaching strategies is a key part of ongoing CPD. Teachers also need to be aware of the wide range of accessible materials to help them with their language teaching; in the absence of a MFL teaching scheme, having a network with others can share best practice, and possible sources for lesson materials.

Thirdly, pupils need to participate in lessons that have strong role modelling from confident and enthusiastic teachers, that can then instil confidence in them. The authors of this chapter recommend using a 'funnel method' for participation, which ensures that pupils feel supported through their learning journey, to lead to individual and independent learning and performance. This Language Learning Funnel method is illustrated in the model in Figure 10.3. The teacher role modelling must begin with whole class participation, to avoid any feelings of isolation, anxiety, or awkwardness amongst pupils. As confidence grows, task design moves down the funnel from top (whole class), through group/paired activities, to individual performance.

The LLF model can be seen as part of the wider school values and teacher skill (themes drawn from the two case studies in this chapter) by positioning it within the framework as shown in Figure 10.4.

To give a taster of lesson ideas to engage and enthuse pupils, some practical activities are shared below. Please see the 'Further reading' box for recommended books that can provide further ideas.

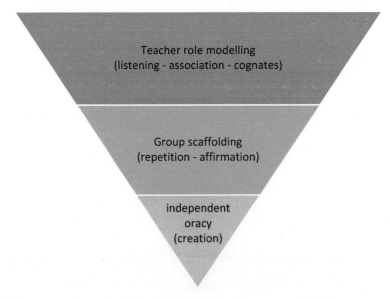

Figure 10.3 Language Learning Funnel (LLF) method for successful MFL

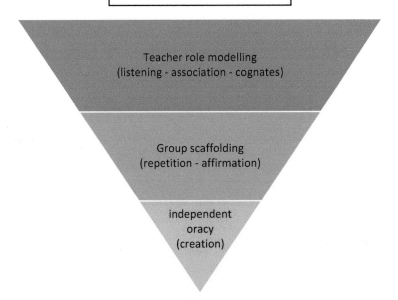

National Curriculum Policy
School ethos, vision and values
Teacher experience and skill

Teacher role modelling
(listening - association - cognates)

Group scaffolding
(repetition - affirmation)

independent
oracy
(creation)

Figure 10.4 Language Learning Funnel (LLF) in context

Practical strategies and excellent ideas to inspire pupils in MFL

- Listen to radio stations from around the world
- Download the TuneIn radio app. Click 'By Location' > Europe > France/Spain then choose either the type of music (genre) you want to listen to or the area in France or Spain
- Try the activities listed below

Vocab hunt

Pupils are given an empty vocab grid. Blu-tac the words in the target language around the room. Pupils work in pairs or small groups and with only one person being able to leave their seat at a time, they have to fill their table. The one pupil who leaves the group has to memorise the word and the spelling, come back and share with partner and group members. The other pupil(s) look up the Spanish word in the dictionary. Pupils take it in turns until all words are found and translated.

Language bingo

This is ideal as a starter activity to practise numbers or colours in target language. Give each pupil a blank card with, for example, six spaces. The pupil can write in six chosen words from a longer list of vocabulary such as Spanish colours or French animals. Pupils listen carefully to the teacher and cross off a word if they hear it. This will develop listening skills. The winner is the first pupil to cross off all words.

Find your end

Pupils are given a question/answer, start/end of sentence, word in the language and have to find their partner.

Global pen pal

Find a school in a country that speaks your target language – seek headteacher permission and consider setting up a pen pal exchange. Parental consent can be easily gathered, and safety about pen pal connections could be discussed with pupils. A simple process of pupils writing lessons in the target language (e.g. Spanish) and then scanning and emailing their letters over to the school can be carried out with little cost or effort. The children in the other school, who may be developing their English, could perhaps write back in English, and their teacher can scan and email back the letters for you to print and hand out to the pen pals in your class. Who knows, you may even inspire your pupils to travel the world or work overseas one day as a result of their primary pen pal exchange!

Further activities and ideas can be found in the books promoted in the 'Key readings' box below.

Key readings

Hunton, J. (2015) *Fun Learning Activities for Modern Foreign Languages: A Complete Toolkit for Ensuring Engagement, Progress and Achievement.* Carmarthen: Crown House Publishing.

Learning languages isn't always fun and games. But these aren't games – they are fun learning activities, and they can help revolutionise language teaching by enabling teachers to authoritatively impart knowledge while fostering a thirst for knowledge and love of learning in their students.

Based on the author's extensive classroom experience, and underpinned by research into how students learn best, each activity comes complete with a detailed explanation and plenty of ideas for variations, differentiations, and extensions. The activities come with example vocabulary lists in French, German, and Spanish as a starting point, which are all available for download via a link provided in the book. However, the activities will work effectively in any language and with any vocabulary list of the teacher's choosing, and can be adapted to suit every topic, learning objective, and age range.

Discover ready to use activities which will make for outstanding lessons in every class and ensure engagement, motivation, rapport, progress, and attainment over time.

Smith, S. (2017) *Becoming an Outstanding Languages Teacher.* London: Routledge.

With a key focus on learning, this book contains a wealth of common-sense advice and well thought out strategies which actually work in the MFL classroom.

The National Curriculum Languages programmes of study for Key Stage 2:
https://assets.publishing.service.gov.uk/government/uploads/system/uploads/attac hment_data/file/239042/PRIMARY_national_curriculum_-_Languages.pdf

Summary

Teaching languages can inspire and motivate pupils to dream of a bigger future with endless possibilities.

- Pupils need to understand the relevance and importance of learning about other languages and cultures for it to have meaning.
- MFL can help achieve the NC's goal for cultural development and can promote the Fundamental British Values (2014). In a world where we hope for our pupils to be tolerant, respectful, and accepting of others, MFL can promote global mindedness.
- Three key themes should be considered when implementing a successful MFL scheme in school: The united school community, teachers that are part of a learning network, and pupils that receive strong role modelling to develop confidence and autonomy.
- The use of strong role modelling when teaching MFL can help to make the learning effective and enjoyable for all pupils, including those with EAL and SEND.
- Following the Language Learning Funnel Model (presented in this chapter) from whole class participation, to group work to pairs to individuals, can provide successful teaching and confident learners.

Further reading

Sharpe, K. (2001) *Modern Foreign Languages in the Primary School: The What, Why and How of Early MFL Teaching.* Paperback 1 Aug 2001.

Although an older text, published in 2001, this book is worth reading as it provides an overview of the place of modern languages in the primary school in the 21st century. It is written for anyone with an active role in teaching languages in schools today, either at primary or secondary levels. It discusses the practical issues involved in teaching MFL to primary students.

Cave, S. (2016) *100+ Ideas for MFL in the Primary Classroom Book.* Dunstable: Brilliant Publications.

The 137 activities in this book can be used to develop oracy and literacy skills in almost any language.
The activities use flashcards, puppets, and bean bags. You will never be stuck for ideas. Guaranteed to get an enthusiastic response from pupils!

https://www.tts-group.co.uk/100-ideas-for-mfl-in-the-primary-classroom-book/MFLP
    MFL.html?gclid=CjwKCAiAyrXiBRAjEiwATI95mWvfgVK4qUiHOzjxjiHVjt_ktLarUQu
    ka2Xpl7OTIKXY7iDScF17hRoC9bcQAvD_BwE#

Kirsch, C. (2008) *Teaching Foreign Languages in the Primary School*. London:
    Bloomsbury Publishing PLC.

The definitive textbook *Teaching Foreign Languages in the Primary School* shows that
language teaching can be both highly effective and immediately enjoyable. The book
uses numerous ideas and approaches that are reinforced with activities, methods for
developing understanding, assessment techniques, and how to ensure continuity and
transition into secondary school. This is the textbook that all primary school language
teachers should not be without. *Teaching Foreign Languages in the Primary School*
advises Modern Foreign Language trainees and qualified teachers on how to teach
MFL successfully at primary level. This book offers full information, including sections
on: Children's ideas about how to learn languages; the current situation of MFL in the
UK, Europe and elsewhere; research into second language acquisition (e.g. behaviourist, cognitive, and sociocultural perspectives); different approaches to teaching foreign languages (e.g. audio lingualism, communicative language teaching, task-based
instruction); the use of games, songs and stories; ways of developing speaking, listening, reading, and writing skills; ways of developing intercultural understanding; knowledge about language and language learning strategies; and, assessment, continuity
with secondary school, and ways of facilitating transition.

   Brimming with case studies and tried and tested ideas from a multilingual language
teacher and ITE lecturer, *Teaching Foreign Languages in the Primary School* shows that
language teaching at primary level can be both effective and enjoyable – no matter
what language the pupils have as their first and no matter what level the teacher has
reached in their own language learning.

References

Arnot, M., Schneider, C., Evans, M., Liu, Y., Welply, O., Davies-Tut, D., Forbes, K. and Sutton, D. (2014)
    *School Approaches to the Education of EAL Students: Language Development, Social Integration and
    Achievement*. The Bell Foundation: London.
Bialystock, E., Craik, F., Green, D. and Gollan, T. (2009) Bilingual minds. *Sage Journals* 10(3), pp. 9-129.
    Available at: http://commonweb.unifr.ch/artsdean/pub/gestens/f/as/files/4740/38302_130737.pdf
Bunting, R. (2000) *Teaching about Language in Primary Years*. 2nd ed. David Fulton Publishers: London.
Coleman, J. A. (2009) Why the British do not learn languages: Myths and motivation in the United
    Kingdom. *Language Learning Journal* 310(1), pp. 111-128. Available at: https://www.tandfonline.com/do
    i/full/10.1080/09571730902749003
Costley, T., Gkonou, C., Myles, F., Roehr-Brackin, K. and Tellier, A. (2018) Multilingual and monolingual children
    in primary-level language classroom: Individual differences and perceptions of foreign language
    learning. *The Language Learning Journal* 48(5), pp. 643-655. doi: 10.1080/09571736.2018.1471616
Cummins, A. (2005) BICS and CALP: Empirical and theoretical status of the distinction, in Street, B.
    and Hornberger, N. H. (Eds.), *Encyclopedia of Language and Education*, 2nd ed., *Vol 2: Literacy* (pp.
    71-83).Springer Science + Business Media LLC: New York.

Department for Education (2013) *Primary National Curriculum Languages*. Available at: https://www.gov .uk/government/publications/national-curriculum-in-england-languages-progammes-of-study

Department for Education (2014) *Languages Programmes of Study: Key Stage 2 National Curriculum in England*. Available at https://assets.publishing.service.gov.uk/government/uploads/system/uploads/ attachment_data/file/239042/PRIMARY_national_curriculum_-_Languages.pdf

Department for Education and Skills (2003) *The National Language Strategy: Languages for All, Languages for Life*. DfES publications: Nottingham.

Dobson, A. (2018) Towards 'MFL for all' in England: A historical perspective. *The Language Learning Journal* 46(1), pp. 71-85. Available at: https://doi.org/10.1080/09571736.20110.1382058

European Centre for Modern Languages (2017) Live stream von ECML Colloquium. ECML Colloquium, 13-14 December 2017. *Teacher Education for Linguistic Diversity: The Contribution of the ECML*. Available at: https://www.youtube.com/watch?v=2axeZFDubTA&feature=youtu.be&t=41m15s

Finch, K., Theaktson, A. and Serratrice, L. (2018) Teaching modern foreign language in multilingual classrooms: An experiment of key stage 2 teachers experiences. *The Language Learning Journal*. Available at: https://www.tandfonline.com/doi/abs/10.1080/09571736.2018.1448432

Holmes, B. (2017) Global Britain require more and better language skills. *Language, Society and Policy*. Available at: https://doi.org/10.17863/CAM.16839

Issa, T. and Hatt, A. (2013) *Language Culture and Identity in the Early Years*. Camden: Bloomsbury Academic.

Longlands School (2019) *Longlands School Website*. http://www.longlands.herts.sch.uk/ [Accessed 15th February 2019].

McLelland, N. (2018) The history of language learning and teaching in Britain. *The Language Learning Journal* 46(1), pp. 6-16. doi: 10.1080/09571736.20110.1382052

Myles, F. (2017) Learning foreign languages in primary schools: Is younger better? *Languages, Society and Policy*. Available at: https://doi.org/10.17863/CAM.9806

Nuffield (2000) *Languages: The Next Generation*. Nuffield Foundation: London.

Sharpe, K. (2001) *Modern Foreign Languages in the Primary School: The What, Why and How of Early MFL Teaching*. Routledge: London.

Sutton, D. (2017) Multilingual Britain - Towards a coherent policy framework for children with EAL. *Languages, Society and Policy*. Available at: https://doi.org/10.17863/CAM.16841

Swanwick, R. A. (2016) Deaf children's bimodal bilingualism and education. *Language Teaching* 49(1), pp. 1-34. Available at: http://eprints.whiterose.ac.uk/96878/3/SWANWICK%20FINAL%20SoA%20LT %20Paper.pdf

Tinsley, T. (2017) *Discussion Paper for the European Commission's Fourth Thematic Panel on Languages and Literacy: 'Rethinking Foreign Language Teaching and Learning'*, 23-24 January 2017. The cost of linguistic exclusion: language skills as a key competence for all. Available at: https://ec.europa.eu/ education/sites/education/files/document-library-docs/tinsley_en.pdf

Tinsley, T. and Doležal, N. (2018) *Language Trends 2018: Language Teaching in Primary and Secondary Schools in England Survey Report*. Available at: https://www.britishcouncil.org/sites/default/files/ language_trends_2018_report.pdf

Vetrinskaya, V. V. and Dmitrenko, T. A. (2017) Developing students sociocultural competence in foreign language classes. *Training Language and Culture* 1(2), pp. 22-39. doi: 10.29366/2017tlc.1.2.2

Woodgate-Jones, A. (2015) Primary teachers in times of change: Engaging with the primary modern foreign language initiative in England. Thesis for the degree of Doctor of Philosophy. Available at: https://eprints.soton.ac.uk/378157/1/__userfiles.soton.ac.uk_Users_slb1_mydesktop_Final%2520ver sion%2520whole%2520PhD.pdf

11 Religious Education
A creative freedom to teach innovatively

Robert Morgan

Critical questions

After you have thought and given your responses to the following questions, it would be worth reading the Commission on Religious Education's report (2018) entitled 'religion and worldviews: a way forward' (notably its recommendations) to see how your thoughts match the aims of this document.

Is Religious Education still valid in your interpretation of today's local, national, and global population?

Do you feel confident as a teacher of Religious Education?

Does Religious Education have a place in your school's timetable?

What are your thoughts on parents'/carers' rights to withdraw children from the opportunity to learn Religious Education?

How would you define what is meant to be 'religiously literate' as we approach the decade of the 2020s in modern England?

Introduction

Religious Education (for it should not be trivialised and called merely RE) is not a national curriculum subject but it must be taught in all community schools as enshrined in the 1988 Education Reform Act. Owing to the secretary of state for education having almost no influence in the subject, the curriculum for Religious Education is to be determined locally by Agreed Syllabus Conferences (Bastide, 2007), formed under Standing Advisory Councils for Religious Education (SACREs) with:

> Every agreed syllabus shall reflect the fact that the religious traditions in Great Britain are in the main Christian whilst taking account of the teaching and practices of the other principal religions represented in Great Britain.
>
> (Great Britain. Education Act, 1996, section 375)

Most community schools will follow the local authority's Agreed Syllabus, which is posted on its website. Schools designated with a religious character (faith schools) will usually follow a syllabus derived from that particular faith background, for example a church diocese, whereas academy schools and free schools will have to comply with the funding agreement between the individual academy trust and the secretary of state (Long and Bolton, 2018).

This chapter is not going to spend too much time as to the purpose of why Religious Education should be taught in a pluralistic society within England (I write England, because of the way that devolution in other parts of the United Kingdom has allowed Religious Education to be designed and taught slightly differently); there are plenty of reasons why that should be (see 'A Curriculum Framework for Religious Education in England' by The Religious Education Council of England and Wales, 2013). That said, however, good Religious Education, which shall be the underpinning rationale for this chapter, can only be achieved if you, as the trainee teacher, understand the importance of the subject:

> All children need to acquire core knowledge and understanding of the beliefs and practices of the religions and worldviews which not only shape their history and culture but which guide their own development. The modern world needs young people who are sufficiently confident in their own beliefs and values that they can respect the religious and cultural differences of others and contribute to a cohesive and compassionate society.
>
> (Gove, cited in The Religious Education Council of England and Wales, 2013: 5).

This chapter will then allow you to consider Religious Education's importance before allowing you, as a trainee practitioner, to confidently prepare and be enthused to teach the subject by exploring innovative and current pedagogical approaches. I will declare here, that within Religious Education, this will come to mean the study of faith, belief, and worldview because everyone will seek to understand their position within the world by using one of these three thought systems.

Principles for pedagogy

This chapter aims to inspire, enthuse, and equip you with the relevant pedagogical skills to teach Religious Education creatively but with a meaningful purpose. The last Ofsted report examining the condition of the subject (Ofsted, 2013) was not wholly complimentary, stating that little had improved since its last 2010 inspection (Ofsted, 2010) in both primary and secondary schools, in terms of low standards, weak teaching, confusion about the purpose of the subject, and gaps in training. The report went on to declare:

> The teaching of RE in primary schools was not good enough because of weaknesses in teachers' understanding of the subject, a lack of emphasis on subject knowledge, poor and fragmented curriculum planning, very weak assessment, ineffective monitoring and teachers' limited access to effective training. The way in which RE was provided in many of the primary schools visited had the isolating effect of the subject from the rest of the curriculum. It led to low-level learning.
>
> (Ofsted, 2013: 5)

Religious Education matters and there is a need to fight for it by evolving your pedagogy and implementing it in your school which is more likely than not to have a curriculum and assessment system that favours subjects, notably mathematics, English, science, and computing (unless you are in a school designated with a religious character). The pedagogy you require will be underpinned and defined by the concept of what is meant and understood by 'good Religious Education'. So, what is this? Maybe the application of the acronym 'SACRED' may be useful:

- Subject knowledge
- Attainment targets
- Creativity
- Relevance
- Empowerment
- Design

Subject knowledge

Teachers' Standard 3 makes the point clearly in that there is an imperative need to 'have a secure subject knowledge of the relevant subject and curriculum areas, address misunder-standings and demonstrate a critical understanding of developments in the subject' (DfE, 2013). This is not surprising but often it may be difficult to acquire sufficient subject knowl-edge in the six world major faiths, other world faiths, other beliefs and worldviews; from ancient faiths such as Hinduism, more modern faiths such as Bahá' í, to newly growing beliefs such as Humanism or ethical veganism. There is no shame in not knowing, only shame in doing nothing about it. Subject knowledge may call for study, even a 'just-in-time' principle but it should be more than that. Subject knowledge will be enhanced by an empathic under-standing of faith and belief. As Ninian Smart wrote:

> To understand religious and secular worldviews and their practical meaning we have to use imagination. We have to enter the lives of those for whom such ideas and actions are important.
>
> (Smart, 1989: 10)

Subject knowledge is not only linked to reading. It must be developed by liaising with associ-ated subject bodies (I shall provide a list later) and preparing to attend subject specific con-ferences as you engage with your professional development.

Attainment targets

The QCA (2004) non-statutory guidance for Religious Education is a worthwhile read that demonstrates Religious Education's necessity and how it can be effectively taught. It raises the importance of Attainment Target 1 (AT 1 - learning about religion) and Attainment 2 (AT 2 - learning from religion).

AT 1 - Learning about religion

- Enquiry into, and investigation of, the nature of religion: beliefs, teachings, and sources, practices and ways of life and forms of expression
- The skills of interpretation, analysis, and explanation
- Knowledge and understanding using specialist vocabulary
- Identifying and developing an understanding of ultimate questions and ethical issues

AT 2 – Learning from religion

- Developing pupils' reflection on and response to, their own experiences and learning about religion
- Developing pupils' skills of application, interpretation, and evaluation of what they learn about religion
- Developing pupils' ability to communicate – particularly in relation to questions of identity and belonging, meaning, purpose, truth, values, and commitments

(QCA, 2004: 34)

If the teaching of Religious Education does not address either/or AT 1 and AT 2 then it could not be considered 'good Religious Education'.

Creativity

Creativity is not new, yet it raises the obvious question to you as the trainee teacher, 'are you creative and do you allow your children to be creative?' Perhaps there are constraints to your creativity, such as a crowded curriculum or a squeezing out of Religious Education from the timetable (which will be discussed later). Reflecting on creativity calls your pedagogy into question, or even the favoured pedagogy in your school, whether that be behaviourist or constructivist attitudes toward teaching and learning. Religious Education is philosophical in nature; it requires the promotion of thought (meta-cognition) and associated articulate language. It needs to inspire and transform children's attitudes as they begin their process of enquiry and assimilation. How might you do that using all the resources, especially available digital media and platforms? Attainment Target 2 provides a starting point in your contemplation of being creative with this subject because it asks you to design learning opportunities for children to 'apply, evaluate and interpret'. Webster (2010) in her book *Creative approaches to teaching primary RE* explores creativity in a cross-curricular fashion through art, dance, drama, and music with a focus on planning and assessment. Her message is clear:

> To develop creativity in children, you need to open up your professional imagination and enable your class to delve into the creative learning process.

(p. 5)

One word of caution! Try not to fall into the trap of the fixed ability misapplication through cross-curricular learning. For example, if you wish children to engage in a written activity (for we should not dismiss writing as a creative engagement) do not allow them to write according to their ability sets as determined by their English lessons. It does not follow that the skills, knowledge, and understanding from one subject would automatically follow in another. This is a subject that promotes critical thinking and enquiry. It calls for you to provide 'thinking time' and to create a mutually respectful classroom in which ideas can be offered, shared, evaluated, and reasoned. McCreery, Palmer and Voiels (2008) give a checklist for planning to consider how thinking skills can be used in a Religious Education lesson:

- Use a stimulus to get an investigation started
- Create the opportunity for asking questions (using what, when, who, why, and how)

- Record the questions
- Discuss where answers might be found (sources of information from the internet, visitors, artefacts, places of worship)
- Allow children to investigate sources
- Discuss the reliability of the source
- Record answers
- Discuss how the various answers fit together
- Identify further questions arising from the questions

(2008: 61)

From this rich source of learning, ensure it is assessed as well as considering how to cater for the next stages of learning during your planning.

Relevance

You are preparing primary-aged children for their future education in the 2020s and for the decade in which they are likely to enter the workplace or global life – which could be in the 2030s decade and obviously beyond. It is impossible to predict what that world will look like then politically, economically, socially, and ecologically, especially when one remembers the Apple smartphone was only invented in 2007. At the time of preparing this book chapter, United Kingdom politicians are in frantic discussions with European Union politicians about the UK withdrawal from the EU27 club (Brexit). There is uncertainty now, so there will be uncertainty in the future. The subject of Religious Education fits perfectly into such a situation. Religious Education's aims beyond learning about faith and belief can include:

- Making informed judgements about religious and moral issues.
- Enriching spiritual experience.
- Searching for meaning, purpose, and a faith [belief or worldview] to live by.
- Explore fundamental questions of life in a religious context.
- Reflect upon own beliefs and values in a positive way.
- Develop empathy with people who hold different beliefs and to respect and value those beliefs.

(Bastide, 2007, p. 21)

As a teacher, aim to teach Religious Education by making it relevant to children in their own locality, using creative and available technologies, using resources and identifying with people and concepts the children will recognise. That child will then develop the skills and understanding as outlined in the two attainment targets. This will hopefully enable the child to be confidently equipped to face the uncertain future in a local, national and a global sense.

Empowerment

Being empowered works for you as the trainee teacher and for the children. It is a matter of having confidence. Confidence for you as a teacher will come from you being equipped with:

Having accurate subject knowledge; being aware of relevant subject-focused associations or having access to quasi-organised teachers' groups (for example, WhatsApp or a Facebook page); by being aware of the two attainment targets as you plan and assess the children's learning; know how to make the subject relevant, engaging and inspiring for children (think Teachers' Standard 1); by making you reflect on your own pedagogy and hopefully by not making you wonder whether 'you will cause offence by getting it wrong'. With this checklist in place you won't! Confidence for the children in their learning will come from their autonomy and from this will be not only good learning but enjoyment too. Christian Schiller (1979) once wrote how creativity and freedom were linked. For him choice came with a power to do so and the restriction of the children's opportunity to choose inhibited growth and freedom. Such a freedom allows for agency to be channelled into producing creative learning. Therefore, as a trainee teacher, have the confidence to empower children in autonomous choices, decision making, organisation, and structure and allow for a flourishing of output. This does, however, call for you to be empowered by your own school.

Design

There is a need to carefully consider the designing of the teaching of Religious Education. This begins from an objective view of the curriculum and how Religious Education fits into a crowded primary curriculum, especially in Year 6. It may be that this is beyond your remit and power as a trainee teacher or a Newly Qualified Teacher/Recently Qualified Teacher, but it is something that should be discussed with the Religious Education subject co-ordinator, or, should you become that person, then you will know what to anticipate. All schools by law must publish the Religious Education syllabus on their websites (as well as the information regarding withdrawal) but a school needs to implement more than just that. Does the syllabus for Religious Education fit and meet the needs of the school's catchment area and surrounding community? Is there an audit of faith adherents, places of worship, or a list of approved visiting speakers? But there are some measures which will be in your control. There will be some time allocated to the study of this subject and here are some points you can reflect on:

- When planning for a Religious Education lesson ask 'where is the most effective place for this lesson to be taught?' Do not assume that it should be the classroom because that is where you always teach or because that is where the tables are! Why do you need tables? If you do not necessarily need to write or draw, then is there a need for tables? Could they be moved, or could the learning be done in the hall, the sports field, or somewhere in the local community? You may rely on subject knowledge to come from a child, parent, or visitor
- How can I include all leaners? Earlier, I drew your attention to the myth of transferring writing skills ability through cross-curricular learning. What works for children with special needs or with English as an additional language can work for all children (the social model of inclusion). If you move beyond the need to always record progress by writing and focus, for example, on developing thinking skills or role play or designing innovative responses to capture progress, then it could give other children a chance to shine. (Remember the dominant form of assessment is in the English language, in the subjects of English and Mathematics, and through the written word!)

I finish here with an extract of the introduction from the Royal Borough of Greenwich's agreed syllabus conference, introducing its new 'faith and belief' content for March 2019. Would aspects from the 'SACRED' approach be evident here?

Religious Education is fundamental in our multicultural and multi-faith society. Therefore, representatives from within the Royal Borough of Greenwich have updated its Agreed Syllabus in order to inform, educate, and enrich the lives of all its learners.

This new syllabus is designed to teach learners to be increasingly literate in their understanding of religions, faith, and belief within knowledge-rich nurseries, schools, and colleges. Teachers will feel confident that their learning programmes can be designed from a document of quality that has been crafted with care and is underpinned by secure subject knowledge.

The syllabus has been designed to be enacted through a creative pedagogy that enables teachers the freedom to meet the needs of critical-thinking learners – whatever their faith and belief. Good Religious Education throughout all 17 wards in the borough will be contemporary, innovative, inclusive, thought-provoking, and challenging. It will deepen understanding, develop skills, and show how all learners can live and learn in a cohesive community.

I am grateful to all who have contributed to this document, to ensure that this Agreed Syllabus will enable pupils and teachers alike to explore and celebrate the ever-growing, rich diversity within the Royal Borough of Greenwich. It will produce confident and mature learners who can explore faiths and beliefs within their community to prepare and equip them for the national and global challenges of the present and the future.

(Royal Borough of Greenwich, 2019)

The following two case studies will hopefully be an attempt to show what is meant by 'good Religious Education' and how it can be taught in a contemporary, engaging, meaningful, and inclusive method. The case itself is bounded by two primary schools within the Royal Borough of Greenwich and are both located in the town of Thamesmead located in South East London: Bishop John Robinson Church of England Primary School and Heronsgate Primary School. This faith school and community school both work in partnership with the University of Greenwich. Thamesmead is a modern town comprising approximately 35,000 inhabitants, with a high percentage of inhabitants of Black African origin, approximately 35%. I conducted a semi-structured interview with each Religious Education subject co-ordinator during February 2019.

Case study: Bishop John Robinson CE Primary is a Church of England School

Bishop John Robinson CE Primary is a Church of England School, which views Religious Education as a core subject and was awarded the RE Quality Mark GOLD Standard in spring 2018 (see http://reqm.org/). The Religious Education lead in this school is the Deputy Headteacher, Jo Richardson. The school's Christian values are taught within Religious Education lessons with their children achieving in line with other core subjects and particularly their SEN children.

So what does Bishop John Robinson do well?

The school concentrates on placing children and the subject at the heart of its curriculum, concentrating on an inclusive approach. There is a focus on needing excellent subject knowledge but that its Christian ethos is used to explore and understand the faiths and beliefs of all children within the school and its community (see Figures 11.1 and 11.2).

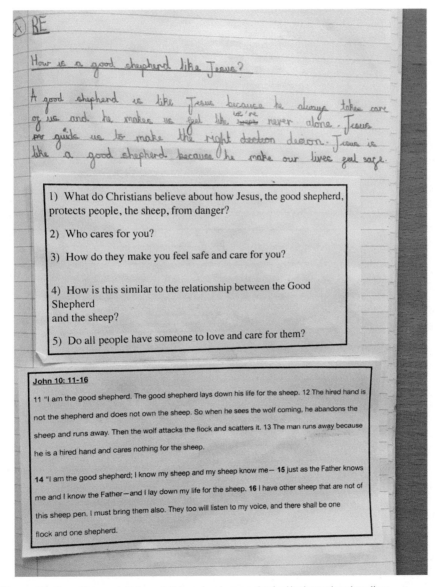

Figure 11.1 Questions enabling children to demonstrate their understanding

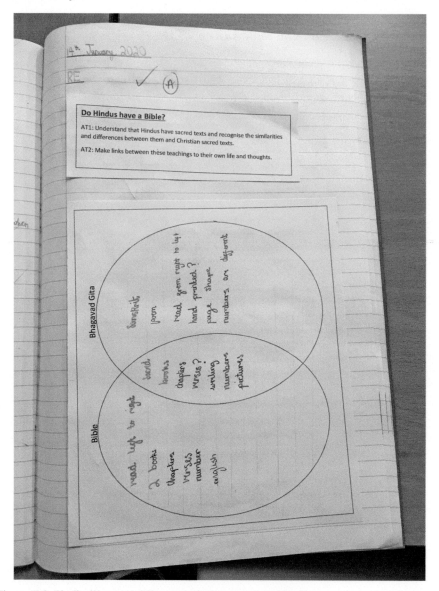

Figure 11.2 Similarities and differences between sacred texts

RE is very, very important in the curriculum I want my children to be rounded. I want my children to be able to understand everyone else. Particularly in a church school … I want my children when they go out of here to understand people; understand faiths; understand why people have different opinions on things; why people might do things differently.

The design of the whole curriculum reflects the centrality of Religious Education. You may think that would be an obvious point for a school of religious character to make but it is manifested in a cross-curricular approach:

so we are very creative with the curriculum, so we will do weeks, we will allow teachers to block areas of the curriculum if needed and RE will be part of that but everyone must build RE into their curriculum. So our staff produce *WOW RE* books which showcases some of their best RE. And also they all have some RE displays in the classrooms ... and all of our hall displays are RE based so that there's a real celebration of work and that the work that they do is meaningful. They are also expected to do a piece of extended writing in RE so that it becomes cross-curricular.

What does good Religious Education look like and how is it defined?

Good RE in our classrooms fits the needs of the children. So good RE meets everyone's needs. One of the things the teachers organise are differentiated packs for children that have very low attainment. There is a focus to ensure that by the end of the unit all children have a good knowledge set of that unit. Importantly there is a focus on Attainment 1 and 2 but with the realisation that Attainment 2 becomes more abstract as the child moves through the year groups. The subject receives a high profile in the school. All of the staff are on a post-graduate qualification in order to teach RE which becomes essential for the teachers to be able to use a range of teaching techniques that promotes learning which subsequently becomes monitored and moderated in the same way as other subjects.

Examples

Underlying the inclusivity for all learners of the subject the school Religious Education is brought to life by the fact that teachers are empowered to be creative; which enables the staff to be committed. In one Religious Education learning walk it was observed that: One class was doing Drama, another class had out some artefacts, exploring Passover and looking at the Seder Plate, while another still was researching a unit on local faiths using iPads. Year 5 was studying an Islamic naming ceremony and one of the parents, who recently had a baby, came in to talk about her experience. Externally, all of the classes go on an educational visit every year. Recent visits in the previous year included: A visit to the synagogue; a Jewish museum; Key Stage 1's unit on baptism allowed them to baptise a teddy bear at the local church; a visit to the mosque; and a trip to the Victoria and Albert Museum to look at Islamic art.

How does the school know the teaching of Religious Education is effective?

Owing to the subject being treated equally within the curriculum there is still a focus on 'data drops' with data analysis allowing for intervention measures to be effected. Children reveal positive comments during monitoring and the appreciation of the child's voice matters. Children enjoy learning about different people and different faiths and how people live. The focus dwells on the similarities of people's faiths and beliefs. For example, when Year 5 studied Islam, in the past children would say:

'we do this and he does that', now it's very much more 'this is what people of the Christian faith do and this what people of the Muslim faith do and this is a very similar process, we learn about the Christian value of forgiveness but in the story we had just seen through Islam they also learn about the value of forgiveness'.

It is the creativity of the teaching whereby teachers are planning for the most creative and engaging ways to put it across to the children which leads to them growing in confidence:

I think they used to feel that maybe they didn't always want to share because they were different whereas, as I say, whilst we were celebrating similarities that's helped to encourage everyone to share because we look at things that people do that are similar but obviously they are differences within that but there are reasons for it, it allows discussion people to sort of air their views.

Case study: Heronsgate Primary School

Heronsgate Primary School is a community school that has the following 11 values infused in its curriculum: Co-operation, responsibility freedom, democracy, peace, respect, love, tolerance, honesty, simplicity, and humility. The Religious Education lead in this school is specialist teacher, Renu Partap.

So what does Heronsgate do well?

The school has a clear focus on the need for teacher to acquire subject knowledge and this will enable them to become confident practitioners within the subject. If teachers are empowered, it is felt they can take ownership of the planning and assessing which will raise the profile of Religious Education in the school which will then have an impact on children's learning:

We give RE at least as much importance as the creative curriculum: History or Geography so the teachers will have to take ownership of at least planning their RE even if it is given to somebody else to teach. So teachers know what their children are learning, so planning is always done by the teachers ... I think RE is really crucial in development of children's skills in not only faith-related but it is about linking it to PSHE their development.

The subject's importance is about children learning the knowledge about a particular faith and then making links to their own experience. The subject is brought alive by not just doing worksheets but with a more practical purpose: Handling artefacts, listening to visitors, visiting places of worship, and plenty of discussion – there are lots of talk partners used in the lessons. Technology is used to capture children' attention and to do research especially in Year 6, for example, when the students were learning about faiths in community. The school endeavours to link everything that is in Religious Education to other curriculum areas. For example, at the end of a topic or unit of work one time in an English lesson is devoted to the writing for Religious Education learning. Therefore, children get that opportunity to reflect upon what they have learnt in that unit.

What does good Religious Education look like and how is it defined?

All children have equal access to RE except the children who are withdrawn. Religious Education is about asking or provoking challenging questions about the ultimate meaning and the purpose of life. The aim here is to learn about beliefs and values of major religions and non-religious worlds, to cater for everybody – not just people who believe in God. There is a need to contribute to moral and spiritual development. The objective is to develop a sense of faith/belief values in children by linking it to the school's values. There is more of a focus on the similarities, not ignoring the differences, but a study of the similarities. The common values of faiths and beliefs are explored before the differences. For example, religions have festivals, they celebrate things, but how are they different?

Examples

Incorporating lots of visitors from different faiths and lots of visits. For example, the year 4 children visited St Paul's cathedral in London. A Buddhist representative came in talk about children's learning rather than being addressed by a PowerPoint detailing how Buddhists live their life. It is more relevant and engaging when somebody visits children in their classroom and tells them 'I'm a Buddhist that's how I live my life'. The school has bought many artefacts from different faiths, a good collection that children can actually touch and engage in a kinaesthetic way which brings learning to life. The point made by Heronsgate is that confident teachers who have excellent subject knowledge will be able to inspire children to want to learn more and increase the autonomy within children's learning.

> Having teachers who are confident in teaching RE in front of the class ... is inspiring and thinking about activities outside of the box I would say [is necessary] rather than just writing in a book, writing something in thought bubble ... So thinking about creative way of recording I think [is] quite inspiring for the children. Talking to each other, maybe visiting ... if one class has leant about one religion they can go and perform in assembly then [the] whole school can learn about that ... I think that's inspiring ... then children will [realize] 'I think I will need to go and find something more about it'.

Autonomous learning is valued at this school by giving children opportunities to research and having the resources to do so at school and at home. It is not being afraid to give the children a 'what if' question because Religious Education does lend itself to a philosophical and wonder-based learning. That will enable a teacher to incorporate the children's finding into the next lesson and be ready to encounter inspired children.

How does the school know the teaching of Religious Education is effective?

This is judged by conducting a search for 'pupil voice' through a questionnaire or talking to two or three children from each class to talk about their learning. One of the children said, for example: 'I like RE because I like to know what other people believe. This time we are learning about losing someone, this means I am able to relate to my own experience like when my grandpa died'. This is an indication that what is being learnt in Religious Education is helping children to understand themselves and others. There is rigorous assessment of understanding ahead of the next steps in learning to keep the focus alive.

Through concentrating on good subject knowledge the outcome should be how it is relating to the child's real life and for children who live in communities where people from different faiths, different communities are. It needs to be connected to other subjects because the children get the most of it because of its increased relevance. Effectiveness is also judged by the drive to teach Religious Education from the teachers. The subject's value is recognised because it is hardly given to PPA cover. The subject co-ordinator supports teachers' planning and delivers staff meetings to ensure that teachers do not feel that they don't know something about a particular aspect of the subject. Team-teaching is a pedagogical technique employed team-taught with teachers who are less confident to give them that confidence. Confidence matters and the school has dealt with developing this when teachers say:

> 'I don't know enough, I might say something wrong' and 'Am I allowed to say this?' They worry too much! But having someone in school who can alleviate their fears about that and go through step-by-step and say 'OK you can say this, you have nothing worry about' or 'I can come and do that for you' let's say and then I think then that really helps. I'm really proud that our staff here ... most of them, I would say, are now confident in teaching RE.

That issue of confidence is linked to the need for subject knowledge to prevail. Knowledge needs to be taught – regardless! A topic needs to be taught with knowledge in place in order for Attainment Targets 1 and 2 to be realised.

Questions

- After reading these two case studies can you identify aspects of the 'SACRED' approach in either school?
- How does each school define 'Good Religious Education'?
- How are teachers prepared to teach Religious Education in each school?
- How is Religious Education innovative in each school?
- How is Religious Education assessed in each school?
- How can children prepared to be religiously literate and articulate in each school?

These two case studies offer insights into good and effective practice for the planning, teaching, and assessing of Religious Education. Both schools value the subject and have designed for it to receive a high prominence with each school's curriculum. Inclusion matters in that all children are catered and planned for. The values of Religious Education are clearly presented to the children through innovative and creative learning opportunities. Both case studies emphasise the necessity of subject knowledge, empowered teachers, and engaged children who can articulate the key learning from studying the subject and an importance on assessment. Religious Education for both schools is studied by children who are allowed to think and discuss.

Conclusion

This chapter has been written to enthuse and confidently prepare you to teach Religious Education to primary-aged children who will need to evaluate a local, national and global picture. Exploring the concept of 'SACRED' and seeing elements of it within the two chosen case studies will inspire you to teach this fascinating subject. In order to prepare to enjoy teaching this wonderful subject:

- Remember there are not necessarily any right or wrong answers; it is a subject of faith/belief-based reason. That is where confidence fits the picture
- Good Religious Education teachers are prepared and innovative and supported by senior leaders and a school that values the rightful place of this subject
- When supported, good Religious Education teachers will design their own interpretation of what is meant by 'good Religious Education' by having the freedom and empowerment to plan, teach, and assess the subject to produce meaningful outcomes that children are easily able to articulate in whatever medium suits their desired learning and to fit their learning need
- Such learning is then to be celebrated and shared inside and outside the school, making full use of community relationships allowing the child to grow up and make their presence in the future world – whatever that may be
- Use the pedagogical freedom to be creative and innovative. Explore the world with the children

Important subject-based associations

AREIAC	The Association of Religious Education Inspectors, Advisers and Consultants	http://www.areiac.org.uk/
AULRE	Association of University Lecturers in Religion and Education	http://aulre.org/
Culham St Gabriel's	Dedicated to educational work in support of Religious Education (RE).	https://www.cstg.org.uk/about-us/
NASACRE	National Association of Standing Advisory Councils on Religious Education	http://www.nasacre.org.uk/
NATRE	National Association of Teachers of Religious Education	https://www.natre.org.uk/
RE: Online	Supporting school-based teachers of Religious Education	http://www.reonline.org.uk/
RE Today Services	Working nationally and internationally to support Religious Education in schools	https://www.retoday.org.uk/
The Interfaith Network	Advancing public knowledge and mutual understanding of the teachings, traditions and practices of the different faith communities in Britain	http://www.interfaith.org.uk/

Recommended reading

Bastide, D. (2007) *Teaching Religious Education 4–11*. 2nd ed. Abingdon: Routledge.

Also your own 'SACRE' agreed syllabus.

References

Bastide, D. (2007) *Teaching Religious Education 4–11*. 2nd ed. Abingdon: Routledge.

Commission on Religious Education (2018) *Religion and Worldviews: The Way Forward. A National Plan for RE*. Religious Education Council of England & Wales. [Online] Available at: https://www.commissiononre.org.uk/wp-content/uploads/2018/09/Final-Report-of-the-Commission-on-RE.pdf   [Accessed: 23 February 2019].

Department for Education (2013) Teachers' Standards. [Online]. Available at: https://assets.publishing.service.gov.uk/government/uploads/system/uploads/attachment_data/file/665520/Teachers__Standards.pdf [Accessed: 23 February 2019].

Great Britain. *Education Act 1996: Elizabeth II. Chapter 3 (1996) Agreed Syllabuses, Section 375*. London: The Stationery Office.

Long, R. and Bolton, P. (2018) *Faith Schools in England: FAQs* (BRIEFING PAPER Number 06972, 6 June 2018) House of Commons Library. [Online] Available at: file:///C:/Users/mr90/Downloads/SN06972%20(1).pdf

McCreery, E., Palmer, S. and Voiels, V. (2008) *Teaching Religious Education*. Exeter: Learning Matters.

OfSTED (2010) *Transforming Religious Education*. OfSTED. [Online] Available at: https://webarchive.nationalarchives.gov.uk/20141107041843/http://www.ofsted.gov.uk/resources/transforming-religious-education [Accessed: 23 February 2019].

OfSTED (2013) *Religious Education: Realising the Potential*. OfSTED. [Online] Available at: https://assets.publishing.service.gov.uk/government/uploads/system/uploads/attachment_data/file/413157/Religious_education_-_realising_the_potential.pdf [Accessed: 23 February 2019].

Qualifications and Curriculum Authority (2004) *Religious Education: The Non-statutory National Framework*. [Online] Available at: https://webarchive.nationalarchives.gov.uk/20090608220227/http://www.qca.org.uk/libraryAssets/media/9817_re_national_framework_04.pdf   [Accessed: 23 February 2019].

Royal Borough of Greenwich (2019) *Agreed Syllabus Conference*. (March 2019).

Schiller, C. (1979) *Christian Schiller in His Own Words*. National Association of Primary Education. London: AC Black.

Smart, N. (1989) *The World's Religions*. Cambridge: Cambridge University Press.

The Religious Education Council of England and Wales (2013) *A Curriculum Framework for Religious Education in England*. The Religious Education Council of England and Wales. [Online] Available at: http://resubjectreview.recouncil.org.uk/media/file/RE_Review:Summary.pdf [Accessed 23 February 2019].

Webster, M. (2010) *Creative Approaches to Teaching Primary RE*. Harlow: Pearson Education Ltd.

Part 2

Wider issues and debates

12 Relationships and Sex Education

Richard Woolley and Sacha Mason

Critical questions

What kinds of relationships should children be taught about in schools?

How can family relationships be discussed without making any children feel different or that their family isn't 'normal'?

Should Sex Education be included in the primary school curriculum, and if so, should it be more than the physical changes experienced at puberty or the mechanics of sex? Should the emotional and enjoyable aspects of sex be indicated?

How can relationships and sex be discussed in a way that is inclusive of children's families and their own developing identities?

Does early Sex Education have a positive or negative impact on children's behaviours?

How might your own experience of relationships, including sexual relationships, affect your ability and willingness to discuss information and issues with children? What strategies or sources might you draw on to gain support?

Introduction

Sex and Relationship Education has been an optional part of the curriculum in primary schools for many years. At the start of this millennium guidelines were introduced to support its implementation, although they were never statutory (DfEE, 2000). It has always been our contention that the subject should be named Relationships and Sex Education (RSE), we believe this for three main reasons:

- Relationships should come first in the curriculum title, because developing healthy relationships is a fundamental part of human development, and ideally should precede sex
- Relationships should be plural in the title, so that myriad engagements with others including strangers, acquaintances, friends, and family can be explored

- Sex Education should be included within the curriculum in primary schools so that children learn about the changes associated with puberty before they experience them, and they understand why such changes occur rather than merely being taught the mechanics

Relationships Education is statutory in primary schools in England from the autumn term of 2020. Its introduction is in a context where media products have never been more freely available to the general population, including soap operas where diverse and sometimes violent relationships are shown; social media and electronic devices provide opportunities for cyber bullying, sexual exploitation of children, and young people and potentially easy access to pornographic materials; and magazines and websites aimed at children and young people encouraging them to aspire to being 'teenagers' at a younger age.

This context makes equipping children for safe, respectful, and positive interactions with others essential in order that they develop into confident and healthy individuals with positive self-esteem and sense of self-worth. Relationships Education thus has the potential to impact all areas of their lives and well-being, as the new statutory guidance notes:

> Everyone faces difficult situations in their lives. These subjects can support young people to develop resilience, to know how and when to ask for help, and to know where to access support.
>
> (DfE, 2019: 8)

A fundamental aim of the new curriculum for Relationships Education in England is on:

> teaching the fundamental building blocks and characteristics of positive relationships, with particular reference to friendships, family relationships, and relationships with other children and with adults.
>
> (DfE, 2019: 19)

It seeks to achieve this by focusing on five key areas (DfE, 2019: 20–22):

- Families and people who care for me
- Caring friendships
- Respectful relationships
- Online relationships
- Being safe

Principles for pedagogy

This chapter seeks to explore and discuss the why, how, and what of the pedagogical approach we advocate for the teaching of Relationships Education in primary schools. It is important to note that whilst Relationships Education is to be made statutory in 2020 in primary schools and Relationships and Sex Education in the secondary phase of schooling, those primary schools who wish to include Sex Education as part of their curriculum may do so. We are committed to all primary schools making RSE a core aspect of their provision. In terms of *why* this should be the case, we consider five key principles for RSE as fundamental:

1. Children of all ages have a right to information about matters that affect them:

    > The right to education includes the right to sexual education, which is both a human right in itself and an indispensable means of realising other human rights, such as the right to health, the right to information and sexual and reproductive rights.
    >
    > (UN General Assembly, 2010)

2. The values that are taught in schools need to be reflected in all areas of the curriculum, both explicitly and intrinsically. RSE is a values-based aspect of the curriculum and school teaching teams need to recognise those that are important to them. These may be subjective and objective and linked to attitudes and behaviours which need to be acknowledged, examined, and on some occasions challenged. Teams need to understand and agree the values that collectively guide them as a strong system of beliefs that underpins their approach.
3. Children are deeply interested in sexual matters (Halstead and Reiss, 2003).
4. Children are active learners and are agentic in their capacity to understand their world.
5. Children should be afforded access to a broad and balanced RSE curriculum that acknowledges and meets their needs to be able to have healthy, fulfilling, and respectful relationships.

To explore *how* this subject may be approached, we have included two case studies; one relevant for Key Stage 1 (children aged 5-7 years) and the other for Key Stage 2 (children aged 7-11 years). These have been selected to illustrate some of the teaching approaches that can be adopted in teaching a Relationships Education and RSE curriculum. The activities should form aspects of a whole school approach that considers a spiral curriculum; from the Reception class to Year 6, so that children have opportunities to build their knowledge and understanding. The content of the curriculum needs to be relevant, differentiated to children's needs, and appropriate to their stage of development and maturity. Key considerations are embedded within these case studies in how children and parents/carers are consulted. Children's views should be sought and inform lesson plans and teaching through assessment of prior knowledge. In turn, high quality RSE depends on a partnership between home and school.

Meeting the needs of children

The government has made clear that Relationships Education has been made compulsory in all primary schools from 2020 in order to meet the needs of children and young people who are 'growing up in an increasingly complex world and living their lives seamlessly on and offline' (DfE, 2019: 4). Its intention is to help them live healthy and safe lives. There is acknowledgement that for some people making the subject compulsory, and the nature of some of its subject matter, will be contentious leading to a need for content to be age- and stage-appropriate and for it to be 'taught sensitively and inclusively, with respect to the backgrounds and beliefs of pupils and parents' (DfE, 2019: 4). In the primary phase of education this will involve:

- A focus on strong and positive relationships
- Appreciation of both family and friendships
- Understanding of relationships both on and offline
- Being able to know how to get help if problems arise, in order to support positive mental health
- Developing children's resilience and well-being
- Fostering self-belief so that children can achieve goals, including distant goals
- Developing personal attributes 'including kindness, integrity, generosity, and honesty' (DfE, 2019: 5)

The latter point is particularly interesting. In earlier versions of the guidance it included reference to self-sacrifice, which was later omitted. We prefer the concept of self-respect and would add this to the list of personal attributes in the guidance.

Parents and carers continue to have the right to withdraw their child from Sex Education, but not from Relationships Education (DfE, 2019). All schools must have a written policy for Relationships Education, developed in consultation with parents and carers: 'Schools should ensure that the policy meets the needs of pupils and parents and reflects the community they serve' (DfE, 2019: 11). This is an interesting requirement, and opens up the possibility of there being a tension between the needs and views of children, their parents, and the community. The policy document for Relationships Education should:

- Define Relationships Education
- Set out subject content
- Outline how it will be taught and by whom
- Describe how it will be monitored and evaluated
- Indicate why parents do not have a right to withdraw their child
- Identify a date for reviewing the policy

Statutory guidance includes a reminder that religions and beliefs are protected characteristics under the Equality Act (Legislation.gov.uk, 2010) and as such must be respected when developing the policy. That said, within religions there are diverse views about relationships (e.g. divorce, same-sex partnerships, the role of marriage) and as such there needs to be an understanding that there is no single view representative of any particular religious faith. Similarly, sexual orientation, sex and gender reassignment are protected characteristics under the Act, and will also need to be afforded respect.

The 21st century context

The ever-changing context of the 21st century, each child is worthy of consideration when thinking about an RSE curriculum. In many homes, children have access to a range of different sources of information via the media which is available 24/7 in various forms such as television, social media, and the internet. This means that unlike any other generation, children today have exposure to often unregulated or vetted information and imagery. Equally, older siblings may openly discuss certain topics that they engage with via the media around the home that younger children may hear. Family relationships and structures have also changed over the last 30 years and more children now live with single parents, in re-constituted family structures where they may not live with both their biological parents but with step parents and siblings, or in families with same-sex parents. This is of critical importance in understanding the prior knowledge that children bring into the school setting to inform planning and teaching. Schools can provide an essential role in providing factually accurate information as part of the RSE curriculum and one that is inclusive of all difference to discuss, for example, relationships, family structures, and sexualities relevant to the children's worlds in school, home, and beyond.

Preparing for emotional, physical, and social changes

The current average age for a girl to have her first period is at 12.9 years (Kelly, Zilanawala, Sacker, Hiatt and Viner, 2016). This means that many children experience significant body changes during their years in primary school. Therefore if children are to be prepared for the emotional, physical, and social changes that are associated with puberty, it is essential that discussions around what children can expect and how they might feel in order to learn to manage these are necessary well before these occur to avoid any 'mystery, confusion, embarrassment and shame' (Brook, PSHE Association, and SEF, 2014). Any changes in puberty should be normalised, openly discussed, and prepared for. We also contend that it is both positive and healthy for children to understand the changes experienced by each other: In other words, for RSE to be provided for all children rather than in gender-specific groupings. This should help to remove some of the mystique created by segregated learning and ideally will lead to greater understanding and empathy between genders.

Strategies to support effective RSE

A range of strategies can be used to seek prior knowledge and understandings to inform an RE and RSE curriculum:

- The use of picture books can stimulate discussion, in whole class or smaller group work about the complexities of interpersonal relationships. Story books offer a range of diverse opportunities to share with children. For example, traditional fairy tales such as Cinderella can stimulate conversations with children in Key Stage 1 about stepfamilies and the complexities of relationships. The unkind treatment of Cinderella by her stepmother and stepsisters may allow for discussion about why these behaviours, albeit in a fictional story, occur – and equally about why Cinderella does not feel able to challenge their behaviours. Role play may be used to present alternative ways of behaving to illustrate how children, particularly girls, may be empowered to express their feelings and views. The reframing of traditional tales can be undertaken with a more contemporary relationship dynamic

- A questions box can provide an ideal opportunity for Key Stage 2 children where an open forum for discussion based on these questions can be provided, whether in small or whole class groupings. This strategy may also allow for preparation time for the teacher to read the questions in advance. For example, a child may pose a question that asks how two dads or two mums can make a child
- Examples that the children bring with them to school – for example, local or national incidents or events may happen (such as a Royal wedding), a new baby in a family, the death of someone famous or a family pet, friendship upsets between members of the class – can all provide rich discussion points about communication, love, families, care, pleasure, and loss

These suggestions are not exhaustive and teachers can utilise many different opportunities for discussion beyond these.

Inclusive Relationships Education

Relationships Education must be inclusive, not only to meet the requirements of the Equality Act (Legislation.gov.uk, 2010) in England, but also to represent diversity within society and appreciate difference (whether seen or unseen) within a school. Hellen (2009: 88) contends that 'the majority of transgendered people were aware that they were transgendered well before puberty' whilst sexual orientation is felt more strongly after the onset of puberty. Thus, there may be children in our classrooms who are questioning their gender identity, and some who have awareness of their sexual orientation. RSE should acknowledge such diversities in how people identify can provide positive messages and role models, modelling the celebration of difference to all children however they identify.

Case study

Rebecca has been exploring different kinds of relationships with her class of Year 2 children (aged 6–7 years). Using a Taxonomy of Relationships (Table 12.1), the children have considered a broad range of relationships – from those with strangers to best friends. In the most recent lesson the discussion has focused on what makes a great best friend and the children have drawn attributes to highlight the personal traits and characteristics they associate with the concept.

Rebecca explains:

Jason drew the outline of a person, and around it added illustrations to show he felt a best friend should be kind, friendly, always share, help when you are in trouble, make you feel happy, and play both at school and at the weekends. He wanted a best friend who shared his interest in trains and railways as he loves to find out facts about locomotives of all different types. Sarah drew two friends, stating that: 'A good friend is for playing with. Making sure you don't be alone' as is shown in Figure 12.1.

Table 12.1 Taxonomy of Relationships

Myself	A healthy relationship with oneself is essential for all other relationships to function effectively. This is essential for positive self-esteem and sense of self-worth.
Special friend	A person to whom we commit at a deeper level, sometimes indicating this through a ceremony or legally binding act.
Best friends	Someone we might confide in and spend quality time with.
Friends	People we choose to spend time with, and with whom we have common interests, socialise with or engage in shared activities.
Family members	Those with whom we live or who we share some biological connection, and those related to these people.
People who help	Those we can turn to for help in a difficult situation; people we can usually trust because of their particular role in society.
Acquaintances	Those we know of or meet occasionally.
Strangers	People we don't know.

Source: Adapted from Mason and Woolley, 2019.

Figure 12.1 Children identifying what makes a good friend

Mandy drew a cloud and around it placed different kinds of weather. She explained that a best friend should be there to help you when you are feeling sad (when it is raining), should be good fun and enjoy playing (when the sun shines), can help you feel better when you feel all alone (when it is snowing), and can help to calm you down when you are angry (when the thunder and lightning come). She drew the different types of weather around the cloud and explained her thoughts verbally: 'A best friend should stick with you whatever happens' she explained, 'even though it will not always be easy to do'.

Reflecting on Rebecca's description of the views of Jason, Sarah and Sharon consider:

- How this activity might help the children to appreciate friendships, including close friendships.
- Whether the notion of a 'best' friend is helpful, and how it might suggest the need to have one more special friend than others.
- How a child who finds interaction with others difficult might engage with the activity and whether it might be adapted to meet their particular needs.
- Could the activity be structured in other ways, so that those who find representing their ideas in visual form difficult can access it more easily?
- How your own view of friendship, including the notion of having a best friend, might impact on the way in which you would facilitate this discussion.
- Is Sarah's drawing (Figure 12.1) indicative of her stage of development, or her perception of ideal body image?

The framework provided through the taxonomy (Table 12.1) provides a continuum of relationships to help structure discussion. Importantly, it includes the relationship with oneself, as we suggest a positive self-view and sense of self-worth are essential in order to have the confidence to appreciate and value difference in others. This is reinforced by the revised Statutory Guidance in England, which states that Relationships Education is most effective when set in the context of:

> deliberate cultivation of character traits and positive personal attributes, (sometimes referred to as 'virtues') in the individual. In a school wide context which encourages the development and practice of resilience and other attributes, this includes character traits such as helping pupils to believe they can achieve, persevere with tasks, work towards long-term rewards and continue despite setbacks.
>
> *(DfE, 2019: 20)*

Research focus

In order to meet the five key principles for RSE that we argue for, when talking about designing and teaching this aspect of the curriculum, there is a need to be brave as a whole school team. Mason (2010) draws on research findings undertaken in two primary schools. This study is a comparative multi-method investigation of the provision of Sex and Relationship Education (SRE, as it was then called) in the two schools. It involved a documentary analysis of the school SRE policies, observations of the taught sessions, interviews with the teachers delivering the sessions and of the PSHE coordinators in each school, along with a draw and write session with the Year 5 and 6 pupils where the children were asked what they understood to be the changes that happen during puberty. The draw and write activity provided the children with opportunities to share their understandings of puberty by drawing or writing a non-gendered outline of a person. The draw and write activity was then repeated following the taught input as part of the SRE curriculum and this allowed for a comparison between the before and after. In this way the activity provided evidence of prior learning alongside an assessment of learning at the end. Alongside the draw and write activity, the class teacher was asked by the researcher to pose questions to the children which the children could draw or write responses to. One of the questions asked was 'Can you write down or draw how someone might know when they are ready to have sex and a relationship with someone?' (Mason, 2010: 165). These questions elicited some insight into the how children aged 10–11 viewed the world of relationships. Responses focussed on being ready both emotionally and physically, being old enough, and being in love. One particular response stated 'when they have left home and have a driving licence!' These data provide rich (and often charming) evidence for adults to appreciate the capacity of primary aged children to make sense of their world and the relationships that surround them. It also supports our underpinning principles for a comprehensive RSE curriculum within primary schools.

Children need to be viewed as agents in their own learning who have the capabilities to understand and make sense of experiences both inside and outside of school regarding complex interpersonal relationships. A critical role for the school and home is to respond to these understandings; to hear and act on them. In acting on them, we afford children the right to accurate legal and biological information that enables clarity where interpretations have become muddled. This may apply to the child whose understanding about being ready to have sex and a relationship is dependent on having a driving licence!

Key reading

A key source that supports thinking and discussion about the RSE curriculum is *Fifteen Domains of Healthy Sexual Development* (developed by the RSE Hub from McKee et al., 2010). The *Fifteen Domains* align with the key principles identified in this chapter and provide a clear overview of the breadth of content, starting within the primary phase of education, which can frame the design of a relevant RSE curriculum:

- Respect and understanding of consent
- Understanding of anatomy, physiology, dysfunction, fertility, and sexual response
- Ability to maintain safety (legally, physically, and emotionally)
- Understand how to achieve, maintain, and negotiate healthy relationships with peers, family, partners, and the wider community
- Openness to exploring sexuality, gaining knowledge, and asking for help as part of life-long learning
- Celebrate sexuality, pleasure, and the joy of sex and healthy relationships
- Understands own values/beliefs and how they impact on decision-making and behaviour
- Ability to comprehend, establish, and respect boundaries

- Build resilience to be able to manage any unwanted outcomes
- Developing personal skills and an understanding of agency
- Having an awareness of the diversity of sexual behaviour throughout the lifespan
- Appreciation of the diversity of sexual orientations and gender identities
- Understanding of varying gender roles in culture and societies
- Applying critical analysis to media representations
- Developing a positive attitude to their own concept of self

In order for these to be differentiated appropriately, we have divided them into relevant content across the primary school key stages (see Table 12.2) and mapped to the themes of content identified in the statutory guidance document of 2019. The mapping of these together allows for an overview of how the *Fifteen Domains* (SRE Hub, undated) are embedded within the themes across all the primary school phases and the relevant content specifically for KS2.

The government has recommended that all primary schools should have a Sex Education programme, although they can choose not to, and this should be 'tailored to the age and the physical and emotional maturity of the pupils' (DfE, 2019: 23) taught through a whole school approach (DfE, 2019: 39). This programme should complement other school approaches for behaviour, inclusion, bullying, safeguarding, and promote respect for equality and diversity.

Table 12.2 Mapping the *Fifteen Domains* to Key Themes in RSE

DfE (2019: 20-22)	*15 Domains (RSE Hub, undated)*
Families and people who care for me Caring friendships	Understanding of varying gender roles in culture and societies Developing a positive attitude to their own concept of self Understands own values/beliefs and how they impact on decision-making and behaviour Developing personal skills: Developing an understanding of agency Understand how to achieve, maintain, and negotiate healthy relationships with peers, family, partners and the wider community Ability to comprehend, establish and respect boundaries Respect and understanding of consent For KS2 specifically
Respectful relationships	Openness to exploring sexuality, gaining knowledge and asking for help as part of life–long learning Celebrate sexuality, pleasure and the joy of sex and healthy relationships Understanding of anatomy, physiology, dysfunction, fertility and sexual response Having an awareness of the diversity of sexual behaviour throughout the lifespan Appreciation of the diversity of sexual orientations and gender identities
Online relationships Being safe	Build resilience to be able to manage any unwanted outcomes Ability to maintain safety (legally, physically and emotionally) Applying critical analysis to media representations

The statutory guidance (DfE, 2019: 19) indicates that:

> Families of many forms provide a nurturing environment for children. (Families can include for example, single parent families, LGBT parents, families headed by grandparents, adoptive parents, foster parents/carers amongst other structures.) Care needs to be taken to ensure that there is no stigmatisation of children based on their home circumstances and needs, to reflect sensitively that some children may have a different structure of support around them; e.g. looked after children or young carers.

A further key resource to support such an inclusive approach is the second edition of the *Family Diversities Reading Resource* (Morris and Woolley, 2017) which provides an array of high-quality picture books appropriate for use with children in the primary phase of education, illustrating a wide variety of models of family life. This is freely available online.

Case study

The second case study in this chapter focuses on Key Stage 2 and discusses the approach a teacher, Jeevan, took with a Year 3 class in the final summer term (see Figure 12.2). The children had been revisiting content covered in Year 2 where the biological names for different external body parts had been discussed as part of the school RSE scheme of work. Jeevan's Year 2 colleague had asked the children, in mixed ability groups, to name the different body parts specific to males and females in as many ways that they could. The children had identified a range of 'family' names for these parts of their body along with some more biological terms. Jeevan revisited the biological terms (for example breasts, testicles, vulva, penis, vagina) with the class and then asked the children, using a non-gendered outline of a person, to draw or write the changes that the children knew happened in puberty. The children's prior knowledge from Year 2 learning (as discussed earlier) was clearly visible and Jeevan was able to build on these understandings in further lessons to teach more fully the emotional and physical changes that different genders experience during puberty.

Observing the lesson we saw that groups were very engaged with the activity and Jeevan and the class teaching assistant moved from group to group to speak to the children. Jeevan noticed that children in one of the groups were giggling. Jeevan had taught a session like this in the previous academic year and recognised that children often giggle with each other initially, although this does soon settle once they realise that the teacher acknowledges this very normal response. He asked the class to stop and then took a moment to remind the class of this:

> Thank you everyone, I can see some really interesting work going on in your groups. I wanted to just remind you all that sometimes we feel a bit uncomfortable, or strange, thinking about these very personal and private parts of our body and this feeling makes us want to giggle because perhaps we feel a bit embarrassed. This is very normal and we are not going to worry about that as along as it is not laughing or giggling about anyone else in the group as that would not be kind, would it?

The class returned to its work. The strategy of setting ground rules and acknowledging the feelings that the class may have is an effective way to open up discussion about

Figure 12.2 Children engaging in the Draw and Write activity

how children feel and normalises these responses. Jeevan was able to analyse the work that the children had done and to build on where any misunderstandings were evident and to extend the children's knowledge.

The differences in the changes for boys and girls are important for all children to learn about, for example menstruation and the use and management of sanitary protection. Jeevan expressed his concern regarding the planned session to the female class teaching assistant, Molly. His worry was regarding talking to the class about the use of sanitary protection as he felt it would be more authentic to be discussed with the children by a female. Molly felt very comfortable doing this and prepared for the session by purchasing a range of different products such as sanitary towels of all different sizes, the various tampons available, sanitary product bags, and holders. She also checked where the sanitary disposal bins were in the school toilets so that she could direct the children to them.

Jeevan and Molly then devised a series of lessons that discussed the internal body parts for men and women. Following the lesson where the class were taught about the reproductive organs for women, Molly talked to the children about periods and how the girls might manage sanitary protection. Some of the girls said that they had seen tampons before because their mums use them but they were not quite sure how they were to be used and why. Molly was able to talk through all the emotional and physical changes during menstruation such as feeling tearful, angry, or sad. She was also able to explain how the body produces chemicals to make the process of menstruation happen and that these cause, for some, difficult emotions. Molly was clear to point out that in understanding that this may be a reason for some girls feeling different on different days, that boys can be sensitive to how the girls may be feeling. During the lesson, one of the girls asked how often Molly needs to change her sanitary towels when she has her period. This question may pose some difficulties for teachers during where children may venture into more personal arenas of a teacher's life. Typically a distancing technique can be used. Molly replied:

> That's a really good question and the answer is that it is very individual to the person. Some women's menstrual flow is more heavy than others. What many women do is check whether they need to change their sanitary towel when they use the toilet so it is a good idea to take them with you when you go. You might want to use one of the special cases or have a little bag, or to put a spare towel in your pocket of your school skirt. When girls first start their periods they sometimes find it difficult to know as it is all new to them and the way they might feel more comfortable is to change regularly for the first few periods to feel secure. Sometimes girls bring a spare pair of pants and tights in their PE bags, just in case they don't quite get things right to start with. If any of you find that you have forgotten anything, then you can always come and talk to me or one of the other teachers for help if you need it. You really don't need to feel worried about this as we really understand and want to help you.

In responding in this way, Molly has not shared anything about herself although she has given a full answer to the question. The normalising of body changes and ensuring that children have an 'open door' access to trustworthy information and practical support is essential. Much of this information given to the child by Molly will be part of many lessons of this kind in schools across the world and its inclusion as part of this chapter is to either reaffirm or offer insight into an approach that can support teachers in RSE lessons. The children were given an individual home-school folder where they could take home the activity they had done in class. This supports dialogue between the child and parents/carers, if both are willing, about the issues covered.

At the start of the year for those in Key Stage 2, an open event can be held to invite parents to hear and ask questions about what content the children will be covering as part of the RSE curriculum and this provides an opportunity for the home-school folder to be introduced. Schools need to be transparent about the issues they plan to cover, and teachers can prepare parents for tricky questions from children both at home and at school that are beyond the expected content that should be anticipated. The government outlines that 'the school's policy should cover how the school handles such questions' (DfE 2019: 23). Teachers who are uncomfortable with answering a question or are unsure of how to do this, should thank the child and say that they need to think about what they have asked before they answer. The teacher can then seek support from senior staff. It is important to return to the child to offer a response, or a reason for not answering it. Depending on the question and whether it raises any safeguarding issues, a consultation with the parent can be a purposeful way of having a joint approach to support the child's knowledge and understanding in developmentally appropriate way.

The case study of Jeevan and Molly explored how activities that establish prior under-standing can assist teachers in knowing the level of knowledge that children in their classes have. These can then be a starting point to plan out further sessions. The changes associated with puberty are part of the statutory Science curriculum and as such are an entitlement for children. However, we argue that the emotional changes during adolescence are less well explored and discussed in mixed-gender groups and before they occur. The series of les-sons discussed may well provide the foreground to introduce sexual intercourse, pregnancy and childbirth, contraception, masturbation, sexualities, and sexual responses as the children progress through Key Stage 2.

Chapter summary

In order to develop effective Relationships Education in primary schools it is important to:

- Focus on equipping children for safe, respectful, and positive interactions with others
- Promote a positive relationship with oneself, as a firm foundation of self-respect and secure personal identity support effective relationships with others
- Develop a spiral curriculum to support learning throughout a child's time in primary education, that is reflective of a whole-school ethos
- Help children appreciate not only how they will develop physically, socially, and emotion-ally with the onset of puberty, but to give this a sense of context and purpose
- Ensure that Relationship Education is inclusive and respects the broad range of beliefs, experiences, and identities
- Involve children and parents/carers in the design of the curriculum, building on children's prior knowledge
- Deal with children's questions in an open and honest way

Further reading

Alien Nation is a picture book by Matty Donaldson, published by the Proud Trust, pro-viding a very useful resource to explore gender roles, gender expectations, and gen-der identity.

The *Expect Respect* toolkit from Women's Aid, available at: https://www.womensaid.org .uk/what-we-do/safer-futures/expect-respect-educational-toolkit/

This toolkit includes a range of downloadable lesson plans to use across the primary phase (and across all years of schooling) and resources to support the discussion of gender and conflict resolution.

The *Family Diversities Reading Resource* (2nd edition) developed by Janice Morris and Richard Woolley (2017) Lincoln: Bishop Grosseteste University and University of Worcester. Available at: http://libguides.bishopg.ac.uk/childrensliterature

This resource provides an annotated bibliography of over 150 high-quality children's picture books for use across the primary phase of education, celebrating a wide range of models of family life. It is freely available to educators online.

PSHE Association (2018) *Preparing for Statutory Relationships Education. PSHE education lead's pack: key stages 1 and 2*. Since loco: PSHE Association. Available at: https ://www.pshe-association.org.uk/curriculum-and-resources/resources/preparing -statutory-relationships-education-pshe

This resource provides support with both policy and curriculum development in schools, with practical support to embed this in a comprehensive programme of PSHE. It is available to members of the PSHE Association.

Mason, S. and Woolley, R. (2019) *Relationships and Sex Education 3-11*, London: Bloomsbury.

This book explores key issues within the context of the new guidance for Relationships Education in primary schools in England, drawing on research case studies and policy.

References

Brook, PSHE Association, and SEF (2014) *Sex and Relationships Education (SRE) for the 21st Century: Supplementary Advice to the Sex and Relationship Education Guidance*. DfEE (0116/2000). Sine loco: Brook, PSHE Association and Sex Education Forum.

DfE (2019) *Relationships Education, Relationships and Sex Education (RSE) and Health Education: Statutory Guidance for Governing Bodies, Proprietors, Head Teachers, Principals, Senior Leadership Teams, Teachers*. London: Department for Education.

DfEE (2000) *Sex and Relationship Education Guidance*. Nottingham: Department for Education and Employment Publications.

Halstead, M. and Reiss, M. (2003) *Values in Sex Education: From Principles to Practice*. Oxon: Routledge Falmer.

Hellen, M. (2009) Transgender Children in Schools. *Liminalis: Journal of Sex/Gender Emancipation and Resistance*, pp. 81-99. Goldsmiths Research Online. Available at: http://eprints.gold.ad.uk/3531/ [Accessed 5th August 2018].

Kelly, Y., Zilanawala, A., Sacker, A., Hiatt, R. and Viner, R. (2016) Early Puberty in 11-Year-Old Girls: Millennium Cohort. *British Medical Journal. Open* 102, pp. 232-237.

Legislation.gov.uk (2010) *Equality Act 2010*. [Online] Available at: http://www.legislation.gov.uk/ukpga /2010/15/contents. [Accessed 31 March 2018].

Mason, S. (2010) Braving it Out! An Illuminative Evaluation of the Provision of Sex and Relationship Education in Two Primary Schools in England. *Sex Education: Sexuality, Society and Learning* 10(2), pp. 157-169.

Mason, S. and Woolley, R. (2019) *Relationships and Sex Education 3-11*. London: Bloomsbury.

McKee, A., Albury, K., Dunne, M., Grieshaber, S., Lumby, C. and Matthews, B. (2010) Healthy Sexual Development: A Multidisciplinary Framework for Research. *The International Journal of Sexual Health* 22, pp. 14-19.

Morris, J. and Woolley, R. (2017) *Family Diversities Reading Resource*. 2nd ed. Lincoln: Bishop Grosseteste University and University of Worcester.

RSE Hub (undated) *Fifteen Domains of Healthy Sexual Development*. Since loco: Sex Education Forum. Available at: http://www.rsehub.org.uk/resources/15-domains-of-healthy-sexual-development/?page =1&keywords=&area=Policy%20and%20Guidance&schoollevel=&suggesteduse=

UN General Assembly (2010) *Report of the United Nations Special Rapporteur on the Right to Education*. Sixty-fifth session Item 69 (b) of the provisional agenda: Promotion and protection of human rights: human rights questions, including alternative approaches for improving the effective enjoyment of human rights and fundamental freedoms. Available at: https://www.right-to-education.org/sites/right -to-education.org/files/resource-attachments/UNSR_Sexual_Education_2010.pdf

13 Reading for pleasure

Roger McDonald

Critical questions

How can a 'reading for pleasure' pedagogy be embedded within school practice?
What strategies could a class teacher use to ensure a reading for pleasure culture?
Where can I access research, focused on reading for pleasure?

Introduction

Reading for pleasure is essential to developing lifelong, critical, and engaged readers. It has been defined by the National Literacy Trust as:

> reading that we do of our own free will, anticipating the satisfaction that we will get from the act of reading. It also refers to reading that, having begun at someone else's request, we continue because we are interested in it.
>
> (Clark and Rumbold, 2006: 6)

It can involve any kind of text, in electronic or printed form, and can take place anywhere. Cremin et al., (2020) notes that reading for pleasure can be solitary and/or social and/or interactive but at its core is the reader's volition, their agency, and desire to read, their anticipation of the satisfaction (Clark and Rumbold, 2006) gained through the experience and their interaction with others. It is, or can be, 'transformational' (Cremin et al., 2014: 5).

We can probably all recount instances in our lives where we experienced true pleasure from reading. This could be a book that transfixed us, a letter from a loved one, a congratulatory e-mail, or maybe following a set of instructions leading to a new accomplishment. The experience of wallowing in every word on the page or screen, waiting to see where the author will take us, and using our own imagination alongside creating possibilities, is an emotional experience which can draw us back time and again to the text.

The pleasure, however, does not necessarily need to be joyful. We can experience pleasure from reading which causes us unease, concern, or sadness. Intrigue and curiosity feature in many stories by the excellent children's author Gary Crew. I can remember the atmosphere in my own classroom as I read *The Bent Back Bridge* by Gary Crew as, together, we journeyed with Lola to an isolated telephone box in a clearing hoping against hope that we could keep her safe. As a class we had a shared text and a shared experience which led to discussions, predictions, and possibilities. There was a real desire to read, not for any objectives set but through the satisfaction the reading gave us.

Developing a reading for pleasure pedagogy is probably something we all desire to achieve within our classes and schools but crucially is not something we can just tell children to do. We need to model it, experience it ourselves, be authentic, and also be knowledgeable about the diverse range of children's literature.

The benefits of reading for pleasure

It is important for us to be able to identify the benefits of reading for pleasure. This chapter will argue that we should dedicate time every day specifically for reading for pleasure but also that it becomes embedded as valued behaviour across the school. It is therefore important to know what the impact of this approach can be.

Research evidence has highlighted the benefits of reading for pleasure. A frequently quoted source identifying the benefits of reading for pleasure is the Organisation for Economic Cooperation and Development (OECD) which promotes policies that will improve the economic and social well-being of people around the world. Evidence from OECD (2002) found that reading enjoyment is more important for children's educational success than their family's socio-economic status noting that being a frequent reader 'is more of an advantage than having well educated parents' (OECD, 2002: 3). In addition, Clark and Rumbold (2006) argue that reading for pleasure could be one important way to help combat social exclusion and raise educational standards.

BookTrust (https://www.booktrust.org.uk/) identified a range of research highlighting the benefits of reading for pleasure including social, emotional, attitudinal, and grammatical impact.

- Reading for pleasure has many non-literacy benefits and can increase empathy, improve relationships with others, reduce the symptoms of depression, and improve well-being throughout life (The Reading Agency, 2015)
- Reading for pleasure has social benefits as well and can make people feel more connected to the wider community. Reading increases a person's understanding of their own identity, improves empathy, and gives them an insight into the world view of others (The Reading Agency, 2015)
- Students with more positive attitudes towards reading are more likely to read at or above the expected level for their age (Clark, 2013)
- There is a strong association between the amount of reading for pleasure students say they do and their reading achievement (Twist *et al.*, 2007)
- Students who read for pleasure make significantly more progress in vocabulary, spelling, and Maths than children who read very little (Sullivan and Brown, 2013)
- Teachers who encourage students to read books of their choice for pleasure add a major contribution towards students developing a positive attitude towards reading and a life-long interest in reading

Clark and Rumbold (2006) in their review of literature on reading for pleasure carried out for the National Literacy Trust identified how developing a reading for pleasure culture can impact on a range of areas including:

- Reading attainment and writing ability
- Text comprehension and grammar
- Breadth of vocabulary
- Positive reading attitudes
- Greater self-confidence as a reader
- Pleasure in reading in later life
- General knowledge
- A better understanding of other cultures
- Community participation
- A greater insight into human nature and decision-making

In addition, a literature review, commissioned by The Reading Agency between March and June 2015, found that reading for pleasure was an essential prerequisite for other outcomes of reading to be achieved. It noted the importance of choice and the desire to read, through intrinsic motivation. The impact of reading for pleasure identified by The Reading Agency related to personal, social, and external outcomes of reading for pleasure. To read their full report, which explores reading for pleasure from infants to adults, follow this link: https://readingagency.org.uk/news/The%20Impact%20of%20Reading%20for%20Pleasure%20and%20Empowerment.pdf

The benefits of reading for pleasure have been well documented. As well as the sample of research studies indicated above the Department for Education (2012) has also published a comprehensive review of literature into the benefits of reading for pleasure. There can, it seems, be no doubt that developing a culture of reading for pleasure has massive benefits. Within our own practice it is thus interesting to question the prominence we give to reading for pleasure. From my own teaching experience, I know the time we often give over for test preparation – for example, in Year 1 for the phonics check and then in Year 2 and Year 6 for the Standardised Assessment Tests. I don't think there is as an abundance of research, as there is for reading for pleasure, showing the impact of test preparation.

Decline in reading for pleasure

Although the benefits are clear, research is accumulating that suggests that a growing number of children do not read for pleasure (Clark and Rumbold, 2006). Indeed, internationally OECD (2011: 4) notes that 'fewer students today are reading for pleasure, even though daily reading for pleasure is associated with better performance in school and with adult reading proficiency'.

The national picture is similar, showing that children's attitudes to reading are comparatively low and although had improved slightly (Twist et al., 2007, 2012) have remained unchanged in 2019. The 2019 National Literacy Trust surveyed 56,906 children aged 8-16 and found that, compared to the year before, fewer enjoyed reading and fewer said that they read regularly in their own time. Of those surveyed 53% of children said they enjoyed reading either very much or quite a lot. The report noted that while enjoyment levels had been rather stable between 2005 and 2012, they are now at their lowest since 2013 (Clark and Teravainen-Goff, 2019).

Ensuring that the percentage of children reading for pleasure rises is at a pivotal point. National policies acknowledge the importance of reading for pleasure with it becoming statutory within the national curriculum (DfE, 2013) and reading aloud is expected to gain prominence in the revised Ofsted inspection framework from 2019. In addition, the Open University and the United Kingdom Literacy Association (UKLA) have together created a space for teachers to access and act on the current research through setting up over 90 professional development groups as well as organising a range of conferences dedicated to reading for pleasure across the United Kingdom.

Principles for pedagogy

Underpinning this chapter is evidence from the 'Teachers as Readers: Building Communities of Readers' project (Cremin et al., 2014). Carried out in two phases, funded by UKLA and the Esmee Fairbairn Foundation, the project aimed to:

*   Widen teachers' knowledge of children's literature.
*   Develop teachers' confidence and skilful use of such literature in the classroom.
*   Develop teachers' relationships with parents, carers, librarians, and families.
*   Develop 'Reading Teachers' – teachers who read and readers who teach.

(Cremin *et al.*, 2009)

The findings of the research highlighted the importance of developing both the skill and the will to read. Within the education system currently, an emphasis may have been placed on the skill where 'the pressure to raise standards can lead to transmission type teaching, to atomised skills which are amenable to measurement and to the proliferation of learning outcomes which can be enumerated and audited' (Alexander, 2006: 104). However, the research pointed to the need for an approach where the will to read influences the skill and vice versa (OECD, 2010). It may be useful to reflect on your own approach to reading in your class by noting whether you are more disposed towards reading instruction or reading for pleasure.

Reading instruction is orientated towards	Reading for pleasure is orientated towards
Learning to read	Choosing to read
The skill	The will
Decoding and comprehension	Engagement and response
System readers	Lifelong readers
Teacher direction	Child direction
Teacher ownership	Child ownership
Attainment	Achievement
The minimum entitlement	The maximum entitlement
(The expected standard)	(A reader for life)
The Standards Agenda	The reader's own agenda

Distinctions between reading instruction and RfP (Cremin et al., 2014: 157)

The two phases of the Open University and UKLA research (phase one – comprising of a survey of 1,200 primary teachers' knowledge and use of children's literature – and phase two – qualitative research over the period of a year working with 43 primary teachers from 27 schools in five local authorities) found that in order to develop reading for pleasure effectively teachers need:

1   Considerable knowledge of children's literature and other texts.
2   Knowledge of children as readers and their reading practices.
3   An RfP pedagogy, encompassing:
    • social reading environments
    • reading aloud
    • informal book talk, inside-text talk & recommendations
    • independent reading time
4   To be Reading Teachers: teachers who read and readers who teach and explore the consequences.
5   To develop reciprocal and interactive reading communities.

Further information about each of these areas can be found at https://researchrichpedagogies .org/research/reading-for-pleasure which is a comprehensive website comprising research findings, examples of classroom practice relating to each of the findings, whole school development support, staff meeting resources, surveys, and practical classroom activities.

This chapter has reviewed the research highlighting the impact of reading for pleasure and sign-posted resources to support and enable class teachers and schools to embed a culture of reading for pleasure. The final part of the chapter will put this into practice by showcasing three examples of teachers who have adopted the reading for pleasure agenda.

Introduction to the case study examples

Even a cursory exploration of the reading for pleasure website shows the number of teachers and students responding and implementing elements of reading for pleasure within their own settings. With a growing number of contributions from across the United Kingdom, the website offers the opportunity to view and share ways in which teachers and students have actioned each of the research findings.

Since 2017, Egmont Publishing in partnership with The Open University and UK Literacy Association, have recognised teachers and schools whose practices make a real difference to children's RfP through the Egmont Reading for Pleasure Awards. There are three award categories: Early Career Teacher, Experienced Teacher, and a Whole School Award.

The three case study examples will therefore offer three distinct perspectives on developing a reading for pleasure pedagogy within the classroom and throughout the school. The first case study explores how an early career teacher embedded reading for pleasure within her class. The second case study is from the perspective of an experienced teacher and literacy lead who explains strategies she used for enriching the school's practice for reading for pleasure. The final example is from a headteacher and explains the strategic approach to reading for pleasure across a school.

Case study: Marianne Mitchell – early career teacher

In this case study early career teacher Marianne Mitchell shares ways in which she has embedded reading for pleasure within her class. At the time of the interview Marianne was coming to the end of her second year as a class teacher. Marianne is a keen reader herself and has been dedicated to inspiring a passion for reading within her class. I interviewed Marianne about what the concept reading for pleasure means to her and how she has embedded it in her class.

What does the term 'reading for pleasure' mean to you both personally and professionally?

At its essence, 'reading for pleasure' (RfP) is the act of voluntarily picking up a book for the sole purpose of finding gratification through reading it. The purpose of the reading may be for entertainment, the pursuit of knowledge (involving a level of cognitive effort that is not necessarily immediately enjoyable), or it may simply be a means of occupying the mind when passing time (e.g. in a waiting room). The reading material could be anything from traditional books (fiction or non-fiction) to magazines, newspapers, digital texts, or even leaflets and pamphlets.

I have found that linked to the act of reading itself is the importance of the accompanying conversation with other readers including discussion of material already read, in the process of being read or that the reader is considering reading.

For me, RfP personally and professionally is very similar. In the classroom, I strive to nurture the process of finding gratification in reading in my students. I model reading behaviour for the children and create a positive reading culture in the room where the children begin to discover their own preferences and find their own happiness within the pages.

Could you give two examples of how you have implemented reading for pleasure in your classroom?

There are so many important elements for developing reading for pleasure and it can be quite daunting in the first year of teaching when there is so much to learn. However, I would select the following two aspects of RfP as the most important cornerstones of my classroom practice.

1.   Reading aloud daily to the class

It is my view that reading aloud at least on a daily basis to the class is the single most important aspect of RfP for a teacher to adopt. The choice of text is crucial to the success of the experience. I believe it is essential to read a text that the teacher already knows. This allows selection of an appropriate text. I have found that the benefits of reading aloud for my class have included:

- Generating enthusiasm for class story time by reading in an entertaining way which the children enjoy

- Providing opportunities for the children to talk about the text in a relaxed atmosphere where everyone's input is valued, thus nurturing critical thinking skills
- Creating a shared reading history as a classroom community which allows intertextual links and commentary amongst readers (natural mutual book blether)
- Providing children with access to texts beyond their own technical reading ability
- Modelling of 'good' reading fluency. Children can hear the tune of the text and may imitate the reading
- Natural broadening of pupils' vocabulary through exposure to new words in context
- Exposure to authors and literary genres that the child may not otherwise experience

2.   Access to books

The second area I have developed is to ensure all children have access to a wide range of texts. Without access, in my experience, a child has little chance of learning to love to read for pleasure. Ideally every school would provide a well-stocked central library for the enjoyment of all pupils as well as a regularly updated classroom library.

I provide my own well-stocked classroom book corner so that children have unrestricted access to books every day at school. Children may take these books home to read in addition to school library books and reading scheme books. I timetable RfP sessions (at least once per week) to ensure that the book corner is actively used, the books are regularly read, and I encourage children to take a comfortable reading position during this time. When I reflected on my own reading habits, I noted that I rarely read for pleasure sat up at a table so I wanted to reflect this in my classroom. Children can sit or lie wherever they wish and may choose to share books with friends or read to teddies. Some prefer to adopt a more formal seating position at a desk and read in silence. This is part of discovering our own preferences as readers – not only what we enjoy reading, but how we like to read it.

Books do go missing and occasionally become damaged (or worn out!), so I aim to replenish books on a regular basis. Many of the books I personally provide are sourced from charity shops and second-hand book shops to minimise the outlay. I also make a point of giving books to children as end of year or Christmas presents to show them how special books are to me and to ensure that every child owns at least two books when they leave my class.

What has been the impact of the reading for pleasure pedagogy for you and your class?

The impact of RfP for me, since beginning my teacher training, has been a renewed passion for children's literature. I considered that I had a good knowledge of children's literature for younger children and had been an avid reader myself as a child so therefore knew 'classic' children's literature for KS2. However, I quickly realised that my knowledge of new texts for KS2 was limited. I took action by shadowing the UKLA book awards with my class which enabled us to delve into up-to-date texts.

I have read voraciously in this area for the past three years and have embraced the online reading teacher community, participating in Twitter reading forums including 'PrimarySchoolBookClub', 'ReadingRocks', and Twitter 'readalongs'. I met several children's authors, poets, and illustrators at reading seminars and literary festivals and regularly listen to children's book podcasts (e.g. *In the Reading Corner*, *Down the Rabbit Hole*) as well as following children's book awards.

The impact on me has been huge. I am able to make bespoke recommendations not only to children but to staff as well. My increased knowledge of children's literature means that I am interested in and know about new publications and aim to read as widely as possible. I have earned a reputation in my workplace as a well-read teacher amongst children, parents, and other teachers.

By trialling research-based strategies in my classroom and leading by example, I have shared good practice, which other members of staff are adopting, building a whole school ethos of reading for pleasure. I have seen a marked change increase in RfP activities across the school including:

- Increased book talk between pupils and staff
- Improved enjoyment of reading sessions
- Children now say they enjoy and choose to read poetry
- An active reading community
- Cognitive proficiency is improving (fluency and comprehension) along with vocabulary (verbal and written)

What advice would you give an early career teacher who says they do not have time for reading for pleasure?

Reading is fundamental to every area of the school curriculum. When children read for pleasure it usually leads to them wanting to read even more thus creating a virtuous circle that positively impacts on performance in all subjects. Not only does reading empower children to access information in all subjects, it also benefits general analytical and thinking skills transferable across the whole curriculum. Giving children time to read, reading with them, and promoting reading for pleasure will empower them as scholars, but creating life-long readers will empower them for life beyond school as well. Reading can empower children and even raise their socio-economic status. It can also make children kinder, more empathetic people, equipped for a mentally healthy life ahead as adults. It is our duty as teachers to nurture the reader in every child.

In what ways has the OU/UKLA research informed your pedagogy?

Entering the Egmont Open University RfP award last year helped me to consolidate three years of research and practice and consider what I was doing in my classroom and the impact of it. I entered the classroom with a profound and life-long love of reading but considering OU/UKLA research allowed me to break down my own reading habits and map out how I had become such a reader. I began to think about why I read, how I read, what I read, and who had encouraged and empowered me to become the reader I am. Then I was able to begin to transfer this energy and passion for literature to emerging readers in primary school. The OU/UKLA website is full of examples of how to improve teaching practice. The newsletter highlights key findings each month and following key personnel on Twitter keeps me abreast of the latest discussions and ideas in this field. Attending the conference last year was a highlight which only served to further renew my enthusiasm.

Marianne gives a wonderful insight into embedding a reading for pleasure pedagogy in her class. Reading the case study shows how, even within a contested space of education with various pushes and pulls from a variety of sources, she ensures that RfP is core within her pedagogy. Marianne shows us how she has reflected on her own RfP habits by, in a sense, holding a mirror up to her own preferences and has tried to replicate the notion of agency, freedom, and choice for the children within her class.

In the next case study, we meet Sadie Phillips who is an experienced teacher and literacy lead. Sadie offers her perspective on developing a RfP culture across the school.

Case study: Sadie Phillips – Literacy Lead

Sadie Phillips has worked at Canary Wharf College Eastferry for over three years. The school is an independent free school for boys and girls aged 4-11 years. Sadie is the Year 5 class teacher and also part of the literacy team. She has a passion for promoting literacy and is dedicated to ensuring the very best experiences and opportunities for readers and writers at the school through a purposeful, engaging, creative curriculum. Sadie shares her practice through the OU/UKLA reading for pleasure groups as well as through her own website which can be accessed via this link www.literacywithmissp.com

In this case study Sadie explains how she has developed a reading for pleasure culture through her work as the literacy lead.

What does the term 'reading for pleasure' mean to you both personally and professionally?

Reading for pleasure means finding those moments of pure joy when reading something that you find irresistibly interesting, something that exercises and excites your imagination. It's being completely immersed and engrossed in those un-put-down-able texts that transport you to another time, another place, or another world.

As teachers, we hold the key to unlocking children's ability to decode and decipher the meaning of words but it's also our duty to shine a light on reading for enjoyment.

Our aim should be to inspire and excite children to read, encouraging them in their pursuit of a real, deep knowledge and understanding of language, and how authors make choices that impact the reader. It's about developing a love of literature that stretches far beyond the reach of the classroom; it's about igniting that spark which will last a lifetime.

Could you give two examples of how you have implemented reading for pleasure in your classroom.

Example one: Cosy reading spaces

I began reflecting upon where and how I read for pleasure myself - usually on the sofa, a sunbed by the pool on holiday, in a comfy armchair in front of the fire or curled up with a blanket in bed - and I started thinking about how I could make the classroom spaces and environment a little more inviting and cosy.

I have never once sat at a desk upright reading a book. It would be uncomfortable and unsustainable; I'd probably end up moving or getting distracted. Yet, this is what I was asking the children to do in my classroom during reading time in school. It was a bit of a light-bulb moment and I knew something had to change.

I wanted to encourage reading for pleasure by creating a comfortable, calm, relaxing atmosphere in the classroom, allowing children to choose where and how to sit and read.

- I collected lots of blankets, cushions, and throws from home and placed them in a bucket in the book corner
- I brought in some teddies which we called 'reading buddies' and placed them in the book corner too
- Sometimes, I gave out baskets of torches and dimmed the lights, with a roaring fire on the interactive whiteboard (this worked well during winter afternoons when it was quite dark already) to allow the children to read by torchlight
- We started calling it 'cosy reading' instead of 'independent reading'
- I put up some fairy lights and switched them on whenever it was cosy reading time and this became an instantly recognisable sign that it was happening
- I would often set the room up whilst they were out of the classroom (in another lesson or outside playing) so that they walked into 'cosy reading' and were excited by it
- I read for pleasure myself during cosy reading time (this was an important factor)
- I allowed the children to choose where and how they wanted to sit and read - some chose to pop their feet up on a chair, lay underneath a table, cosy up in the book corner or on the rug. They were encouraged to get cosy. Book talk was allowed

We negotiated all the options and discussed how we could manage the most popular areas (the sofa bed in the book corner) to make it fair for all. The children decided that if they had sat in the book corner last time, they would find somewhere new to sit this time. We have not had any arguments about reading spaces and the children are very considerate.

Impact:

- The children's reaction to 'cosy reading' was incredible. They were clearly excited about it and enjoyed snuggling up with a blanket and a book
- Time and space were made for reading for pleasure within the classroom and this promoted reading for enjoyment
- Children could sustain independent reading for longer periods of time and we had much less movement/book swapping happening during cosy reading
- Feedback from the children was overwhelmingly positive
- It has been so successful that we now have cosy reading almost every day
- When the weather gets warmer, we'll also consider alternative spaces such as the playground with beanbags and blankets or 'reading picnics'

Example two: Becoming a Reading Teacher

As well as *where* and *when* independent reading happens, we also need to consider *how* it happens to ensure that it does not simply become a boring, routine procedure, void of authentic reader engagement and interaction. Tempting as it may be, reading time should not be seen as time to catch up on a bit of marking or answer emails. Instead, make your reading time in class really effective by ensuring that the adults in the room are engaged in reading for pleasure too! Developing enjoyable independent reading time is central to building rich reading communities, where children take pleasure in reading and are motivated to read on their own. If they are able to see you, the teacher (or indeed teaching assistant), participating in independent reading they will see that reading is valuable. It will also allow you to engage in further discussions about reading and recommend books to children too. Most importantly, it allows the children to see you as a reader and a reading for pleasure role model.

What advice would you give a teacher who says they do not have time for reading for pleasure?

It's no secret that the benefits of reading aloud are manifold. Yet, in the current climate of curriculum pressure and jam-packed timetables, many teachers still view reading aloud as an 'added bonus' rather than a crucial part of the curriculum – often an end-of-the-day activity, squeezed out due to increasingly busy schedules.

What would I say to those who say they do not have time for reading for pleasure? Make time. Just because it doesn't have a learning objective attached to it, does not mean it isn't valuable. It's arguably our moral obligation to set aside daily time and space for reading (without any follow up work) and to nurture children's enjoyment of it. Reading aloud has *many* advantages that silent reading lacks. Perhaps most importantly, reading aloud to children reinforces the sheer enjoyment of sharing a story together, it shouldn't be presented to them as a chore. In order to foster and future-proof a love of reading, we need to make time to read for enjoyment.

As a useful starting point for teachers, I would highly recommend using the Open University's 'Review your Practice' survey for reading aloud. It's a short reflection task, which will help you to identify key areas to focus on initially. The OU website also has a plethora of useful documents to help improve your practice, including: practical classroom strategies for reading aloud, a reading aloud PowerPoint for staff CPD (with accompanying guidance notes) and, perhaps most useful of all, plenty of examples of practice from other teachers. There is a whole library of fun, creative ideas that are sure to inspire your own reading aloud practice!

In what ways has the OU/UKLA research informed your pedagogy?

The OU/UKLA has opened my eyes to a range of research-informed, practical strate-gies, and quality children's literature to support reading for pleasure in the classroom. Not only has the OU/UKLA research highlighted the importance of reading for enjoy-ment, reinforcing my own pedagogical thinking, but it has also helped me to recognise personal areas of development and new strategies for moving forward.

It is easy to hear the passion Sadie has for developing a reading for pleasure pedagogy across the school and the impact the work has had on the children and the wider community. Her vision is embedded in the research carried out by Cremin et al., (2014) and forms the foundation of the developments within the school.

In the final case study, we hear from Sonia Thompson who is the headteacher of St Matthew's Church of England Primary School in Birmingham. Sonia became the headteacher in 2018 and has further developed and embedded a reading for pleasure culture across the children, staff and parents. In addition, the school have partnered with Just Imagine (https:// justimaginestorycentre.co.uk/) to provide quality reading and writing CPD opportunities for schools.

Case study: Sonia Thompson - Headteacher

What does the term 'reading for pleasure' mean to you both personally and professionally?

Personally, reading for pleasure (RfP), means the right to not only become a reader, but it is the right to become a willing, volitional reader. I refuse to not allow children to access this powerful opportunity within my school.

Professionally, it means that regardless of whatever else in happening in education, I will allow teachers within my school the time and space to create/nurture research-informed, transformative, two-way communities of readers.

What would be your top the actions for a school wanting to adopt a reading for pleasure pedagogy?

- Put reading for pleasure on your School Development Plan (SDP) and do not take it off … ever! All leaders and stakeholders need to be heavily invested in keeping the RfP agenda at a high profile level within the school. Having it on the SDP will raise its profile and give leaders the opportunity to request/ring-fence funding for reading for pleasure to thrive
- Use the RfP Research Rich Pedagogies website. I was part of the original TaRs project, so I was familiar with the reading pedagogies, which made the difference. For schools that are not, the site is invaluable. It provides a school with all the research and resources to support the creation of a coherent plan of action, for moving sustainable and embedded RfP practices forward, within any school
- Timetable regular RfP insets. This will allow leaders to take staff through the research around the impact of RfP – it is the biggest single indicator of a child's future success – teachers need to know that! Staff meetings will also provide opportunities for leaders to train staff on all the key RfP pedagogies. The aim is always to hopefully develop a community of 'Reading Teachers', who begin the journey of holding up a mirror to their own reading practices and using their findings, to begin meaningful, reciprocal dialogues about reading practices and preference, with their own classrooms (see Figure 13.1)

Could you give three examples of changes you have made to implement a reading for pleasure pedagogy in your school?

- **We have timetabled independent reading, in both KS1 and KS2.** This means that children have volitional reading opportunities within the school day. These are not an add on, or an incidental; they are non-negotiable. Teachers use this time to create a community of readers within their own classrooms. They model reading behaviours and create a space, where children have reading rights and can own their reading choices and motivations to read
- **Reading for pleasure at my school has benefitted greatly from outside involvement.** One of the most successful was a **BookTrust** programme called **Story Hunters**. It involved each child in a lower KS2 year group receiving a book package each month. This created an amazing personal library (18 books), to keep, take home, and share. We currently run two **Just Imagine Centre** programmes. **Reading Gladiators** is for our higher attaining Year 2, Year 4, and Year 6 readers. These reading clubs are, amongst other things, an empowering reading for pleasure programme, which equips the children with the knowledge to influence and guide other children's choices. This has made a big difference. **The Reading Journey** involves themed reading spaces, which contain three copies of each books. Having multiple copies has had striking results. It has improved the social and reciprocal nature of reading interactions, between children and children and children and teachers (see Figure 13.2)

Figure 13.1 Teacher's reading space

Figure 13.2 Themed reading spaces

Figure 13.3 Building a community of engaged readers

- **Building a community of engaged readers amongst the staff.** RfP is the beating heart of our school and all staff know that. Its importance means that we now make time to fully support teachers to position themselves within this and take ownership of this agenda within their classrooms and across the school. This involves in school CPD, out of school CPD, and an opportunity to attend the OU/UKLA Teacher Reading Group
- We are passionate about ensuring that our children read widely and deeply. We want them to get lost in a plethora of books from a plethora of authors, both new and old. We also want children to own their diverse choices and find 'their' author, book, or series. Regular reading surveys and discussions have helped to locate preferences, such as newspapers and magazines, and the impact of changes. Alongside this, **Daniel Pennac's** popular **Rights of the Reader** declaration is a manifesto, which we display around the school. We actively make time to discuss, enact and model it, so that our children understand that all reading has value and is valued at our school (see Figure 13.3)

What has been the impact of the reading for pleasure pedagogy for you and your school?

- I have no hesitation in saying that a rich reading for pleasure culture within my school has directly had an impact on our reading attainment data. We have been consistently well above national averages in our SATs data, at both KS1 and KS2, for a number of years. Although I do not feel that I have to validate the time we allocate to reading for pleasure, this data does help to do so
- Our reading for pleasure practice was recognised nationally, when we entered and won the OU/UKLA Whole School Reading for Pleasure School of the Year 2018. This award has given me a platform to enthusiastically share

- The impact of our consistent and persistent drip-feeding of reading for pleasure in our school continues to draw our parents. Our parents have really appreciated knowing why reading for pleasure is so crucial. Through sharing the research with them – that reading for pleasure impacts on all of children's learning, across the curriculum – our parents saw the wider, intrinsic, affective value; beyond the book bag and the home reading journal

What advice would you give a school who says they do not have time for reading for pleasure?

- I would really encourage the school to make time. As I previously said, the research is clear. Balancing the teaching of the skills of reading, alongside nurturing the will to read, will have impact. My school, in one of the most deprived areas of Birmingham, has proven that

In what ways has the OU/UKLA research informed your pedagogy?

- In every way! Through using the five key findings we were able to slowly move the pedagogy forward. The website supported us to formulate our school development plan, which then went on to shape our 'CDP for RFP' journey. The wealth of high quality CPD materials, including PowerPoints, handouts, film clips, further reading, and of course the examples of practice, meant that we were able to build our school reading community, immersed in practice, which was research informed and evidence-based (see Figure 13.4)

Is there anything else you want to note specific to your experience?

- I have been involved in RfP discussions and research for over ten years. I refuse to stop championing it. I have seen the value and importance of reciprocity. Finding out about children's reading identities has been key in ensuring our engagement with our children and families is authentic

We have to challenge ourselves to make authentic space, value and build on children's agency as readers. This was particularly poignant when a group of boys, who loved reading *The Beano*, then went on to create and sell their own comic to both children and staff. One of these boys said he could not afford comics in his house. **We would have never uncovered this without making space for discussions.** These integrations are our privilege and our children's right (see Figure 13.5).

School Development Plan...

- *To ensure that every child in the school learns within the context of a social reading environment* (ensuring pathways to challenge for the most able as well as support for the less confident).

- *To ensure that every child is regularly read to* (in acknowledgement of studies showing that children who are regularly read to do better in school socially and academically).

- *To ensure that children have access to a wide range of books from which they can choose to read independently, for pleasure.*

- *To encourage and develop informal book talk and recommendations so children learn to be courageous and discriminating readers.*

Figure 13.4 School development plan

Figure 13.5 Boys' creation of their own comic based on their love of *The Beano*

Chapter summary

This chapter has sought to explore the importance of developing a reading for pleasure peda-gogy within our lives, classrooms, and schools. We have heard how an early career teacher, a literacy lead, and a headteacher have ensured that reading for pleasure is central to their practice. Their commitment is so strong due to the impact reading for pleasure has on the lives of children and also the wider school community. Each case study used the research by Cremin et al., (2014) as central to their development, drawing on the research evidence, prac-tical classroom examples, and support to review their own practice. They all highlighted the importance for teachers to know a diverse range of texts which in turn gives opportunities for reading conversations, authentic recommendations as well as enriching the community of readers in the class, school, and wider area. Developing a reading for pleasure pedagogy in our classrooms and schools is one of the greatest gifts we can offer the children we teach.

Further reading

Clark, C. and Rumbold, K. (2006) *Reading for Pleasure: A Research Overview*. London: The National Literacy Trust.

Cremin, T., Mottram, M., Collins, F., Powell, S. and Safford, K. (2009) *Teachers as Readers: Building Communities of Readers 2007-08 Executive Summary*. Leicester: The United Kingdom Literacy Association.

Pennac, D. (2006) *The Rights of the Reader*. London: Walker Books.

References

Alexander, R. (2006) Dichotomous Pedagogies and the Promise of Cross-Cultural Comparison. In A. H. Halsey, P. Brown, H. Lauder, and J.-A. Dillabough (Eds.), *Education: Globalisation and Social Change*. Oxford: Oxford University Press, 722-733.

Clark, C. and Rumbold, K. (2006) *Reading for Pleasure: A Research Overview*. London: The National Literacy Trust.

Clark, C. and Teravainen, A. (2017) *Celebrating Reading for Enjoyment*. London: The National Literacy Trust.

Clark, C. and Teravainen-Goff, A. (2019) *Children's and Young People's Reading in 2019: Findings from the 2019 Annual Literacy Survey*. London: National Literacy Trust.

Cremin, T. (2020) Reading for Pleasure: challenges and opportunities. In: Daly, C. and Davison, J. eds. *Debates in English Teaching. Debates in Subject Teaching*. London: Routledge, (In Press)

Cremin, T., Mottram, M., Collins, F., Powell, S. and Safford, K. (2014) *Building Communities of Readers: Reading for Pleasure*. London: Routledge.

Cremin, T., Bearne, E., Goodwin, P. and Mottram, M. (2008) Primary Teachers as Readers. *English in Education* 42(1), 1-16.

Cremin, T., Mottram, M., Bearne, E. and Goodwin, P. (2008) Exploring Teachers' Knowledge of Children's Literature *Cambridge Journal of Education* 38(4), 449-464.

Department for Education (2013) *The national curriculum in England: key stages 1 and 2 framework document*. Available at: https://www.gov.uk/government/publications/national-curriculum-in-engl and-primary-curriculum

Hurd, S., Dixon, M. and Oldham, J. (2006) Are Low Levels of Book Spending in Primary Schools Jeopardising the National Literacy Strategy? *The Curriculum Journal* 17(1), 73-88.

OECD (2002) *Reading for Change: Results from PISA 2000*. www.pisa.oecd.org

OECD (2010) PISA 2009 *Results: Learning to Learn – Student Engagement, Strategies and Practices*, Vol.III.

OECD (2011) Do Students Today Read for Pleasure? *PISA in Focus*, No. 8, OECD Publishing, Paris. doi: 10.1787/5k9h362lhw32-en

Sullivan, A. and Brown, M. (2013) Reading for Pleasure and Attainment in Vocabulary and Mathematics. *British Educational Research Journal* 41(6) pp. 971–991.

The Reading Agency (2015) *Literature Review: The Impact of Reading for Pleasure and Empowerment*. London: BOP Consulting.

Twist, L., Schagen, I. and Hodgson, C. (2003) *Readers and Reading: The National Report for England PIRLS*. Slough: NfER.

Twist, L., Schagan, I. and Hogson, C. (2007) *Progress in International Reading Literacy Study (PIRLS): Reader and Reading National Report for England 2006*. London: NFER and DCSF.

Twist, L., Sizmur, J., Bartlett, S. and Lynn, L. (2012) *PIRLS 2011: Reading Achievement in England*. Slough: National Foundation for Educational Research.

14 Writing for pleasure

Ross Young and Felicity Ferguson

Critical questions

Do you identify as a writer-teacher?

Have you attended a writers' workshop?

Does your class use the same practices and processes as writers do outside the school gates?

Do the children in your class live the writerly life?

Introduction

There is strong evidence that, historically, too many children in England underachieve in writing (Ofsted, 2009, 2012). The DfE (2012: 3) remarks that 'writing is the subject with the worst performance compared with reading, maths and science at Key Stages 1 and 2'. In 2017, we read that 'attainment at the expected standard, as measured by teacher assessment … is lowest in writing' and that this is similar to the pattern in 2016 (DfE, 2017, 2018). The National Literacy Trust (Clark, 2016; Clark and Teravainen, 2017) has in recent times shown that English children's enjoyment of writing, coupled with their drive and motivation to write both in and out of school, has for many years been in steady decline, with 49.3% of children reporting feelings of indifference to or active dislike of writing (Clark and Teravainen, 2017). The same researchers found that 'eight times as many children and young people who do not enjoy writing write below the expected level compared with those who enjoy writing' (Clark and Teravainen, 2017: 14), a fact supported by Ofsted's (2019) latest research, which points out that positive attitudes towards writing are important predictors of attainment. According to some studies, the most significant pointers to high achievement in writing come from the affective domains of motivation and volition (Alexander, 2009; Beard, 2000; Hillocks, 1986; Clark, 2016), with the best motivator being agency (Au and Gourd, 2013; Dyson and Freedman, 2003; Ketter and Pool, 2001; Lave and Wenger, 1991; Watanabe, 2007). Agency, volition, and motivation have very clear links to the experience of pleasure in writing.

Graham and Johnson (2012: 11), in a review of perceptions of writing in their classroom in the UK, state that:

while 75% of the children demonstrated a positive attitude towards their reading experiences, only 10% of the same children described positive or happy associations in their writing memories. The majority of children … associated the writing experience with incompetence or anxiety; even those children who were perceived by me to be able writers did not consider the experience to be emotionally rewarding … children who were competent in their literacy skills, who met their targets, who could write successfully in a variety of genres, failed to express any sense of joy in their written achievements.

These are sobering words. It seems clear that in England children are underachieving largely as a result of their dislike of writing. The National Literacy Trust conclude in their 2017 annual survey that their findings 'highlight the importance of writing enjoyment for children's outcomes and warrant a call for more attention on writing enjoyment in schools, research and policy' (Clark and Teravainen, 2017: 15). Our own research (Young, 2019) set out to do exactly this.

Defining writing for pleasure

As literate adults, most of us would have little difficulty in defining what we mean by *reading* for pleasure and indeed this is now a statutory part of the English National Curriculum (2013). Cremin et al., (2014: 5) state: 'at the core of reading for pleasure is the reader's volition, their agency and desire to read, their anticipation of the satisfaction gained through the experience and/or afterwards in interaction with others'. However, little consideration has been given to what *writing* for pleasure might mean, particularly in the context of the classroom.

It is known that children who enjoy writing and are motivated to write are seven times more likely to achieve well academically (Clark and Teravainen, 2017). Therefore, writing for pleasure is a vital consideration when teaching young writers. If we examine what professional writers have said on the subject (Cremin and Oliver, 2017) and Cremin et al.'s, (2014) definition of reading for pleasure, we can define writing for pleasure as a volitional act of writing undertaken for enjoyment and satisfaction. The specific sources of enjoyment and satisfaction in and of writing are many and varied, and will be different for individual writers in different contexts.

In our book *Real-World Writers: A handbook for teaching writing with 7-11-year-olds* (Young and Ferguson, 2020), we consider some of the reasons why writers are *moved* to write. They include the following:

- To **teach** others by sharing their experience and knowledge, and teach themselves by writing to learn
- To **persuade or influence** others by sharing their thoughts and opinions
- To **entertain** themselves and others by sharing stories – both real and imagined
- To **paint with words** to show their artistry and the ability to see things differently, or to simply play around and have fun
- To **reflect** in order to better understand themselves, their place in the world or their response to a new subject
- To **make a record** of something for the future

Writing can of course involve a variety of these simultaneously. Pleasure in writing, then, is the satisfaction that can come from seeing the writing through to a conclusion. We argue that there are two types of pleasure in writing, namely, writing *as* pleasure (enjoyment) and writing *for* pleasure (satisfaction).

Writing as pleasure

- Feeling a need to write and experiencing enjoyment in practising the craft of writing
- Feeling confident and happy when engaging in the different processes of writing
- Enjoying being part of a writing community, discussing your own writing, and how it feels to be a writer

Writing for pleasure. Pleasure is gained from practising the craft of writing, from engaging in the process or in particular parts of the process, whether it be: generating ideas; dabbling; getting the words down on paper or screen for the first time; revising a section till you get it just so; editing to perfection or publishing the final product with care. Joyce Carol Oates and Ernest Hemingway both recorded that, for them, the pleasure was all in the revising, while Ellen Goodman likens editing to cleaning up a house. For some, no doubt, pleasure ends with the completion of the act of writing; the idea that it will be seen by others can fill them with dread.

Writing for pleasure

- The sense of a purpose fulfilled
- The expectation of a response
- The sharing of something in which you feel pride
- The discovery of your own writing voice

This type of pleasure is the satisfaction that comes *after* the act of writing. It is knowing that you will receive a response from your audience and that your writing will be put to work through sharing your memories, knowledge, ideas, thoughts, artistry, or opinions with others. There can also be a pleasure in hearing the different meanings that others may make from your text. Writing *for* pleasure gives children a sense of empowerment and the feeling that their writing has enriched their life and the lives of others.

A working definition of a 'writing for pleasure' pedagogy

Writing for pleasure is a volitional act of writing undertaken for enjoyment and satisfaction. Therefore, a Writing For Pleasure pedagogy is any research-informed pedagogy which seeks to create the conditions in which writing and being a writer is a pleasurable, purposeful and satisfying experience. It has as its goal the use of effective writing practices with young apprentice writers and the promotion of the affective aspects of writing and of being a writer.

(Young, 2019: 13)

Critical questions

- How do you know whether the children in your school or classroom enjoy writing?
- Do your children enjoy the craft of writing?
- Do your children regularly get to feel the sense of satisfaction that comes from publishing or performing their writing for a genuine purpose and to real and varied audiences?

The principles of effective writing teaching

In the context of increasing interest in writing for pleasure as an effective writing pedagogy, The Goldsmiths' Company, and with assistance from The University of Sussex, funded a project that sought to observe the impact a 'writing for pleasure' pedagogy had on children's enjoyment, satisfaction and, importantly, on excellent academic progress in writing. The principles described below are grounded in the latest educational research into the most effective writing instruction (Young and Ferguson, 2021) and are the ones that are put into practice by the best 'writing for pleasure' primary school teachers. To find out more about this research and its findings, visit www.writing4pleasure.com.

1. Creating a community of writers

If we want to create life-long writers, then we need to treat them as genuine apprentices in an environment which reflects the way writers work. The classroom should feel like a sociable **writer's workshop** whose aim is to create a community of writers in which teachers write alongside children and share their own practices, and in which children are shown how to talk and present their writing to others in a positive and constructive way. Children are seen as participants in determining writing projects, as opposed to passive recipients of someone else's choice. The community of writers takes part in meaningful practices and writing projects they can identify with. Importantly, in a contemporary writing workshop (Young and Ferguson, 2020), children are involved in actions, discussions, and reflections that make a difference to how they are taught and undertake their writing.

2. Every child a writer

In the writing workshop, effective writing teachers hold high achievement expectations for all writers. They see every child as a writer and a member of the community and, from the first, teach strategies that lead to greater independence. They emphasise the need to be clear about the purpose and audience for every class and personal writing project undertaken, and also model and promote the social aspects of writing and peer support in their classrooms.

3. Reading, sharing and talking about writing

Children are given ample opportunity to share and discuss with teachers and peers both their own and others' writing in order to give and receive constructive criticism and celebrate achievement. When the writing environment is positive and settled in tone, the community begins to build its own ways of talking and thinking as *writers*.

4. Purposeful and authentic writing projects

Meaningfulness affects learner engagement and outcomes to a considerable extent. Writing projects are most meaningful to children if they are given the opportunity to generate their own subject and purpose, write at their own pace, in their own way, with agency over how they want to use the form, and with a clear sense of a real reader. Given these circumstances, writers are likely to remain focused on a task, have self-determination, maintain a strong personal agency over and commitment to their writing, and so produce something significant for themselves and in keeping with teacher expectations. In short, when children care about their writing, they want it to do well.

5. Explicitly teach the writing processes

Effective writing teachers give direct instruction in the different components of the writing process (how to generate an idea, plan, draft, revise, edit, publish). They scaffold children's understanding of these processes through demonstration, discussion, modelling, and sharing exemplars written by themselves. The ultimate aim is for children to relinquish their dependence on this scaffolding and develop their own preferred writing process.

6. Setting writing goals

To maintain children's self-efficacy, commitment and motivation during a class writing project, teachers should ensure that children know and keep in mind the **distant goal** of the project, that is to say the future audience and purpose for the writing. The class, as a community, should have a say in setting **product goals** – what they will have to do to ensure their writing is successful and meaningful. Setting shorter-term **process goals** benefits learners in terms of cognitive load, focus, motivation, and achievement; for example: 'Make sure you finish your draft by the end of Thursday's writing time'. However, once experienced enough, children should be able to use their own writing process and only need to know the final deadline for completing the project; for example: 'You have eight more writing sessions before your piece has to be ready for publication'.

7. Reassuring consistency

A well-organised classroom facilitates learning, ensures focus, and builds writing confidence. Writers will be enabled to work largely independently, with readily accessible resources communicating strategies clearly. Children need the reassurance of knowing how a writing lesson will proceed. A **mini lesson**, followed by **writing time**, and then **class sharing** is the most effective routine teachers can adopt. A mini lesson is a short instruction on an aspect of writing which is likely to be useful to the children during that day's writing. Conferencing between teacher and groups or individuals takes place during writing time, and children will know that, once they have finished working on a class writing project for the day, they may concentrate on their personal projects.

8. Personal writing projects

It is essential that children are given time to write for a sustained period every day and to work on both class and personal writing projects. Personal projects should be seen as an important part of the writing curriculum since it is here, through exercising their own choice of subject, purpose, audience, and writing process, that they have genuine autonomy and come to understand the true function of writing as an empowering and pleasurable activity which they can use now and in the future. Teachers will hold equally high expectations for both personal and class writing projects. Finally, personal projects can give the teacher insights into children's personalities and help build relationships, and can of course provide evidence for the assessment of their development as independent writers. When children see their teachers as positive, caring, and interested in their lives, they are more likely to engage in writing at a high level of achievement.

9. Balancing composition with transcription

Studies emphasise that transcriptional skills are best learnt in the context of a child's purposeful and reader-focused writing. Spelling and punctuation should be largely self-monitored as children write, marking their text for items to be checked and corrected at the editing stage. Invented spellings should be seen as acceptable in the drafting stage, and handwriting skills are most meaningfully practised when publishing a completed piece. Research shows that there is no evidence to link the formal teaching of grammar with improvements in children's writing (Graham and Perin, 2007). Successful writing teachers know that if grammar is to be understood in a meaningful way, it must be taught functionally and applied and examined in the context of real purposeful writing. Grammar teaching should therefore take place within mini lessons and should, as far as possible, be useful and relevant to the children's writing that day. It is important that children also have mini lessons in writing study, when strategies and craft knowledge are taught, such as techniques for editing the manuscript, 'dabbling' around a writing idea, or how to develop a character.

10. Teach daily 'mini lessons'

Feeling you can write well on your own is very important to children, and while they need guidance, advice, and individual instruction, they also need to be taught self-regulating strategies (Young and Ferguson, 2019). This can be done through mini lessons on how to generate ideas, use of planners and checklists, or what to look for when improving and revising a draft. Self-regulating writers work independently to a large extent, freeing up their teacher to conference with individuals or small groups.

11. Being a writer-teacher

Just as it would be hard to teach children the tuba if you've never played one, so it is difficult to teach children to be writers if you never write. Become a writer-teacher who writes for and with pleasure and use your literate life as a learning tool in the classroom. Write and share your own pieces in class in relation to the projects you are asking the children to engage with, but be sure to maintain reciprocal relations when discussing and modelling your own writing processes and the exemplar texts you have written. Sharing the strategies that you really employ in your own writing is highly effective instruction, and children also gain from knowing that their teacher faces the same writing challenges that they do.

12. Pupil conferencing: Meeting children where they are

A rich response to children's writing is crucial. Research particularly emphasises the usefulness of 'live' verbal feedback, which is immediate, relevant, and allows children to reflect on and attend to learning points while actually still engaged in their writing. It is seen as superior to 'after-the-event' written feedback. Verbal feedback is given during short conferences which are most successful in a settled, focused, and self-regulating classroom. Teachers focus initially on composition and only attend to transcriptional issues at a later stage in the child's process. Finally, writer-teachers are better able to give constructive feedback and advice because they understand from personal experience the issues children encounter when writing.

13. Literacy for pleasure: Reading and writing connecting

Successful writing teachers know that children who read more, write more and write better. A reading for pleasure pedagogy (Cremin et al., 2014; Hansen, 2001) assists a writing for pleasure pedagogy since the individual reading of good texts available in school and in class libraries provides children with models, and continually suggests and inspires ideas and themes for personal writing projects. Successful writing teachers also know that reading aloud poems and whole texts to the class in an engaged way has a significant effect on children's vocabulary and story comprehension, and increases the range of syntactic structures and linguistic features children will use in their writing.

14. Successful interconnection of the principles

Research cannot emphasise strongly enough that all these principles, so critical to the effective teaching of writing, are powerfully interconnected and should be considered as such.

Case study: Creating our own publishing houses

Having read *Back and Forth: Using An Editor's Mindset To Improve Student Writing* by Lee Heffernan (2017), I was inspired to create a class publishing house in my own classroom. With children fully participating in the setting up of the project, it was my belief that their sense of a writing community would be enhanced, and that having responsibility for the publishing house would encourage them to read, share, and talk like writers (see Figure 14.1).

Aims: The principal aim on this occasion was to sharpen children's writer identities. I wanted them to feel like genuine writers who go through the authentic processes to become published authors. By promoting cooperative learning, I wanted to increase

Figure 14.1 Our whole-class publishing house

children's sense of self-regulation and self-efficacy since they would need to work with and use one another to be successful.

Description: We were now about halfway through the academic year and the children were settling into the idea that they could publish personal writing projects, including writing being undertaken at home, into the class library. They were increasingly talking about writing and writing collaboratively. Confidence had been built and a stronger sense of writer identity established. The children were beginning to believe in themselves as writers and to feel they had many things to say and share with each other.

At the time, I was fortunate enough to have accepted a publishing deal and so took the opportunity to explain the process I was going through and the relationship I was building with the publishing house and my 'editor'. What I've come to realise is that a *compositional* editor is a very critical friend. They look to push your ideas and your writing to its maximum potential. They support and champion you, but they also tell you when things need untangling. A publishing house, I also discovered, has a certain identity, a certain statement of intent, and a reputation for producing particular types of books. I decided to talk about it a little with my class.

We discussed which publishing houses were publishing our favourite books in the class library and we decided that, in many ways, I was the children's chief 'editor' and, as a writer-teacher, they were mine too! But we didn't have publishing house. We asked ourselves: What does our class library stand for? What sort of texts do we want to publish for each other? Importantly, what sort of texts do we *need* to publish for each other? What's our mission? We discussed this and created our own mission statement for our newly forming publishing house. Now we needed a name and a logo.

The children got together and came up with a variety of ideas. We took a vote and agreed on 'Banger Books Publishing: Books With A Wizz And A Bang!' We agreed on a logo which we felt everyone would be able to draw and add to their published pieces easily.

However, there was some disappointment in the class. Some of the children felt that maybe minority preferences weren't visible in our whole class mission statement. So with that, we decided that we could also have smaller, independent houses and that these would need mission statements, brand names, logos, and an editor too. It was also agreed that these independents should avoid encroaching on Banger Books Publishing.

The result was this poster showcasing the independents and what sorts of books they were looking to publish on their label (see Figure 14.2). Children met and conferred with the editors when they felt they had something to publish with them. They shared

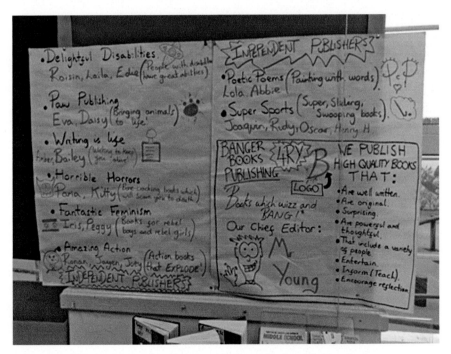

Figure 14.2 Posters showcasing the class' independent publishing houses

any revision or editorial ideas for the manuscript before it went to press. I was also around to offer advice and an independent voice too.

Here is our initial list of independent publishing houses which made up our community of writers at that time:

- Delightful Disabilities: *People with disabilities have great abilities*. We wish to publish: Stories, poems, faction, memoirs, and lots of other things about disabilities
- Paw Publishing: *Bring animals to life*. We are looking to publish high-quality texts which have strong animal characters and an environmental message
- Writing Is Life: *Writing that keeps you alive*. We are looking for memoirs that entertain, are well written, and include lots of people and loads of info
- Horrible Horrors: *Bone-cracking books that will scare you to death*. We publish high-quality books that are well written, powerful, have a meaning, are scary, entertaining, or surprising
- Fantastic Feminism: *Books for rebel boys and rebel girls* We want our books to include an amazing girl! Something that the girl does to save the day, to be thoughtful, to have a moral
- Amazing Action: *Books that explode*. We publish high-quality texts that are scary with lots of action and are well written
- Poetic Poems: *Painting with words*. We publish high-quality books that are well written, very artistic, entertain readers, not boring, poems about the things you like
- Super Sports: *Super sliding swooping books*. We publish high-quality books that are well written, about sport, are funny, and are adventurous
- 4RY Book Review: *Sharing the book love*. We publish high-quality reviews which inspire you to pick up a book and read

Impact

Creating a community of writers – children felt empowered to create and maintain their own inclusive writing community. *Every child a writer* – all children could access the publishing houses and feel they had something to say. *Reading, sharing, and talking about writing* – this is where I saw the biggest changes. It was wonderful watching children gather around a text and discuss its strengths and what it might need before it could be published. Hearing children be both critical and supportive friends has been inspiring. *Explicitly teach the writing processes* – the project helped children better understand the recursive nature of the writing processes and what manuscripts have to go through before they are published. *Personal writing projects* – it gave a high status to and created high expectations for personal writing projects. *Balancing composition with transcription* – it ensured that children attended to both the composition and the transcription of their pieces before publishing. Revision and editing were taken very seriously and were done to a much higher standard than I usually saw. *Pupil conferencing: Meeting children where they are* – this process helped me as a writer-teacher understand my role as a *compositional* editor and editor-in-chief of Banger Books Publishing. The way I spoke with the children about their projects changed dramatically. We were talking about the quality of their manuscripts on a much deeper level and I was giving genuine writerly advice and sharing my craft knowledge.

This example of practice and others like it can be found at www.writing4pleasure .com.

What is it writing for pleasure teachers do that makes the difference?

Our own research (Young, 2019) found that young writers interviewed as part of the study explicitly made a significant connection between self-efficacy, agency, and self-regulation. The children's interview and questionnaire data showed that agency was really important to them. Those who felt that they had a degree of ownership and control over the topics for their projects had a generally more positive disposition towards writing and perceived what they wrote as being more personally meaningful.

Some children stated clearly that they felt more self-efficacy when they were able to choose their own topic for a class writing project. For example, 'We don't have to write what the teacher says. It's actually better if you choose what you're going to write because you know about the thing you're going to write about' (see Figure 14.3). Others felt that their sense of self-efficacy and motivation were much diminished when their teacher chose the ideas for a class project. For example:

> If we are writing about something I don't know about – if we are writing and I have no idea what it is – I just don't know what to do; I don't like writing when it's things I don't like or it's something I'm not interested in – I'm like do I really have to write about that? If we weren't asked what we wanted to write about – it could be a bit boring; when you haven't been learning much and you don't know what to write … when you haven't really learnt about the thing you're writing like in topic and science.

However, it was very apparent from children's comments that agency over their ideas and their writing process did not by itself guarantee that they wrote well and for pleasure. They understood that they also needed instruction to help them believe that they *could* write and that they *knew how* to write successfully. The following interview statement by a Year 4 boy shows clearly that he knew exactly what he needed: 'When I know what to do, and when I can write about what I feel inside, kind of – I know I can write and I want to write'. It seems critical, therefore, that agency must sit alongside self-efficacy and self-regulation to bring about pleasure and better progress in writing.

The teachers in the research project ensured children knew about the writing processes, knew how to set themselves process goals, and knew what their own favoured processes and strategies were. They gave children explicit instruction in techniques and strategies for generating ideas for class and personal writing projects. One teacher introduced class writing

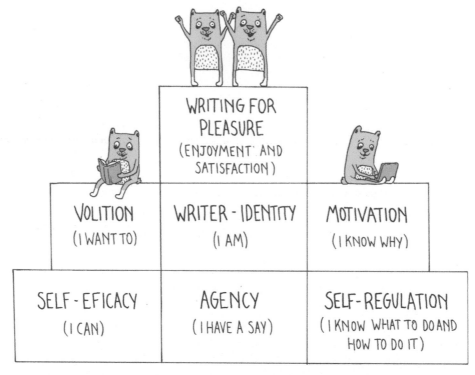

Figure 14.3 The affective domains involved in a writing for pleasure pedagogy

projects with a 'genre week' comprising a series of lessons which included discussions of genre, what genuine purpose published pieces were going to serve, and what product goals the children would need to set in order to write something successful and meaningful. Children were then given agency over the writing topic and audience. In this way, teachers ensured that their pupils had a sense of self-efficacy, agency, and self-regulation in rich combination.

Key reading

Wyse, Dominic. (2018) *Choice, Voice and Process – Teaching Writing in the 21st Century: Revisiting the Influence of Donald Graves and the Process Approach to Writing.* UCL Institute of Education.

   In this paper, Dominic Wyse re-evaluates the once influential process approach to writing and its teaching developed by Donald Graves (1983), and recommends its return as a pedagogy relevant to the contemporary primary school. Throughout, he reminds us that 'more than 30 years later there is compelling experimental evidence that process approaches to teaching writing are effective'. The paper is informed by his reporting on two empirical projects which were part of a four-year multidisciplinary study entitled How Writing Works. Firstly, the qualitative data analysis of interviews with celebrated expert writers, and secondly, an account of the teaching of writing to novice adult writers based on previously published experimental research.

Wyse is able to show that the accomplished writers' reflections on their processes match many aspects of Graves' process approach, particularly in terms of creating writing ideas, and the necessary skill and hard work involved in seeing a text through to final publication. He compares the evidence relating to novice writers with the much more extensive research into the most effective writing teaching of younger children, and finds that the key elements of the process approach to writing that work for young writers also seem to work for adult writers. He refers in particular to:

- Having ample time to write
- Providing meaningful contexts for writing in a variety of genres (especially if these are linked to writers' life experiences)
- Allowing children choice and ownership over their writing ideas and writing processes
- Collaborative and dialogic talking about writing
- Individual feedback through pupil-conferences while children are in the act of writing

All these too are promoted by Graves in his seminal work *Writing: Teachers and Children At Work*.

Of particular interest in this paper will be the very timely drawing of the reader's attention to the currently questionable state of writing teaching in English schools. Wyse says with some irony: 'In the country where the English language originated, it might be reasonable to expect an evidence-informed and enlightened approach to teaching the English language and writing in its national curriculum'. He deplores the extent to which education policies fail to reflect the abundance of research evidence that is available, and singles out for comment 'approaches that assume an undue emphasis on imitation, copying and reproduction' and the insistence on the teaching of formal grammar.

Finally, Wyse suggests that there is much to be learnt from the comparisons of music composition with text composition that were part of the 'How Writing Works' study. Parallels between the compositional process of music and words, with their required skills and knowledge (derived from other sources of reading or listening) of intonation, melody, or theme, and layered meanings or harmonies, provide a rationale for such comparisons. And, as Wyse points out, when the ear of the writer or composer is well-tuned, it enables precision, fluency, and the technical skills necessary to create and craft writing or music.

Case Study: A description of one writing for pleasure teacher's practice

I feel like if I never wrote - life would be a bit boring wouldn't it - having loads of thoughts but never being able to show it.
When he says 'time for writing' I don't go errrr, I go 'ooo writing!'

I really really enjoy writing. It's just my pleasure. I love *it*.

(Year 4 children)

The following account describes the practices of one writing for pleasure teacher, as observed and recorded by the researcher (Young, 2019). His class were achieving outstanding progress in writing, as testified by his school data.

Creating a community of writers

Mr Hayden teaches a Year 4 class in a large primary school in London. The school has a higher proportion than the national average of children entitled to Pupil Premium, children with special educational needs, and children with English as an additional language. His young apprentice writers see him as positive, caring, and interested in their lives and this undoubtedly contributes to their engagement in writing at a high level of achievement. They are a community of writers in which their teacher teaches and writes alongside his class and shares his own writing practices. The community of writers take part in meaningful practices and in writing projects they can identify with. For example, during the observation week children were engaged in writing a memoir of something from their own lives, to be shared with peers, and published into the class library for all to read. Mr Hayden has shown them how to talk and present their writing to others in an outstandingly positive and constructive way. Importantly, children are involved in actions, discussions, and reflections that make a difference to how they are taught and undertake their writing.

Every child a writer

I like to do writing because it's one of my hobbies
I like to write something that is really strong.

In his writing workshop, Mr Hayden holds high achievement expectations for all members of his class. He sees all children as writers and, from the first, teaches strategies that lead to greater independence and ensures that everyone remains part of the writing community. He also models and promotes the social aspects of writing and peer support through his manner around the class and in his mini lessons.

Reading, sharing, and talking about writing

I try to like draw and entertain with my writing. I normally share my writing and I want it to be reader-ready and really good for them (see Figure 14.4).

In Mr Hayden's writing workshop, children are given ample opportunity to share and discuss their own and others' writing (including his) in order to give and receive constructive criticism and celebrate achievement. The sophistication, maturity, and commitment children showed in these discussions was striking. The writing community had developed their own ways of talking and thinking as writers and this was a beautiful thing to observe.

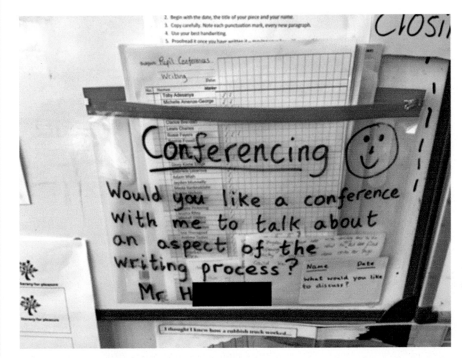

Figure 14.4 Mr Hayden's conferencing folder

Purposeful and authentic class writing projects

> There is a day where we do idea generation and we think of loads of ideas and then we pick one we want to write about. It's not really strict that you have to write about that one. You can choose.
>
> He doesn't really rush you. He helps. He makes it slow. Take your time with it and it will go smoothly.

The class writing projects Mr. Hayden introduces are seen as meaningful by his class. Children are first taught about a particular genre and are then given the opportunity to generate their own subject and purpose, write at their own pace, in their own way, and with a clear sense of a real reader. Given these circumstances, his writers remain focused on a task, maintain a strong personal agency over and commitment to their writing, and so produce something significant for themselves and in keeping with his expectations. In short, his class care about their writing and want it to do well.

Explicitly teaching the writing processes

Mr Hayden gives direct instruction in the different components of the writing process (how to generate an idea, plan/dabble, draft, revise, edit, publish). He supports children's understanding of these processes through discussion, modelling, and sharing exemplars which he has written himself. As a result, his class respect and trust him

Figure 14.5 Mr. Hayden's display showcasing the recursive nature of the writing processes, different approaches to the writing process and the class' distant, product and process goals.

as a fellow writer. He is able to show them that the writing process is not necessarily linear but discursive, and he encourages them over time to develop and use their own process. The writing posters he and his class produce collaboratively are always on display and are referred to by the children until they are able to relinquish dependence on them (see Figure 14.5).

Setting writing goals

> I kind of had a plan before of what I wanted to do today.

To maintain children's commitment and motivation during a class writing project, Mr Hayden ensures that they know the distant goal (the future audience and purpose) for their writing (see Figure 14.6). The community also has a say in setting product goals – what they will have to do to ensure their writing is successful and meaningful. They also discuss what not to do by looking at ineffective examples and deciding together what they need to avoid. Mr. Hayden sets loose process goals which keep his class on track without forcing them to write at a certain pace or rush their work. For example, he will say 'remember that your pieces need to be published into the class library in three weeks' time, so plan your writing time with that in mind'. This means children write responsibly, happily, in their own way and without negative pressure.

Figure 14.6 Children's suggestions of product goals for writing a successful football report

Personal writing projects: Writing every day

> We don't have to write what the teacher says. It's actually better if you choose what you're going to write because you know what you're going to write about.

Mr Hayden knows how essential it is that children are given time to write for a sustained period every day and to work on both class and personal writing projects. Personal projects are seen by him as an important part of the writing curriculum since it is here, through exercising their own choice of subject, purpose, audience, and writing process, that his class has true agency and come to see writing as an essentially empowering and pleasurable activity which can be used both now and in the future. Not surprisingly, Mr Hayden sees this as a social justice issue and therefore holds equally high expectations for both class and personal writing projects. He is aware, too, that personal writing projects offer him an insight into children's personalities and help build relationships. He also appreciates their value in contributing to the assessment of children's development as independent writers.

Balancing composition with transcription

The children in Mr Hayden's class know that transcriptional issues can be attended to after the act of drafting and during the revision and editing stages. Spelling and punctuation are largely self-monitored; as they write, they mark their texts for items to be checked and corrected later. He promotes the idea that children's handwriting skills are best practised in a motivating context, such as when preparing their completed pieces for publication. Mr Hayden knows that if grammar is to be understood in a meaningful way, it must be taught functionally, and examined and applied in the context of real composition. He teaches grammar through mini lessons and invites the children to try and use a particular grammatical feature in their writing that day. Decontextualised grammar exercises do not feature in his classroom.

Teach self-regulation strategies

While Mr Hayden appreciates that children will often need guidance and advice, he also believes in the importance of self-regulation strategies and how these allow his class to write with confidence and independence. He has taught them techniques on how to generate ideas, use story maps, planners and checklists and writing 'tricks and tips' for revising their compositions. His class also have easy access to resources for editing and publishing. Impressively, he discusses with the community their rights and also responsibilities when producing their texts (see Figure 14.7).

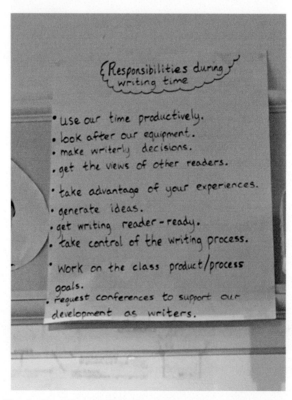

Figure 14.7 Mr Hayden's poster produced in conjunction with his class explaining their responsibilities during class writing time

Being a writer-teacher

It is impossible to underestimate just how much Mr Hayden's class gain from knowing that their teacher faces the same writing challenges that they do. He writes in and out of the classroom and shares his writing regularly with the children in the spirit of seeking constructive criticism. The researchers felt that the sorts of conversations they observed taking place during this sharing were inspirational. He maintains genuine reciprocal relations when discussing and modelling his own writing processes and the exemplar texts he is writing himself. He shares the 'tricks, tips and secret strategies' that he genuinely employs in his writing and invites the children to give them a try too.

Pupil conferencing: Meeting children where they are

> He actually gives us fun tricks and tips of things you can do and how to do it.
> Sometimes he comes and prompts us and he gives us advice to pick and it's really fun.

Mr Hayden's rich response to children's writing is crucial. During the planning and composition stages he gives conferences and provides immediate, relevant and non-judgemental feedback to individuals in his class, drawing on his own experiences as a writer. He allows them time to reflect on his suggestions and to attend to learning points while they are still engaged in their writing. Only later in a child's process does he give support with transcriptional issues. Because he is a writer-teacher, he is seen by his class to be well-placed to advise and give feedback; they know he understands the issues they encounter when he writes himself. They feel that they can talk to him as writer-to-writer and he reciprocates this feeling.

Conclusion

> My pedagogical stance is best exemplified by a Writing for Pleasure pedagogy which is why I pursue it faithfully. One of the unexpected benefits of implementing this approach is that it has reignited my passion for learning about writing and the teaching of it and I am now a voracious reader of the literature which underpins the approach. From Ralph Fletcher to Lucy Calkins; from Donald Graves to Michael Rosen, I now have a small library's worth of wisdom to work my way through knowing that next year's teaching will surely be even better than this year's.
>
> *(Mr Hayden)*

The researcher (Young, 2019) was in no doubt that Mr Hayden's class wrote for pleasure and genuinely felt themselves to be writers and not simply producers of text – a rare thing in the current climate of children's writing at school. That he was able so successfully to create a writing for pleasure community together with the achievement of exceptionally high progress data in a very diverse class of children suggests that writing for pleasure as a pedagogy has huge potential.

Chapter summary

In order to develop a writing for pleasure approach in primary schools, it is important to:

- Recognise that children are more likely to underachieve if they dislike writing
- Recognise that writing for pleasure is based on principles of effective writing teaching
- Attend to children's affective writing needs, for example their self-efficacy, agency, self-regulation, volition, motivation, and writer-identities
- Participate in action-research and CPD, for example by submitting an example of practice at www.writing4pleasure.com

References

Alexander, R. (2009) *Cambridge Primary Review*. London: Routledge.

Au, W. and Gourd, K. (2013) Asinine Assessment: Why High-Stakes Testing Is Bad for Everyone, Including English Teachers. *The English Journal* 103(1), pp. 14–19.

Beard, R. (2000) *Developing Writing 3–13*. Oxon: Hodder and Stoughton.

Clark, C. (2016) *Children's and Young People's Writing in 2015*. London: National Literacy Trust.

Clark, C. and Teravainen, A. (2017) *Writing for Enjoyment and Its Link to Wider Writing*. London: National Literacy Trust.

Cremin, T., Mottram, M., Collins, F., Powell, S. and Safford, K. (2014) *Building Communities of Engaged Readers: Reading for Pleasure*. London: Routledge.

Cremin, T. and Oliver, L. (2017) Teachers as Writers: A Systematic Review. *Research Papers in Education* 32(3), pp. 269–295.

DfE (2012) *What is the Research Evidence on Writing?* London: Education Standards Research Team, Department for Education.

DfE (2013) *The national curriculum in England: Key stages 1 and 2 framework document*. Available at: https://www.gov.uk/government/publications/national-curriculum-in-england-primary-curriculum

DfE (2017) *National Curriculum Assessments at Key Stage 2 in England, 2017 (revised)*. London: Department for Education.

DfE (2018) *National Curriculum Assessments at Key Stage 2 in England, 2018 (provisional)*. London: Department for Education.

Dyson, A. H. and Freedman, S. W. (2003) Writing. In J. Flood, J. Jensen, D. Lapp, and R. J. Squire (Eds.), *Handbook of Research on Teaching the English Language Arts* (pp. 967–992). Mahwah, NJ: Erlbaum.

Graham, L. and Johnson, A. (2012) *Children's Writing Journals*. Royston: United Kingdom Literacy Association.

Graham, S. and Perin, D. (2007) *Writing Next: Effective Strategies to Improve Writing of Adolescents in Middle School and High Schools*. New York: Alliance for Excellent Education.

Graves, D. (1983) *Writing: Teachers and Children at Work*. New Hampshire: Heinemann.

Hansen, J. (2001) *When Writers Read*. 2nd ed. New Hampshire: Heinemann.

Heffernan, L. (2017) *Back and Forth: Using an Editor's Mindset to Improve Student Writing*. New Hampshire: Heinemann.

Hillocks, G. (1986) *Research on Written Composition: New Directions for Teaching*. Urbana, IL: National Council of Teachers of English.

Ketter, J. and Pool, J. (2001) Exploring the Impact of a High-Stakes Direct Writing Assessment in Two High School Classrooms. *Research in the Teaching of English* 35(3), pp. 344–393.

Lave, J. and Wenger, E. (1991) *Situated Learning: Legitimate Peripheral Participation*. London: Cambridge University Press.

Ofsted (2009) *English at the Crossroads*. London: Ofsted.

Ofsted (2012) *Moving English Forward*. London: Ofsted.

Ofsted (2019) *Education Inspection Framework: Overview of Research*. London: Ofsted.

Watanabe, M. (2007) Displaced Teacher and State Priorities in a High-Stakes Accountability Context. *Educational Policy* 21(2), pp. 311–368.

Wyse, D. (2019) Choice, Voice and Process – Teaching Writing in the 21st Century: Revisiting the Influence of Donald Graves and the Process Approach to Writing. *English in Australia* 53(3), pp. 82–92.

Young, R. (2019) *What is it Writing for Pleasure Teachers Do that Makes the Difference?* UK: The Goldsmiths' Company and The University of Sussex [Online] Available at www.writing4pleasure.com

Young, R. and Ferguson, F. (2019) *Power English Writing: Teacher's Guide Year 6.* Oxford: Pearson Education.

Young, R. and Ferguson, F. (2020) *Real-World Writers: A Handbook for Teaching Writing with 7-11 Year Olds.* London: Routledge.

Young, R. and Ferguson, F. (2021) *Writing for Pleasure: Theory, Research and Practice.* London: Routledge.

15 Creating a dynamic and responsive curriculum

Janet Morris and Rachel Wolfendale

Critical questions

What are the current ideological drivers of curriculum development?

What are the foundations of a dynamic and relevant curriculum?

How can a curriculum be implemented to maximise engagement and inspiration?

How can a curriculum be designed and planned?

How can teachers implement the curriculum with autonomy?

How are the interests of parents, children and community represented in curriculum design?

What is the impact of delivering the curriculum in this dynamic way?

Introduction

The content, purpose, and nature of the curriculum are current hot topics for primary schools. This chapter aims to explore, with three of our partner schools, their intent around the development of curriculum and the practical ways in which it is implemented by individual teachers and their impact. We further aim to explore current practice within the parameters of the national curriculum (DfE, 2014), the most recent Ofsted framework (Ofsted, 2019b) as well as curriculum research and academic discussion (Alexander, 2010; Barnes and Cremin, 2018; Myatt, 2018; Swann et al., 2012). Our aim is to support teachers and students in implementing a dynamic, responsive curriculum that represents the children in their class. We argue that the current impetus around a broad and balanced curriculum offers opportunities for teachers, believing that they 'Can still exert autonomy (despite external pressures) over what they teach through the ways in which they interpret the statutory curriculum' (Chamberlain and McDonald, 2018).

Critical question

What are the current ideological drivers of curriculum development?

Although recent interest by Ofsted (Ofsted, 2019b) is clearly a key driver to schools' current focus on curriculum, this only acts as confirmation of teachers' and educationalists' accumulated concerns over the narrowing of the curriculum in recent years.

Published by the last Labour Government, 'Excellence and Enjoyment' (DfES, 2003) recognised that 'high standards are obtained through a rich, varied and exciting curriculum which develops children in a range of ways'. It was envisaged this would be achieved through empowering primary schools to take control of their curriculum, to be 'more innovative and to develop their own character' and to 'make the most of links between different areas and provide opportunities for children to have a wide range of learning experiences' (DfES, 2003).

Many schools have also been influenced in developing a 'principled' pedagogy by the findings of the Cambridge Primary Review, 'a comprehensive and independent enquiry into the condition and future of primary education' (Alexander, 2010: 1). In this summary of the review's priorities there is an emphasis on the creation of a 'true entitlement curriculum' where 'learning in one area enhances the learning in others' (Alexander, 2014: 161).

In the national curriculum (DfE, 2014) the department for education itself recognises that 'The school curriculum comprises all learning and other experiences that each school plans for its pupils. The National Curriculum forms (only) one part of the school curriculum'. This implies a freedom to go beyond the national curriculum and develop the wider school curriculum to represent and serve the idiosyncratic character of individual schools. The document also recognises the importance of the 'spiritual, moral, cultural, mental and physical development of pupils at the school and of society, and prepares pupils at the school for the opportunities, responsibilities and experiences of later life'.

In the research sitting behind the most recent Ofsted framework (2019a) it was highlighted that there was a tendency for many schools to narrow the curriculum, with too much emphasis on core subjects to the detriment of the quality and quantity of curriculum coverage of the foundation subjects. There will now be a greater emphasis on knowledge, local needs, and contexts as well as an emphasis on seeking to address disadvantage. Other important principles include the need to emphasise equity and empathy, challenge, relevance, exploration, and freedom (Ofsted, 2019a). In the findings it was recognised that in successful schools teachers' subject knowledge was found to be important, as was professional development in foundation subjects in order to bring about depth and coverage of the curriculum on offer. However, leaders in these schools also ensured that the curriculum was appropriate to the context of the school and were clear about how the curriculum meets their unique aims and values. They also 'prioritise the curriculum, make it their business to ensure that the planned curriculum is implemented successfully across a wide range of subjects so that curriculum quality is high. By doing this, they ensure curriculum coherence'. The impact of high quality teaching on addressing the attainment gap is also recognised by the Education Endowment Foundation who summarise that 'What happens in the classroom makes the biggest difference: Improving teaching quality generally leads to greater improvements at lower cost than structural changes' (Education Endowment Foundation, 2018).

Taken together we argue that these drivers *could* set the scene for schools and teachers to confidently adapt the curriculum to support the diverse learning needs of their children. We now show examples of where our partner schools are working to address these issues as they explain the principles that underpin their approach to offering a broad, rich curriculum. The following case studies show how the discreet teaching of subject knowledge considered throughout the rest of this book, can be woven together to create a cohesive, connected, and relevant curriculum. This is based on a foundation of clearly identified values and learning characteristics.

Critical question

What are the foundations of a cohesive, connected and relevant curriculum?

Case study one: Values and learning characteristics as the foundation of the curriculum

Sam and Rebecca are curriculum leads in Forster Park and Coopers Lane Primary Schools in the London Borough of Lewisham. Both are larger than average in size, with a high proportion of pupils from minority ethnic backgrounds and an above average number speaking English as an additional language. Both schools have a high level of economic disadvantage with a large percentage of their pupils supported by funding through the pupil premium.

At Forster Park, the national curriculum requirement for a broad and balanced curriculum is underpinned with a consideration of children's spiritual, moral, social and cultural development (SMSC). In this way SMSC is at the centre of all of the learning, with children being provided with opportunities *from* real life and *for* their future lives. Rebecca, the curriculum lead, emphasises that this 'puts the children first and at the core of the curriculum'.

Teachers plan around five characters who embody the key life skills of: *Leadership, organisation, resilience, initiative, communication* and a sixth character, *adventure,* suggesting that the children use all of these skills to 'go on an adventure in learning'. Planning also takes into account their school values of *energy, respect for diversity, ambition, creativity, adventure, and community*. Each half term one of the skills is paired with one of the values as a focus for the planning. For example, *energy* and *organisation* are chosen at the beginning of the year to get you going!

Similarly, Coopers Lane School have developed their vision for The Coopers Lane Learner, created by the whole teaching staff during dedicated staff meeting time. The schools' behaviour system also works effectively alongside promotion of the schools' core values so children learn about the value of perseverance and their responsibility to produce their best work. This focus on learning characteristics highlights children's entitlement to and attitude towards their own learning, with 'creativity inspiring them to have a commitment to learning that lasts'. Explicit teaching focuses on curiosity and wonder and critical thinking and aims to build resilience and aspiration. The emphasis is on them as a whole-rounded child, encouraging them to embrace their own education. Teachers are encouraged to offer 'a range of opportunities that create lasting memories'.

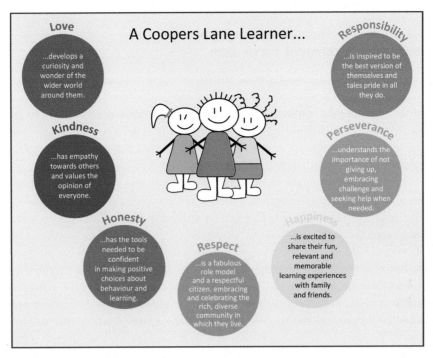

Figure 15.1 A Coopers Lane Learner

This recognition of the importance of teaching core values and learning behaviours as a foundation for the delivery of the curriculum is a common factor in both Forster Park and Coopers Lane and is continually promoted in the environment, the language used and specifically in teachers' plans. This approach mirrors the emphasis on learning behaviours highlighted in the Ofsted (2019) framework where inspectors will judge whether learners' attitudes to their education or training are positive. This case study demonstrates how two schools in our partnership seek to develop children who are committed to their own learning, know how to study effectively, are resilient in the face of setbacks, and take pride in their achievements (see Figure 15.1).

However, it is also important to note that such prominence of SMSC, core values and learning behaviours must *co-exist* with the teaching of knowledge and skills:

> Attainment and personal development are like two strands of a rope intertwined and depending on each other. Too much attention to 'personal development' may lead to a lack of mental and intellectual challenge, while too little may result in children not learning life-skills and how to relate to other people. We all need both.
>
> (Wilson, 2014 p. 60)

Critical question

How is the curriculum designed and planned?

Case study one: Building on the foundations and creating a coherent curriculum

At Forster Park School the national curriculum expectations are taken apart and the objectives allocated to particular terms and year groups so that each subject is divided up over six half-terms across the year to ensure progression. The aim of the curriculum plan is to ensure coverage of all subject areas where 'every child can shine in their environment' and have the opportunity to develop skills in different areas, with these often overlapping. However, it is also important to the planning process that teachers' voice is superimposed on top. Class teachers add their own ideas and have creative freedom to decide how the objectives could be achieved and pieced together logically with the learning characteristics, school values and their own children in mind.

Curriculum design at Coopers Lane follows a similar pattern with the emphasis on topic-based learning, with each component piecing together to ensure complete coverage over the year. In each topic, subject areas are brought together in a logical way with the learning objectives presented as key questions for the children to explore, thereby prioritising the development of children's curiosity. Time is allocated in staff meetings for teachers to work together in year group teams to plan each topic and to consider where core subjects such as Literacy might link. Subject leaders have also developed their knowledge and expertise in the foundation subjects and can provide support as well as detailed knowledge trackers to support progression.

Rebecca gives a lovely example of how this all comes together in a Year 4 lesson where the objective was: 'to use a range of materials creatively to design and make products'. This activity was paired with the learning characteristic of 'initiative'. The children were encouraged and facilitated to volunteer and trial ideas, carry out research, suggest and create resources leading to a whole class performance. The children auditioned for roles in their final piece, complete with their own props and scenery, etc. This project, or topic-based approach, leads naturally to cross curricular planning where the children are engrossed in their learning (Barnes, 2018). A further example saw children exploring the Romans in Britain. The speech of Boudica to rally her troops offered a vehicle for learning about persuasive language. The children became so engrossed in the drama of this lesson that they questioned if this was 'actually English teaching'.

As can be seen in this case study, each school emphasises the importance of 'connecting the dots'. As Rebecca points out 'These are not individual isolated lessons, they are all feeding into one big picture'. This approach offers relevance and opportunities for the application of transferrable skills and knowledge while being careful to avoid tenuous links being forced into the planning. Each week the plans consider what the main focus question will be with all of the topic work directed towards that same question. Key vocabulary is identified and explored alongside the main focus question in order to improve children's comprehension skills. Myatt endorses such explorations of language and suggests that learning is further enhanced by discussing the meaning and roots of these words as they are often conceptual. This enables children to develop confidence and expertise in subjects and will 'take pupils deeper into the richness of the subject' (Myatt, 2018: 97).

Critical question

How can the curriculum be implemented to maximise engagement and inspiration?

Creative teaching should not be viewed *in contrast* to the teaching of essential knowledge, skills and understandings as 'creative teaching involves teaching the subjects in creative contexts, that explicitly invite learners to engage imaginatively and that stretch their generative, evaluative and collaborative capacities' (Cremin and Barnes, 2018: 428). This is achieved in different ways between schools and even within schools. Teachers may launch a new topic with theme days, Drama activities, role play, or use artefacts to inspire questions and a desire to find out more. These are sometimes referred to as 'creative entry points'.

In Coopers Lane School, for example, a Year 4 class was learning about Greek myths so the launch day involved dressing up, storytelling, role-play, arts and crafts, and construction. As the topic evolves children are encouraged to come up with new questions or may be presented with a problem to solve by carrying out their own research. Children complete 'KWL grids' at the beginning and end of a topic which stands for: What I know, what I want to know and what I've learnt. Sam explains this is then built into the medium-term plan and 'centres the children within the planning'. At the end of a topic teachers and children revisit these grids and reflect on that term's learning. The grids are stuck into the topic books so children can add questions and keep a log of what they are learning. Depth is ensured with further prompts relating to subject knowledge and vocabulary. At Forster Park, teachers often plan lessons where children become the 'experts' in different aspects of the topic and then share their learning with each other. This facilitates a child-led approach to the learning where children's individual interests can be taken into consideration.

Alongside this, teachers across each of the schools are encouraged to utilise their *own* knowledge and expertise as well as sharing this with colleagues and subject specialists. This will then enable a sharing of subject knowledge and associated vocabulary to ensure children can be exposed to knowledge at a more profound level. Immersive sessions of deep learning can be planned in as the children's understanding of the topic expands and their favourite creative activities are repeatedly returned to in order to maintain engagement and inspiration. With this approach to curriculum delivery, ample time is needed to allow for extended study and space provided to facilitate unexpected learning opportunities.

The topic is then brought to a close with a 'finale', offering a chance to apply the accumulated knowledge and skills. This is sometimes attended by other children in the school or by parents and gives the day a sense of purpose, pride and audience. These events may involve exhibitions, performances, or immersive experiences such as – at Forster Park – creating a royal banquet, complete with feasting and dancing!

A further example given by Coopers Lane is of a Year 3 class learning about India. Parents were invited to an end of term event in the playground to celebrate the festival of Holi, wearing white T-shirts with paint being thrown by all! The learning journey leading up to this event involved children taking on the role of travel agents, researching places in India, and potential city holidays. They prepared keynote presentations and flow diagrams on India to apply computing skills. These examples illustrate the importance of rejoicing in, and respecting the production of, carefully considered work that reflects the joy and inspiration experienced by children and is an important part of the curriculum delivery.

Critical question

How can teachers implement the curriculum with autonomy?

In planning for a dynamic and relevant curriculum it is essential to continuously evaluate the purpose of each piece of teaching that will be adopted and implemented from the wider curriculum plan. There are a series of questions below (Myatt, 2018) that may help the teacher to frequently reflect on the purpose and wider meaning of their planned teaching:

Prompt questions for reflecting on purpose:

* Why am I teaching this lesson?
* Where does it fit into the bigger curriculum plans?
* What are my pupils meant to take from it?
* Why is it important for them to know this and master this?
* What difference would it make to the learning if we did not do this?
* What is it for?

(Myatt, 2018)

It would be useful to consider these prompts for each planned lesson in order to ensure the teaching relates to the wider overall curriculum as well as the values and driving foci of the school. Enabling children to recognise and explore the connections between subjects helps them understand the purpose of their learning and how this links to the bigger picture (Myatt, 2018). Nothing can beat the joy, for both teacher and child, when the pieces fit together and it all makes sense!

In order for the creation of a dynamic and relevant curriculum to be implemented successfully by teachers, the role of the leadership team in the school is critical. In the examples used in this chapter, the leadership team has been instrumental in inspiring and educating their staff as to the values underlying their vision and supporting them with the logistics of turning this into workable classroom plans. Time allocation is crucial to enable planning to be comprehensive and ensure logical coverage across subjects as well as to allow for collegiate working to share ideas, knowledge, and inspiration. This also allows for systematic evaluations and improvements to keep the curriculum dynamic.

Subject leaders play a key role in assisting teachers to plan for depth of knowledge by consistently enhancing and updating their own specialism through tailored training opportunities that can be transmitted to the wider staff. In her interview, Sam talks of curriculum leadership team meetings held twice a term and how these offer opportunities to evaluate and reflect on curriculum delivery and adjust where necessary.

With this support and guidance in mind, it is most beneficial for children if teachers, once armed with the information, guidance, resources and time allocation they need, are also provided with creative autonomy to make the learning relevant for themselves and to the children they are teaching.

> Professionally independent and curious, creative teachers are aware of themselves as creative beings, although for some this may be a relatively new insight. They model, demonstrate and foster a questioning stance and the making of connections, and a marked degree of autonomy and ownership: in the process they value and nurture originality and the generation/evaluation of ideas. Through such practice they seek to develop the creative dispositions of their students.
>
> (Peacock, 2015: 41)

As Peacock (2015) notes, it is essential that school leaders encourage teachers to develop and share their expertise, creativity and knowledge with each other. In Coopers Lane, teachers are encouraged to team teach and carry out their own peer observations free from a sense of performativity. The school also encourages staff to deepen their subject knowledge and broaden vocabulary. An example of this is to take advantage of the expertise provided by education departments of local museums, galleries, and other places of interest.

As teachers become increasingly knowledgeable and confident in a wide variety of subjects the more they are able to gain autonomy and creative licence to adjust the delivery of the curriculum to suit their own individual style, expertise and passions.

Critical question

How are the interests of parents, children, and community represented in curriculum design?

Making learning relevant for children

A common thread in each school is in recognising children as co-constructors of their learning. There is an emphasis on creativity, encouraging questioning and ensuring relevance to the children and community of the school. All teachers are encouraged to spend time getting to know their classes really well so they can identify children's interests and strengths based on the assumption that these may be varied and therefore form a fascinating basis on which to personalise the learning. This recognises that, within a topic, there will be aspects of the learning that really appeal to some children or that others may find more challenging. With this in mind, it is crucial to plan opportunities for all the children to excel. As Rebecca points out, if the curriculum were too narrow 'it would be a shame. If you're not teaching art, if you're not teaching DT, if you're not teaching Computing, they may never have a moment to shine'.

Similarly, in Coopers Lane teachers are encouraged to find out about their children's preferred learning environments and adjust their planning to suit these. For example, video blogging, role play, learning outside, or construction offer a varied menu of learning opportunities. Sam explains that an integral part of their curriculum development involves asking teachers to complete an 'A-Z of what their children love before they even start planning'. This is then referred to alongside the topics so that 'they and the children can enjoy the learning more'. This demonstrates that it is possible for teachers to consider involving children in *how* they would like to learn, and perhaps learn better, as well as *what* they would like to learn.

The importance of making the learning relevant to 'real life' is also imperative. In Forster Park for example they have introduced a *real* bank in the school where children and their families can deposit money for savings. This project was launched in 2018 and has been a real success with the community. The bank is staffed by children who were interviewed for their posts following the completion of job applications. They were then given uniforms and responsibility to present the project to the school, plan marketing strategies and other 'real life' job experiences. Banking both their own and their parents' money proved a successful way of showcasing how children can take ownership and become experts, through being grounded in authentic and relevant experiences.

Making learning relevant to families, local community, and the wider world

The contribution that parents can make to the learning in schools is often underestimated or underutilised. Their expertise and unique experiences offer an opportunity to enhance and enrich the learning and the impact on children's sense of identity and representation in the curriculum can be substantially enhanced by adopting this approach.

In each of these partnership schools, parents, school staff, and local community members are invited in to talk about their jobs, such as a local basketball player or mayor, in order to raise aspirations and inform children of the vast opportunities available to them as they grow up. Parents are kept informed as the learning progresses over the year so that they can offer their involvement or request support themselves in certain subjects such as maths. Community days are held at the end of the year to celebrate the learning together. In each school there is a rich and diverse fusion of cultures and languages and the acknowledgement of each family's value and opportunity to engage with the school is paramount.

Plumcroft Primary School in Woolwich demonstrates these principles of inclusion and community collaboration in practice. Each year, Sophie, the curriculum lead, applies for funding and coordinates an Arts-based, community-focused project in order to 'do something that makes us a community'. She explains that the school intake draws from an area of South East London traditionally seen in deficit terms, which can impact on the way the children perceive themselves and their families. The intent is to design a whole school project with the key aim of children feeling that their community is valued – that it is in fact, 'Brilliant!' Furthermore that they, the children, have potential and ideas and can develop skills that could be used to improve their area.

The project, carried out in the final term, is designed to offer opportunities for the children to learn about and through their communities. It further aims for the children to learn in a different way, through interaction with their area and the people within it; express their ideas in a wide range of ways and for the creative Arts to bring the school, families, and community together.

Case study three: Representing children, parents, and community in the curriculum

'The Londoners Project' at Plumcroft Primary School Woolwich.

The project began with 'Maybe it's because I'm a Londoner', a song that encapsulates post-war pride in the people and localities that survived the Blitz. Sophie explains that they started with the Blitz as this is 'a very strong part of the identity of London, but one which the children knew very little about'. The launch assembly focused on the experience of children just like them; showing photographs of children making go-carts, playing on bomb sites, or sleeping in underground stations. They then moved on to thinking about changes in their community in the post-war period and the arrival of the Windrush Generation from the Caribbean. This led the project into an enquiry to find out about *their* London and themselves as Londoners, through interacting with *their* place and *their* community.

Parents were asked to contribute from the outset. The funding provided by Awards for All from the National Lottery for community-based projects requires community participation in the planning. Parents were asked for their ideas on the project and the types of activities it should involve, giving a valuable starting point. They were asked for their stories of what it was like growing up in London or what London was like when they arrived, what they like about London and what they would like to see improved. Teachers then shared these stories with the children so that they had lots of different ideas about people growing up in their area or what it was like being a new arrival. A range of visitors were also invited into school, many of these were contacts of teachers and staff. Teachers had freedom to organise appropriate visits and design activities to address this enquiry and were encouraged to use the 'three Vs' (visits, visitors, and voices).

One example of this was a group of Year 4 children developing and using their data handling skills through their consideration of big local issues. Children went out into their local shopping centre and interviewed the local residents asking them to indicate their concerns about the community; crime, pollution etc. They then displayed this information visually in different types of graphs. The children developed confidence, as they became the experts – with their clipboards; demonstrating and explaining their knowledge to the shoppers.

A design activity, a 'Dragons Den' competition, involved the children creating new structures as solutions to some of the problems identified. One lovely suggestion was for 'a place for grown-ups who were having a hard time or had a hard life, somewhere for them to relax'. Written materials, produced to support their 'pitch', included beautiful language about community and making their area better.

The Londoners Project culminated in an Arts week where each child had the opportunity to develop their creative skills, facilitated by specialist tutors, in their chosen art form (music composition, drama, dance) or through journalism. Working towards a whole school performance, with parents invited and involved, the children explored and found ways to express, 'what's so great about *their* London'.

Dixon and Hales (2013) explain how deep learning, particularly of History, can be achieved through interacting with 'the local' in this way. Furthermore, Leat and Thomas (2019) suggest that such a community-based curriculum is not only highly motivating and engaging but enables consideration of global concerns and how children can contribute towards the United Nations Sustainable Development Goals (https://www.un.org/sustainabledevelopment) The example of the design solutions to locally identified issues offered by the children at Plumcroft indicate children's sensitivity to, and affinity with, their surroundings and the people within it as well as their creative and imaginative approaches to solving problems.

The project also shows how the performing arts and the consideration of popular culture as well as 'the familiar' can engage children, enabling them to make links and keeps their learning relevant.

Although the children enjoyed 'Maybe it's because I'm a Londoner' (perhaps not as much as the older members of staff at the school), it was their enjoyment of the song 'London's the Place for Me' that really captured their imagination. It was introduced to them accompanying the footage of the famous Calypso artist, Lord Kitchener, arriving in London on HMS Windrush in 1948. However, the children recognised it from the film *Paddington* and made their own connections to the theme of new arrivals.

It is important when discussing culture, that this is seen as something that is shared, something we all have, not different, exotic or 'othering' which can be divisive and breed resentment. Overall, this project gave children an opportunity to focus on expressing what they shared together as Londoners; great food, great parks, great museums, and learning through community experiences, as well as the common goal of making their area better. The finale of the performance saw the whole school singing a new verse of 'London is the Place for me' inspired by one of the children's poems and reflecting their joy in the diversity of their community (see Figure 15.2).

The example of the Londoners Project highlights the value of visits and extra-curricular activities. These should always be purposeful and linked to the learning as they are often costly and time consuming. They should be consistently evaluated to ensure they are providing rich and engaging experiences that feed into the long-term plans discussed earlier. Local resources such as the local parks, libraries, mosques, or synagogues for example, should be

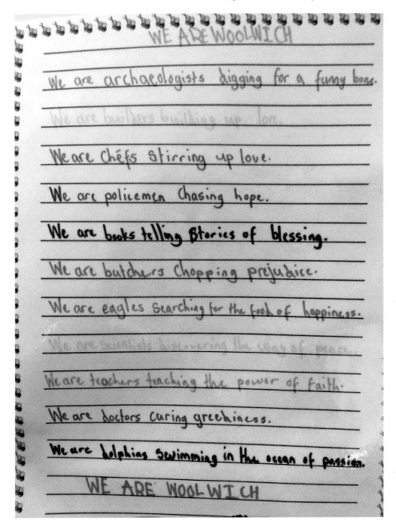

Figure 15.2 Celebrating the local

utilised to give meaning to the experiences. Parents and local community members can also be asked to share their cultural experiences or subject knowledge with the children.

The significance of local and global current affairs is also important when creating a dynamic curriculum that is relevant and inspiring for children. Rebecca from Forster Park emphasises that localised issues have become increasingly prominent in the last year. She suggests that knife crime or the current concern over county lines, for example, create a challenge for schools when refreshing their curriculum objectives. The importance of focusing on the school's core values and the promotion of children's spiritual, moral, social, and cultural development becomes ever more significant. She stresses that, should there be topics in this context that they deem to be vital, teachers should be encouraged to have the confidence to veer away from the timetable in order to address these issues properly and in a timely manner.

This disposition towards flexibility and reacting to meaningful wider contexts is essential to the embedding of an authentic, relevant, and engaging curriculum that sits alongside the requirements of the national curriculum (2014). The aim is not to lessen the intentions of this curriculum, but to recognise how the meshing together of cultures from the wider community, home, and school would enrich a child's educational experience. Dyson (2016) notes how this type of curriculum 'seeks to acknowledge and respect the complexity of children's social worlds and cultural materials. And it attempts, not only to create bridges between worlds, but to support children's own naming and manipulating of the dynamic relationships among worlds' (Dyson, 2016: 57).

Critical question

What is the impact of delivering the curriculum in this dynamic way?

Impact on engagement and enjoyment

Undoubtedly the impact of the curriculum is of key importance in our discussion. Rebecca recollects how, before their recent changes to create a more connected curriculum were implemented, the books in school were showing a 'lack of joy'. However, the enthusiasm and excitement that she is now witnessing when she visits lessons has become more evident in children's work.

There is value in planning sufficient time and variety of opportunities to enable children to fully immerse in new learning. For example, carrying out a Science project over an extended period and concentrating on the importance of making relevant connections allows children to deepen understanding. As Rebecca explains, 'I see primary school as "making memories"'.

A possible barrier to implementing a more creative approach to teaching and learning can be teacher's anxiety over the production of evidence or how to document this approach in a way that matches the learning experiences. Mobile technology, such as tablets, can be used to record learning through photographs, videos, and recording of children's voices as additional evidence to support the topic books. This has the added benefit that children's work can be respected and celebrated through displays. A clear expectation of high standards and an encouragement for them to produce their *finest* work, with pride, helps children value their learning.

Sam at Coopers Lane notes that: 'When we visit classrooms, children can always tell you what they are learning about and topics are given the same value as discreet subjects such as maths and English'. She adds that some children who are usually less engaged, or have had behavioural difficulties in the past, will often now talk animatedly about their topic and what they have learnt. It is evident that there are lessons they have really engaged in. Sam observes that, 'as reflective practitioners we can think about what was good about that learning that engaged these children, and made them want to come to school, and try and teach more in this way'.

Impact on learning and long-term skills

The schools' emphasis on curriculum relevance to the wider community and career-related learning ought to positively impact on children's application of skills in the future. Forster Park's bank for example, and associated 'economics curriculum', provides children with financial awareness and opportunities to apply Maths skills in concrete and meaningful scenarios. This has particular significance in a school where 'The majority of pupils are disadvantaged and supported by funding through the pupil premium' (Ofsted, 2015). Here, the impact of this curriculum approach, although qualitative in nature and more difficult to capture through data, could have long-term positive repercussions on how children engage with learning throughout their lives. The important qualities taught through such a curriculum including resilience, confidence and independence, go beyond the academic and prepare children for contemporary life.

Impact on teachers' pedagogy

The impact on teachers themselves is also important to consider. As Rebecca points out that, 'for some, this is a shift which is ahead of the curve, where previously they were delivering schemes of work'. Teachers need to be supported in learning how to react and adapt to children's interests and learning attributes which in turn increases teacher's own pedagogical skills and enjoyment in teaching. Subject leaders offer suggestions or guidelines to help with the planning and structure within the framework. Rebecca reiterates that within their approach 'it is, essentially quite free for teachers to adapt plans to the children's interests and their own strengths, which keeps it exciting and not repetitive'. This unhindered approach to planning and recognition of teacher's own unique skills and knowledge, alongside the professional support afforded, has a positive impact on a teacher's sense of creative autonomy and professional self-esteem. Collegiate working and sharing of ideas, resources, and expertise supports workload as well as developing confidence and may increase job satisfaction and longevity in the profession.

Chapter summary

Sir Ken Robinson identified three crucial characteristics that should be present in a curriculum: 'Diversity, Depth and Dynamism' (Robinson, 2015: 157). These encapsulate much of what has been discussed in this chapter where the individual strengths and interests of children and teachers are recognised alongside building relationships with the wider community through opportunities to pursue subjects with relevance and depth.

Each school that we visited has implemented their own approach to the curriculum that ensures wide coverage and depth in all subject areas, not just discreet teaching of core subjects. The approach is characterised by topic or project-based learning that has been carefully mapped out in advance to ensure comprehensive coverage of the national curriculum (2014). Here we can see that the teachers and children together have brought the topics alive. They have taken ownership and control of their own curriculum to ensure it is relevant to their particular children and communities and is aligned with their own and their schools' core values.

Further reading

Barnes, J. (2018) *Applying Cross-Curricular Approaches Creatively: The Connecting Curriculum.* Oxon: Routledge.

Department for Education (2014) *The National Curriculum in England: Complete Framework for Key Stages 1 to 4.* Available at: https://www.gov.uk/government/publications/national-curriculum-in-england-framework-for-key-stages-1-to-4 (Accessed: 18 March 2020).

Myatt, M. (2018) *The Curriculum: Gallimaufry to Coherence.* Woodbridge: John Catt Educational.

Ofsted (2019) *Education Inspection Framework Overview of Research.* Available at: https://assets.publishing.service.gov.uk/government/uploads/system/uploads/attachment_data/file/813229/Education_inspection_framework_references.pdf (Accessed: 18 March 2020).

References

Alexander, R. (2010) *Children, Their World, Their Education. Final Report and Recommendations of the Cambridge Primary Review.* London: Routledge.

Alexander, R. (2014) The Best that Has Been Thought and Said. *Forum* 56(1), pp. 157–166.

Barnes, J. (2018) *Applying Cross-Curricular Approaches Creatively: The Connecting Curriculum.* London: Routledge.

Chamberlain, L. and McDonald, R. (2018) Investigating the Aims, Values and Purposes of Primary Education: The Case of the Cambridge Primary Review. In Cremin, T. and Arthur, J. (Eds.), *Learning to Teach in the Primary School.* Oxon: Routledge.

Cremin, T. and Barnes, J. (2018) Creativity and Creative Teaching and Learning. In Cremin, T. and Burnett, C. (Eds.), *Learning to Teach in the Primary School.* Abingdon: Routledge, pp. 428–442.

Department for Education (2014) *The National Curriculum in England: Complete Framework for Key Stages 1 to 4.* Available at: https://www.gov.uk/government/publications/national-curriculum-in-england-framework-for-key-stages-1-to-4 (Accessed: 18 March 2020).

Department for Education and Skills (2003) *Excellence and Enjoyment: Learning and Teaching in the Primary Years: Introductory Guide: Supporting School Improvement.* Available at: https://webarchive.nationalarchives.gov.uk/20040722022638/http://www.dfes.gov.uk/primarydocument/ (Accessed: 18 March 2020).

Dixon, L. and Hales, A. (2013) *Bringing History Alive through Local People and Places: A Guide for Primary School Teachers.* London: Routledge.

Dyson, A. H. (2016) *Negotiating a Permeable Curriculum: On Literacy, Diversity, and the Interplay of Children's and Teachers' Worlds.* New York: Garn Press.

Education Endowment Foundation (2018) *Attainment Gap Report, 2018.* Available at: https://educationendowmentfoundation.org.uk/public/files/Annual_Reports/EEF_Attainment_Gap_Report_2018.pdf

Leat, D. and Thomas, U. (2019) Community Curriculum Making: Mixing the 'Local' with the National Curriculum. *Impact: Journal of the Chartered College of Teaching.* May 2019. Available at: https://impact.chartered.college/article/community-curriculum-making-mixing-local-national-curriculum/

Myatt, M. (2018) *The Curriculum. Gallimaufry to Coherence.* Woodbridge: John Catt Educational.

Ofsted (2019a) *Education Inspection Framework Overview of Research.* Available at: https://assets.publishing.service.gov.uk/government/uploads/system/uploads/attachment_data/file/813229/Education_inspection_framework_references.pdf (Accessed: 18 March 2020).

Ofsted (2019b) *School Inspection Handbook.* Available at: https://assets.publishing.service.gov.uk/government/uploads/system/uploads/attachment_data/file/843108/School_inspection_handbook_-_section_5.pdf

Peacock, A. (2015) The Art of the Possible. In A. Wilson (Ed.), *Creativity in Primary Education.* 2nd edn. London: Sage, pp. 25–32.

Robinson, K. and Aronica, L. (2015) *Creative Schools: Revolutionizing Education from the Ground Up.* London: Penguin.

Swann, M., Peacock, A., Hart, S. and Drummond, M. J. (2012) *Creating Learning Without Limits.* Berkshire: OUP.

Wilson, A. (2014) *Creativity in Primary Education.* London: Sage.

16 Creating inspiring displays

Anthony Barlow

Critical questions

Who decides what goes on your classroom wall? Why?

How many learning spaces you have seen, have been inspirational?

Which classroom display elements are essential or non-negotiable?

How often have you considered what ethos would be suggested by a classroom where nothing was displayed?

Are you a charismatic teacher, competent craftsperson, or reflective practitioner?

Introduction

This chapter will explain and discuss classroom display. It will put display into a wider context and consider the environment for learning in settings working with pupils 3–11 and how different elements interact. Using a historical and societal perspective, it will consider how things have come to be and how we have developed norms of practice that we perhaps should now question. This is not least to ensure we are being inclusive teachers. This chapter will show possibilities for creative display and how 'display for learning' might be developed through case study examples to help frame the debate.

Do you remember the first time you backed a classroom display board with paper? This rite of passage will occur as soon as you are given your classroom keys. This simple act shows that this is *your* domain, *your* room, and *you* are going to be in charge of what will happen here. With many things that we cannot control in this challenging profession, this small act will make your bare classroom become a place where all *your* hopes and dreams about being a teacher can be realised.

Display: We love it!

Non-teachers reading this might think this is over the top, but as Thom (2017) suggests 'The classroom is a teacher's arena; it projects powerful subliminal messages to the young people in it. Its make-up will, in part, influence their responses to our teaching and their motivation in our subjects'. This 'arena' is somewhere you will spend upwards of 30 hours a week. The bold primary colours can quickly change the look and acoustics of what might at first be an echoey and uninspiring space. Our usual leap of imagination is the pupils' happy faces when they see all the hard work: *You* worked hard doing all this, so *they* will work hard for you might be how our thought process goes, right? You imagine this might just be the key to the trust that you so dearly crave as a teacher.

Critical question

If you work hard, pupils will work hard as well – right? Is this something you recognise? Is this your motivation? Or was it just me, a naive 21-year old, desperate to do something to assuage my nerves. This was it. They were going to trust *me* with the class and this group of children?

Display: The context

This urge to create wonderful spaces where learning might 'ignite' is perhaps one of the few things that has remained unchanged over the past 50 years of education. It was certainly important to me when I set up my first classroom almost two decades ago. Why? Does it matter? This chapter will contextualise this so you can start to think again about this most usual of classroom chores.

Reading back what's written above, much of it is about **you**, the teacher rather than **them**, the learners. There are many presumptions of display practices in primary schools that have underlying presumptions about learning and pedagogy. Increasingly, we need to question these practices and follow some sort of justification (or hopefully evidence) that these practices are at least effective. Having interviewed hundreds of candidates for teaching courses over the past years, the response to the question 'If this was your classroom, how would you make learning come alive', relates most often to the physical space not the role of the teacher. As many in the world of education now agree, it is the quality of teaching – not the quality of poster, triple-backed pupil work and bright, colourful walls – that leads to great learning. Sometimes, in some schools, it can feel like we are preparing teachers for an interior design course!

Critical question

Any classroom space should be set up for the learners and everything we do should be considered in this light. The risk is, in our wish to take control, we might make it suitable for us: An Instagram- or tweet-friendly space?

Think about the classrooms you have been in and the teachers you have worked with and their relationship to what is on the wall. Who put what was there and why? Were you part of this discussion or saw who played a role in the creation of this? Was there any pressure from others as to what should be there? Is the potential for display taken for granted?

Display: Context

The classroom environment is an exciting and creative space where learning takes place. It is therefore important to take time to think about our own classroom environment and consider how effective it is at supporting, developing, and enhancing learning opportunities. Slade (2014) offers a list for class teachers to consider when reflecting on their own classroom environment.

Does your classroom have:

- Working wall(s)
- Prompts and examples of work to support future learning
- Wall for Science, Discovery Time (topic)
- Children's targets displayed
- Next steps for learning
- Learning Objective clearly displayed (on IWB)
- Steps to success on the IWB
- Self/ Peer Assessment on AfL
- Names on children's trays
- Class Charter
- Clear and visual writing display
- Key words and subject-specific/technical vocabulary displayed (Ofsted Priority)
- Key questions displayed and referred to in lessons (not only important for children but also enables adults working with children to be clear about teacher expectations)
- X Table grids (either large on display or individual all tables)
- Number lines (again differentiated for year group)
- Alphabet/sounds/phonics/blends displayed
- Visual timetable (particularly important for SEND pupils)
- Motivation display (ie: Stars of the Week/Golden Time points/Team Points, etc)
- Exciting and enticing reading corner
- Plants
- Birthday information
- Posters – taking account of children's interests
- Class monitors
- Noticeboard with groups on?

This is a way that one school supports its staff in developing their classroom environment; there are often many ways that schools support their staff but as a tick list it might be judged a step too far. *How has it come to this?*

Display: Some history to the context

If we go back in time and think of how humans inhabit spaces, we feel the need to adorn them and give them a sense of belonging. We have been doing this for up to 65,000 years as examples of wall art in caves in Spain particularly show. Evidence of ladder-like shapes, dots and handprints were painted and stencilled deep in caves at three sites in Spain. Although 'their precise meaning may forever be unknowable … they were almost certainly meaningful to our lost kin. It wasn't simply decorating your living space … People were making journeys into the darkness' (Pike cited by Marris, 2018). The idea of making *journeys into darkness* is a particularly powerful idea. Consider this in relation to the ideas cited above. Until most of us decorate our own teaching rooms and personalise them, this is perhaps what we have been doing. It is also a great metaphor for what we want children to be able to do, hopefully we can provide the light!

Humans have been a distracted species for a long time. All around us things vie for our attention. The reason why advertising slogans work lies, perhaps, in the etymology of the word: Advertise has a root in the Latin verb 'advertere' – *to turn towards* (Doyle, 2011). Historical parallels we could consider might be citizens gazing at the Athens' Parthenon friezes, Roman mosaics spread liberally around Europe or, closer to home, Henry VIII's Hampton Court Palace Tudor tapestries. All can be said to be ways to tell stories and explain the world through the technologies available at the time by those who had the means, the wealth and power. Consider today though: We are spoiled with ways to turn towards displays, screens or printed paper. Pupils' homes are filled with pictures, lists, or 100 TV channel menus. Their streets are full of adverts, signs, and pitches for attention. In the doctor or dentist's office there are posters giving advice and even a walk in the woods might be disrupted by information boards or an app explaining what you can see. Our world is full of display, so perhaps our classrooms should be no different?

The problem is, as teachers, what we really crave is our pupils' attention. We are the 'more knowledgeable other' as Vygotsky coins it (Vygotsky, 1978) and are the teacher who is supposed to be leading the learning. As we are gatekeepers to some aspects of knowledge, dispositions and skills, it is perhaps odd that we fill the teaching space with distractions. Consider that children are spending six hours plus per day *away from* the distracting world. The graphics below show what this means in practice (see Figures 16.1 and 16.2).

If school simply emulates the busy-ness of the rest of their lives, does this 'noise' help them learn? Fisher et al., (2014: 1362), argue that the research suggests that young children 'with immature regulation of focused attention are often placed in elementary-school classrooms containing many displays that are not relevant to ongoing instruction' and that the evidence is that focused attention is needed for encoding (understanding what's going on) and subsequent task performance.

3-4s

1% have their own smartphone, 19% have their own tablet.

96% watch TV on a TV set, for **14h a week.**

30% watch TV on other devices, mostly on a tablet.

36% play games, for nearly **6¼h a week.**

52% go online, for nearly **9h a week.**

69% of these mostly use a tablet to go online.

32% watch TV programmes via OTT services (like Netflix, Now TV or Amazon Prime Video).

45% use YouTube, 80% of these say they use it to watch cartoons while 40% say funny videos or pranks.

1% have a social media profile

5-7s

5% have their own smartphone, 42% have their own tablet.

97% watch TV on a TV set, for around **13¼h a week.**

44% watch TV on other devices, mostly on a tablet.

63% play games, for around **7½h a week.**

82% go online, for around **9½h a week.**

67% of these mostly use a tablet to go online.

44% watch TV programmes via OTT services (like Netflix, Now TV or Amazon Prime Video).

70% use YouTube, 65% of these say they use it to watch cartoons while 61% say funny videos or pranks.

4% have a social media profile.

Figure 16.1 Screen time of children aged 3-7 (Ofcom, 2018)

8-11s

35% have their own smartphone, 47% have their own tablet.

94% watch TV on a TV set, for nearly **13h a week.**

43% watch TV on other devices, mostly on a tablet.

74% play games, for around **10h a week.**

93% go online, for around **13½h a week.**

45% of these mostly use a tablet to go online, with 24% mostly using a mobile.

43% watch TV programmes via OTT services (like Netflix, Now TV or Amazon Prime Video).

77% use YouTube, 75% of these say they use it to watch funny videos or pranks while 58% say music videos.

18% have a social media profile.

40% who own a mobile are allowed to take it to bed with them, it's 28% among tablet owners.

Figure 16.2 Screen time of children aged 8-11 (Ofcom, 2018)

The wider built environment in schools

We need to consider ourselves as the teacher competing with other stimuli in the classroom. Displays are just one aspect of this. What we should consider is, what is the optimum environment for children to learn in? Most of us will draw from both our peers, as teachers, and our own childhood experience of how teaching was modelled to us. As might become clear, this is often not the best starting point if we are to become evidence-informed teachers. The principles 'built into' teaching today might usually be said to be broadly social constructivist in ethos. This suggests that learning is transmitted actively and socially through language and social interaction with pupils. Indeed, as soon as compulsory schooling started (in the 1870s), the standardised classroom layout supported this, with a display/'performance' area for the teacher at the front (Wall et al., 2010: 3). Brighouse and Woods suggest that ever since the 1930s a school's visual environment has been important.

In later years, influential headteachers like George Baines (said to be responsible for 'open-plan' 1970s schools) interestingly talked of the building itself being a teacher. Baines talked of children acquiring the six selves:

- Self-awareness
- Self-confidence
- Self-direction
- Self-discipline
- Self-criticism
- Self-esteem

The school itself was encouraged to work with 'industry, integrity, and imagination'. If the 'three Is' and 'six selves' were developing well, with good teaching, he believed the 'three Rs' would follow (Burke, 2009). Such a view would be frowned upon by many today with a series of skills not necessarily leading to a literate and numerate set of pupils as government ministers have been keen to point out (Gibb, 2017). Such schools additionally had specialist areas such as a craft kitchen, cooking bay, practical maths bay and a science bay which were all suitably equipped in terms of the type of furniture and floor coverings. The big open areas were lovely with higher ceilings than the bays which were all on a domestic scale (Dyer, 2015).

Critical question

Think about the schools you know and work in and consider when they were built – did they afford space and value to developing learning beyond the classroom, where pupils could develop skills beyond those being sat at a table? What impact did this have on the education that was provided for them?

Consider how much this informs the classroom you intend to set and this might affect your view of how to do and what to do in relation to display.

Interestingly, in the years post-2000, significant amounts of money were spent on schemes in the *Building Schools for the Future* programme and dialogues between building and architectural practices happened (CABE, 2003). You might think this is self-evident: The designers and builders of schools need to know what the best way to set up the learning space is. However, in more recent times there have been criticisms that such dialogues do not happen when money is tighter and schools will all be made from the same kit (Booth, 2012). Much of the debate was not over the individual classrooms but more about overall cost price and 'starchitects' (Marrs, 2016). Some recent thinking has suggested a more fundamental change is needed where a 'learning space' in the 21st century might mean modifications where 'rows of desks and chairs are replaced with a range of furniture that can be configured in various ways to facilitate teaching and learning' (Kariippanon, et al., 2018: 301). How much this is ever going to happen with a return to a more teacher-instruction mode of teaching being advocated (Gibb, 2017b) from the age of five years in England remains to be seen.

Critical question

How many of the learning spaces you have seen have been inspirational? To whom did they appear so? The teacher, the parents, visitors such as Ofsted? What about the children? Would their views, ideas, or the effect on them have been judged?

Pedagogy and the relationship to teaching space and display is important. Featherstone and Bayley (2006) talk about the Italian Reggio schools' spaces for the under five-year-olds, which include:

- Being skilfully and thoughtfully adapted to the children
- A spacious feel, plenty of light and muted colours on walls – colour is provided by the children and their work
- Good storage
- Clearly delineated areas
- A range of resources, including boxes and displays of natural objects
- A room for role-play in the central piazza and areas for construction with bricks

Much of this echoes what can be read into Baines' descriptions (above) of learning in past decades and what the research suggests about open-plan designs built in the 1960-1970s. The jury is out if this does change teaching practices (Wolner, 2012).

What is the evidence for the way we set up our classrooms and their effectiveness?

Many texts on education (and educational commentators) discuss education in general. What we should do is consider developmental ages and stages in relation to display. Younger children are said to prefer bright colours and older children more subdued colours. Jarman (2019) argues that the targeted use of colour is one of the most challenging aspects to get right in a learning environment. They note that over the years, many teachers have taken to the idea that children thrive in a brightly coloured environment. However, Autistic Spectrum Disorder children also have a particular relationship between colour, mood, and behaviour which might be different to non-ASD children. Pile, in contrast, (1997) advocates using strong but warm colours (and not intense primary colours) for younger children. Colour preferences also exist for older students and may be 'gender and age related among adults' (Wall *et al.*, 2010: 18).

Similarly, Fisher et al., (2014) argue that maintaining focused attention in classroom environments may be challenging for under five-year-olds because the 'visual features in the classroom may tax their still-developing and fragile ability to actively maintain task goals and ignore distractions' (Fisher et al., 2013: 19).

Children's ability to maintain attention plays a 'critical role in learning and adaptive behaviour' (Fisher et al., 2013: 290) and Goswami concurs with this saying that brain-based factors such as learning anxiety and attention deficits can also disrupt an individual's capacity to learn (Goswami, 2006). One other set of parameters around effectiveness we might wish to consider could be Hattie and Yates' prescription for learning in general. In their book *Visible Learning and the Science of How We Learn* they talk about human learning requiring time, goal-orientation, supportive feedback, accumulated successful practice, and frequent review. Unless the material is strongly meaningful, it is subject to rapid forgetting (Hattie and Yates, 2014: 113).

Key reading

Barrett, P.S., Davies, F., Zhang, Y. and Barrett, L. (2015) *The impact of classroom design on pupils' learning: final results of a holistic, multi-level analysis*, Building and Environment, 89, pp. 118–133.

Barrett et al., (2015) made assessments of 153 classrooms in 27 schools in order to identify the impact of physical classroom features on the academic progress of the pupils. They came up with a conceptual model around the ideas of Simulation, Individuality, and Naturalness (SIN). They found that 16% of the variation in pupils' learning progress can be explained by the physical attributes of the classrooms.

Stimulation: Appropriate level of complexity and colour. How do the different elements in the room combine to create a visually coherent and structured or random and chaotic environment?

Naturalness: Light sound, temperature, air quality and links to nature.

Individuality: Ownership, flexibility and connection. Does the classroom meet the needs of children or groups of children? How personalisable is the room? Does it allow for 'changing pedagogy'?

Adapted from Barrett *et al.* (2015).

It is argued that intimate and personalised spaces are better for absorbing, memorising, and recalling information (EEF EYFS toolkit, 2014, cited in Barrett 2015: 19). Barrett also found that it may be particularly challenging for the youngest children to actively maintain task goals and ignore distractions. As they note, the youngest children have the busiest and most colourful learning environment (Fisher et al., 2014: 136). They note that:

when placed in a decorated classroom, the children were more likely to be distracted by the visual environment, and when placed in a sparse classroom, they were more likely to be distracted by themselves or by peers. Second, the classroom visual environment affected the overall amount of time the children spent off task: They spent significantly more instructional time off task in the decorated-classroom condition than in the sparse-classroom condition.

(p. 1367)

We are not advocating sterilising the learning environments of young children by removing all decorations, artwork, or educational displays. However, further research is needed to examine the optimal level of visual stimulation in primary-grade classrooms to develop evidence-based guidelines for classroom design.

Display: *Some starting points*

Display can be both a verb and/or a noun. The Oxford dictionaries notes that 'to display' is to 'put (something) in a prominent place in order that it may readily be seen [and] to show (data or an image) on a computer, television, or other screen'. It also is 'a collection of objects arranged for public viewing'. This, perhaps, sums up the reasons why we display in classrooms: make learning seen, to show images/ text or to showcase an object or collection.

What we need to remember about classrooms in settings working with 3–11-year-olds is how different each one is. Consider an EYFS setting compared to a Year 6 classroom and how learning artefacts are displayed and how indoor and outdoor spaces are used. Consider the amount of light, whether it is more likely to be on the ground floor or upstairs, and how much space there is to display. Some rooms might have two or three outside walls, while others might have just one. Some rooms might have learning displayed in different subject areas, while others might have topics or themes.

Through this chapter, I recount my own reflections on my first classroom displays when teaching Year 5 children. At this time, 3D displays and 'big display' was a theme that we were being encouraged to think about. The idea was that interactivity would lead to pupil engagement and pupil learning. The process and choices in creating these displays have stayed with me ever since. The case study in this chapter focusses on literacy teaching and focuses on 'working walls' in particular. Reflecting now on these early attempts at display, it wasn't ever something explicitly taught to me or learnt from others. It is interesting now, having worked with hundreds of student teachers, that students still seem to value 'doing displays' and also instinctively know how they would want their classrooms to be set up. It is important here to broaden out what we mean by display – it is much more than just the fixed bulletin boards that feature in most EYFS and primary classrooms.

Critical question

Which classroom elements are essential or non-negotiable?

Look at this list. Consider which are non-negotiables and which are essential. Maybe there are things that you could do without. In the example shown in Table 16.1, I have highlighted the ones which I would consider could contribute to display in the primary classroom and then, in Table 16.2, I have given examples of how you might do this.

Table 16.1 Elements of most 3–11 classrooms

Chairs	Grouped tables that interlock	Carpet area/Outdoor area	Easy access to water
Natural light and **windows**	**Display boards**	**Computer**	**Screen or interactive whiteboard**
Bookcase and small library	Dictionaries, atlases and other key texts such as textbooks	**Whiteboard/ display paper**	Equipment for teaching maths such as calculators
Basic stationery: pencils, rulers, pens	Teacher's desk	Trays for children/ storage	All-purpose storage
Posters, quotations or more permanent wall-text	**Rules and reminders**	**Other 3D displays or artefacts**	**Instructional/Fire notices**

Table 16.2 How these elements might embody display

Classroom feature	How display could be embodied	Classroom feature	How display could be embodied
Grouped tables that interlock	Might feature times tables or other displays to support writing.	**Screen or interactive whiteboard**	The key display tool for most lessons.
Natural light and **windows**	Windows are often used to stick all manner of pupil learning and notes/ information.	**Whiteboard/ display paper**	These are used regularly to display timetables, the date, Learning Outcomes, Success Criteria or vocabulary.
Bookcase and small library	These display books often spine or cover facing to attract attention.	**Rules and reminders**	These are specific for your children.
Display boards	The main location for displaying pupil learning or directing towards topic work. Display boards might feature calendars or other key basic skills information.	**Other 3D displays or artefacts**	Some settings might have a thematic display area (nature table). This is an area where pupil resources may be placed.
Posters, quotations or more permanent wall-text	Indoor/outdoor posters might feature books or feature inspirational poems (e.g. Google 'Footprints poster'). Walls might have permanent slogans (e.g. Einstein, JK Rowling, Martin Luther King). Older year groups might have thoughts for the day and younger groups might have indoor/ outdoor number lines, alphabet.	**Instructional/Fire notices**	These direct pupils or staff to keep them safe.

Table 16.3 How teachers use visual displays

Academic	Non-academic	Behaviour materials
Organising the class: goals for the day, group assignments, job charts, labels, schedule day/week, yearly schedule, skills, and homework.	*General information:* school policy, teacher information, and decorative items.	Behaviour materials aim to influence student behaviour (e.g., good behaviour charts, book challenge points).
Specific content learning materials: content specific, procedures, resources, calendars/clocks, and other.	*Non-academic items:* motivational slogans, decorations, decorative frames, student art, and other non-academic.	Behaviour was subdivided into four subcategories: behaviour management progress charts rules other behaviour

Research focus: How teachers use visual displays

Almeda (2014), in research from the United States, tried to find clusters in design decisions in classroom visual displays. The research found that there were three decisions usually made: academic, non-academic items, and behaviour materials (see Table 16.3).

At the equivalent schools in England (which might be said to be academies), there was an emphasis on literacy development which was more likely to encourage print-rich environments and colourful decorations and functional text. In contrast, the relatively visually sparse classrooms were largely from private schools which suggested that 'private school teachers in this region may consider visual displays distracting' (Almeda, 2014: 4).

Display: Another way to categorise it

Another way of categorising display and which shows the richness that it might encompass is around the two ideas of 'valuing' or enforcing and reminding pupils to do things.

Valuing

There are many ways to use display to show how you value the children within your class. It is important to remember that we are not only valuing the 'work' but valuing the children as they spend most of their time within your classroom. Some of the ways you may want to do this is by:

- Changing displays to reflect the interests of children within your class.
- Displaying themes from the current news agenda (appropriate to the age of your class).
- Showing the best examples of learning.
- Showcasing aspects of learning (e.g. promoting reading by displaying award winning books).
- Promoting types of books related to topic work.
- Having an area where children's models or other constructions can be displayed.

Enforce and remind

Displays within the classroom can also provide comfort for the children as they can reassure them that it is a safe place to be where their safety has been prioritised. You may want to consider including:

- A description explaining how a space should operate (e.g. rules, reminders).

- Window displays to explain routines for parents or children.
- A changing display showing the day of the week or weather.
- Newsletters and other long-term information posted on the wall.
- The alphabet, times tables, or key mathematical symbols to support memory or teaching.
- Pictures of pupils can support teachers in remembering pupils if they are not their full-time teacher (the children could draw these themselves!).
- An aide-memoire for pupils and teachers (key vocabulary).
- A birthday/celebration chart.

Display: What we are encouraged to do

There is a great deal of 'folk wisdom' surrounding classroom environments in school which is clear from books supporting a display-rich environment. Other books celebrating the virtues of display are Gormley and Andrew-Power (2009) where positive display is said to encourage positive behaviour and Muijs and Reynolds (2005) who suggest teachers use display to 'cheer up' classrooms and make them 'more pleasant'. They also find it improves 'peripheral' and 'subliminal' learning and classroom 'climate' and promoting 'pride' (2005: 110–111). Quite some claims! What all these suggest is that display creates an all elusive classroom ethos.

Critical question

How often have you considered what ethos would be suggested by a classroom where nothing was displayed?

There is limited research on something as important as the optimum way to set up your classroom. The same can be said for what and how we should display in our primary classrooms. One study by Thomson et al., (2007) is useful as it is based on a three-year ethnographic study in one (unnamed) school. This study cites previous government documents (e.g. Excellence and Enjoyment, DfE, 2004) which suggest official sanction that a good school is one that 'looks good'. This same document suggests that, in best practice case studies, there is 'evidence on display of everyone's achievements'. Another DfE document from the same year suggests that 'The physical environment has a significant influence on learning. It gives children clear messages about how we value them and how we value their learning. It can be supportive of independent learning' (DfE, 2004). It is interesting going back through documents from the past twenty years to see what other guidance was produced. There are documents from the National Strategies (DCSF, 2008) explicitly producing materials for display in the classroom on matters such as 'rules for talk', 'rules for listening', and 'talking well and talking better', all predicated on an idea that once taught, pupils need reminders so that things will 'sink in'.

Thomson et al., (2007) argue similarly in their findings that walls (re)produce and promote normative meanings of 'good work', the 'good student', the 'good teacher', and the 'good school', which serve both internal and external purposes. External purposes in this case being anyone viewing the school being able to see how good it is just by what has been put on the walls. They find that what is on the walls is seen to promote an inclusive culture. Finally, they find that there is a sense of the collective in what is displayed; walls constitute resources to construct narratives about their collective and individual histories in the school (Thomson, et al., 2007). It is a powerful idea – that the narrative of the school or a collective history should be able to be expressed and seen, as presented on its walls.

> ## Critical question
>
> Are you a charismatic teacher, competent craftsperson, or reflective practitioner?

Thomson, *et al.*, (2007) contends that there are three discourses about teachers in the UK (Think about which of these most accurately reflects you. How might this affect how you display work? Ultimately, when we put anything on the walls of our classrooms, we are putting ourselves 'on display'. You might have met the larger than life *charismatic* teacher, the one who is loved by the children and lavishes them with praise. Their classrooms are pristine, with regularly changed displays, and an environment which we would think could not help but lead to learning. Equally, you might have seen the hardworking and dedicated 'early to arrive and late to leave' *craftsperson*, dedicated to the job and the children. Displays are there but they are matter of fact – bland but functional. Finally, there is the questioning and *reflective* teacher who does not waste time on fripperies, who is a really deep thinker, and likely a great teacher who the children respect rather than love. They won't adopt new ways of working easily but are very consistent in the practice that they adopt. Stereotypes are never fully like teachers you know but as Thomson et al., (2007) argue, displays (like many other parts of the teacher's realm) can help signify and send messages about change, control, and performance in a performative sense. Thus, as displays are a clear way to signify one part of this, it could be the reasoning behind many schools' continuation of display practices.

Workload and display

As has been argued so far, the way we set up our schools have often been directly influenced by who has trained and influenced us. There are impressive books on display (see below) and many sources online such as Instagram or Twitter where we can get inspiration for creating displays in our classrooms. However, such workload is not something we need to do. One of the tasks teachers are expressly *not* supposed to do, in a deal brokered with unions in 2005, is 'routinely to participate in any administrative, clerical and organisational tasks which do not call for the exercise of a teacher's professional skills and judgement'. Display is described as 'Preparing, setting up and taking down classroom displays in accordance with decisions taken by teachers'. This suggested 21 tasks is not currently part of the official 'School Teachers' Pay and Conditions' document (2018) but should still be considered. It is interesting to look at the other ones too.

Interestingly, in the more recent workload survey (2018) data collection, marking practices, and lesson preparation time were the top three causes of excessive workload. Also, senior leaders are advised to ensure that the highest quality resources are available, valuing professionally produced resources as much as those created in-house.

Indeed educational researcher John Hattie has weighed in on the debate saying that there are a 'million resources available on the internet and creating more seems among the successful wastes of time in which teachers love to engage' which does not leave enough time for teachers time 'to focus on the intellectual exercise of planning sequences of lessons'. (DFE, 2016: 9).

Case study: The 'working wall'

The concept behind the working wall is that learning is a continuum. I see a working wall as the epitome of a social space, an ongoing dialogue to remind pupils of what they are learning. Adams talks of social constructivist learning needing to provide authentic and collaborative tasks in a safe environment as it supports student knowledge construction and they see it as a 'journey towards understanding' (Adams, 2006: 250).

The following case study is edited from a blog post by Sadie Philips, a teacher working with KS2 in London. It is recommended you read the full blog as this is an edited extract where elements have been re-ordered for reasons of space. It can be found here: https://literacywithmissp.com/2018/08/07/harnessing-the-power-of-working-walls/ Sadie notes that when she started teaching, it was easy to confuse Pinterest-perfect classrooms with those that had an impact on learning. With thought and planning, an effective classroom environment is used as an interactive support to engage children in discussion and promote independent learning through accessible tools and scaffolding. Sadie argues that a working wall can model, celebrate, and explain the writing journey. It is not a static display that celebrates what's finished; working walls are a perpetual 'work in progress' that adapts and grows: Modelling of writing, images, key vocabulary, and prompts quickly pinned as you go.

What are the essentials?

Sadie argues that a working wall should be close to where you teach, contributed to by everyone, a place for acknowledgement and celebration. Ultimately, it is a teaching tool that reinforces and is an invaluable resource for building confidence, independence, and interest in a subject. Some of the benefits of a working wall are:

Vocabulary – Immerse children in relevant vocabulary and use it to introduce new words. Use topic word banks and vocabulary word mats from online.

Examples – What good writing looks like through teacher modelling, quality texts and children's own writing shows what you are looking for. Children love if their work is added and label why it's good adding sticky notes to highlight features.

Learning Objectives – Ensure progression. It might be a ladder or arrows on the display showing the journey and progress. This allows children to see how far they've come and motivates them to reach for the next step.

Purpose and Audience – Children need to understand what/who their writing is for. It needs to be purposeful and meaningful with clear short-term and summative goals. Include success criteria generated by the children (What do I need to include in my writing to make it effective?) and targets.

Useful resources and scaffolding – Resources encourage greater independence and could be word banks, synonyms, or sentence starters to take away for support. In my classroom, there is always movement around the room as children independently seek resources: Dictionaries, thesauruses, or words from the working wall.

In addition, a working wall can create surprise and curiosity for the children in your class. It is a space which children will regularly go to for support and help so can be used to increase interaction through, for example, responses to a question or by encouraging children to add to the working wall through captions and sticky notes. Also a working wall can build surprise and wonder. For example, if learning is focused on a text, you could add the next illustration in the book which always creates a buzz around what might happen within the next chapter.

To read more about working walls, follow this link where the full blog can be found: https://literacywithmissp.com/2018/08/07/harnessing-the-power-of-working-walls/

What is clear from this case study is the idea of learning being a journey, a joint enterprise where ideas, the process, and the scaffolds to get there are worthy of. It is not a 'done today, forgotten tomorrow' activity. This is especially important in a subject that promotes composition of sustained pieces of writing and, as the national curriculum calls it, stamina to write at length (DfE, 2014: 10). As any writer knows, returning to your plan and having a dialogue about the process is a very useful thing.

Research focus

Displays, like the example of the working wall above, might support what Robin Alexander describes as *dialogic teaching* (Alexander, 2018 and see various references in the article below). This will lead to interactions which encourage learners to think and do so in different ways. While he talks of 61 indicators, here is a succinct summation of the kind of talk they are looking for:

- Questions which invite more than simple recall
- Answers which are justified, followed up, and built upon rather than merely received
- Feedback which, as well as evaluating, leads thinking forward
- Contributions which are extended rather than fragmented or prematurely closed
- Exchanges which chain together into coherent and deepening lines of enquiry
- Discussion and argumentation which probe and challenge rather than unquestioningly accept
- Scaffolding which provides appropriate linguistic and/or conceptual tools to bridge the gap between present and intended understanding
- Professional mastery of subject matter which is of the depth necessary to liberate classroom talk from the safe and conventional

- time, space, organisation, and relationships which are so disposed and orchestrated as to make all this possible

(Alexander, 2018: 10-11)

Many of these aspects link in with Goswami's research around the type of talk most appropriate for children and the ability for children to embed memories where she argues they improve when a carer or teacher adopts an elaborative conversational style:

> to help them to make sense of temporal and causal aspects of their experiences. Adapting our dialogue with young children leads to more organised and detailed learning and memory. These findings suggest that using elaboration in classroom dialogues will aid retention and understanding.

(Goswami, 2015: 11)

Bransford et al., talk of learning as a bridge between the taught and the learner so teachers can understand what students know. They note that accomplished teachers give learners reason, 'by respecting and understanding learners' prior experiences and understandings, assuming that these can serve as a foundation on which to build bridges to new understandings' (Bransford et al., 1999: 124).

Baeten et al., (2016) describes such learner-centred environments (founded on constructivist ideas) as being particularly prevalent in education (Baeten et al., 2016: 44) and Hattie and Yates talk of the difficulty in coping with unrelated materials. Finally, as Maxwell and Chmielewski (2008) found, there is a clear causal relationship between certain types of visual displays and increased self-esteem in young children. They also compared with other literature and said children should participate in the process of creating any such displays. They note that:

> it is critical that we understand more about what the physical environment may be 'teaching' children, and what they are learning. The messages that children receive from the physical environment, and the way in which they interpret these messages, may have a profound effect on their socio-emotional development.

(151-152)

Chapter summary

While this chapter does not come to any firm conclusions and the jury is still out as to the effectiveness of the best way to create an optimum learning environment, displays in the primary classroom are something we should begin to question. As the Design Council points out, they are perhaps one of our biggest 'blind spots' and might be one answer to some of the ills said to beset us in our classrooms around behaviour, attention, and the ability to sustain learning. Which ways are most effective and why? Is there a possible measure of effectiveness? Should we have any displays at all? Ultimately, what so much research does not do is ask what the pupils think and carry out studies in more controlled environments so that the full impact of display-rich environments can be assessed.

Display is dominant in our ideas of what makes a good school, sanctioned from the highest educational authorities, and a 'must do' for many decades. There is some (often unspoken) pressure on teachers today to conform to folk wisdom and stereotypes of what a good class-room looks like; these are perhaps outdated and certainly against current workload agreements in English schools. There is some evidence that particular colours are more effective than others and that too many/busy displays having a less than positive effect. As in many areas of school life, it is worth questioning the status quo – should we have display at all? Is it a good use of our time?

References

Adams, P. (2006) Exploring social constructivism: Theories and practicalities. *Education*, 34(3), 243–257.

Alexander, R. (2018) Developing dialogic teaching: Genesis, process, trial. *Research Papers in Education*, 33(5), 561–598.

Almeda, M. V., Scupelli, P., Baker, R., Weber, M., and Fisher, A. V. (2014) *Clustering of Design Decisions in Classroom Visual Displays*. Available at http://www.upenn.edu/learninganalytics/ryanbaker/LAK201 4_v6_OK.pdf

Andrew-Power, K. and Gormley, C. (2009) *Display for Learning*. London: Bloomsbury.

Baeten, M., Dochy, F., Struyven, K., et al. (2016) *Learning Environments Research* 19, 43. doi: 10.1007/ s10984-015-9190-5

Barrett, P. S., Davies, F., Zhang, Y. and Barrett, L. (2015) The impact of classroom design on pupils' learning: Final results of a holistic, multi-level analysis. *Building and Environment*, 89, 118–133.

Booth, R. (2012) *New Schools to Be Smaller after Coalition Cuts Building Budget*. Available at https://ww w.theguardian.com/education/2012/sep/30/new-schools-smaller-coalition-budget

Bransford, J. D. ed. (1999) How people learn: Brain, mind, experience, and school, edited by John D. Bransford, et al., National Academies Press, 1999. ProQuest Ebook Central, https://ebookcentral.proq uest.com/lib/roehampton-ebooks/detail.action?docID=3375627

Burke, C. (2009) George Baines Obituary. *The Guardian* Online https://www.theguardian.com/education /2009/oct/27/george-baines-obituary [Last Accessed 27.10.20]

DCSf (2008) *What Makes a Good Listener?* https://webarchive.nationalarchives.gov.uk/20101008094119 /https://nationalstrategies.standards.dcsf.gov.uk/downloader/printpdf/21117

DfE (2004) *Excellence and Enjoyment*. https://webarchive.nationalarchives.gov.uk/20040722022638/ht tp://www.dfes.gov.uk/primarydocument/

DfE (2016) Eliminating unnecessary workload around planning and teaching resources. *Report of the Independent Teacher Workload Review Group*. https://assets.publishing.service.gov.uk/government/ uploads/system/uploads/attachment_data/file/511257/Eliminating-unnecessary-workload-around-pl anning-and-teaching-resources.pdf

Doyle, C. (2011) *'The Real Thing'? The Language of Advertising Slogans* https://blog.oxforddictionaries .com/2011/10/20/language-of-advertising-slogans/

Dyer, E. (2015) *Interview with Judith Baines*. https://architectureandeducation.org/2015/06/23/interview -with-judith-baines/

Featherstone, S. and Bayley, R. (2006) *Foundations for Independence: Developing Independent Learning in the Foundation Stage*. 2nd revised edition. London: Featherstone Education Ltd.

Fisher, A. V., Thiessen, E. D., Godwin, K. E., Kloos, H., Dickerson, J. P. (2013) Assessing selective sustained attention in 3- to 5-year-old children: Evidence from a new paradigm. *Journal of Experimental Child Psychology*, 114, 275–294.

Fisher, A. V., Godwin, K. E. and Seltman, H. (2014) Visual environment, attention allocation, and learning in young children: When too much of a good thing may be bad. *Psychological Science*, 25(7), 1362–1370.

Gibb, N. (2017) *The Importance of Knowledge-Based Education*. https://www.gov.uk/government/speec hes/nick-gibb-the-importance-of-knowledge-based-education

Gibb, N. (2017b) *The Evidence in Favour of Teacher-Led Instruction*. https://www.gov.uk/government/ speeches/nick-gibb-the-evidence-in-favour-of-teacher-led-instruction

Goswami, U. (2006) Neuroscience and education: from research to practice? *Nature Reviews Neuroscience*. AOP, published online 12 April 2006. Available at https://www.nature.com/articles/nrn1907

Goswami, U. (February 2015) *Children's Cognitive Development and Learning*. York: Cambridge Primary Review Trust.

Hattie, J. and Yates, G. (2014) *Visible Learning and the Science of How We Learn*. Abingdon: Routledge.

Jarman, E. (2019) *The Communication Friendly Spaces™ Approach: The Targeted Use of Colour in Learning Environments*. Available at http://elizabethj.wpengine.com/wp-content/uploads/2018/04/the-cfs-approach-and-targeted-use-of-colour.pdf

Kariippanon, K.E., Cliff, D.P., Lancaster, S.L. et al. (2018) Perceived interplay between flexible learning spaces and teaching, learning and student wellbeing. *Learning Environment Research* 21, pp. 301–320. https://doi.org/10.1007/s10984-017-9254-9

Marrs, C. (2016) *Gove: 'I Regret Scrapping Building Schools for the Future'*. Available at https://www.architectsjournal.co.uk/news/gove-i-regret-scrapping-building-schools-for-the-future/10015221.article

Marris, E. (2018) Neanderthal artists made oldest-known cave paintings. https://www.nature.com/articles/d41586-018-02357-8#ref-CR1 [Accessed 24th February 2019].

Maxwell, L. E., and Chmielewski, E J. (2008) Environmental personalization and elementary school children's self-esteem. *Journal of Environmental Psychology*, 28, 143–153.

Muijs, D. and Reynolds, D. (2005) *Effective Teaching: Evidence and Practice*. London: Sage.

Ofcom (2018) *Children and Parents: Media Use and Attitudes Report 2018*. Available at https://www.ofcom.org.uk/__data/assets/pdf_file/0024/134907/Children-and-Parents-Media-Use-and-Attitudes-2018.pdf

Slade, C. (2014) *DLA's Guide to a Fantastic Learning Environment 2014-15*. http://www.davidlivingstone.croydon.sch.uk/wp-content/uploads/2014/08/Creating-the-classroom-environment-Sept-2013.pdf

Thom, J. (2017) *How to Be a Minimalist Teacher*. https://www.theguardian.com/teacher-network/teacher-blog/2017/sep/01/how-to-be-a-minimalist-teacher

Thomson, P., Hall, C., and Russell, L. (2007) If these walls could speak: Reading displays of primary children's work. *Ethnography and Education*, 2(3), 381–400. doi: 10.1080/17457820701547450

Wall, K., Dockrell, J. and Peacey, N. (2010) Primary schools: the built environment. In *The Cambridge Primary Review Research Surveys*, 589–622. Interim report summary (2008).

Woolner, P., McCarter, S. Wall, K., and Higgins, S. (2012) Changed learning through changed space: When can a participatory approach to the learning environment challenge preconceptions and alter practice? *Improving Schools*, 15(1), 45–60.

17 Outdoor learning

Michelle Best, Adewale Magaji, and L.D. Smith

Critical questions

What do you understand by outdoor learning?

What do you have in your school playground e.g. garden, animals, plants, ponds, and how are these used to support outdoor learning?

When planning an outdoor learning experience for students can you list the types of skills you want them to learn?

Introduction

This chapter will discuss the importance of children learning outside the classroom and explore how teachers can use this as a tool to enhance teaching and learning. We will explore various types of outdoor learning opportunities and group them into categories to guide our discussion, and safety issues connected to learning outdoors. The chapter will end with an overview of teachers' comments and the student voice to indicate the impact outdoor learning has on students' education.

What is outdoor learning?

Outdoor learning is a planned learning activity that may be organised within the confines of the school environment and beyond, including playful encounters with materials, objects, and equipment and has been planned and framed by the adult's intentions for children learning (Bilton and Waters, 2016). Therefore, engaging students in a learning environment should be more than simply participating in a classroom activity but considering other ways that learning can be promoted among students in a range of outdoor learning opportunities.

Outdoor learning can take place in various places such as botanical gardens, zoos, school playgrounds, art galleries, school trips, homes, museums, and other places of interest that can promote learning among students. Therefore, outdoor learning should not be misconstrued to mere recreational activity, free time, or a waste of learning time as often associated with this type of activity, and more importantly, may be seen as a way of socialising rather than a learning platform. Arguably, students can learn in the process of socialising when it helps in sharing and co-constructing knowledge with their peers and it is with this justification that we could conclude that long, uninterrupted time outdoors allow children to develop strong relationships with nature, teachers, and their peers (Sisson and Lash, 2017) and an opportunity to foster learning and progress. In the same vein, outdoor learning can develop an increased motivation to learn as connecting education to the natural environment, students have context in which to place their learning, and the intrinsic motivation of teamwork and ecological preservation as fuel to increase their desire to study and engage with curriculum (Yancey-Siegel, 2017). Added to this are positive attitude towards sustainable education and the love for the environment and improved well-being. Outdoor learning can also promote skills such as confidence, creativity, enterprise, leadership, and communication, organisation, problem solving, and scientific inquiry – all achieved through interdisciplinary activities used in outdoor education and transferred in other educational and life situations.

Outdoor learning substantially promotes experiential learning as it focuses on the personal and imminent gaining of knowledge and is referred to by John Dewey, Kurt Lewin, and Jean Piaget as an active process of learning through experience which involves a reflective approach. Maynard et al., (2013: 212) refer to experiential learning as a 'play-based approach to learning for children' as it supports their progress and helps to delineate the product of learning by using a process of systematic thinking of what has been learnt. Teachers, therefore, should plan for student growth by considering the 'how' of learning, ensuing a more dynamic learning experience which allows time for reflection. In the quest to captivate students' attention, involve and inspire them, teachers are more frequently considering the creation of knowledge outside of the classroom where an outdoor environment transpires into a 'place embedded with positive meanings' (Maynard et al., 2013: 212). Having said this, we suggest that teachers and schools should identify the type of learning activity they wish to promote outdoors and how this can support teaching and learning. We have made a list of examples of places that outdoor learning can take place (see Table 17.1) and we would ask that teachers and anyone reading this chapter should add to these lists. These activities can take place outside normal school time, however, there are others that can take place in the school playground or garden.

Despite the benefits of outdoor learning provisions, Aaron-Price and Chiu (2018) suggests that there is a need for teachers to be engaged in professional development to support their expertise in organising outdoor learning experience for students. Whilst this is relevant, Bevan et al., (2010) suggest that a collaboration with museums, science centres, and other informal education organisations such as libraries, cultural institutions, after school clubs (see Table 17.1) will be useful in giving teachers the opportunity to create a learning experience for their students. This could improve subject and pedagogical knowledge of the teachers involved. We also recognise that planning outdoor learning activities can be complex and time consuming and in essence, this could discourage teachers in taking part. Likewise, the simple reasons of knowing what skills and learning experiences they would like to encourage among students can also contribute to this disparagement. It is with this intention that we would like to highlight the five essential components of outdoor experience that includes reflecting the local landscape; balancing risks and benefits; reconsidering time, materials, and space; including children's voices and sustaining the natural learning environment (Sisson and Lash, 2017: 14) as a guide to facilitating outdoor learning. In essence therefore,

Table 17.1 Outdoor learning opportunities

Science	Literacy and Mathematics	Art/Humanities	Industry/commercial
• zoo • botanical garden • science learning centre • ecology and field work • museums • nature reserves, seaside • engineering, design and technology centres • sports and exercise science • falconry • planetariums • Walthamstow wetland	• Literacy and numeracy experience in the field • Problem solving • Collaborative learning	• art gallery • natural history museums • music centres • Tate modern • creative play • photography • languages • residential trip and school holiday • church and mosques • archery • rock climbing • cooking • park • stadium	• building and construction site • food processing company

we believe that in order to meet the requirements of these components of outdoor learning, a simple categorisation of the various skills and learning epistemology is relevant to guide teachers as seen in Table 17.1 and this would form the basis of our discussion in the next section. However, while you are considering those outdoor learning opportunities, we would like you to engage with the questions in the box below.

Task 1: Questions to think about

Can you think of other outdoor learning opportunities and locations and include in the list in Table 17.1?

Are there opportunities for students to carry out field work in your school and what are they?

Record the outcomes and discuss with your colleagues

To explore how outdoor learning may be approached, we have included two case studies; though mainly relevant for Key Stage 1 (children aged 5–7 years) the focus of the activities can be attuned with Key Stage 2 curriculum (children aged 7–11 years). The case studies illustrate materials and plant topics and different teaching approaches that can be adopted cross-curriculum. The activities also enhance transferable skills such as team building, communication skills, responsibility, and respect. Activities need to consider health and safety and individual allergies but the most positive aspect of participating in an outdoor learning experience is that it builds 'opportunities that the children would not normally receive in a classroom environment' (Teacher, 2019). Outdoor learning lessons are carefully planned to enhance the individual outdoor learning experience whilst considering both children's needs and parents' concerns.

Introduction to the case studies

The following case studies explore how different subjects are embedded in outdoor learning activities. The activities should be considered as a whole school approach in terms of curriculum, opportunity and learning development. Key questions for students (see below) guided the children's voice which inform the themes and are further supported by the teachers' views.

1   What is your favourite experience of learning outdoors?
2   What did you learn from your favourite experience?
3   Why is it useful to do that kind of activity outside?
4   Which other activities would you like to do (more of)?

Case study: Outdoor learning (materials)

The lesson started in the classroom with the teacher outlining facts about materials. Children sat on the mat and identified different materials (plastic, wool, leather, rubber) from images on flash cards and the use of props. Children explored and referred to how they looked and felt. This was followed by discussing key adjectives (bendy, brittle, waterproof, squashy, bumpy, and rigid) which linked to the different materials. All key words were on laminated strips and were to be discovered and used outside of the classroom in the next activity. The link to experiential learning and taking indoor learning outside wherever possible was a key focus.

Once outdoors, the aim of the lesson discussing and using key words was reinforced by children exploring the outdoor environment to find objects, identify different materials and then use key words and adjectives to describe them. Students explored the bug nest and wooded areas (photos) and placed laminated key words next to the material they had found.

To further consolidate learning, students were asked to explain how the outdoor learning experience was useful to their learning and were encouraged to share findings and ideas with their friends. The lesson ended back in the classroom with a discussion and summary of the four key questions (see Appendix 1).

Scientific enquiry was embedded as students found materials and described their physical properties (hard, soft, bendy, and brittle).

Literacy was embedded using key words where children acquired a wide vocabulary and used discussion to learn e.g. by finding out if the material is hard or soft, smooth or rough, waterproof or non-waterproof.

Humanities was referred to in terms of the history of the island and reference to visiting the Fleet, a wood and river area along a pathway to partner school (see Figure 17.1).

Industry/commercial aspects were referred to when passing by the construction site as part of the play area in the school. Students were able to relate to wheelbarrows and shovels and what they were made and their uses. Some children were talking about the health and safety aspects of climbing ladders and what the 'keep out' tape meant.

The DfE (2013) states that children should be able to describe key characteristics and be familiar with, and use, technical terminology accurately and precisely and build

Figure 17.1 Local landscape provides space and materials with a historical and community influence

an extended specialist vocabulary. These activities allowed children to explore the properties of materials indoors and outdoors and differentiate between an object and what it is made from (Year 1). To add a challenge, more-able students can be questioned about objects made from different materials used together. For example, a bench can be made from wood and plastic and metal. In the lesson the concept of a stick being bendy as opposed to brittle was explored which encouraged children to investigate how wood can bend (Year 2 studies). One of the main features of outdoor learning is the concept of learning in different contexts. Insect houses, bird cameras, and inspiring signs such as 'Take me to the moon and back' support learning as well as a keen focus on the history of the surrounding areas.

Teachers and children are proud to be part of a distinct history and underlying dynamics of the Isle of Sheppey. The area named the Fleet links to a partner school via a short pathway and includes a river and pond life featuring ducks, wind turbines, trees, and tadpoles. One teacher indicates how 'bringing the community spirit into the school so the students see the relevance of it' is an important part of outdoor learning.

Therefore, creating such a learning environment for pupils become an essential component of outdoor experience that arguably reflects the local landscape, space, and materials (Sisson and Lash, 2017) that are required to provide a sustainable learning environment that pupils can thrive in, and become custodians of their environment and may be friends of the planet in whatever way or form that may inspire and lead them to fulfil their full potentials. In a way also promoting curiosity and scientific inquiry skills that has been reiterated if not directly but indirectly from the activities in the environment that may have inspired them (see Figures 17.1, 17.2 and 17.3).

Figure 17.2 Insect house

Figure 17.3 Tree trunk chairs create a log circle for discussion time

Case study: Outdoor learning (plants)

The lesson started by teachers and a Forest School leader asking the children to change into their protective suits and wellington boots and make their way to the outdoor learning area. Children were able to sit on tree-trunk chairs (log circle) and began talking about health and safety (no licking, no picking, and staying in the boundary). Children talked about the trees and the buds and the teacher questioned if there were any changes in the outdoor learning area today. The teacher probed for links to the seasons and students referred to spring and changes in the trees and buds, noticing the shapes, sizes, furriness, and colours.

Activities included two challenges:

- Rope tying (reef knot and P and Q knot)
- Stick finding and building a shelter

There were two groups differentiated by the fact that Group 2 had already learnt how to do knots the previous week. All tasks were focused around building a shelter for shade and working as a team.

Teachers promoted independent thinking and discovery learning by asking children to 'go and find out' about buds, trees, and insects. Collaborative learning was promoted by children working in pairs and small groups to collect sticks and using fir tree branches as cushions and fans. Sticks tied together with rope were used to assemble the shelter and some children were rubbing sticks together to try and create a fire (bush craft tool/fire activities). The groups came together to assemble and enjoy the shelter whilst others investigated the workings of worms, climbed trees, and created decorations with fir cones and string.

Scientific enquiry was embedded as students related to changing seasons and demonstrated familiarity with common names of trees (willow) and examples of deciduous and evergreen trees. In line with the curriculum, students were able to relate to plant structures (including leaves, blossom, roots, buds, trunk, branches, and stem).

Literacy remained a key focus through discussion and communicating as a team. There was a clear focus on inclusion highlighted by the opportunities outdoor learning brings particularly for inner city children who may not have visited the countryside. These key experiences ensure that children can draw on a wider scope of knowledge particularly when reading and writing in the classroom. Mathematics was also included when making knots as students were required to measure and position the P and Q knot.

Humanities was related to in terms of creative play as students made ornaments and furnishings out of woodland materials to decorate the shelter. There was a discussion about visits to a local park and garden allotments too.

Industry/commercial aspects were referred to when relating to building a shelter and the skills that are transferable in industry.

These energetic activities teach technical skills of knot tying as well as communication and problem-solving skills. As part of Year 1 studies children identify seasonal change and how plants have changed over time, for example, the leaves falling off trees and buds opening; and compare what they have found out about different plants e.g. the furry buds on some of the trees. In terms of Year 2 studies children can observe and describe how plants and trees grow and relate to their need for water, light, and temperature.

The DfE indicates that pupils in Years 1 and 2 should explore and experience different practical activities, which promote children to compare objects, materials, and living things. Teachers should challenge students to observe changes over time and notice patterns and relationships. These concepts also relate to Key Stage 3 where students 'draw simple conclusions and answer questions' (DfE, 2013: 15) and classify animals into commonly found invertebrates (such as insects, spiders, snails, and worms).

Teachers outlined the importance of outdoor learning and categorised a range of skills and learning opportunities. The lesson was designed with clear learning objectives and schemes of work have been designed so that learning could be taught outdoors wherever possible. One teacher indicated how outdoor learning helps students to 'use taught skills and put into practical situations [by looking] at real subjects and transferring skills to different tasks'. In essence, these outdoor learning experiences allowed the pupils to be involved in working with various elements of nature that they may not come across in the confines of the classroom, thereby giving them opportunity to link their experiences to real life situation. This type of connection is what makes a lasting impression in the way they accept and embrace their environment and take care of nature in its organic form (see Figures 17.4 and 17.5).

Figure 17.4 Building a shelter, collaborative learning

Figure 17.5 Rope tying, teaching knots

Science

Outdoor learning is crucial in promoting scientific inquiry and problem-solving skills among students, creating opportunity for them to explore, investigate, ask questions, and create their own knowledge in a constructivist learning environment. Therefore, the need to support teachers in promoting such skills may be relevant in improving teaching and learning. It is in response to this that Aaron-Price and Chiu (2018) carried out a study of a museum-based, Science professional development programme's impact on teachers and their students. The programme focuses on teacher subject and pedagogical content knowledge, increasing confidence, and creating a community of practice to provide stability and support for teachers (Aaron-Price and Chiu, 2018: 945). Overall outcomes show improvement in subject content knowledge of both teachers and their students, increased Science teaching and hands-on activities that are more student-centred, positive impact on self-efficacy and anxiety (relating to how teachers embrace new materials presented to them). We will be under no illusion to postulate that this form of anxiety may be common with primary school teachers, who may consider teaching Science as a weak area in terms of pedagogy and subject knowledge. Hence, such feelings of anxiety may be accompanied with nervousness and the fear of creating more misconceptions among students rather than addressing them.

Teachers indicated though that learning science outdoors allowed students to use 'natural materials [which] enables pupils to learn about nature while thinking outside the box'. This 'allows them to put their learning in different contexts, to make it more relevant'. Learning outside also encourages children to learn skills such as 'understanding and respecting the environment [whilst] recognising it as a learning opportunity'. This was mirrored by the students who indicated that a tangible experience helps their learning. The students talked about what they had seen 'we learn outside about different weather we see – sun and rain and wind' and 'we learn about seasons and looking at trees'. Students also related to tangible sensory skills and things they could do such as 'building a shelter', 'making a fan', 'making knots in rope' and 'learning about birds' and 'watching flowers grow'. These skills are transferred to other learning such as 'labelling a body with sticks and chalk and telling the time' and 'Den building, planting and growing'.

The DfE state that 'most of the learning about science should be done through the use of first-hand practical experiences' (2013: 70) which is mirrored in outdoor activities. However, those tasks which involve secondary sources such as books and photographs are also useful to learning.

Literacy and Mathematics

Teachers stated that learning outdoors 'relates to maths and PE and problem solving' and that 'outdoor learning is embedded in our practice. We plan for provisions in the same way we do inside – i.e. have same areas of learning – Maths, reading, physical development etc'. There were many examples of embedding English and Mathematics and teachers related to how physical activity was also important stating that 'many of our children do not have gardens' and 'modern lifestyles which means that some children have less time outside than prisoners'. This indicates how the school can compensate for those students who do not have access to the outdoors at home, perhaps due to working parents or those with siblings who need extra care. Teachers indicated the value of learning English outdoors as this environment acted as a 'stimulus' to learning. One teacher commented on how stories were shared outdoors and how children were inspired by the outdoor environment. This indicates that outdoor learning develops 'speaking and listening skills and encourages pupils to make curriculum links'. Teachers identified that 'children have an opportunity to extend and reinforce classroom learning' so tasks which are started in the classroom could be taken outside for further learning. This was reinforced by some students who stated how they use 'phonics outdoors' and this helps them to learn. Students also commented on how they 'measure the trees to see how tall they are' and 'play hide and seek [and] practise counting'. This indicates how learning is discreet, not added on but embedded in the outdoor learning opportunities.

There is a plethora of activities which embed English and Mathematics outdoors, but it is important to remember that learning outside of the classroom is not just for one day, it is to be planned throughout the year across the curriculum. Outdoor learning allows children to tackle their learning in new and exciting ways which makes it more relatable and therefore memorable so that they can apply their learning in different situations. To promote English, teachers can plan a word hunt, develop story ideas, and use role play to develop expression. To enjoy Mathematics outdoors, children can measure areas of the playground and explore the link between centimetres and metres – create a giant clock using hoops and sticks and combine problem solving with their knowledge of time on analogue clocks. The Institute for Learning Outdoors states that 'Outdoor Learning is at its most potent when it is interwoven within the formal school curriculum' (2018). If you are short of ideas, Creative STAR Learning (2019) offer a range of Literacy books and resource packs which you can download. There is also a blog where you can share ideas and good practice.

Art

Teachers indicated how outdoor learning enhances social skills through teamwork and communication skills. Discussion was particularly prevalent not only in the lesson or during activities but also on the way to the outdoor area where students chatted with peers and teachers. Teachers use outdoor learning as a tool to enhance learning through a 'multi-sensory approach and building creativity' as 'children become familiar with their local environment and the history and importance of the area'. Teachers stated how activities such as 'creating African shelters and their own pencils' develop imagination and enhance learning. Students echoed this creativity by outlining things they had made such as 'making fans and … decorations' and 'we make things like shelters and bird feeders, we have fun'. One teacher summarised that they enjoyed delivering art activities outdoors because 'using natural materials enables pupils to learn about nature while thinking outside the box' (Teacher, 2019).

Visits to the Natural History Museum, Science Museum, and Horniman Museum add breadth and diversity to the curriculum. Activities such as 'School journey, local walks, and sports day at the park' develop a range of skills and geographical awareness. One of the schools offer a Peace Garden where children can go and sit at any time. This allows for reflection and timeout which contributes to well-being and as the DfE indicates is a recommended school provision in relation to personal, social, health, and economic education (PSHE). The principles of PSHE are taught in schools and are fundamental in all areas of the curriculum. PSHE can be embedded in outdoor learning activities which essentially encourage:

> young people to reflect on their learning and the progress they have made, and to transfer what they have learnt to say and to do from one school subject to another, and from school to their lives in the wider community.
>
> (PSHE Association, 2019)

This indicates the relevance of individuals experiencing a range of learning environments. Another important aspect of PSHE relates to providing 'a safe and supportive learning environment where children and young people can develop the confidence to ask questions, challenge the information they are offered, draw on their own experience, express their views and opinions and put what they have learnt into practice in their own lives' (PSHE Association, 2019). Learning outdoors provides the opportunity for children to question things they may not have experienced before and may not get the opportunity at home.

If teachers are looking for ideas to promote the arts in outdoor learning, the Council for Learning Outside the Classroom (CLOtC) offer a bank of resources and CPD opportunities for teachers and there is a specific area on arts and creativity.

Industry/commercial

Teachers ensure that skills are planned for such as 'enquiry, reasoning and observation' and 'teamwork, problem solving and speaking and listening'. Peer learning was noted in one of the case studies where one girl commented on her fear of worms, so a small group of children encouraged her to have a go at holding one. This peer support was as natural as the environment and she conquered her fear of worms in one lesson. In terms of industry relevance 'collaboration, responsibility and respect' are recognised as key transferable skills.

It is also important for children to learn outdoors to 'allow them to move freely in a different environment. To develop fine/gross motor skills in natural areas and benefit from space and fresh air'. One teacher indicated 'I enjoy delivering activities which include large scale mark making, construction, water play and mud kitchen' as this adds relevance to learning and the world of work. Students related well to learning about 'where the buds come from' and 'learning about birds' and how 'we find things together' which links well to enquiry, problem-solving, and teamwork. Outdoor areas were signposted well, and areas can be divided into different types of trade – e.g. construction, kitchen, earth and space, and greenhouse/planting area. This promotes children to learn about the world of work and different industries. This is reinforced by the recent work of Kashefpakdel (2018: 1) who refers to the 'In the Career Strategy: making the most of everyone's skills and talent' report published by the Department for Education in 2017. This report acknowledges 'the role of primary schools in introducing children to the world of work and the government's plan to test and fund career activities that works'. Kashefpakdel (2018) also refers to how schools should consider career-related learning activities and employer engagement. One of the case study schools include the role of dads to enhance the awareness and development of 'enterprise' and 'employability' skills by bringing your dad to school and is supported by the 'Dads matter' initiative.

Kashefpakdel (2018: 6) refers to the positive impacts of engaging children with career learning activities as 66% of the teachers 'agreed that introducing children to the world of work can challenge gender stereotyping about jobs and subjects'. This relates to the types of jobs that children are inspired to do at primary school which 'in turn has an impact on their decisions about who they want to become when they grow up'. Introducing children to the world of work therefore broadens aspirations and brings learning to life.

Health and safety in outdoor learning relates to how children 'learn about the world around them' and therefore reference to 'safety when outside e.g. poisonous plants, staying with others, safe structures, road sense' are important. The main point teachers make about outdoor learning is that 'activities can be cross-curricular – it is less restrictive outside and natural resources can be used'. There is also a clear focus on environment, safety, litter collections and recycling and how venturing outside to learn every week allows children to connect to their school and care for their local environment. If the school is looking for a more futuristic look Solardome Industries, the UK's only manufacturer of glass and aluminium domes for education, create multipurpose outdoor classrooms and dome buildings that inspire learners. These glasshouses and rooftop classrooms offer a learning environment for every type of weather and one which 'stimulates creativity and brings learning alive'.

Conclusion

The importance of children learning outside the classroom has been highlighted throughout this chapter and examples and tools have been shared so that teachers can develop their approach to outdoor teaching and learning. The triangulation of teachers' comments and student voice (Appendix 2) indicates the impact outdoor learning has on students' education. The Natural Connections project:

provides strong evidence that learning outdoors has multiple benefits for school children. 92 per cent of teachers surveyed said that pupils were more engaged with learning when outdoors and 85 per cent saw a positive impact on their behaviour.

(Natural England, 2016)

It is important to remember that schools must offer a curriculum which is balanced and broadly based and which 'promotes the spiritual, moral, cultural, mental and physical development of pupils [and] prepares pupils … for the opportunities, responsibilities and experiences of later life' (DfE, 2016). Part of this is the ability of the teacher to be creative and exploit the locality of the school; its geography, history, and natural resources. Teachers should therefore plan for a diverse range of activities which consider the wider curriculum when learning outdoors. By adapting a whole-school approach to outdoor learning there are opportunities to promote a future generation of sustainability, whilst increasing emotional intelligence, behaviour, and motivation to learn.

The Council for Learning Outside the Classroom (CLOtC) aims to raise the profile of learning outside the classroom by promoting how these educational experiences 'expand the horizons of young people, opening their eyes to the wonders of areas such as art, heritage, culture, adventure and the natural world' (2019). The CLOtC provides support and facilitates good practice and state that outdoor learning raises attainment and aspirations by 'reducing truancy and re-motivating those who are disengaged from their education' (2019). 'To understand learning outside is still an opportunity to learn and extend knowledge in a different environment' (Teacher, 2019).

Critical questions

Now that you have read this chapter, make a list of all the benefits that students can derive from outdoor learning. Include any other benefits that you think may not have been stated in this chapter.

Are there any barriers to you planning an outdoor learning experience for your students? Make a list and discuss with your colleagues.

Do you think CPD in outdoor learning would be useful to help you plan for your students?

Recommended reading

Alves, A. (2017) *Ideas to Make Outdoor Learning Work for Your School*. Available at: http://www.headteacher-update.com/best-practice-article/ideas-to-make-outdoor-learning-work-for-your-school/154990

Bentsen, P. and Jensen, F. G. (2012) The Nature of Udeskole: Outdoor Learning Theory and Practice in Danish Schools. *Journal of Adventure Education and Outdoor Learning* 12(3): *Cultural Perspectives on Experiential Learning in Outdoor Spaces*, 199–219.

Blenkinsop, S., Telford, J. and Morse, M. (2016) A Surprising Discovery: Five Pedagogical Skills Outdoor and Experiential Educators Might Offer More Mainstream Educators in this Time of Change. *Journal of Adventure Education and Outdoor Learning* 16(4), 346–358. Available at: https://www.tandfonline.com/doi/pdf/10.1080/14729679.2016.1163272?needAccess=true

Department for Education (2015) *Statutory Guidance. National Curriculum in England: Science Programmes of Study.* Available at: https://www.gov.uk/government/publi cations/national-curriculum-in-england-science-programmes-of-study/national -curriculum-in-england-science-programmes-of-study

Dillon, J. and Dickie, I. (2012) *Learning in the Natural Environment: Review of Social and Economic Benefits and Barriers.* Available at: http://tinyurl.com/go5y6da

Richardson, M., Sheffield, D., Harvey, C. and Petronzi, D. (2015) *The Impact of Children's Connection to Nature RSPB Report.* http://tinyurl.com/zaoy23h

Waite, S. (2010) Losing Our Way?: Declining Outdoor Opportunities for Learning for Children Aged Between 2 and 11. *Journal of Adventure Education and Outdoor Learning* 10(2), 111-126. Available at: http://hdl.handle.net/10026.1/5476

References

Aaron-Price, C. and Chiu, A. (2018) An Experimental Study of a Museum-Based, Science PD Programme's Impact on Teachers and Their Students. *International Journal of Science Education* 40(9), 941-960.

Bevan, B., Dillon, J., Hein, G. E., Macdonald, M., Michalchik, V., Miller, D., Root, D., Rudder, L., Xanthoudaki, M. and Yoon, S. (2010) *Making Science Matter: Collaborations between Informal Science Education Organisations and Schools. A CAISE Enquiry Group Report.* Washington, DC: Center for Advancement of informal Science Education (CAISE). Conference: NARST Annual International Conference.

Bilton, H. and Waters, J. (2016) Why Take Young Children Outside? A Critical Consideration of the Professed Aims for Outdoor Learning in the Early Years by Teachers from England and Wales. *Social Sciences* 6(1), 1-16.

Creative STAR Learning (2007-2019) *Literacy Outdoors.* Available at: https://creativestarlearning.co.uk/ c/literacy-outdoors/ [Accessed on 9 April 2019].

Department for Education (2013) *The National Curriculum in England Framework Document.* Available at: https://assets.publishing.service.gov.uk/government/uploads/system/uploads/attachment_data/ file/381344/Master_final_national_curriculum_28_Nov.pdf [Accessed on 9 April 2019].

Kashefpakdel, E. (2018) Introducing primary children to the world of work. *Education and Employers Research.* Available at: https://www.educationandemployers.org/wp-content/uploads/2018/07/Intro ducing-children-to-the-world-of-work-FINAL.pdf [Accessed on 30 April 2019].

Maynard, T., Waters, J. and Clement, J. (2013) Child-Initiated Learning, the Outdoor Environment and the 'Underachieving' Child. *Early Years, An International Research Journal* 33(3), 212-225.

Natural England (2016) *England's Largest Outdoor Learning Project Reveals Children More Motivated to Learn When Outside.* Available at: https://www.gov.uk/government/news/englands-largest-outdoor-learning-project-reveals-children-more-motivated-to-learn-when-outside [Accessed on 30 April 2019].

PSHE Association (2019) *Ten Principles of Effective PSHE.* Available at: https://www.pshe-association .org.uk/curriculum-and-resources/resources/ten-principles-effective-pshe-education [Accessed on 30/04/2019].

Sisson, J.H. and Lash, M. (2017) Outdoor Learning Experiences Connecting Children to Nature: Perspectives from Australia and the United States. *YC Young Children* 72(4), 8-16. Available at: https ://www.jstor.org/stable/90013699?seq=1/subjects

Solardome Industries. (1995-2019) Available at: http://www.solardome.co.uk/education/ [Accessed 30 April 2019].

The Council for Learning Outside the Classroom (2019) *Learning Outside the Classroom.* Available at: https://www.lotc.org.uk/about/ [Accessed on 30 April 2019].

The Institute for Learning Outdoors (2018) Available at: https://www.outdoor-learning.org/Good-Practice/Dev elop-your-Organisation/Outdoor-Learning-in-Schools/Teaching-Outdoors [Accessed on 30th April 2019].

The School Run (2019) *What Are Materials?* Available at: https://www.theschoolrun.com/what-are-ma terials [Accessed on 9 April 2019].

Yancey-Siegel, W. (2017) *How Outdoor Education Can Prepare Students for the Future.* Available at: https://www.opencolleges.edu.au/informed/features/outdoor-education-prepare-students-future/ [Accessed on 19 October 2018].

18 Pedagogy for imagination

Roger McDonald

Critical questions

How can opportunities for imagining be fostered in the primary classroom?
What are the indicators of imagination?
With all the pressures on a primary school teacher why should I promote the imagination?

Introduction

I can remember, in my first year as a teacher, the deputy headteacher coming into the staff room exasperated announcing that 'children just don't have any imagination anymore!' She had just come from a writing session with her Year 5 class where they were redrafting an extended piece of writing about a ghostly experience on the London Underground.

The parallel Year 5 class were also writing an extended piece on the same theme, but their teacher was praising the imaginative ideas the children had conjured. Since this incident, I have had an interest in the imagination. What was it about the teacher in the parallel Year 5 class that enabled imaginative engagement? Was the teacher aware of facilitating opportunities for imagining? What beliefs did the teacher hold about education and how were these shown through her practice?

These questions led me to explore imagination and opportunities for imagining in more detail. In this chapter I present some of my findings from an interpretive study of a Year 4 class in a primary school located in South London. The focus of the study, which took place over the course of one academic year, was to identify opportunities for imagining created by the teacher.

A contested space

The study took place at a time of considerable change in primary education. Teachers were experiencing increasing pressure related to the performance agenda as schools were tasked with 'narrowing the gap' and ensuring all children reached the 'expected level'. This was after a time of supposed growth in creativity which occurred at the start of the 21st century with cross curricula and creative practices encouraged (Craft et al., 2014). A tension existed (and exists) between the need for a creative approach and the pressure to achieve targets set by the school, academy chain, or government.

Teachers are therefore working within a *contested space of education* where their actions are influenced by a range of factors at work – both within the space and acting externally upon it. These factors range from statutory aspects which demand compliance such as the teachers contact, Department for England regulations, and school policies, to influencing factors such as the 'risk' of the school in relation to an Ofsted inspection, the pedagogical principles from the headteacher and senior leadership team and the influence of parental expectations. Figure 18.1 shows some of the possible factors influencing the pedagogic practices of any primary school teacher. In the diagram, all the arrows are the same size and same colour but you may want to think about your own contested space and consider which arrows have the greatest influence and whether you feel that influence has a positive or negative affect on your own pedagogy. The figure shows how the range of factors in the arrows will influence the pedagogy in the classroom. You can see that different approaches may be taken within the contested space and different decisions made due to, for example, the beliefs the teacher holds about education. Figure 18.1 indicates that these decisions made by the teacher and the influencing factors could mean that the pedagogy in the classroom could lean towards one with imaginative features, one which focuses on measurement or maybe one which is related to curriculum entitlement.

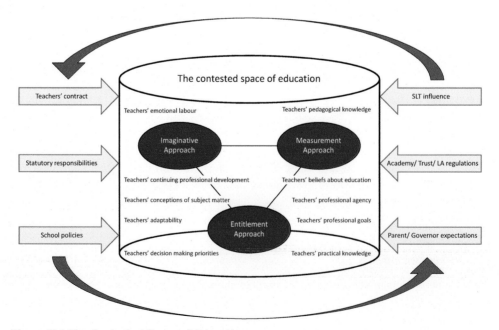

Figure 18.1 The Contested Space of Education

Some of the factors in Figure 18.1 will, in effect, distort the practices in the classroom. This may be due to the perceived pressure from the high stakes accountability system some teaches find themselves working in, where targets and objectives have taken precedence over principled, child-focused, and value-led teaching. Much has been written regarding the political influences on primary education in England (Moss, 2010; 2013, and Flewitt and Roberts-Holmes, 2015) and how the drive to 'raise standards' has led to an increasingly target-driven pedagogy in the classroom. Within the subject of literacy this shift is evident as Alexander (2007: 104) notes that:

> the literacy juggernaut appropriates and shapes teaching schemes, learning goals and assessment. Pedagogy is also twisted into a kind of 'service'. The pressure to raise standards can lead to transmission type teaching, to atomised skills which are amenable to measurement and to the proliferation of learning outcomes which can be enumerated and audited.

Within the contested space therefore a teacher could find themselves teaching in a way that they feel their pedagogy has been, as Alexander (2007) notes, twisted and where compliance and conformity have become the dominant practice over creativity and creativity (Cremin, 2015).

The relegation of a creative pedagogy has drastic repercussions for the imagination which, according to Kearney (1988), is in danger of extinction. I argue that imagination is crucial; it is a human attribute which must be valued, understood, and developed within the primary classroom. In the seminal work undertaken by Warnock (1976) the 'cultivation of imagination' was identified as what should constitute 'the chief aim of education' (p. 9) and that, as educators, we 'have a duty to educate the imagination above all else' (p. 10). This is due to that fact that imagination is situated centrally in our lives as we experience the world (Zittoun and Gillespie, 2016). Possibly each day we make choices, ponder on courses of action, speculate, emphasise with others, daydream, remember past events, consider future events, and wish we were in other places. Sometimes these are within our own realm of experience and at other times these may be when engrossed in a book, a film, music, or the world of art. Imagination is therefore a core psychological process which is key to our understanding of ourselves and the world, without which humans would be 'enslaved by their immediate situation' (Zittoun and Gillespie, 2016: 52).

Before identifying aspects of pedagogy for imagination it is important to briefly look at what imagination actually is.

Defining imagination

The concept of imagination and its definition is complex. The purpose and function of imagination are difficult to clearly define, meaning that there are often a variety of, sometimes conflicting, interpretations of the term (Warburton, 1998). Indeed, a specific definition of imagination has perplexed researchers and academics with the imagination becoming 'the junkyard of the mind' (Carroll, 2015; Kind, 2016: 1).

Education philosopher John Passmore (1980) notes the powerful nature of the imagination, especially through teaching and illustrates how an understanding of the imagination can: Create a more meaningful relationship with learning (Van Alphen, 2011), be the source of the flexibility of thinking (Egan, 2005) and can form the basis of our ability to project, to plan, to design and to create (Warburton, 1998).

Van Alphen (2011: 17) develops the concept by noting that imagination is:

- The ability to picture something in the mind that bears a relationship to a phenomenon from the physical world or other human experience such as the psychological, mythical, spiritual, or philosophical
- All human endeavours to understand the universe and our lives require the activity of the imagination, a process of thinking in which we create images that 'picture' the phenomena that confront us
- Imagination is able to go beyond the limitations of physical objects, stereotyped thinking, literal concepts, and is open to exploring associations, the development of ideas, broader formulations of concepts, perceiving deeper and richer meanings, creating original artefacts and probably a host of other activities that constitute human endeavour

Van Alphen's (2011) definition is useful to us as primary school teachers as it reminds us that imagination is rooted in experience. It is vital that we offer our children a vast array of experiences through educational outings, experiences within school and also a rich and varied reading environment where children can encounter new worlds on a daily basis through the stories they read, and the stories read to them.

My own definition of imagination draws together the key themes from the historical accounts written regarding the imagination, including Kant's transcendental imagination, Coleridge's primary imagination, Vygotsky's creative imagination and Passmore's notion of being imaginative. In addition, the definition draws on the theory and ideas from Egan (1992), Warnock (1976), and Currie and Ravenscroft (2002). My definition situates imagination within a socio-cultural context and proposes that:

> Imagination is the ability to conjure images in the mind which can be manipulated in order to go beyond actual experiences and construct alternate possibilities where something new is created in thought, emotion or action.

The definition can of course be debated. Imagination itself is such an all-encompassing term, any definition will need to focus on specific aspects of imagination and be clear about the context the definition derives from. In my definition the key aspects are the way in which imagination enables the creation of alternatives or possibilities where something new is created in the three specific areas of thought, emotion, or action.

I have so far argued that, as teachers, we are working within a contested space of education where our practices are influenced by the factors at work within that space. I have shown that the imagination is a crucial attribute which must be nurtured, valued, and developed but, within the contested space, imagination is in danger of being squeezed out or compartmentalised to make way for a performance agenda.

I will now exemplify the practice of one teacher working in a school in South London whose pedagogy within the classroom gave opportunities for imagining. Julie, the teacher taking part in the study, worked in the same contested space but her practice was distinct as she ensured that opportunities for imagining were core to her practice.

Introduction to the case study

This interpretive study took place over the course of one academic year and focused on the practices of one teacher, Julie, to identify the opportunities for imagining apparent for the children in her class. I was interested in how a teacher, within the contested space, with all the pressures, which for others had led to a skill-based pedagogy, was true to her beliefs about education, and did not veer from her principled approach. Julie embodied the principles outlined by Alexander who called for: Pedagogy of repertoire and principle rather than recipe and prescription where teaching is 'fully rather than selectively informed by research' (Alexander, 2010: 4).

Julie is an experienced teacher, is part of the senior leadership team and is the literacy lead in the two-form entry primary school. Julie had also worked for a number of years in university teaching students and had been involved in a number of literacy-related research projects as well as being an active member of the United Kingdom Literacy Association (UKLA). Julie was therefore situated centrally in the contested space. She had school pressures for literacy standards, collective responsibility as part of SLT, influences from the newly incorporated academy chain, as well as the responsibility of her own Year 4 class. One distinguishing attribute for Julie however, was her immersion in research. She knew and understood the principles underpinning child development, specifically development in reading, writing and speaking, and listening. This knowledge and understanding meant that Julie was able to base her decisions in the classroom and decisions in SLT on principled practice rather than being drawn into short term 'initiatives'.

There were many aspects of Julie's pedagogy which led to opportunities for imagining. Within the examples for this chapter I have chosen to focus on the role of talk within the classroom and how that led to opportunities for possibility thinking and emotional engagement.

The importance of talk

The enrichment of talk within the primary classroom and our understanding of it is important, as talk is crucial to thinking and learning (Barnes, et al., 1969), to making meaning (Vygotsky, 1978) to empowerment (Clay, 1998) and for motivation (Alexander, 2010). To explore Julie's use of talk in the classroom, I will use Alexander's (2008) identification of teaching talk and the five features he identifies.

- **Rote** (teacher–class): The drilling of facts, ideas and routines through constant repetition.
- **Recitation** (teacher–class or teacher–group): The accumulation of knowledge and understanding through questions designed to test or stimulate recall of what had been previously encountered, or cue pupils to work out the answer from clues provided in the question.
- **Instruction/exposition** (teacher–class, teacher–group, or teacher–individual): Telling pupils what to do, and/or imparting information, and/or explaining facts, principles or procedures.
- **Discussion** (teacher–class, teacher–group, or pupil–pupil): The exchange of ideas with a view to sharing information and solving problems.
- **Scaffolded dialogue** (teacher–class, teacher–group, teacher–individual, or pupil–pupil): Achieving common understanding through structured and cumulative questioning and

discussion which guide and prompt, reduce choices, minimise risk and error, and expedite 'handover' of concepts and principles. There may, or may not, be a correct answer but justification and explanation are sought. Pupils' thinking is challenged and so understanding is enhanced. The teacher is likely to share several exchanges with a particular child several times in order to move the thinking on.

(Alexander, 2008: 30)

Alexander (2008) notes that although all five types of teaching talk will be apparent in a teacher's repertoire it is the discussion and scaffolded dialogue where most learning takes place. In the case study box below, I will highlight some of the aspects of discussion and scaffolded dialogue which were apparent in Julie's class.

Case study: Talk as an analytical lens

One of the features of the talk within Julie's class was the conversational style to the discussions taking place through which Julie would support, develop, and sometimes challenge the children's thinking. The response below from Julie was in the context of a discussion about a child's work in response to the book *The Daughter of the Sea* by Berlie Doherty. Preceding Julie's comment a child had just given feedback about another child's writing. Julie responds by saying:

> Absolutely, you've picked up another important issue. It was structured so well; we actually understood the timeline of the story. And George, that was a really important reason that made that piece of letter-writing so amazing. So, Amanda, once you've written Fred a comment, could you take that back to George, please? We need to capture that. So, the timeline, the structure, also made that letter brilliant. I thought fabulously brilliant, and then let's have – let's finish with, let's finish with Susan.

The extract shows an openness between Julie and the children where space is offered for celebration of the work being developed. There is a collaborative nature as three or four children are involved in the discussion and support reviewing a child's response to the main text. There is an encouraging tone form Julie, as well as an acknowledgement that the important issues identified had come from the children themselves.

The children and Julie listened to each other and valued the knowledge and ideas each other brought to an understanding of the text. This was not teacher-dominated or prescriptive in nature, instead being collaborative and learning together within a community of writers. The extract below shows the way Julie motivated the children by recognising them as writers where their ideas, thought, opinions, and decisions are as valuable as hers as the teacher.

> How clever is that? How really clever was that? I understand what brilliant writers you are. You take ideas, and you twist them, and you do all sorts of clever things with them. I thought that was really brilliant. There were some lovely greetings

and lovely, lovely suited and booted language over there. So, thank you for that idea, as well.

Cumulative talk was evident where knowledge was being built between Julie and the children in the class. They were learning together, finding out thoughts and feelings about the text together, and sharing together as a community. The extract below exemplifies the way in which Julie and the children build on each other's ideas, culminating in excitement as new knowledge about the text is discovered:

T: We've just found out. All this time. So she's not as stunned in the head as a salmon, or whatever it was. A herring, wasn't it? She's actually got the wisdom, the wisdom of …I think. Yes?

P: In the reading, we get a picture of the Lord of the Ocean which we thought was Hill Marliner. And on mine, I wrote – we had to write questions – and one of my questions was, "Does he have a Lady of the Ocean?"

T: ((Gasps)) I remember that question!

P: I was thinking, and I was thinking, just then, maybe Eilean is the Lady of the Ocean, 'cause she knows all about the wailing sound and she's able to … and she knows about …

T: I think we are having a bit of one of these moments, again, aren't we, when things are slotting into place. Oh my goodness!

Throughout the lessons Julie knew exactly what the intentions were for the learning taking place. She was flexible in the way she built and developed the knowledge the children brought to the learning as well. The children were integral to the learning; they were not incidental to it whereby they were expected to meet standard learning objectives. The learning therefore was dynamic. It was exciting, purposeful, and changeable rather than static, formulaic, and measurable.

I have briefly introduced the type of teacher talk in Julie's class and focused on how it was based in discussion and scaffolded dialogue. This was enabled due to the beliefs Julie held about education and the central place children's own ideas and experience had within the class meaning that a community of learners was developed with Julie learning from the children as well as the children learning from her and each other.

There was a stark contrast to what Alexander warned regarding the 'proliferation of learning outcomes' which has been a feature of many classrooms with children needing to tick off a range of objectives and success criteria in their books at the end of a lesson. Often these objectives and success criteria have been predetermined by the teacher, or in some cases a teaching scheme, and the teaching manipulated to ensure the targets are not only met but can be evidenced. The evidencing is an indicator of the pressures within the contested space as still, in some schools, teachers are de-professionalised by processes such as the scrutinising of their books, learning walks, and lesson observations without advance notice, designed to 'check' that teachers are following school or academy policies.

Within processes such as these, the voice of the child is lost. The child as a knowledgeable learner who brings experience to the class is negated in favour of a school-centric policy where the objectives set are seen as the most important learning. We should, as a profession, rise up against such practice where fear, conformity, and compliance are seen as paramount in order to 'raise standards'. Creating an education for our primary school children which is creative, imaginative, taught with passion and purpose for the empowerment of the children is attainable and in itself will lead to increase standards but it is not an 'easy fix'. I will now highlight two aspects of Julie's pedagogy which exemplify how, within a culture of learning talk, possibility thinking, and emotional engagement can lead to opportunities for imagining.

Case study: Possibility thinking and emotion

Through the talk taking place in Julie's class there was space created for possibility thinking which is an indicator of opportunities for imagining. Possibility thinking is a term coined by Anna Craft (1999) and is seen to be at the heart of creativity (Craft, 2002). Possibility thinking was in part evidenced through the types of question posed by Julie and the responses from the children.

The questions posed by Julie were characterised by words of possibility such as 'what', 'how', and 'why' which gave space for children to offer their own thoughts and ideas through their answers. These 'as if' questions (Craft el al., 2013) enabled the children to enter into the realms of possibility and imagining (Passmore, 1980), supported and scaffolded by Julie but which opened up opportunities for the children. In the example below Julie is encouraging a child to respond to the feelings of one of the characters through what Craft (2014) calls 'as if thinking'.

> So, if I said to you, 'How is Jannet feeling?' all that tells us is, 'Her blood ran cold to hear it'. So, is Jannet feeling like cold blood? Is that how you think Jannet is feeling? Like cold blood? Would that explain that to us? Come on, ok, let's hear some of your amazing imagination. Do you think – 'cause you use phrases like this in your writing all the time, and I never say, 'What do you mean?' So is that saying Jannet feels like cold blood? Can you help us, say, use that phrase to infer how Jannet's feeling?

The extract shows clear opportunities for possibility thinking through the language of possibility used by Julie by using phrases such as 'if I said …', 'So, is …', 'Is that how you think …', 'would that …', and 'do you think…'. Opportunities were given for exploring the possible rather than the actual (Egan, 1992) where, within the given context, freedom was given to the child for their responses based on their imagining.

There was a similar situation for the responses from the children in the class where I noted how the responses were valued and built while the learning which was taking place. Question responding is defined by Craft et al., (2013) as responding to questions through 'testing, predicting, undoing, accepting, rejecting, evaluating, compensating, completing or repeating' (p 16). The response is only possible as a result of the degree of possibility within the question posed. The children in Julie's class were adept at responding to questions in a conversational style where there was exploration taking place and the class community were discovering together.

There was an emotional connection between Julie and the children which enabled opportunities for imagining. Emotions, as Hargreaves (1988) notes, are 'at the heart of teaching' (p. 835) and through my time in Julie's class it was clear that both Julie and the children invested emotionally not only with the subject matter of each lesson but with each other. Egan (2005) identified emotion as a crucial element of imagination and I was able to identify three key parts which made up the emotional experience in Julie's class. There was a purpose to the teaching which was taught with passion for the empowerment of the children.

The purpose was evident through the authentic nature of the learning taking place. All the children and the teacher were invested in the learning. It was not 'being done to them' from detached learning objectives or 'steps to success' but was instead driven by a desire to explore, discover and lean together. The children were drawn into the learning through the skill of Julie – who was also learning alongside the children. Learning alongside the children was a key aspect of Julie's practice. Her pedagogical knowledge meant that she was able to, in effect, remove the power hierarchy so common in many classrooms. Julie was no longer the 'font of knowledge' but was instead the learning guide, the more experienced 'other', who was also immersed in the learning but invested in guiding and supporting the children as they discovered together.

The short extract below shows the subtleties in the way in which Julie would respond with the children. The class are continuing in the exploration of *The Daughter of The Sea* and are discovering together as they near the end of the story. Julie is as excited as the children; she shares in their discovery as a community of learners.

T: Does Munroe know Eilean's got the rag?
P: (.) No.
T: Does anybody know? (.) So I kind of am hearing your inferences and predictions for the, kind of, big, big dramatic ending of this story. We know, as the reader, we know more than any of the characters know. Apart from ... Eilean knows. Eilean knows (.) most of it, doesn't she? Eilean –
P: Maybe that's why she's always so quiet.
      [Excited background chatter]
P: She doesn't wanna expose herself.
      [Excited background chatter]
T: Oh my goodness, Eilean knows all! Munroe's just confessed to Jannet, so now Jannet knows a little bit more than she did before this terrible incident. The other crofters know nothing. Go on?

The atmosphere in the classroom was positive due to the constant encouragement given by Julie. This meant that the children had a safe space in which to experiment with their thoughts and were able to use their imagination to seek out possibilities. Some of the language used by Julie included:

Absolutely.
I thought that fabulously brilliant.
What amazing, amazing thing to do.
Brilliant. I love that comment.
You've picked up another important issue.
That was a really important reason that made that piece of letter writing so amazing.
You've really captured them because of the way you've used that emotive language
    and taken us through the event so clearly.

Through her responses Julie reinforced the emotional experience by responding positively to the children's discoveries, emphasising the point that the class were exploring and responding to the text as authentic readers where their thoughts and ideas were as equally valued and valid as her own. Julie picked up on what the children said and encouraged the emotional link between them and the characters enabling the children to experience the 'as if' thinking.

The extract above also shows the passion Julie had, which was infectious and gave purpose to the learning. Julie opened herself up emotionally to the class which in turn offered a safe space for the children to invest emotionally with the lessons. It was clear that Julie had a caring disposition towards every child in her class. Within the contested space she actively chose to demonstrate the care through the language she used which in turn was based on her beliefs about effective teaching. The love, care, and positive relationships identified meant that there was what the literature refers to as 'emotional labour' (Hargreaves, 1988; O'Connor, 2008; Uitto et al., 2015) exerted by Julie. The emotional labour relates to the effort Julie used to ensure all children were emotionally supported through the way she spoke and acted in the lessons. In effect Julie needed to perform every day, showing care and concern which, although real, needed to be evident to the children and come across in an unbiased way.

The purpose and passion led to the empowerment of the children. They were empowered to create possibilities, to engage emotionally within a safe environment and to use their imaginations. Children were empowered by the choices and freedom they experienced which in turn gave them space to ponder, think, imagine, and reflect as they created their own alternatives and possibilities.

Reflecting on the case study

Over the course of a year I was able to gain an in-depth understanding of the beliefs and practices Julie had in relation to what she saw as effective teaching. These beliefs and practices directly impacted the opportunities for imagining by the children. It is clear that Julie has a secure pedagogy. She understood what she did and why she did it. When new initiatives were proposed she would robustly challenge them, ensuring any changes were made for the learning interests of the children and not for any short-term school-centric quick-fix solutions. In summary, I suggest that it is fruitful to consider these aspects of Julie's pedagogy:

- Children are active participants in the learning
- Children's background and interests influence the curriculum
- The teacher learns alongside the children, valuing their contributions
- Learning Objectives are derived from multiple sources and are relevant to the children
- Success criteria (if used) are created by the children with direction from the teacher
- Possibility thinking is enabled through the teaching and learning talk
- Emotional labour is exerted by the teacher, creating trust, unity and a safe space to create alternatives
- There is a clear purpose to the learning which is shared and influenced by the children
- Learning is guided by the teacher in order to empower the children
- The classroom is a learning community

Chapter summary

Imagination and creating opportunities for imagining are crucial aspects of classroom practice. It is important that we provide the space for children to think, reflect, adapt, plan, predict, and create. We need to be adept at following new lines of interest and learning from our children and creating learning opportunities from them. We must engage emotionally with the children in the class where they feel the purpose of the learning they are involved in and are empowered by it. Above all, we should create an authentic community of learners in our class where – we as the teacher – are learning alongside the children. We do all this whilst working in an educational space which is contested, where our pedagogy, determination, and drive will be continually tested. However, if we have firm pedagogical roots we will stay strong and create classrooms which are purposeful, where the teaching is passionate, and the community of learners are empowered through opportunities for imagining.

References

Alexander, R. (2008) *Towards Dialogic Teaching: Rethinking Classroom Talk*. 4th ed. York: Dialogos.

Alexander, R. (2010) *Children, Their World, Their Education. Final Report and Recommendations of the Cambridge Primary Review*. Abingdon: Routledge.

Barnes, D. (1969) The Language of the Secondary Classroom. In D. Barnes, J. N. Britton and H. Rosen (Eds.), *Language, the Learner and the School*. Harmondsworth: Penguin.

Clay, M. (1998) *By Different Paths to Common Outcomes*. York, ME: Stenhouse.

Craft, A. (1999) Creative development in the early years: Implications of policy for practice. *The Curriculum Journal* 10(1), pp. 135-150.

Craft, A. (2002) *Creativity and Early Years Education*. London: Continuum.

Craft, A. (2014) Wise, Humanising Creativity: A Goal for Inclusive Education. *Revista Nacional e Internacional de Educacion Inclusiva* 7(1), pp. 3-15.

Craft, A., Cremin, T., Burnard, P., Dragovic, T. and Chappell, K. (2013) Possibility Thinking: Cumulative Studies of an Evidenced-Based Concept Driving Creativity? *Education 3-13* 41(5), pp. 538-556.

Craft, A., Cremin, T., Hay, P. and Clack, J. (2014) Creative Primary Schools: Developing and Maintaining Pedagogy for Creativity. *Ethnography and Education* 9(1), pp. 16-34.

Cremin, T. (2015) *Education for Creativity*. Accessed at https://cprtrust.org.uk/cprt-blog/educating-for-creativity/

Currie, G. and Ravenscroft, I. (2002) *Recreative Minds: Imagination in Philosophy and Psychology*. Oxford: Oxford University Press.

Egan, K. (1992) *Imagination in Teaching and Learning: Ages 8 to 15*. Abingdon: Routledge.

Egan, K. (2005) *An Imaginative Approach to Teaching*. San Francisco: Jossey-Bass.

Flewitt, R. and Roberts-Holmes, G. (2015) Regulatory Gaze and 'Non-sense' Phonics Testing in Early Literacy. In R. Hamilton, K. Heydon, K. Hibbert and R. Stooke (Eds.), *Multimodality and Governmentality: Negotiating Spaces in Literacy Education*. London: Bloomsbury/Continuum Books, pp. 95-113.

Hargreaves, A. (1988) The Emotional Practice of Teaching. *Teaching and Teacher Education* 14(8), pp. 835-854.

Kearney, R. (1988) *The Wake of Imagination*. Abingdon: Routledge.

Kind, A. (2016) *The Routledge Handbook of Philosophy of Imagination*. Abingdon: Routledge.

Moss, G. (2010) Remaking Primary Education: Reading 'Children, Their World, Their Education: Final Report and Recommendations of the Cambridge Primary Review. *Literacy* 44(3), pp. 144-148.

O'Connor, K. (2008) "You Choose to Care": Teachers, Emotions and Professional Identity. *Teaching and Teacher Education* 24(1), pp. 117-126.

Passmore, J. (1980) *The Philosophy of Teaching*. London: Duckworth.

Uitto, M., Jokikokko, K. and Estola, E. (2015) Virtual Special Issue on Teachers and Emotions in Teaching and Teacher Education (TATE) in 1985-2014. *Teaching and Teacher Education* 50, pp. 124-135.

Van Alphen, P. (2011) Imagination as a Transformative Tool in Primary School Education. *Research on Steiner Education* 2(2), pp. 16-34.

Vygotsky, L. S. (1978) *Mind in Society: The Development of Higher Psychological Processes*. Cambridge, MA: Harvard University Press.

Warburton, J. (1998) Reasoning and Imagined Possibility: A Role for Imagination in Education. *Prospero: A Journal of New Thinking in Philosophy for Education* 4(2), pp. 89-92.

Warnock, M. (1976) *Imagination*. Los Angeles: University of California Press.

Zittoun, T. and Gillespie, A. (2016) *Imagination in Human and Cultural Development*. Abingdon: Routledge.

INDEX

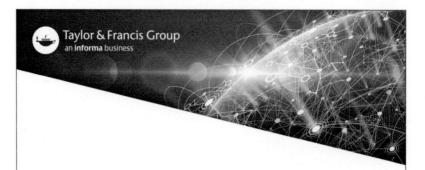